Scraping the Barrel

Scraping the Barrel

The Military Use of Substandard Manpower, 1860–1960

Edited by Sanders Marble

Fordham University Press | New York 2012

Fordham University Press has no responsibility for the persistence or accuracy of URLs for external or third-party Internet websites referred to in this publication and does not guarantee that any content on such websites is, or will remain, accurate or appropriate.

Fordham University Press also publishes its books in a variety of electronic formats. Some content that appears in print may not be available in electronic books.

Library of Congress Cataloging-in-Publication Data

Scraping the barrel : the military use of substandard manpower, 1860–1960 / edited by Sanders Marble. — 1st ed.
        p. cm.
    Includes bibliographical references and index.
    ISBN 978-0-8232-3977-1 (cloth : alk. paper) — ISBN 978-0-8232-3978-8 (pbk. : alk. paper)
1. Recruiting and enlistment—History—20th century. 2. Recruiting and enlistment—History—19th century. 3. Sociology, Military—History—20th century. 4. Sociology, Military—History—19th century. I. Marble, Sanders.
    UB320.S43 2012
    355.2'230904—dc23

                                                        2011037012

Printed in the United States of America
14 13 12   5 4 3 2 1
First edition

Contents

Scraping the Barrel

Introduction

Sanders Marble

Using less-able men in the military is an ancient tradition, but it is one almost ignored by scholars. A Roman law of A.D. 372 provided that men who were too short or weak for service with field armies should be assigned to auxiliary military units, such as river patrol troops.[1] Clearly, the Romans saw some military utility in weaker men, yet their definition of weaker was purely physical and did not involve age or race.

This book is both military history and disability history. It is obviously military history, since it comprises case studies of how armies have used various groups of servicemen to accomplish broader military aims. But it is also disability history. Since militaries reflect the views of their underlying societies, they construct disability both in physical and in social terms: "substandard" is a value judgment. While it is relatively straightforward to say that someone missing a foot has a disability, there are also groups (typically racial or ethnic ones) that societies view as lesser. And for the military, the normal reduced physical ability from increasing age can render someone substandard.

The people who make up armies are products of their societies, largely sharing their society's ideas about disabilities, but armies also have a separate and unique requirement. Fighting wars requires things not generally necessary in civilian life: military-specific training, order and discipline, and physical fitness for the demands of battle. Thus armies have imposed physical standards that have excluded a fair proportion of their societies, but the standards themselves have fluctuated, especially during longer wars. The changing face of armies in the twentieth century (with the shift in emphasis to more technical specialists instead of infantry) has further altered the requirements, as it became accepted that soldiers be able to do *their* job but not *all* of the jobs in the army. Furthermore, if an army

accepted special-purpose units, then those units could have different standards. Overall, there are two basic utilization patterns:
either scattering substandard men across the military in small numbers so they will not drag down the performance of their unit or
forming units of substandard men for specific purposes.

Yet these case studies might not truly be disability history,
because in many cases these men would not be considered disabled
outside the military. Military standards usually exclude at the outset
a large percentage of the population. For example, the American
military of 2009 (with no racial or sex exclusions) estimated that
only 30 percent of the population would meet its entry standards.[2]
Flat feet, poor uncorrected vision, or being forty-two years of age
might disqualify people for military service but would not stop
them from holding most jobs or from rising to high positions in
society. This may be why disability historians have paid no apparent interest to groups such as these while they were serving; disabled veterans have a substantial literature but not substandard
personnel in service. For example, a recent three-volume history of
disability in America does not mention the disabled in uniform,
only as veterans.[3] Military historians, conversely, have focused inor-
dinate attention on elite units (the other end of the spectrum from
the "scrapings"), on women in the military, and on racial minorities.[4] These are valid topics, but casting a wider net would have
brought up more varied examples to consider and not overlooked
the service of hundreds of thousands of men.

All of these case studies are drawn from a period before the
rights of the disabled became a significant issue. Disability rights
groups hardly existed, and since military fitness standards have
long lists of disqualifying conditions, there would be little common
ground between rejected men and men shunted into some form of
limited service. An army might list flat feet, weak stomachs, poor
vision, and arthritic shoulders as disqualifying conditions, but it is
hard to imagine much common ground between men with those
conditions or them clamoring to serve in the military. And even
when there were disabled rights groups, there seems to have been
no pressure to allow service in the military; by the time it is necessary to "scrape the barrel," military service is often unpopular. These
case studies have one full and one partial exception: American
blacks wanted to serve in the military to advance their standing in
society, and the Veterans' Reserve Corps consisted of volunteers
who chose to stay in the military.

For centuries, armies have been willing to compromise their physical standards for Invalid Corps that generally performed various garrison duties. The English had these shortly before 1500, and France, Russia, Austria, Spain, the Honourable East India Company, the Confederate States of America, and Prussia followed suit. The United States had a small Invalid Corps during its Revolutionary War, and the Veterans Reserve Corps that Paul Cimbala describes in Chapter 1 was a revival, with its own special features. These units typically produced clerks and guards but could provide fortress garrisons or even see field service if war came to them.

By the industrial age, armies had more formal criteria than ever before. This was partly attributable to great advances in medicine that could differentiate among (and sometimes treat) a variety of conditions. This allowed the elaborating state bureaucracies to compile longer lists of disqualifying criteria. Populations had increased, and the mass armies common from the 1880s had quite different definitions of substandard men. With conscription bringing in plenty of young men each year and given the conveyor belt that transported men from active duty to reserve service and then to second-reserve responsibility, age became the main distinction between standard and substandard. France and Germany both had conscripted mass armies, but their armies had different views on the utility of reservists. These ideas were based partly on politics, but they had substantial impact in the planning for World War I. In Chapters 2 and 3, Dennis Showalter and André Lambelet look at the German and French experiences leading up to World War I.

Wars also increase manpower needs and threaten standards, which can be lowered or redefined. "Redefined" is not necessarily a euphemism for lowered, because it could include wider roles for ethnic/racial minorities and women. In World War I, the British decided that short men could serve in the army, in special units organized on that basis. Their mediocre performance suggested that better standards were needed than simply height, and in Chapter 4 Peter Simkins chronicles what happened with the "Bantams." The United States would change its standards in two ways in World War I, first accepting more blacks, as Steven Short describes in Chapter 5. The U.S. Army was convinced that blacks were substandard, and made it hard for them to succeed—then blaming them for their failure. In contrast, in Chapter 6 I describe how, when manpower apparently ran short very soon after America's entry into the war, the Army adopted flexible standards under the

"Limited Service" rubric, under which a man's technical qualifications could balance his physical shortcomings.

During World War II, other challenges faced other countries. In the face of enormous losses, the USSR threw away many of its prewar standards, making use of women, ethnic/national minorities, and political prisoners to fill units. David Glantz describes that process and some of its results in Chapter 7. Nazi Germany faced many fronts but had a finite manpower pool, and it quickly reached for two groups. More traditionally, men with physical limitations were brought into uniform much as the various Invalid Corps had been centuries earlier. Walter Dunn looks at policy and one unit in Chapter 8. And although the Nazis also had strict ideological standards, the more men the Moloch of war demanded, the more they bent those standards. Valdis Lumans describes this in two chapters, looking in Chapter 9 at the recruitment standards and policies for "ethnic Germans" according to Nazi racial theory, then looking at the battlefield performance of the men who were brought in under varying levels of compulsion in Chapter 10.

Just as a military's standards are affected by its society, the military can be used to affect society. President Harry Truman used the military to signal to the American public and the world that racial segregation was wrong, although he moved slowly in that regard. From this it was a fairly short step to using the military to engineer social changes, such as those of the sort described by Tom Sticht in Chapter 11, which discusses Project 100,000, a deliberate use of the military to educate young men who would have been ineligible for service, habilitating them rather than rehabilitating them. The premise was that they were not stupid but ill-educated and that, with teaching, they could perform adequately in the military and then have brighter prospects in civilian life. He looks at how they performed in the service and after. Again, disability studies seem not to have examined this group of men.

1   Federal Manpower Needs and the U.S. Army's Veteran Reserve Corps

Paul A. Cimbala

In April 1863, the War Department established the Invalid Corps, later known as the Veteran Reserve Corps, as part of the United States' Civil War army.[1] The purpose of the organization, as Secretary of War Edwin Stanton explained, was to put to work enlisted men and officers who "have been disabled for active service who are yet able to perform duty in garrison, or as depot and prison guards, military police, and in the arrest of skulkers and deserters." Furthermore, the corps would "give honorable employment to this meritorious class, who have suffered in the service of their country" and "to liberate able-bodied soldiers from duty that can well be performed by the invalids" so that they may fight at the front.[2]

Stanton might have given some consideration to the new organization as a means by which the nation could reward men who had served honorably in the federal army and suffered for it. Even so, making use of these war-damaged men foremost revealed the insatiable demand for manpower by federal forces fighting in a conflict that had already continued longer than most Americans had expected. As Capt. John De Forest reported to the Provost Marshal General in the fall of 1865, the needs of the Union armies had placed a strain so great "on the able-bodied manhood of the American people that an intelligent economy of the public forces demanded that some portion of the vast number of men who are unfit for field service should be utilized for military purposes." To that end, thousands of men who had been wounded or who had suffered from camp illness but could still handle a weapon or push a pen remained in the federal army. Some of these men eagerly volunteered to participate in the new Invalid Corps, because they accepted continued military service as a way to support their families or as a patriotic obligation. Others had no choice but to serve out their enlistments despite their protests of having already done their part. Regardless of the reasons, by the end of the summer of 1865, 60,508 enlisted men and 1,096 officers had served in the Veteran Reserve Corps' twenty-four regiments and various independent companies, releasing during the last two years of the war a like number of fit soldiers from behind the lines for duty at the front.[3]

Given the potential pool of fit Northern men and the size of the Yankee army, these numbers would appear to be relatively inconsequential in the final determination of the outcome of the conflict. Nevertheless, the demands of a long war forced officials to resort to alternatives that extended beyond enlisting young, healthy, white, patriotic volunteers. Every additional man in uniform, including invalids, became an important and even necessary contributor to the defeat of the rebellion.

The Manpower Needs of the Federal Army

Numbers alone suggested that the federal government would easily outgun the rebellious states. Along with its growing industrial might, the Northern states had a larger population, offering a much deeper pool of manpower than that enjoyed by the Confederacy; indeed, after adjusting for the real ability to tap into their respective populations, the Northern government had access to around 2.5 times more military-aged men than did its Southern counterpart. By the end of the war, probably over two million men had served in the U.S. military, while various estimates suggest that only approximately 900,000 men had fought for the Confederacy.[4]

These figures, however, obscure the greater needs of the invading federal forces and the difficulties that the Northern government encountered as it strained to keep in the field the substantial armies necessary for achieving a decisive victory. A merely adequate army would not be sufficient to maintain the Union, because the job before the U.S. government required powerful offensive forces to conquer its determined enemy. Additionally, there were behind-the-lines distractions that added to the Northern military burden and diminished the numbers available at the front. Fighting Native Americans in Minnesota, manning forts around Washington and elsewhere, guarding prisoners of war, policing disloyal communities, and performing various additional provost duties all kept men away from combat. All the while, the war dragged on, inflicting unprecedented casualties, thus weakening the army, discouraging volunteering, and forcing the government in March 1863 to initiate conscription.[5]

The federal government used incentives such as bounties to encourage enlistments in the Northern states, but it also shifted its attention to sources other than untested white civilians to answer its manpower needs. Short-term recruits, veterans who reenlisted, loyal white men from the Confederacy, African American men, Native Americans, and even some Confederate prisoners of war all added strength to the Northern armies.[6] Some Northern commentators believed they had discovered another source of manpower in the soldiers they saw taking their ease doing light duty in hospitals or enjoying extended leaves at home allegedly recovering from their wounds. Capt. Samuel Fiske, writing in a Massachusetts newspaper, argued that at least a third of the men on the sick rolls were fit for battle but were malingering in hospitals or even working their farms back home when they should be at the front.[7] Even officials in the War Department were aware of the problem developing in its military hospitals. In the spring of 1862, the army authorized the use of invalids for light duties in military hospitals but realized that these men, lacking any real organizational coherence, "ceased to be soldiers in fact and spirit." Indeed, upon later reflection, one officer admitted that "in too many instances" invalids under such circumstances "continued to be mere hangers-on of hospitals long after they were able to resume the musket."[8]

In March 1863, the War Department attempted to bring some military organization to these hospital workers when it placed their detachments under the command of officers other than the local hospital surgeons. The men continued to perform services in and around the military hospitals, but the arrangements still remained ad hoc, temporary, and without an overarching military rationale. Also, military officials realized that surgeons were discharging large numbers of semihealthy men who were unfit for rigorous campaigning but could still perform garrison and police duties. It was this latter class of men that the War Department decided to keep in the service under the formal organization of an invalid corps.[9]

Organizing and Filling the Invalid Corps

Stanton authorized the establishment of the new Invalid Corps on April 28, 1863. This effort to hold on to invalids for military duty was not an innovation of the federal bureaucracy. European countries such as France and England had engaged in the practice, and the United States itself offered a more immediate historical precedent.[10] In June 1777, during the American Revolution, the Continental Congress had established an Invalid Corps.[11] The War Department, however, was not so much concerned with past practice in justifying its actions as with the "urgent national need."[12]

By late May 1863, the army began transferring men into the ranks of the Invalid Corps, under the supervision of Col. Richard H. Rush, a former cavalry officer from Pennsylvania, who answered directly to the Provost Marshal General and, through him, the Adjutant General of the Army.[13] The organization quickly took shape. By the fall of 1863, the new Invalid Corps contained sixteen regiments made up of 203 companies. The rolls totaled 18,255 officers and men, the majority of them coming from the easily accessed hospitals and convalescent camps of the capital region.[14] A year later, Col. M. N. Wisewell, who replaced Rush in November 1863, looked back on the corps' organization and pronounced the "experiment . . . a success."[15]

The army understood that in tapping into the ranks of invalided soldiers, it would necessarily be relying on men who could perform military tasks at various levels of competency. Consequently, the War Department initially provided that the new Invalid Corps would consist of three battalions with differing degrees of physical limitations. First Battalion men were the "most efficient and able-bodied, and capable of using the musket, and performing guard duty, light marches, &c." A Second Battalion would be the home of "the next degree of physical efficiency, including all who have lost a hand or an arm." A planned Third Battalion was to contain men "who are least effective, and including all who have lost a foot or a leg." That battalion never became a reality and was abandoned in early July 1863. Instead, those men who might have been assigned to the Third Battalion were placed in the Second Battalion.[16] Thus, soldiers with obvious battlefield injuries as well as infirmities ranging from flat feet, poor eyesight, hernias, chronic diarrhea, chronic rheumatism, deafness, and "Confirmed nervous debility or excitability of the heart, with palpitation, great frequency of the pulse, and loss of strength" would find themselves in the new corps, doing service instead of being discharged. Syphilis, insanity, and epileptic seizures, along with "Habitual or confirmed intemperance, or solitary vice, sufficient in degree to have materially enfeebled the constitution," and some other serious maladies and injuries would prevent the transfer of the suffering individuals into the corps.[17]

In the process of filling the two battalions, the Provost Marshal General's office expected to draw particularly on the more able invalids, thus organizing a First Battalion that would be much larger than the Second. Indeed, within a year of the corps' establishment there was about a three-to-one ratio favoring the First Battalion. Men were shifted between the two battalions as their conditions improved or worsened, but the numbers always favored the healthier battalion. When first established, these battalions did not have units larger than companies, which ideally but not always had up to one hundred enlisted men and officers on their rolls.[18] The War Department deployed these individual companies when needed, such as during the Gettysburg campaign in the summer of 1863.[19] In September 1863, however, the War Department authorized the formation of regiments made up of ten companies, along with the appointment of an appropriate number of regimental officers.[20] Initially, four Second Battalion companies joined six companies of First Battalion men to form an Invalid Corps regiment. The Second Battalion companies, despite their regimental affiliations, remained scattered by their various hospital assignments. This organizational structure proved impractical, and the Second Battalion companies eventually became detached from their regiments along their way to their final transfer in March 1865 to the Surgeon General's command.[21] The corps' regiments were almost exclusively organized as infantry and held to discipline under the standard army regulations for that branch. On occasion, however, members of the corps served as mounted patrols, in artillery formations, and in two provisional regiments of cavalry.[22]

Invalids could enter the new organization either as direct transfers from their regiments or as transfers from military hospitals or convalescent camps where they were recuperating and already performing light duties. For example, in the spring of 1863, the immediate and foremost source of men came with the disbanding of the earlier hospital companies; the army simply moved these invalids directly into the new corps, which accounted for the rapid growth of the new organization.[23] Men who came into the corps by transfer retained their rank and were expected to serve out their original enlistments.[24]

Medical transfers were always the foremost source of men for the Invalid Corps. From the inception of the organization down through the end of the war, formal examining boards consisting of surgeons and officers who had served in the field judged the suitability of hospital inmates for transfer. The boards did yeoman's work, maintaining exhausting schedules as they tried to fill the corps' companies and help to alleviate the manpower needs of the army.[25] For example, during early 1865 Capt. James M. McMillan headed a board that examined thousands of patients over a broad geographical area. During February, he was at work at hospitals in Pennsylvania, Ohio, Indiana, and Illinois; in March, he visited hospitals in Wisconsin, Iowa, Illinois, and Missouri; and in April, he traveled to Indiana, Ohio, Michigan, Pennsylvania, and Maryland. At one point in February, he reported examining over 23,700 men in forty-four hospitals in Tennessee and Kentucky and early the next month over another nine thousand in fourteen hospitals in Wisconsin, Iowa, Illinois, and Missouri.[26]

While the examining boards combed the hospitals for suitable men, their superiors in the War Department authorized assistant provost marshals general throughout the Northern states to explore another source of men for the Invalid Corps. The officials in Washington charged the officers to recruit honorably discharged invalids who could perform moderately demanding military chores for three-year enlistments. The provost marshals, usually assisted by disabled and invalided officers, employed common recruiting tactics, such as placing newspaper ads and circulating broadsides, but they were never as successful as the hospital examining boards in filling up the invalid companies. By the end of October 1863, for example, boards transferred 16,448 enlisted men into the corps, while only 1,431 enlisted men volunteered for service. From the inception of the corps down to the fall of 1865, over 45,037 men had been transferred into the organization, while 5,275 enlisted and another 3,493 had reenlisted.[27] Later, the corps opened its ranks to all honorably discharged veterans, which better suited a Veteran Reserve Corps, the organization's new name as of March 18, 1864. The bureaucrats hoped the change of name would encourage volunteering from among the growing ranks of discharged veterans, not just the permanently disabled, who might have viewed the original designation with "repugnance."[28]

Officers in charge of organizing the invalid companies did their duties well but ran into all sorts of difficulties before they were able to send their men on to their new assignments. Inadequate paperwork, procedural uncertainties, and a lack of uniforms, weapons, and other equipment, along with poor housing conditions, all hindered their efforts. However resourceful officers were in overcoming these problems, they often encountered one organizational inadequacy that ingenuity or improvisation could not overcome: the lack of sufficient numbers of company-grade officers. During the fall of 1863, officers sent anxious requests to Washington, pleading with the bureaucrats to assign to them the captains and the lieutenants that they needed before they could put their invalid companies to use.[29]

The shortage of officers resulted not from a lack of interest. Rather, headquarters was simply unable to expedite applications for commissions in the corps to meet the needs of the new units. There were almost 1,400 applications at the Provost Marshal General's Office in late September 1863 and at about the same time only 491 officers on duty when new companies were rapidly taking form.[30] Yet the bureaucratic machine moved at a slow pace, leaving eager officers pondering their futures. A frustrated Orson Woodworth, a former lieutenant with the 74th Indiana Volunteer Infantry, for example, finally concluded that "the war would probably be ended before a final decision would be reached, i.e. if the celerity of action on my application thus far may be taken as a criterion."[31]

Sometimes such delays resulted from the incomplete applications of the officers, who scrambled to fulfill all of the bureaucratic requirements. The more significant cause, however, was the Invalid Corps' desire to be certain that the applicants were worthy of commissions, especially given the fear that men in the volunteer regiments would continue to view the new organization as a dumping ground for worthless soldiers. After September 10, 1863, officers seeking a place in the Invalid Corps could no longer transfer from their old regiments directly into the organization; instead, they had to submit to the Provost Marshal General's Office formal applications that contained their complete military history, along with recommendations from at least three officers under whom they had served.[32]

In selecting officers from the applicant pool, the army scrutinized their past records, expecting to find evidence of moral character, good judgment, and careful attention to their previous duties. By early January 1864, the Provost Marshal General's Office, which had received approximately two thousand officers' applications by early January 1864, gave preference to men wounded in battle and then looked at those applicants disabled by disease.[33] Also in January 1864, the army ordered all officers of the Invalid Corps, including those men already commissioned and on duty, to report to an examination board that would test their knowledge of military matters, assess their general intelligence, and review their "record of sobriety."[34] The applicants' bodies might have been ravaged by the war, but the army did its best to make sure that the officers of the new organization remained capable of conducting themselves as exemplary soldiers.

Reluctant Transfers and Eager Heroes

Most enlisted men went into the corps understanding that it was their duty to complete their terms of service despite whatever inconvenience it would bring. Some of them might have even felt the continued tug of duty and patriotism. At the same time, there were an uncounted number of men who resented their transfers, and many more veterans once discharged from the service refused to reenlist in the organization.

There were a number of reasons why enlistments did not exceed transfers from hospitals. Once discharged, invalids could receive a pension, which led some men to reason that if they could earn "eight dollars a month without duty and thirteen with," the extra money was not worth the effort.[35] Discharged invalids or other veterans no doubt believed that they had already sacrificed enough for the Union cause. That belief certainly influenced even those men who had no choice but to accept their transfers into the Invalid Corps when they would rather be discharged. Also, once willing and proud volunteers now objected to their transfers because, as R. H. Welch complained, they were being "placed in this Branch of the Service contrary to . . . [their] will."[36] Feeling ill-used by their government, they complained to friends and politicians, including the secretary of war and the president.[37]

Transfers also felt particularly aggrieved to be forced to continue their service when they believed that other obligations, such as supporting their families, demanded their attention. Some men reasoned that if they were well enough to be placed in the Invalid Corps, they were well enough to return to their old regiments to complete their enlistments with familiar comrades.[38] A number of transfers simply did not wish to be part of the organization and probably shared the prejudices of soldiers who considered the corps a home for shirkers and thus something less than an honorable organization. Enlisted man E. C. Fisk of Michigan, for example, went reluctantly into the Invalid Corps by way of a transfer. It was against his will, and he preferred to be sent back to his old regiment. His unhappiness and prejudice about the corps prompted him to refer to it as "that stinking concern." His initial experience, he complained, confirmed his impression that "in great part" the Invalid Corps was "filled up with *dead beats*! cowardly sneaks, & scalawags that would disgrace any service, & a set of officers that would disgrace any government for commissioning them." While he admitted some exceptions, "I was never ashamed of my uniform when in my regiment, but there was nothing connected with that miserable concern I was transferred into . . . but what I was ashamed of[.] They were a set of condemned & and in great part useless men, which made it much harder for those who did the duty."[39]

Potential officers, unlike their enlisted subordinates, considered a place in the corps to be a desirable appointment. They eagerly competed for the limited commissions available even when it usually meant accepting a rank lower than what they had held in the volunteer service. Such men actively pursued appointments for a variety of reasons, some self-serving and others patriotic, with neither being mutually exclusive. There were many hurt or sick officers who believed that the army remained their best possible source of income; disabled in the service of their country, unable to take up their civilian jobs, they expected the government to give them the opportunity to earn their support.[40] Some officers considered a place in the corps as an avenue for continuing the military careers they had come to enjoy, not simply a place to earn a competence. And there were veterans who simply felt incomplete as men without having something respectable to occupy their time, regardless of income or career needs. Nevertheless, even those men who were looking to their own finances and ambitions could also have honorable intentions, such as a desire to finish the fight for the preservation of their nation.

The best of these patriots held sentiments much like those of Benjamin Hawkes, a former lieutenant colonel from Ohio. When Hawkes offered his services to the corps, he pleaded that his application was nothing more or less than an expression of his desire to "render some assistance in sustaining the Government." "I feel craven," he explained, "to remain inactive when my country needs my services."[41] As a result, the organization quickly developed an officer corps staffed by men who were at the very least honestly devoted to the Union cause. As several of the corps' officers stationed in Indiana explained, they were pleased to be able to continue to render service "in this hour of the Nation's need."[42]

A Corps of Honor

The new Invalid Corps was a distinctive organization in several ways, one of them being that it was, unlike the volunteer regiments raised in the various states, a national organization on an equal footing with the regular army. The corps' regimental and company officers received their commissions from the president of the United States and not from state governors. Thus they took command precedent over men holding state commissions of equal rank.[43] Another practice marking the Invalid Corps as a national organization was the general prohibition of forming companies of men all from the same state.[44] Even the uniforms worn by the men were supposed to distinguish them from the ordinary volunteer regiments.

The army outfitted the officers and men of the Invalid Corps in sky blue trousers and matching jackets for the enlisted men and frock coats for the officers, instead of the usual dark blue uniform jackets and coats of the volunteers. The clothing was not only "becoming," according to one officer, but served the purpose of distinguishing men who legitimately spent a large part of their time working behind the lines from the shirkers they might have been escorting back to the front. Also, the bureaucrats in Washington probably assumed that the distinctive uniforms would help build the new organization's esprit de corps. However, both officers and enlisted men disliked the uniform, because it marked them as invalids and opened them to ridicule by other soldiers who considered such troops to be substandard and worthless.[45] Officers soon resorted to wearing their old regimental coats when they could get away with the practice, and in 1864 the army agreed to make the dark blue frock officer's coat their official garb.[46] The enlisted men remained uniformed in their light blue garb until the end of the war, but in 1864 and 1865, depending on the post and regiment, enlisted men were frequently ordered to wear dark blue blouses under certain circumstances, such as when not on duty, when the weather was extremely hot, and while performing guard and fatigue duty or routine drill.[47]

The soldierly ridicule prompted by the unique uniforms was a curse that the Invalid Corps had to endure as it attempted to earn a respectable place for itself in the army, especially given the bad reputation that hospital deadbeats had earned prior to its establishment. During his inspection tour in the fall of 1863, Col. Frank Cahill did his best to convince hospitalized soldiers and volunteer officers that new corps was not "made up of malingerers . . . and worthless men who are too lazy or too cowardly to serve in the field" and that it was in fact a "Corps of Honor."[48] So, too, Col. Wisewell tried to calm invalid soldiers who complained about being abused by their former comrades. In answering one private's concerns, Wisewell reassured him that the man was engaged in an honorable service and that those individuals taunting him were cowards, traitors, or men "who do not come up to the standard in a moral point of view that would entitle them to admission into the Corps of Honor."[49] Indeed, from the first days of the Invalid Corps, Col. James Fry, the provost marshal general throughout the war, and his subordinates expected both officers and men to bring extra measures of devotion, competence, and moral rectitude to the new organization so that it matched if not exceeded all other units in soldierly bearing and performance.[50]

The hospital commissioners, recruiting officers, and officers' review boards did their best to make certain that skulkers and men of poor morals never made it into the ranks of the corps, lest they bring with them the old image of the hospital shirker. For the most part, they were successful. Many of the men who took up places in the organization were indeed battle-tested veterans who continued to do good service. In the fall of 1865, Capt. James M. Davenport, for example, noted that his company of men serving in the 3rd Regiment of the VRC bore "the scars upon their bodies as evidence of their valor and devotion to the country." He believed that he knew "of no body of men more obedient to the orders of their superior officers or better instructed in their various duties" than these soldiers.[51]

Not all enlisted men or even officers, unfortunately, matched Davenport's assessment of his own men. Across the North in cities, towns, and camps, drunkenness, bigamy, petty theft, blasphemy, laziness, and disrespect of local citizens along with other common soldiers' vices shamed the veterans' units.[52] Officers dealt with minor offenses such as drunkenness by fining their men, placing them on extended police duty, or embarrassing the miscreants by giving them a severe dressing down in the presence of their companies.[53] Sometimes, however, nothing worked, and the corps then had to rid itself of its incorrigibles.

By 1864, the corps was regularly transferring undeserving men back to their old regiments for field service or, if incapable of such duty, court-martial. Bad men who had enlisted directly into the corps were court-martialed by their officers. And when those officers did not meet standards, the provost marshall general gave them the opportunity to resign before being subjected to military discipline and public humiliation.[54] Frequently, however, the enlisted men and officers who failed to live up to expectations were not so much maliciously incompetent as they were "physically incapable of performing all the duties."[55] The health of even the best of the men was especially tested when the army demanded more of them than they had originally anticipated upon their entry into the Invalid Corps.

The Second Battalion and Hospital Duty

The Second Battalion consisted of the most unfit men in the Invalid Corps, but nevertheless it contributed in important ways to the Union cause. Not the least of the Second Battalion men's contributions was their taking the places of thousands of able-bodied soldiers who would have remained behind the lines performing clerical work or hospital guard duty instead of fighting with their regiments at the front. By November 1, 1863, there were 7,224 men in the Second Battalion.[56] That number increased to 8,687 men in March 1865, when the War Department transferred the Second Battalion companies to the command of the Surgeon General.[57]

The men of the Second Battalion also provided a worthwhile immediate service for the war effort in the positions they filled behind the lines. These invalids performed clerical and other light duties in offices, storehouses, and supply depots, all necessary jobs for keeping the military machine functioning.[58] The New Jerseyan W. G. Dunn, for example, was detached from his company in March 1864 to work as a clerk under the chief mustering officer of the Eighth Army Corps.[59]

The primary work of the Second Battalion invalids, however, was in and around the nation's military hospitals. There they served under the direct orders of their company officers, who answered to the hospitals' commanding surgeons. They worked as ward masters, nurses, orderlies, attendants, clerks, cooks, and guards, and their superiors generally considered them "indispensable."[60] While there was a great demand for Second Battalion men in the hospital wards, they was also a pressing need for them to serve as guards around the hospitals, because the more mobile inmates were not always the best-behaved soldiers in the army.[61] At Mower General Hospital in Philadelphia, for example, the patients frequently went absent without leave, jumping fences to secure whiskey to bring back to the hospital, along the way "molesting and assaulting peaceable citizens, women and children, upon the Hill, drunkenness, &c &c."[62] Someone had to keep these rowdy patients in line, and the Second Battalion companies generally tried their best, although not always successfully, to serve that purpose.[63]

The First Battalion's Duties

First Battalion men performed a greater variety of duties than the guarding of hospitals. Generally more fit than their Second Battalion counterparts, they shouldered muskets and soldiered in more demanding surroundings. First Battalion men guarded prisoner-of-war camps, rendezvous camps, and bridges. They tended seashore lighthouses and performed garrison duty at forts on the East Coast and fortifications around Washington. They escorted draftees to the front, helped enforce conscription throughout the North, and assisted provost marshals in maintaining order on Northern streets.[64]

The work of the 3rd Regiment, VRC, exemplified the type of routine expected of the invalids. It was a common situation to find companies of the regiments stationed at different posts performing their various duties. The 3rd Regiment followed such a pattern during 1864 and 1865, seeing its men serving in the Washington area; Scranton, Pennsylvania; New York City; Albany, New York; and elsewhere on the East Coast, with detachments further divided up and at one point scattered over at least seventy-five different posts in six states.[65]

The assignments at these various stations generally consisted of guard duty, provost work, and escort duty. The men of Company G, for example, guarded prisoners of war in Washington, D.C., at Old Capitol Prison, where they foiled several escape attempts. They next acted as guards at the rendezvous camps of the 193rd New York Volunteers, which consisted of, according to the 3rd Regiment's commanding officer, "many men of a bad class." During the latter days of the war and in the early days of the peace, Company G continued its duty at Elmira, New York, where it again guarded Confederate prisoners, and then at Brattleboro, Vermont, where it guarded government buildings. While Company G performed its various duties, Company I also stood guard at Old Capitol Prison and at the Baltimore and Ohio Rail Road Depot in the capital. It eventually joined Company G at the 193rd New York Volunteers rendezvous and ended its service guarding government buildings in

Burlington, Vermont. Both Company G and Company F escorted new soldiers to their regiments, while Company H guarded the Soldiers' Rest in Washington as well as government property at the city's wharves, recruits, conscripts, and livestock. During this period, at various times, several companies of the 3rd Regiment guarded the draft rendezvous at New Haven and Hartford, Connecticut, and escorted recruits to their regiments. The regiment also provided men for provost duty, patrols, guards, and detectives in Alexandria, Virginia.[66] At the end of the war, the Provost Marshal General's Office judged the regiment's duty to have been "severe." Guards were on duty "for weeks together . . . every other day." The men worked themselves to the point of exhaustion but maintained an admirable discipline to the very end of their service.[67]

Life Behind the Lines

Invalids such as those of the 3rd Regiment usually found themselves in typical uncomfortable military quarters. Often, that meant that they lived under canvas or in cold, dirty barracks that required repairs.[68] When not worrying about leaky roofs or drafty clapboard buildings, however, the men could easily fill the lulls in their days with various diversions. Gideon W. Burtch, for example, worked in a hospital dispensary, which gave him time to study German and read the Bible.[69] Those invalids stationed in or near towns and cities supplemented their solitary amusements with active integration into the social life around them. W. G. Dunn, for example, used his off-duty hours to attend various balls and musical performances, and Benjamin F. Turley informed his brother that he had "all the fun" he could want, including socializing with the opposite sex and drinking liquor, while stationed in Evansville, Indiana.[70] In such an environment, temptations abounded. The good officers of the corps did what they could to rein in the bad behavior of their men and protect the reputation of their organization, but even the invalids fell victim to the usual soldierly vices, with drunkenness being the most common breach of discipline.[71]

For the most part, the communities that hosted the better-behaved men appreciated their performance of their duties and treated them as welcomed guests. Local women especially expressed their concerns for the soldiers, perhaps using them as substitutes for their boys and men at the front. They fed them and provided them with knitted mittens and other humble items for making their lives a bit easier. Civilians were also well aware of the holiday blues that could fall upon soldiers stationed away from their families and consequently often organized special celebrations for the invalid soldiers on duty in their communities.[72] No wonder soldiers still fighting with their volunteer regiments might have considered such a life behind the lines to be soft duty, but there was no guarantee that the invalids would always have it so.

Strenuous and Dangerous Duties

The invalids had opportunities to enjoy themselves behind the lines, but the demands of the war soon placed them on hard duty, and sometimes under harsh conditions. In the aftermath of the October 1864 St. Albans, Vermont, rebel raid from across the Canadian border, for example, invalids provided the sole guard on the state's northern frontier, according to one officer, without relief "for a long time." Men of the 11th Regiment guarded rebel prisoners at Point Lookout, Maryland, standing on post every other day, while having only canvas tents for winter shelter. And at Camp Distribution in Alexandria, Virginia, men of the 14th Regiment, many of them still hampered by their recent wounds, performed "severe" duty, "the camp being large, the posts numerous, the winter uncommonly cold." The combination of poor health and harsh conditions meant that many of them ended up back in the hospital.[73] No wonder one cranky invalid complained that the organization required its men "to do more severe service from day to day than when in the field."[74]

Many officers would have agreed with the complaining soldier. They grumbled that their men stood guard for long periods with little rest before returning to their posts, a consequence of their detachments being understaffed. The practice took a heavy physical toll on their war-worn men. In November 1863, Captain Lewis Hollman, in command of a Second Battalion company in the Second Regiment on guard duty at an arsenal in Ohio, reported that he had "quite a number of men that are not able to stand on post." They had a variety of infirmities that not only made the duty difficult but were aggravated by it. One stretch of night guard duty left some of Hollman's men "not able to do any thing the next 24 hours and the strength of the company compels me to have them all on duty two hours every night." Superiors at least promised him reinforcements.[75] Other officers simply had to make do with the men they had on hand.

Invalids serving as guards or escorts, assisting provost officers, and helping to enforce the draft not only worked hard but continued to risk life and limb for their country. The 3rd Regiment's Company I had a brush with violence while guarding the Baltimore and Ohio Rail Road Depot in Washington, D.C., during the 1864 presidential election. There they had to deal with disorderly crowds composed of drunken Democrats and "Lincoln men terribly in earnest," barely preventing a serious clash between the two groups.[76] Less successful was the Invalid Corps' earlier encounter with an unruly mob as part of the army's larger effort to calm the New York City draft riots that erupted on July 13, 1863. The corps suffered casualties on the first day: the rioters routed them and severely beat those men they caught.[77]

Draft resistors and deserters in Ohio and Pennsylvania also did not hesitate to use violence to protect themselves from the army, which put more men from the corps in dangerous situations.[78] Sometimes the demands of enforcing the draft and hunting deserters equaled those of a strenuous field campaign. Over a period of six months during 1864 and 1865, members of the Sixth Regiment patrolled "disaffected counties" in Ohio, arresting almost one hundred deserters, usually performing their "hazardous and arduous" duties at night. As a consequence, the men endured "much marching and exposure." The danger involved in such work was real. In November 1864, a group of men attacked and wounded two 6th Regiment men who were escorting a deserter.[79] Farther east, during the cold winter of 1864–1865, companies from the 16th Regiment patrolled mountainous counties in eastern Pennsylvania, tracking down and capturing thousands of draft dodgers and deserters, some of whom offered armed resistance. At times, the men endured significant hardship. Company B, for example, worked under conditions deemed "severe to the extreme" by their regimental commander, sometimes riding but frequently marching twenty to thirty miles in deep snow as they tracked down their prey. These scouting missions lasted six to eight days or until "they secured enough deserters to return" to their base of operations.[80]

On occasion, the First Battalion men and even their Second Battalion comrades actually faced their old enemies on the field of battle. Surgeons had recently judged almost the entire 18th Regiment to be unfit for most duty, but on June 20, 1864, the regiment had no choice but to fight off Confederate raiders at White House Landing in Virginia. And after their Virginia experiences, the men had little time to rest. They returned to Washington and continued to act as guards along a railroad, a duty that placed them in the path of Confederate General Jubal Early's cavalry as it raided toward the federal capital in the summer of 1864.[81]

The men of the 18th Regiment were not alone in learning that when the enemy threatened, even the invalids had to turn out for the fight. Several regiments, including Second Battalion men, were in the defensive line around Washington at the time of Early's 1864 raid, and four of those regiments actually fought the Confederates. The 9th Regiment, for example, repelled rebel skirmishers at Fort Stevens, with one killed and thirteen wounded. Four of the latter eventually succumbed to their wounds.[82] In the western theater in November 1864, Peter S. Ludwig and his Second Battalion comrades stationed at Nashville took up arms and endured some rigorous marching when Confederate General John Bell Hood challenged federal forces in Tennessee, but in the end they avoided combat.[83]

Into the Peace

When the war ended in the spring of 1865, the federal government reduced its military expenditures as quickly as practicable. That included the dismantling of the VRC. Citizens and politicians supported the idea of rewarding the invalids with permanent places in the army and petitioned the War Department to keep the corps active. Their wishes, however, ran up against the opposition not only of the economizers but also of the Union general and hero Ulysses S. Grant, who was dead set against retaining invalid units in his peacetime army.[84]

The corps had already shed its Second Battalion men in March 1865, and, beginning in mid-June, the War Department began mustering out First Battalion members that it had previously transferred into the organization from its hospitals and convalescent camps. For the time being, it held on to the service of the men who had enlisted or reenlisted in the corps and still had time remaining to their military obligations. In the process, it reduced the organization's size by allowing over 12,500 First Battalion men to be mustered out with their original regiments. By October 1, 1865, there were only 5,427 enlisted men remaining, commanded by 658 officers, all of the First Battalion.[85]

While the reductions were proceeding, the invalids continued to perform admirable duty as the nation made its transition from war to peace. The most visible postwar duty of the corps was also its most somber. Members of the VRC served as the honor guard for the funerary rites of the assassinated Abraham Lincoln, including providing the escort for the late president's body on its train journey back to Illinois.[86] The corps' other transitional duties were similar to the work it had performed during the war, generally taking up various positions that would allow the army to muster out the volunteer regiments.

Members of the 6th Regiment stayed in uniform throughout the summer of 1865, continuing to guard prisoners of war at Johnson's Island, Ohio, or act as the Confederates' escorts to some other destination. As late as October 1865, six companies of the 6th Regiment stood guard in Cincinnati. They played an important role in maintaining order while the federal army began to dismantle its volunteer regiments. In May 1865, for example, members of the regiment guarded the railroad depot at Crestline, Ohio, through which approximately fifteen thousand returning soldiers passed on their way home. Later, the 6th Regiment took up posts in Cleveland, Ohio, where it guarded property and maintained order as thousands of happy, celebrating troops traveled to their old points of enlistment.[87]

The duties performed by the 6th Regiment were not extraordinary. Other regiments of the VRC also played an important role in helping the army supervise its homeward-bound volunteers, guarding rendezvous camps and policing the streets and depots of cities along their routes home. Members of the 12th Regiment maintained order in the nation's capital, a hub for soldiers on their way to their discharges, even as its own ranks shrunk to 156 present and absent men by October 1865.[88] Men from the 3rd Regiment, continuing its duty in New England, guarded the rendezvous camp at Hartford, Connecticut.[89] A company of eighty-one men from the 3rd Regiment also assumed guard duties in Burlington, Vermont, where there was a rendezvous for that state's returning volunteers. In June, they found themselves engaged in a violent skirmish with returning soldiers, who destroyed property, started a fire, and generally misbehaved. After restoring quiet, the invalids resumed the less exciting duty of guarding government property.[90]

Many of the corps' enlisted men who lingered on in the service had had enough of soldiering and wished to go home, too. Worried about their wives and future employment, they thought it only fair that they be discharged.[91] Some of them still had to fulfill their enlistment contracts, but the government's desire to reduce expenses after the costly war would eventually lead to their dismissal. Still the VRC endured, but only for a short while longer. By the end of 1866, the War Department consolidated the remaining men into four Veteran Reserve regiments in the regular army, the 42nd, 43rd, 44th, and 45th.[92]

While in these regiments, the remaining invalids continued to perform duties and endure the unpleasant service conditions many of them had experienced earlier during the war. The 42nd Regiment, for example, assumed control of the military depot and prisoner of war camp on Hart Island, New York, off the northeastern shore of Manhattan. There the men moved into drafty, vermin-ridden barracks that were "of the very frailest character." Lt. Col. J. B. McIntosh, the regiment's commander, reminded his superiors that "Soldiers who have been wounded in the line of their duties, should have at least as comfortable quarters" as other men on the regular army.[93] In April 1867, when men from the regiment arrived at their new post at Madison Barracks at Sackets Harbor, New York, on Lake Ontario, they found their quarters to be no better.[94]

The Veteran Reserve regiments continued to recruit men who had been wounded during the war. By 1867, however, they experienced some difficulty filling companies, perhaps because their work was so boring and appeared unnecessary at a time when it was no longer essential for the nation's survival.[95] The 44th Regiment, for example, continued to stand guard in Washington, D.C., during 1867 and 1868. There, as during the war, the regiment was overtaxed, not having sufficient troops to devise a duty roster that did not place a strain on the men.[96] The regiment's burdensome service, however, did not last much longer. By the end of March 1869, the 44th, along with the other three Veteran Reserve regiments, disappeared from the army's rolls, their men either being honorably discharged or, if sufficiently fit, transferred into one of the regular regiments.[97]

Veteran Reserve Corps Officers and Reconstruction Duty with the Freedmen's Bureau

During the latter part of 1865 and into 1866, the army exercised postwar economy by reducing the ranks of the enlisted men in the corps to the point where many of their officers became superfluous. Consequently, in November 1865, the War Department ordered most of the corps' remaining officers to return to their homes and wait for further orders.[98] Once home, many of these officers feared, as Lt. W. F. DeKnight worried in March 1866, that they would be set adrift by the government. They existed in a limbo: how would the reorganization of the peacetime army affect them?[99] Obviously, belonging to a shrinking organization did not bode well for those officers who very much wished to hold on to their commissions.

These officers held a positive opinion of their service that differed from most of their enlisted subordinates. Enlisted men, for the most part, accepted that they had completed their duty with the war's end and happily left the corps. Many officers, on the other hand, eagerly and at times desperately sought out opportunities for remaining in the army. Many of them feared that their wartime injuries would prevent them from returning to their old civilian livelihoods. They believed that the postwar army offered them likely and honorable prospects. Some of the invalid officers admittedly enjoyed army life. The more idealistic among them felt that their duty to their nation was not yet complete as long as the postwar reconstruction of the erstwhile Confederacy still required the nation's attention; not until they had made certain the spirit of rebellion was extinguished and the rights of the former slaves of the South were secure would they feel comfortable returning to quieter pursuits.[100] Regardless of their specific reasons, they believed that their wartime sacrifices entitled them at least to the opportunity to hold on to their commissions. For all of these men, the Bureau of Refugees, Freedmen, and Abandoned Lands offered the best chance for staying in the army.

The Freedmen's Bureau, as the agency was popularly known, had already attracted the attention of VRC officers after Congress established the organization in March 1865.[101] Officers began writing to the bureau's commanding officer, Maj. Gen. Oliver Otis Howard, asking for employment. Lt. D. J. Connelly, for example, requested an appointment "in any capacity in which my services might prove useful owing to the reduced state of my company." He furthered his case by assuring Howard that he "could take a deep interest in the affairs" of his new agency.[102] Howard, desperate for personnel because of the financial limits Congress had placed on the temporary agency, had every reason to look favorably upon such requests. For example, he was without adequate resources for hiring civilian agents, thus restricting the size of the agency during the summer of 1865, when it could have had a significant effect on the future course of Reconstruction.

The reasonable alternative to hiring civilians, as Howard knew thanks to the letters that poured into his headquarters, was to use the VRC officers for bureau service. Late in the summer of 1865, for example, he asked the provost marshal general to keep track of suitable VRC men for the Freedmen's Bureau.[103] Into the spring of 1866, Howard petitioned the provost marshal general for the transfer of VRC officers into duty in the Freedmen's Bureau.[104] Even as Howard came to rely heavily on officers from the VRC, however, he never was able to secure the services of a sufficient number of them to make his agency a success.[105]

Because of the false economy of the national government, the Freedmen's Bureau placed those invalid officers that it did muster into its service in difficult circumstances. The officers routinely accepted responsibility for supervising the affairs of the freedpeople and their employers over a jurisdiction of several counties. Capt. John W. De Forest, the officer who wrote the final report of the VRC, assumed control over the subdistrict of Greenville, South Carolina, on October 2, 1866. His jurisdiction soon grew from two counties to three, covering about three thousand square miles—"an area at least two thirds as large as the state of Connecticut"—with a population of around eighty thousand people, including an estimated thirty thousand African Americans.[106]

De Forest's bureau routine kept him well occupied. As the bureau's sole representative in his three-county jurisdiction, he concerned himself with labor contracts, education, and the civil rights of freed slaves, as well as with tending to black and white destitution, all the while facing a white population with varying degrees of willingness to co-operate with him. Furthermore, he had to handle all of the bureaucratic paperwork that went along with these duties without the assistance of any clerical staff.[107] When he worked to see justice maintained in his jurisdiction, he more often than not had to rely on his powers of persuasion, rather than force, which meant he often failed to accomplish much for the aggrieved parties. As he explained, "Without a soldier under my command, and for months together no garrison within forty miles, I could not execute judgment even if I could see to pronounce it."[108]

The white intransigence that De Forest and other VRC men working with the Freedmen's Bureau faced certainly made their jobs all the more difficult. In Kentucky, a loyal wartime state but one that clung to the institution of slavery until the Thirteenth Amendment became part of the Constitution in December 1865, bureau men encountered whites who resisted Reconstruction whenever possible. In the spring of 1866, Capt. William H. Merrill of the 1st Regiment

VRC, who toured parts of the state in his capacity of acting inspector general for the bureau there, attested to that hard attitude so prevalent among the whites he encountered. He discovered, for example, that the "feeling toward the Freedmen was very bitter." In one county, the black residents would not provide information about "outrages" perpetrated upon them by their white neighbors because they feared retaliation from an organized band of "regulators." Furthermore, whites exhibited an open hostility not only to the freedpeople, including black veterans, but to the Freedmen's Bureau and the national government as well.[109] Such conditions prompted John Ely, Merrill's bureau superior in Kentucky, to ask for direct control of at least one thousand men, preferably from the VRC.[110]

The Veteran Reserve Corps troops requested by Ely could have made at least a small difference in the power equation of the postwar South, especially since throughout the Reconstruction era there never were as many federal soldiers as Southern memory later imagined.[111] The corps, however, was no longer a vital part of the army. Consequently, its officers serving in the bureau, as De Forest's experiences illustrated, frequently had to fend for themselves, often with unhappy consequences. Invalid officers serving with the Freedmen's Bureau were actually engaged in a simmering guerilla war with intransigent white Southerners who did their best to undermine and rid their states of the men who tried to implement Reconstruction. They were ostracized, threatened, and attacked. A few men even paid for their devotion to duty with their lives.[112]

Conclusion

At the start of America's Civil War, census data suggested that the loyal states would handily overwhelm their rebellious Southern sisters with armies rapidly mustered from their large military-age population. A quick victory, however, was not forthcoming, and as the war continued, the federal government learned that raw numbers did not easily translate into fresh regiments. Appeals to patriotism, bribes, and finally the threat of conscription helped encourage recruiting, but the federal government always needed more men to accomplish the extraordinary task it faced. Confronting a determined Confederate resistance, it needed to make use of every available opportunity to bring men into the ranks of its armies. In such circumstances, wounded and sick soldiers could not escape the government's attention, and in 1863 they found themselves in the ranks of a new organization composed of invalids.

The VRC successfully lived up to the expectations of the bureaucrats, proving that even these imperfect soldiers could still make an important contribution to the Union cause. Indeed, at times they exceeded those expectations, not only freeing up thousands of able soldiers for frontline duty but ably performing necessary military service behind the lines. These substandard soldiers also contributed significant service to the nation's transition from war to peace.

The desire to return to a military status quo antebellum, however, deprived the VRC men of an even greater role in the reconstruction of the former slave states. Nevertheless, the war-damaged men of the corps who received assignments with the Freedmen's Bureau continued to risk not only their comfort but their lives in the service of their country. Despite the shortcomings of some of the members of the VRC, the organization earned notice and respect for these duties performed. When John Ely, the Freedmen's Bureau commander in Kentucky and a former colonel of the 21st Regiment VRC, asked for Veteran Reserve Corps men to help him control the resentful white population in his jurisdiction, he noted that he had legitimate reasons for the specificity of his troop request. He explained that his experience "with that organization has satisfied me that a Veteran soldier who has received honorable wounds or disability in active service, after convalescing, makes the best soldier for any service."[113]

2

A Grand Illusion? German Reserves, 1815–1914

Dennis Showalter

At first glance, the German reserve system of World War I seems anomalous in this volume. Most of the other chapters address marginal elements of societies or armies, brought under arms out of desperation. The German army, by contrast, is generally credited with developing a system of organization, training, and command that by 1914 not only could fill its active units to war strength but also form entire divisions and corps effective enough to take the field on the same footing as troops of the line from the campaign's beginning.

But like all historical constructions, this impression of the German army combines accuracy, exaggeration, and pure myth. To begin determining the exact mix, it is necessary to step back a century and consider the Prussian Landwehr. This citizen militia, developed during the Era of Reform (1807–1813), proved sufficiently effective and popular that it was not merely retained after 1815 but became the foundation for a military system intended to blend training with enthusiasm.[1]

I

The Defense Law of 1815 in principle required three years' service in the active army and four in its reserve, then seven more in both the First and Second Categories of the Landwehr. Upon mobilization, each of Prussia's nine army corps would take the field with four active and four Landwehr regiments—regiments not identical in ethos but comparable in quality. However, even before natural increases in population combined with peacetime cuts in the military budget, the Prussian War Ministry recognized the impossibility of financing a full term of active service for every able-bodied man of twenty, except at the expense of everything else the army needed: weapons, equipment, food, and barracks. Shortly after Waterloo, the ministry's solution was analogous to the Selective Service System as practiced in the United States between the Korean and Vietnam Wars. Not only was the term of active service eventually reduced to two years—and often cut another six months as an economy measure—but more and more conscripts were administratively designated Landwehr Reserves and given no formal training at all.

The Landwehr was expected to be so popular that the conscripts' natural enthusiasm would compensate, with voluntary participation in drills and exercises substituting for time not spent in barracks. In the long peace after Waterloo, however, the Landwehr lost its novelty. Commissions in its officer corps were no longer widely sought by socially ambitious young men from the middle classes. Nor did Landwehr units develop social roles in their communities, in the fashion of Britain's volunteers and territorials or the U.S. National Guard. Prussia thus found itself with a reserve force of dubious effectiveness—and with an army whose effectiveness depended on the rapid, large-scale mobilization of those reserves.[2]

The consequences emerged during the German revolutions of 1848. By the summer of 1849, a Prussian government increasingly committed to counterinsurgency had called several dozen Landwehr battalions into active service. Despite widespread revolutionary propaganda, the military establishment tended to believe that at bottom "the people" were sound in heart and faith. A few weeks of barracks life and close-order drilling would be all that was needed to remind them where their true loyalties resided. Instead, from the Rhineland to Silesia public protests escalated into collective refusals of orders, looting and destruction of supply depots, and general indiscipline serious enough that one trainload of Berliners inspired warning telegrams along their route.

Politics had little to do with the disaffection. Assignments far away from their home districts antagonized men with farms or shops to run, and workers had no guarantee that their jobs would be kept while they were gone, nothing promising that their businesses, their work places, and their wives would be well and truly cared for. Admirably fit Landwehr reservists in their twenties, whose lack of training gave them lower priorities for call-up, stood in the crowds that gathered to see the thirty-somethings of the Landwehr on their way to glory. Marches caused blistered feet from ill-fitting boots and thighs chafed raw by the cheap cloth of government-issue trousers worn with nothing underneath—drawers would not become an item of uniform until after the Austro-Prussian War. Open-air bivouacs aggravated rheumatism and arthritis. Poorly cooked food and unboiled drinking water caused epidemic diarrhea. All these things might have been acceptable or at least tolerable in the context of the kind of national emergency thirty years of propaganda had told the Landwehr it was intended to confront. Instead, the future seemed to hold nothing beyond close-order drilling and intimidating civilians—a point by no means lost on the more articulate of the rank and file, who were often men of relative substance in their villages or neighborhoods.

The dichotomy between the political beliefs of the Landwehr officers and those of the active army have often been exaggerated. Men seeking Landwehr commissions, usually drawn from Prussia's commercial and official communities, were inclined to favor law, order, and hierarchy, but that was of no help preserving discipline in a context of chronic low-grade disaffection. The usual result was a tendency to give as few orders as possible and overlook everything that did not involve open mutiny.[3]

The active army had its own personnel problems. The experiences of 1848–1849 reinforced a growing opinion in the active officer corps that the existing system of conscription did not develop trained men but only drilled men, who performed by rote under orders but neither understood nor internalized what they were doing and why they were supposed to do it.[4] The argument that three years in uniform were required to develop an infantryman was apparently demonstrated so convincingly false in the next century that it has understandably been dismissed as a self-serving stalking horse advanced by an increasingly militaristic officer corps.[5] But at midcentury, no army anywhere in the world had developed anything like a functioning method of preparing short-service conscripts for long-range battlefields. It would take decades of trial, error, and experience to approximate the appropriate requirements and techniques. Even then, the results were at best questionable.

A first step toward reform involved brigading each line regiment with a Landwehr regiment, in the hope of improving the latter's training and cohesion by osmosis while giving the active regiment a greater interest in the welfare of its counterpart. That, however, meant that Prussia had to respond to anything but the most minor of crises with a general mobilization, and this at the price of disrupting the stable higher organization that was one of the army's few advantages over the improvised divisions and corps of France and Austria.

Nor did the restructuring address the problem of demographics. Prussia's population had been ten million in 1820. Now it was eighteen million. The annual conscription intake had, however, remained the same: around forty thousand. This discredited the principle of universal service by making the draft an increasingly random process that exempted some men entirely while imposing on others decades of active, reserve, and Landwehr service. Another consequence was the army's enforced dependence on large numbers of men in their late twenties and thirties. Prussia's fundamentally unbalanced conscription system placed in the front ranks men whose civil responsibilities were likely to weigh heavily on their minds and whose diminished physical vitality was uncompensated by increased mastery of the soldier's craft.

To revitalize the field army, the War Ministry proposed in 1858 that only men between the ages of twenty and twenty-six should be assigned to the active formations and their reserves. To keep costs within acceptable parameters, the term of active service would be reduced to two years. Men above twenty-six would serve in the Landwehr and end their military commitment at thirty-two. The Landwehr, in this model, would become the army's second line, to be employed primarily as garrisons and on lines of communication.[6]

Prince Regent William, who assumed formal authority in 1858, had long been a vocal and informed critic of the army's personnel system. He was aware that rapid improvements in the state's financial situation theoretically made more money available for the army. He understood that the Prussian parliament shared in general the opinion that significant military reform was necessary for Prussia to maintain its status (and, for the increasing number of German nationalists, to play a role in unifying Germany) in the face of Austrian and French hostility.[7] That reform, moreover, was generally accepted as involving a major overhaul of the Landwehr—exact nature unspecified.

William was assisted in organizing his thoughts by a memorandum from an officer who had been one of his staff officers earlier in the decade, someone he trusted personally. By his own admission, Albrecht von Roon was less proposing a detailed proposal for military reform than making his case as someone who would push through reorganization at all costs. That point conceded, Roon's document remains useful as a compendium of views widely circulated in the active army's officer corps. The establishment of universal suffrage in Prussia after 1848, Roon argued, had made the Landwehr a political institution by making Landwehr men into voters. That meant that instead of being a tool of state policy, the army in future could be employed only after public debate and consent.

Nor were those fetters compensated by operational effectiveness. Roon's insistence that three years of active service was the minimum time necessary for inculcating a "true soldierly spirit" is generally interpreted as a demand for the "militarization" of Prussia's young men in barracks and on parade grounds. In fact, Roon, like most of his counterparts in the officer corps, entertained no delusions about the possibilities of changing a young adult male's basic convictions via an extra twelve months in uniform. His reasoning was more subtle. In the modern world, the masses followed lines of least resistance. Put ordinary human beings into a coherent structure with an avowed purpose and provide effective leadership, consistent discipline, and fair treatment, and their convictions would not matter—they would behave as the organization wished. Roon agreed that it was fully possible to produce an adequately drilled soldier in less than a year, perhaps no more than six months. Drill and training, however, were not the same; one was the necessary basis for the other. Developing individual skill and group cohesion in an age of firepower required a substantial apprenticeship under arms.[8]

No serious objections were raised in public or Parliament when in 1859 the government took advantage of the mobilization authorized during the Franco-Austrian War to begin restructuring the army. In basic terms, the Landwehr regiments brigaded with the line units were renumbered as active formations, retaining their Landwehr history and honors but otherwise severing all ties with that institution. Terms of service were established as three years in the line, five in the reserve, and eleven in the Landwehr. The Landwehr formations that remained, 116 infantry battalions and a dozen regiments of cavalry, were authorized new cadres and a new mission: second-line duties in case of national mobilization.

From the military's perspective, these innovations were a stride in the direction of a New Model Prussian army combining the traditional Prussian virtues of low cost and high fighting power. The military budget, it was true, would have to be increased by a quarter, at least 9.5 million taler. Still, half this expense could be understood as a one-time investment in infrastructure: barracks, drill grounds, and schools of instruction.

In fact, paying for the reorganization was not a major political problem: the initial funding was readily approved by Parliament. The crucial question was who would control the purse strings: crown or Landtag. The Landwehr question became a wedge issue in that context, a focus for the arguments of both sides. The debate escalated into a constitutional crisis whose scope is outside the limits of this chapter, but it gave Roon his chance as hatchet man.[9]

Of greater direct significance was the smoothness of the army's institutional transformation. The Landwehr officer corps was already strongly acculturated to the line. For years, its tone had been set increasingly by bureaucrats from the lower and middle grades who perceived Landwehr service as useful in their government careers and as a means of social advancement. Far from representing the people as opposed to the aristocracy, far even from representing the rising middle class, Landwehr officers as a body identified themselves as officers of the King, as good as any line officer—and nothing less.[10]

The institutional reorganization shared center stage with (and arguably took second place to) the army's issues with developing functional balances among firepower, shock, and moral force. Preparing the new maneuver regulations issued in June 1861 had absorbed a good deal more of the army's energy than the political squabbling in Berlin. Future infantry combat, the new regulations suggested, should seek to engage the enemy in a fire fight, maneuver him into the open, exhaust his reserves, and then destroy him— a process of stages. Although battalion columns were encouraged whenever it was desirable to get somewhere in a hurry and in large numbers, company columns were recommended as the normal combat formation. Company commanders, however, were repeatedly warned to keep their men well in hand and not allow them to dissolve into an uncontrollable mass of skirmishers. Thanks to the breech-loading needle gun, the standard infantry weapon, fewer skirmishers were needed to screen the column as it maneuvered rapidly, searching for flanks and weak spots and taking maximum advantage of cover as it closed on enemy positions.[11]

As suggested earlier, Prussian officers entertained few illusions regarding the army's capacity to change fundamentally the values and attitudes of a conscript's lifetime in either two or three years. What they sought through the longer term of service instead reflected a fact that the army's liberal critics misunderstood or ignored. Arguably since the beginning of the fourteenth century—certainly since the end of the eighteenth—the demands of war had increasingly diverged from the circumstances of daily life at all social levels. The rise of the modern state had reduced to near vanishing the amount and degree of private, individual violence. The emergence of modern agricultural and industrial economies had reduced the randomness of making a living. Even death was becoming less a matter of haphazard routine and more of a predictable consequence of age or debility. Life, in short, was for the overwhelming majority of Prussian citizens less of a risk and more worth living than at any time in the state's history. What "technicians" among the midcentury army reformers sought was not a return to the good old days of living hard and dying young. They regarded military training as a way of leveling assumptions about the nature of the universe, with specific enlightenment on the nature of war. More pragmatically, the men who would go into future battles under Prussia's flag deserved a fighting chance to emerge alive—or at least to have their deaths not be in vain.[12]

An overlooked statistical anomaly developed from that assumption. The reforms increased the annual conscription intake from forty thousand to sixty-three thousand—not exactly an expansion calculated to shake Europe's balance of power to its foundations. To increase recruits in proportion to the expanded population, the number should have been closer to eighty thousand. It was not a concern for cost that kept the intake lower than it should have been. It was that the higher number could only be reached by lowering physical requirements.[13]

William's adamant opposition to that measure, a sentiment widely shared in the officer corps, reflected the conviction that in a long-service army of the traditional kind, older soldiers were often the most valuable soldiers, not only for their practical experience but from having survived sickness, disease, and privation.[14] The young men on whom Germany proposed to depend would be unseasoned: fitness must compensate. That meant transferring the four youngest classes of Landwehr reserves to the reserve of the active army in order to complete the now-doubled number of regiments upon mobilization.

Dierk Walter sarcastically and appropriately notes that the final result of the reforms (in terms of both institutions and personnel) involved little more than separating the Landwehr name from the field army.[15] Exchanging the shako and its "Landwehr cross" for the spiked helmet was hardly traumatic. The Forty-eighth, Fifty-third, and Sixty-sixth Infantry bore new numbers but had not lost their histories or their local identifications.

The new mobilization system worked smoothly enough in the six-week Austro-Prussian War of 1866. Tested more comprehensively against France in 1870, strains emerged. The front-loaded mobilization system of the Prussian-dominated North German Confederation immediately brought (for practical purposes) the entire active army into the field. It was not enough to finish the war against the grimly determined Third Republic that rose from Napoleon III's destroyed imperium. As casualties and sickness emptied regimental depots, Landwehr men entered the replacement pipelines. No fewer than four divisions built around the Landwehr saw action, with duties ranging from local security in quiet regions to sieges including Belfort and Strasbourg and to taking the field alongside active formations in the war's later stages.

Across the board, the Landwehr did well operationally and demonstrated at least as much endurance as its active-army counterparts. The Landwehr's primary mission remained rear security, and that too was well done. About 130 of the almost 170 nondivisional Landwehr battalions mobilized during the war served in occupied France, and no local commander ever complained of having too many of them.[16]

II

After 1871, it was clear that any future conflict, whatever its nature, would involve even larger armies. The Prussian system of conscription, extended across the new German Empire, increased the pool of reservists with every passing year. But the reserve system developed within two new contexts. Under the conditions of Bismarck's Reich, no significant element of German society, whether defined in economic, political, or ethnic terms, felt itself sufficiently excluded or sufficiently victimized to reject its chances in the system. Bismarck's demonstrated virtuosity at manipulating interest groups and creating new ones, usually described in negative terms, offered hope as well. The middle classes had for decades been pushing into the foci of status and power—a process understood not as selling out but as buying in.[17]

Moreover, after 1871, in a Second Reich lacking obvious common symbols of integration, association with the military experience became central to German self-identification.[18] That Germany had been united by the sword was a postulate unchallenged in the new Reich: to the public mind at least, the intellectuals, the businessmen, the politicians, the diplomats, and even Bismarck himself had ultimately stood aside for the soldiers. In 1898, the *Berliner Illustrierte Zeitung*, a leading popular magazine, polled its readers on significant people and events of the past hundred years. The public's choice as the nineteenth century's greatest thinker was Helmuth von Moltke.[19]

The argument that an increasingly conservative leadership was reluctant to expand the army's size because it feared penetration and corruption of the army by liberals, democrats, socialists, and Jews is familiar but correspondingly clichéd. Economics and demographics did at least as much as social considerations to shape the Second Empire's reserve system. The continuing growth of Germany's population after 1871, combined with falling death and disability rates among young men from a safer, healthier society, generated steadily increasing numbers of conscript-eligibles. At the same time, the political parties of the German Reichstag might agree on very little, but one fundamental point in common was an unwillingness to expand the army budget sufficiently to make universal active service a reality.[20] After 1890, an expanding navy competed vigorously for funding, effectively presenting itself as being at the cutting edge of industrialized warmaking.[21]

In a strategic context, the midcentury Wars of Unification had confirmed the long-standing Prussian tradition of applying maximum force in the pursuit of limited objectives. As a sated power, Germany was also the fulcrum of Europe. Protracted conflict, with its accompanying risk of becoming general, could only threaten both of its positions. The war with the French Republic in 1870–1871 had not changed the conflict's outcome. However, its dragged-out endgame left both combatants materially debilitated to a point where third-party involvement was a rational and dangerous possibility. Germany being in such a situation again could not be risked.[22]

The army's doctrinal and institutional response was to increase the emphasis on decisive battle: the battle of annihilation, *Vernichtungsschlacht*. Despite its apocalyptic ring, the term did not mean literal extermination. *Vernichtungsschlacht* involved the comprehensive defeat, physical and psychological, of the enemy at all levels, from the rank and file to the highest command. It meant the breaking of both will and the capacity for continued resistance.

It was intended as the single hammer blow, delivered by an army superior at its cutting edge to any in Europe, that would guarantee the Reich's future existence in an environment that increasingly did not wish Germany well.[23]

How best to produce soldiers able to fight and win that kind of decisive war? Above all, they could not be processed; they must be engaged. The annual recruit contingents, however, were best described as tractable. Products of a deferential, patriarchal society and an authoritarian state, they were unlikely to stage individual or collective acts of resistance—but neither could they be expected to cooperate proactively with the army system. The army's approach to the challenge reflects a side of its character overlooked or minimized by recent academic emphasis on the army of the Second Reich as being structurally dysfunctional, professionally inefficient, and best at translating apocalyptic ideologies into extreme behaviors from Africa to Belgium, France, and beyond.[24]

The definitive legal statement of conscription on the Second Reich was the Military Service Law of 1888. Remaining in force until 1914, it combined experience and prognostication in addressing the nation's strategic requirements.[25] Immediate liability included all males between twenty and thirty-nine. The law provided for three years of active service and four in the active reserve (in 1893, this was changed to two and five except for cavalry and field artillery), five years in the First Category Landwehr, and eight more in the Second Category. Men from seventeen to twenty and forty to forty-six were assigned to the Landsturm.

The primary innovation, and a major one, was the creation of the Supplementary Reserve. It was light duty: a twelve-year term with three call-ups of ten, six, and four weeks—and not everyone was actually summoned for these token drills. This category included all men between twenty and thirty-two temporarily unfit, excused for specific reasons, or not called up because there was no room for them in the ranks. By 1914, almost half of the theoretically eligible conscripts met one or another of those categories and were assigned accordingly.[26]

The conscription law, as actually administered, correspondingly incorporated an increasing spectrum of special circumstances.[27] Men who were the sole support of families or dependant parents could be deferred or entirely exempted. So could hardship cases among business or professional people able to make a case that military service threatened their livelihood: self-employed craftsmen, for example, or small shopkeepers. Students accepted as one-year volunteers were allowed to postpone that year for academic reasons. Medical students were eligible to serve for a year as aid men and physician's assistants, and *Sanitaetsgefreiter* Neumann entered army lore as a bawdy folk hero, equally capable in his search for love (or its simulacra) and in outwitting in turn conscientious sergeants, watchful chaperones, and outraged fathers.

The large surplus of available men enabled the setting of comprehensively high standards, making unnecessary the eventual French practice of assigning marginally fit men to regimental service companies. Army doctors seldom challenged the system except in flagrant cases of abuse. Unwilling warriors with good connections were known to benefit from wink-and-a-nudge doctors' notes: flat feet was a common diagnosis meriting exemption. Men who failed the physical were reexamined in two successive years, then assigned to the Supplementary Reserve or the Second Category of the Landwehr. It is reasonable to say that most of those who passed a later test wanted to pass it badly enough to implement programs of diet, exercise, and possibly minor surgery.

Conscription authorities tended to be generous, random, or hypocritical, depending on one's perspective. At the same time, not everyone who can meet or exceed the minimal qualifications to serve is necessarily promising military material. The Supplementary Reserve was a convenient way of selecting out those experience suggested would be more trouble than they were worth: the obviously vulnerable, the obviously hostile, the obviously clueless.

Suitability could also have political connotations. The political rise of Social Democracy in particular led to a pattern of discrimination against urban recruits with family or employment profiles indicating sympathies with the Left. Apart from the familiar political reasons, prior to the Great War it was an article of faith everywhere in military Europe that men from small towns and rural areas were better adapted physically and psychologically to the conditions of modern war than the allegedly less physically developed, more emotionally labile townsmen. Countrymen were also increasingly more likely than urban recruits to be more or less familiar with horses—a major factor when warmaking forward of the railheads depended on animal traction.[28]

The loopholes incorporated into the Supplementary Reserve system were generally understood by prospective conscripts. They were correspondingly acceptable, because military service was acceptable at all levels of society in a Reich made by war. The army never became the school of the nation and the hammer of socialism envisioned by right-wing idealists. For the mass of men in the ranks, however, military service did play a major role in certifying and affirming adulthood.[29] The dramatic changes in German society since the 1790s had invalidated or marginalized many traditional male rites of passage. Once completed, military service increasingly became a passport to adulthood: marriage, permanent employment, a place at the men's table in *Kneipe* or *Gasthaus*—all were associated, directly or indirectly, with a certificate of demobilization.

An easy rite of passage is a contradiction in terms. Institutional factors nevertheless facilitated acculturation to the uniform. The army's system of territorial recruiting meant that men were serving not necessarily with their friends and neighbors but alongside men with the same accents and backgrounds. Nor was the prospective recruit entirely a pawn of fate. If he volunteered for conscription, he had some choice of branch and regiment. The cavalry in particular usually had waiting lists, even though it required an extra year of service. The showy uniforms impressed the ladies, and the army was easier than a broad spectrum of entry-level civilian jobs. Commanders sometimes allowed recruits to express preference for a company, battery, or squadron: this was a chance to improve one's specific circumstances, since only a fool failed to inquire among reservists about his regiment's internal dynamics in advance of reporting to duty.

Military service offered an adult latency period. It was a chance to escape from the restrictions of home: to drink, brawl, and lose one's virginity out of sight of parents and pastors. As a familiar army rhyme put it, to become a real solider the recruit had to spend at least three days on bread and water in the regimental guardhouse. Discipline could be harsh, but good officers and NCOs understood when to look away, when to laugh or swear in private over the infinite ability of young men to get themselves in trouble. Especially the country boys seem to have appreciated their opportunities. A high proportion of complaints about the demoralizing effects of conscription came from small-town fathers and pastors as disturbed by their loss of patriarchal authority as by their sons' loss of innocence while serving the state.

For all the horror stories that fathers, uncles, and brothers enjoyed telling about their time "with the Prussians," the conscript found himself part of an institution ultimately designed to enable success. No military system, especially a conscription-based one, can function if its standards are too high for most of its members. Old soldiers hazed new ones, but more in the sense of an initiation, as opposed to the comprehensive, efflorescent brutality that characterized the armed forces of the Soviet Union in the regime's final years. From the system's perspective, hazing that became more than an uncomfortable game was bad for discipline. From the old-timers' point of view, hazing could be expensive in other ways. For example, regulations required certain standards of appearance. They did not specify how they were to be achieved. A man handy with a needle and thread or able to bring boots to an inspection-level shine could put a fair amount of money in his pocket dealing with the *Hammel*. A man who knew the ropes and judiciously shared his knowledge seldom had to worry about paying for his beer and cigars.

Most recruits reported in early autumn, just after the harvest. Fall and winter were devoted to what Americans called "the school of the soldier": instruction in wearing and maintaining uniform and personal equipment, close-order drilling, physical training, marksmanship (surprisingly important in the Kaiser's army), and not least standards of order, cleanliness, and hygiene in barracks that were at best close quarters. The instructors' task was complicated by the recruits' civilian conditioning. The daily routines of barracks (sewing on buttons, washing clothes, scrubbing floors) were woman's work, and the best-willed conscripts required time to learn and apply the new and unmartial skills.

Time and patience played a much larger role in German basic training than most Western accounts credit. Recruits were trained in the companies to which they were assigned. Effectiveness as an instructor was not only a major responsibility but a fundamental standard for promotion for officers and NCOs alike. They were given wide latitude—a peacetime exercise of that individual initiative so important in German operational doctrine. Results, and how they were achieved, were nevertheless closely scrutinized. In practical terms, the demands of the drill ground and the gymnasium were designed to be met by average recruits at an average level of motivation. Underperformance was likely to bring down collective punishment on their comrades, as sergeants and corporals struggled to bring their squads up to unit standards. Extra duty in the kitchens or shoveling manure was frequently accompanied by an after-taps "visit from the Holy Ghost," a beating administered in the barracks room as a motivational exercise. But too much unofficial "instruction," too many entries in a punishment book, too many drill days lost to the guardhouse, and the responsible superior could usually count on an unpleasant session with his own superiors, centering on his fitness for his assignment and his career.

In early May, the recruits in each company were inspected; most moved on to straight duty. The rest of the spring and summer was devoted to higher-level unit training, then maneuvers. With autumn, as recruits crowded the barracks, freshly minted reservists commemorated their active service by purchasing assorted souvenirs and looked forward to intimidating the younger generation with peacetime war stories that improved with every round of schnapps.

The bourgeoisie had a particular *douceur* dating back to 1814: the institution of the one-year volunteer.[30] These were men with higher levels of education, able to pay their own expenses and perform a year of active service instead of the prescribed two or three. As it developed in the Second Reich, the system is usually described in terms of its role as the army's principal source of reserve officers. Reality was more complex. Volunteers were in theory eligible to apply for a commission in the reserve or the Landwehr. It was universally understood that anyone with the wrong political orientations, social origins, or religious affiliations had little or no chance. When all else failed, the active regiments' officer corps had the same right to vote on reservists as on regulars—and unanimity was required for acceptance.

Kaiser Wilhelm II might inform reserve officers as late as 1913 that he did not entertain high expectations of them.[31] As in so many other things, he did not speak for an army that regularly summoned its inactive officers to one- and two-month exercises—nor for most regiments, who, once they approved an officer, usually sought to integrate him into the community. As for the reservists, they had worked hard enough and paid enough dues for their commissions that most took their responsibilities as seriously as their privileges both before and during the Great War.[32]

Being a one-year volunteer had other advantages. It was a mark of middle-class status. It saved a year or two of time for embarking on a profession or learning a business. Not least, it offered prospects of better treatment while in uniform. Such considerations continue to move Western society's privileged classes even in the twenty-first century. Once in the regiments, "one-years" could be in for a rude surprise. They were not really officer candidates but enjoyed enough exceptions and exemptions from routines to be a running challenge to the noncoms. But a volunteer who took some time to build himself up physically before reporting, who knew when to laugh at a dirty joke and buy a round of drinks or a handful of cigars, or who was willing to play Cyrano for a word-shy comrade and take an extra turn on latrine duty could have a memorably enjoyable year—at least in retrospect.[33] And for most of those who did not receive commissions, the army had a consolation prize: appointment as an NCO in the reserve or Landwehr. Schoolteachers, clerks, and other members of a burgeoning white-collar class, welcoming the stripes as part of an upward-mobility starter kit, made up the core of the Imperial Army reserve's enlisted commanders.

This discussion of the active army's institutional culture and training methods is necessary to establish the matrices in which the reserve system functioned. The German army was a citizen force. Military service was expected to enhance loyalty and inspire enthusiasm, not to produce sullen, broken-spirited automata. Lapses and abuses were widely noted in press and Parliament. Internal investigations produced a high rate of courts-martial and convictions. Administrative discipline separated other offenders from the service quietly but permanently.[34] The weak, the clumsy, the "mama's boys" (*Muttersoenchen*), those who did not adapt, and those unfortunate enough to become "designated scapegoats" could be and at times were driven to the edge of collapse or suicide.[35] Nevertheless, between 1871 and 1914 the everyday routines of peacetime military service were not regarded as excessively straining the average man in his early twenties. Exceptions only validated the generalization.[36]

The active-army experience at minimum produced class after class of men who reported for their annual two-week refresher training willingly and on time. The active regiments provided cadres and facilities; men were recalled between February and December. The staggered timeframe was intended to minimize disruption both to the general economy and active-unit training routines. Reserve NCOs and NCO candidates were summoned a week or two early and placed in charge of an active cadre responsible for reinvigorating esprit de corps and restoring the confidence considered necessary to command. Both were considered, reasonably enough, to be eroded by normal civilian experience—especially since most reserve NCOs had gone no higher than *Gefreiter* (Private First Class) during their active service. And there was no time to refresh either on the job.

Even though comprehensive regulations and years of experience provided a tight framework, getting the reservists settled and preparing for their departure, plus the intrusion of at least one Sunday, cut actual training time to around nine or ten days. The stated principle of the training period was to develop effective performance under simulated combat conditions. For individual soldiers, that meant restoring a sense of successful participation by replicating familiar training processes. It began with uniform inspections and close-order drilling. Marksmanship was restricted to single exercises in squad and platoon firing: cartridges were expensive. Sweat was not. Reservists' physical conditioning was restored by constant marching. Distances and loads, initially short and light, were increased until the men were able to march around twenty kilometers a day under full packs with standard rest periods of ten minutes each hour.

Individual refreshment was the preliminary to exercise by units: company, battalion, and eventually in regiments brought close to war strength for the sake of realism. Regimental and battalion commanders, company first sergeants (*Feldwebel*), and key administrative personnel were regulars. Company officers were a mix of regulars and reservists, most of the latter commissioned on completing their volunteer year. Emphasis was on commanding larger units—a war-strength company of over 250 men could be daunting to a captain accustomed to one of half that size. Arguably more than in active units, in principle reservist exercises kept written orders to a minimum in favor of encouraging initiative. Training at the battalion level featured operating as advance, flank, and rear guards, enveloping movements, and when possible cooperation with cavalry, artillery, and eventually machine guns. It also incorporated at least one night exercise, which was usually the low point of the fortnight in terms of performance but, properly evaluated, a major learning experience as well.

Training emphasized offensive action, in part as a means of disabusing reservists of any notion that they were second-line troops with defensive missions. And, not least, attacks against blank rounds and marked enemies nurtured the pride and sense of achievement on which the reserve system ultimately depended. "Attack" did not mean running forward shoulder to shoulder led by sword-waving lieutenants. Like their active-army counterparts, reservists were exhorted to move in deployed lines, taking advantage of terrain, digging foxholes, even constructing field entrenchments if necessary.

The advance was by rushes in small groups, responding to orders when possible, otherwise exercising initiative to close the range for a final assault.[37]

Practice could be disconcerting. Officers regularly reported losing contact with their men in the field as practice attacks dissolved in confusion. No amount of exhortation could keep men from bunching up instead of spreading out, even when the guns were firing blanks. Off duty, the temporary soldiers tended to treat the occasion as a reunion and celebration. When a group of artillery reservists took the opportunity to get blind drunk, their battery commander responded with a paint-peeling lecture and threatened to put the whole outfit through extra drills. His actual, relatively mild punishment of the culprits with a day's arrest probably reflected the exigencies of scheduling discussed above: guardhouse time was not an officially designated learning experience. Nevertheless, in a typically Wilhelmine catch-22, the captain found himself featured in a local Social Democratic newspaper as a brutal militarist.[38]

The two training periods authorized for the Landwehr during their three to five years of service in the First Category were supposed to replicate those of the active reservists. In fact, they left a great deal to memory—especially since men older than thirty-two could not be called up for refresher training in peacetime without a special imperial order, usually depending on a budget surplus that seldom existed. Over forty, with no training to speak of since their Landwehr days, most *Landstuermer* were expected to stay home for summons as needed for emergencies that did not involve strenuous effort.

In the first year of the Great War, the Institute of Applied Psychology in Potsdam began collecting material for a psychographic study of "warriors." One typical respondent declared that he had volunteered on the first day of mobilization, but from patriotism rather than any overpowering enthusiasm for war as such. Another stressed the sense of nationalism cultivated in his student fraternity. A third said he enlisted because he was "ashamed" to remain a civilian while family men were being called to arms. No one spoke of hatred for Germany's enemies or of anticipation of a "fresh and joyful war."[39] Their statements reflect and illustrate the growing body of evidence that the militaristic "hurrah-patriotism" long associated with Germany in 1914 has been greatly exaggerated. Instead, the public mood was sober, reflecting an understanding of Germany's war in quite precise terms: a defensive conflict against a coalition of implacable enemies.⁴⁰ The army might have put "a nation in barracks," but the result had been less a people of warriors than a state of soldiers: citizen soldiers—perhaps even civilians in uniform.

III

How best could those citizen soldiers be used? The mobilization plan of 1875 incorporated "Field Reserve Troops," no fewer than thirteen divisions, each with four infantry and one cavalry regiment plus three or four batteries of artillery—the same as their active counterparts. Their missions were to secure lines of communication, perform occupation duties, and reinforce the active units when needed. And their title of "Reserve" barely camouflaged their origins. All 180 battalions initially came from the Landwehr. Twenty-odd additional independent "Field Infantry Regiments" were also to be built around the younger Landwehr classes as well as active reservists surplus to requirements.

By 1889, the Field Reserves had reached a paper maximum of eighteen divisions and thirteen separate brigades. The number of active reservists had grown to a point where they could provide the bulk of the manpower. Men from the First Category of the Landwehr, aged from twenty-six to thirty-two, made up the balance and formed an increasing number of separate brigades as well. The thirty-somethings of the Landwehr's Second Category were designated for occupation and garrison roles and were structured accordingly: around two hundred infantry battalions and no fewer than forty-eight battalions of foot artillery, along with smaller numbers of cavalry and field batteries. The Landsturm added another two hundred battalions plus support troops, which would be available for home defense and security duties only in a national emergency, given the effect of their mobilization on industry and agriculture.

Ongoing controversies, nurtured and facilitated by Bismarck, between the War Ministry and the General Staff, helped change the Field Reserves' mission. To oversimplify a complex issue, the General Staff favored numbers and was not especially concerned about paying for them. With the passage of time, the General Staff also grew less concerned (at least relatively less concerned) with preserving the caste spirit of the officer corps at the expense of an expanded army. The War Ministry was, in contrast, more socially conscious when it came to officers' civilian origins. It was also materially oriented, favoring allocating funds for developing and purchasing weapons systems and exploring other technological developments as a possible alternative to a one-sided reliance on mass.[41]

The "reserve question" was consistently and often simultaneously a source of contention and an instrument of compromise between the General Staff and the War Ministry. The recent dispute over the existence and nature of the Schlieffen Plan has produced so many statistics on the subject of available forces at specific times that it is easy even for specialists to become confused.[42] After 1871, the German army's cutting edge remained the corps: eight infantry regiments organized in two divisions, plus a steadily increasing amount of artillery and a couple of cavalry regiments for scouting and screening. Behind them came the reserves. But growing doctrinal emphasis on short, decisive war led to questioning the wisdom of holding back trained men who might turn the tide if deployed at the front. Their cadres on mobilization would include serving officers and NCOs transferred from the active battalions. The mobilization process enabled relegating older and less fit men to depots or lower-priority formations. It was only logical that the General Staff began considering reserve brigades and divisions as potential front-line troops to front load the order of battle.[43]

The initiative served the interests of a decisive offensive war without the pain of convincing the Reichstag and the War Ministry to pay for the privilege of changing their institutional minds on the subject of numbers. As early as 1880, Chief of Staff Helmuth von Moltke the Elder incorporated two reserve divisions into the field army facing France, replacing active formations assigned to reinforce fortresses. Since the latter were considered exposed to greater immediate risk, the reservists were still essentially replacement troops. Assigning them to active corps with front-line responsibilities was nevertheless a major difference from the 1860s.

How many reserve divisions could the field army absorb without risking dilution? The rule-of-thumb ratio that developed through the 1890s was one to two. And that posed another problem. The army corps as it developed in Europe was roughly the force able to pass a single point on a single day using a single road: around thirty thousand. Simply adding a third division to each active corps overexpanded command-and-control networks. It complicated logistics by overcrowding roads and wreaked havoc on tactical doctrines and systems based on binary higher organizations.

These were no small problems, given the German emphasis on offensive maneuver. Mobilization plans initially coped by assigning half or more of the reserve divisions to "Army Detachments" deployed in secondary sectors on secondary missions. The 1905 plan, for example, defined the reserves' main responsibility as covering the flanks of the main advance, against Antwerp in the north and Verdun in the south.[44] But the flexible German way of war was designed to make any sector of any front potentially important. Doctrine, training, and organization were designed to foster uniformity, enabling any corps or division to perform the mission of any of its counterparts. The vaunted Prussian Guard was a structural elite, its recruits selected for physical development, its parade drill rigid, and its field training demanding. In no way was it an operational elite in the pattern of its Napoleonic predecessor or its panzer successors, intended for crucial sectors or situations.

An interim solution was to organize the reserve divisions into reserve corps. After the turn of the century, urban districts (Brandenburg and Silesia, the Ruhr, and the Rhineland) increasingly were able to provide enough surplus active reservists for two divisions.[45] Since active-army supporting units were allocated and organized by corps, adopting the corps system for the reserves allowed common tables of organization—an important factor given the already complex and increasingly tight schedules for mobilization and operations. The headquarters would be formed on mobilization, but a new corps was more likely to handle two divisions effectively than an equally ad hoc army detachment would be able to cope with a half-dozen. And sandwiching reserve corps between active ones in a general advance minimized the vulnerabilities of inexperience.

Increasing the number of larger reserve formations was facilitated by the active army's method of expansion. The post-1871 organization of eighteen corps persisted until 1890, when two more were added. Three more in 1899/1900 and two in 1912 brought the total to twenty-five. These were not created out of thin air. The process began with the creation of extra companies, then battalions, in existing regiments, giving them time to find their feet, then assigning some new and some old battalions to the regiments, brigades, and divisions of the new corps.[46] The process took several years, and as a result active corps frequently had extra brigades and regiments awaiting eventual new homes. Leaving them in place on mobilization disrupted loading times, movement schedules, and eventually tactical doctrine. For a few years at the turn of the century, most of the leftovers were initially grouped into ad hoc "war corps" (*Kriegskorps*), the General Staff's substitute for the expanded active army it wanted.[47] By 1914, the extra formations were considered best used by distributing them. Four reserve corps had an active brigade, three an active regiment, as fillers and role models.

Testing reserve divisions in peacetime was anything but stress free. Divisions were large, complex formations. Commanding one was considered a quite respectable capstone to a career. In 1906, VI Corps organized a provisional reserve division as part of its annual exercises. German and foreign observers generally praised the results. Conservatives (and realists) nevertheless warned against overestimating the potential at mobilization of formations existing only on paper.[48] Erich Ludendorff, one of the General Staff's rising stars, was less pleased with the maneuver performance of reserve divisions. But out of necessity, the army devoted more of its energy to improving the reserve formations' effectiveness.

Moltke the Younger, appointed chief of staff in 1906 upon Schlieffen's retirement, was an eloquent advocate for giving reserve formations larger active cadres, increasing field training for reserve officers and NCOs, and raising armament and equipment to active-army standards.[49] That last remained a significant problem in two crucial areas. Even Schlieffen had tempered his enthusiasm for reserve units by warning against organizing divisions and corps unless they could be given a "more or less" adequate number of guns. Not only was the active army increasing the number of guns in a corps to 160, including thirty-six newly designed 105-mm howitzers and sixteen 150-mm medium howitzers, but the Germans, caught behind the technological curve when France introduced *Mademoiselle Soixante-Quinze*, were also forced to replace all their field guns with what amounted to a new field gun of their own. This expensive process remained incomplete at the outbreak of war: reserve corps were mobilized with only seventy-two guns, no field howitzers at all, and no organic medium pieces.[50] Less visibly but tactically no less disadvantageous, twenty-five reserve regiments (almost a fourth of the total number) took the field without a machine-gun company.

On the other hand, mobilization procedures were so polished that both active and reserve regiments were able to leave the same depots within the six to eight days provided by the schedule. The army had been able to lay in more or less full stocks of equipment: uniforms, weapons, vehicles, horses. In most reserve battalions, two or three of the company commanders and first sergeants were active soldiers and thus able to keep routine confusion to a minimum. Boots and clothing were marked and sized to specific wearers. Civilian authorities were engaged to coordinate requisitioning horses, arranging billets, and similar matters involving the community. Students proved indispensable as messengers and errand boys.

A typical reserve regiment began its existence on the second day of mobilization, with its senior officers and NCOs preparing for quartering the newcomers. By the fourth day of mobilization, companies were up to strength. As medical officers weeded out the less fit, those who passed spent the next three days in fitting uniforms (especially boots), target practice, and route marches with rifles, cartridge belts, and full packs. No less important was the simultaneous process of accustoming horses to new drivers and fully loaded wagons. But despite the complexity of the mobilization of the reservists, on August 9, 1914, the Fifteenth Reserve Infantry Regiment was ready for the field: eighty officers, 3,230 enlisted men, and six machine guns.[51]

The smooth and rapid mobilization was more than a strategic advantage and an administrative tour de force. It contributed significantly to morale and, by extension, effectiveness, by demonstrating the army's "culture of competence." The ability to deliver mail, provide reasonably edible food, and generally convey an everyday sense that the system knows what it is doing can compensate for massive levels of tactical ineffectiveness and strategic cluelessness. Germany's first-line reservists took the field in 1914 with a boost unmatched in mass conscript armies.

The Landwehr was the field army's third line, and its basic field formation was the Mixed Landwehr Brigade. Formed by corps districts, they included six battalions, three or four batteries, and a squadron or two of cavalry. These composite units were ideal as flank guards, rear security, and for holding quiet sectors in emergencies. There were nineteen of them, seven being grouped into "Higher Landwehr Commands" 1 and 2. In addition, a Landwehr corps was formed upon mobilization for service in the East: two divisions each of four regiments but only twelve guns.

Once the ranks of the active, reserve, and Landwehr formations and their depot battalions were filled, enough men remained for most regiments to form additional units. The "Mobile Ersatz Battalions" were built around older active reservists and younger Landwehr men still unassigned and completed by the better trained and fittest Supplementary Reservists. The number of men with limited training was kept as low as possible, though a twenty-two year old unmarried construction worker from the Supplementary Reserve was in practice likely to be preferred to a thirtyish Landwehr man with glasses, three children, and a peacetime desk job.

Standard mobilization procedure was that each infantry regiment of an active corps raised a Mobile Ersatz Battalion. Each field artillery brigade contributed two batteries. The result was a Mixed Ersatz Brigade: four or five battalions and four batteries. Most of them were grouped by threes into six ad hoc Ersatz Divisions after completing their individual mobilizations. These divisions were structurally anomalous, with the artillery remaining attached to the brigades, and usually including a battery of field howitzers—the latter not otherwise the case in reserve formations. They were not originally intended to take the field without some time to work up and shake down. The War Ministry had to authorize their commitment to operations. Medical units and supply trains had to be organized from scratch. It took three or four weeks to make up basic shortages of personal equipment—too often by levying on replacement battalions themselves increasingly constrained to make do with the bits and pieces the field units had left behind.[52]

IV

The German army that took to the field in 1914 was in principle built around men who had gone through a full term of active service, even if years earlier. That had been the rationale for the reforms of the 1860s. With the misbegotten Ersatz divisions, Germany's reserve system began to fray around its edges. It all but unraveled with the organization in mid-August of thirteen more divisions, which would enter German mythology as the "innocents" slaughtered at the First Battle of Ypres.

The myth that the new formations' ranks were filled with adolescent volunteers has been well and truly demolished. So has the parallel myth that the volunteers were primarily students or otherwise from the "educated classes." As many as a third of the quarter-million or so "war volunteers" (*Kriegsfreiwilligen*) accepted by the army in August 1914 may have been workers and craftsmen. Their distinguishing demographic feature was youth, as over half were under twenty. Their distinguishing military demographic was random distribution in the "August divisions." Volunteers made up three-fourths of the 201st Reserve Infantry Regiment, and less than

20 percent of the 219th. Whatever the remaining balance, it was made up from men of the Landwehr and the Supplementary Reserve who had remained in the depots, put to work learning or relearning the basics until they should be needed in the replacement pipeline—or, more optimistically, for the victory parades. The Supplementaries were likely to have had no training whatever to speak of. Between them and the volunteers, that was the state of three-fifths of the infantry's rank and file. The Landwehr were mostly leftovers, older men filtered out of the mobilized regiments, their active service long behind them.

Giving such a near-random mixed bag only two months to be ready for combat in the field was an irresponsible gamble. The formations lacked everything from maps to lieutenants. Meals tasted as if the cooks had taken special army courses in how to ruin them. Comprehensive material shortages reduced officers and NCOs to keeping men busy with saluting drills and exercises in foot care and oral hygiene—not so much from peacetime pedantry as for lack of any reasonable alternatives. Once in the field, the junior leaders as a group failed to convey a sense of grip: the air of competence (however assumed!) that remains a major element of controlling fear and confusion among inexperienced soldiers.[53]

The catastrophic results in front of Ypres, however, were remarkable more as an archetype than an exception. Newly raised reserve formations and elite regiments of the Prussian Guard alike were shot to pieces by handfuls of exhausted British troops; frontal attacks and flanking movements both collapsed in bloody confusion.

Results had been no more glorious further south, in the halcyon days of the Schlieffen Plan, when anything seemed possible. Lieutenant Erwin Rommel was a career officer, twenty-three years old and fighting fit. Captain Walter Bloem was a forty-something novelist with an incipient paunch and a reserve commission. Rommel's first experiences kept him twenty-four hours on his feet, then set his platoon to attack a French village in blinding fog. He collapsed on the field of honor: "not least the terrible condition of my stomach had sapped the last ounce of my strength." Captain Bloem lost his innocence at Mons: "Wherever I looked, right or left, were dead or wounded . . . [our] proud, beautiful battalion finished the day an ineffective rabble."[54]

That point made, the German system worked. In the war's opening campaign, there was no significant, systematic difference between the performances of active and reserve divisions.[55] Some were better than others; any one might have a "bad quarter of an hour" or a bad few days. Even at regimental and battalion levels, where active formations might be expected to be smoother and more polished, officers and NCOs made the same kinds of mistakes as their reservist counterparts. Rommel and Bloem both served in well-regarded active regiments.

Did that pattern reflect technology, doctrine, or training? In material terms, at the sharp end, against automatic machine guns, rapid-firing rifles, and shrapnel, the German infantryman had the speed of his two legs and the protection of a fraction of an inch of cloth.[56] As for doctrine, the military theorists of the Second Reich were increasingly convinced that a decisive battle in the literal sense was no more achievable than Clausewitz's corresponding concept of absolute war. Even Schlieffen's more favorable scenarios arguably involved a series of rapid victories on the frontier that would cripple the French army and set the stage for further operations in the interior over six to nine months. By 1914, that period was being extended to as long as two years in some General Staff circles. In any case, victory would take a while, and it would be expensive. The challenge lay in minimizing its cost.[57]

In that context, two schools of thought continue to exist regarding training. One describes a tactical conservatism generated by a mutually reinforcing toxic combination: first, class consciousness generated a belief that a potentially disloyal population needed to be controlled in battle even more than in politics. Second, the maturing industrial era fostered a commitment to the concept of mass *fin de siècle* heroic vitalism and encouraged the belief that willpower and fighting spirit as manifested by aristocratic officers would inspire the rank and file to rise above themselves.[58]

The other side of the debate presents a German army that came to understand and take seriously the battlefield problems posed by modern firepower and mass armies. Specifics varied, but all incorporated some balance of enthusiasm and technique: of drill to instill discipline with instruction to develop initiative, of firepower with shock, of open-order advance using cover and concealment with an ability to come to close quarters at the finish when necessary.[59]

Either paradigm made high demands. Could they be met systematically, predictably? In the specific context of August 1914, any chances for the short, decisive conflict on which German policy and strategy were predicated depended on an "institutional katana"— the kind of tempered blade envisaged, however vaguely, in the

1860s reforms. Instead, Germany went to war with a heavy, blunt instrument created by a conscription system built around numbers, averages, and loopholes. It depended on and was diluted by reservist officers and enlisted men whose training and skills were inevitably blurred by disuse and who were allowed no time for refurbishing. The limited difference in performance between active and reserve formations in the war's first weeks reflected leveling down—not up.

Postscript

In 1915, new divisions were formed by reducing existing ones from four regiments to three; no distinction was made between active and reserve regiments, and no systematic differences were observed in effectiveness. The replacement system became increasingly homogenized. Divisional designations were left unchanged, but their quality and employment were judged by performance. As an indicator, there were sixty-two divisions trained for the 1918 offensives; thirty were (nominally) prewar active formations, fifteen prewar reserves, and seventeen were wartime creations.[60] And the pattern of leveling down persisted. During 1916, the German high command accepted, albeit unwillingly, that the army had become a militia.[61] Many of the new divisions that Ludendorff was forming in 1916 were from garrison troops, now considered good enough for the front—at least quiet sectors—releasing other units for real fighting. Wilhelm Deist commented that by 1918 the army had devolved into a uniformed proletariat that ended the war by a "camouflaged strike."[62]

The hecatombs of the Great War owe at least as much to limited skill at arms, broadly defined, as to defective doctrine.[63] By 1918, events had gone far to establish the mass citizen armies of Europe's age of nation-states as a temporary anomaly, one created by the industrial revolution but rendered at least obsolescent by industrial war. The German army was better prepared for the war that actually unfolded in 1914 than any of its European counterparts. Its strength was nevertheless its critical weakness: the army was a fundamentally wrong tool for the job.

3   Manifestly Inferior? French Reserves, 1871–1914

André José Lambelet

Among the many sins of the French army in preparing for what would become the Great War was the sin of omission: it failed to envision Germany's massive use of reserves from the start and to adequately plan the use of its own reserves. In his memoirs, Marshal Joseph Joffre explained,

> Up to this time we had been convinced that the Germans would assign to their reserve troops only tasks of secondary importance, very much in the way we expected to use ours. "No fathers in the front line," as William II had put it, and his words had been repeated in the Reichstag in June, 1913. The phrase seemed to accord with the theories favoured at this time by the German Army, where it was considered that success must be based upon the intense violence of the first encounter. We were, therefore, justified in accepting that our adversaries would not entrust the fate of the first battles to manifestly inferior troops.[1]

Despite clear indications that the Germans *were* intending reserve units for front-line combat, Joffre continued to believe that German reserve units lacked the "combat power" for an initial offensive.[2] He acknowledged the dire consequences.[3]

If Joffre bears the lion's share of responsibility for France's strategic decisions in 1914,[4] his doubts about reserves reflected long-standing conflicts within France about the nature and role of the military. Prewar projections showed the depth of those suspicions for mobilization: the army's planners expected that up to 13 percent of mobilized men would fail to report for duty.[5] This chapter aims to explain the origins and development of the French mistrust of the reserves, a mistrust that is particularly notable because of the importance that reserves played in French military organization.

Since the Revolution, French military organization had fluctuated between two poles: on the one extreme, the mass armies of the Revolutionary *levée en masse*; on the other, the long-service professional armies of the Restoration and the Second Empire. Mass armies could be justified because sheer numbers were decisive in modern warfare; they could also be justified on the grounds that soldiers fighting for a cause they believed in would be better soldiers than professionals (or mercenaries), whose motivations might be selfish. Quality and quantity could go together. Professional armies, on the other hand, could be justified because long-service regulars, within the rigid disciplinary structures of the army, were better trained, better disciplined, and more amenable to the harsh conditions of modern warfare. Between these two extremes lay a vast territory of compromise: conscription, more or less extensive, for a greater or less duration, combined with a body of trained reserves.

By the eve of the Great War, France had its compromise, a military system in which reserves figured prominently. While all fit men were obliged under the 1913 law to serve three years in the active army, they were also required to serve an additional ten years in the active army reserve, followed by seven each in the territorial army and the territorial army reserve. The fighting core of the army was meant to be the units of its active army, brought to full battle strength by an influx of the younger classes of the reserves, backed by units of older reservists and the territorial army.

Antecedents

A century earlier, the French had been pioneers in mass warfare and relied on armies of enthusiastic citizens. On August 23, 1793, the National Convention decreed the famous *levée en masse*:

> The young men will fight; married men will forge weapons and transport supplies; women will make tents and uniforms and serve in hospitals; children will turn old linen into lint; old men will have themselves carried into the public squares to rouse the courage of those who fight, to preach hatred of kings and the unity of the Republic.[6]

The Revolutionary army, however, would not win because it had mobilized more men but because its soldiers were fighting for a cause, an ideal. Citizen-soldiers would fight harder than mercenaries. Yet while the *levée en masse* was the origin of the idea of the nation in arms, it was not conscription in the modern sense; that came only with the *loi Jourdan* of 19 Fructidor VI (September 5, 1798), which, for the first time, created a regular system of conscription. Men aged twenty to twenty-five could be required to serve for a maximum of five years.[7] However, all military obligations ceased when a man reached the age of twenty-five; there was no reserve commitment.[8]

After Napoleon's defeat, France, bled dry by two decades of virtually continuous warfare, renounced mass armies and moved to the other extreme: a smaller army built around professional officers, NCOs, and long-service troops.[9] The 1818 *loi Gouvion Saint-Cyr* reintroduced conscription to France after a brief hiatus.[10] Military service was compulsory but not universal: only a small fraction of each class was called up. Conscripts were chosen by lot for a term of six years. The system also included "replacement": men who drew a "bad number" could pay someone else to do their military service for them; thus the poor made up most of the troops.[11] The 1832 *loi Soult* increased the duration of conscription to seven years and imposed a new obligation of reserve service—but one without practical significance. Reserves played essentially no role in the military system from 1818 until 1868.

The army, though based on compulsory service, remained a professional one. The length of the term of conscription meant that common soldiers were alienated from life in the villages and towns from which they came. Soldiers stood outside the currents of everyday civilian life; veterans were treated with suspicion and sometimes hostility by civilians.[12] This alienation benefited the army: conscripts often opted to reenlist, so there was an ample supply of experienced NCOs.[13] If their toughness sometimes made soldiers objects of popular suspicion, it also made them an effective force for France's wars. It was a commonplace, reinforced by successes in Algeria, the Crimea, and Italy, that French soldiers had a special kind of fighting spirit, the *furia francese*, which resulted from the happy combination of long service and the putative hereditary martial qualities of the French.[14] Armies of professionals were, the French military insisted, better disciplined and thus better under fire than armies of short-term conscripts.

The realization that reserves might be crucial in modern warfare began to dawn on French military leaders during the Italian campaign of 1859, when France faced a shortfall of active-duty troops and utterly lacked trained reserves.[15] But it was the stunning successes of the Prussian armies in 1864 and 1866 that brought the issue of military reform in general and reserves in particular to the fore.[16] The French military attaché in Berlin wrote agitated reports about the power of the Prussian army, and some prominent military officers began questioning convictions of French military superiority.[17] The French, however, were unable to embark on the kind of wholesale reform necessary to meet the Prussian threat. The only concrete result of the agitation was the 1868 *loi Niel*, which retained the conscription lottery, reduced active-duty service to five years, but tacked on four years of reserve duty afterward.[18] The reserves, however, remained poorly trained, and mobilizing them was cumbersome. By article 30 of the law, a wartime imperial decree was needed for each separate class of reservists. Notoriously, the Niel law also created the *garde nationale mobile*, a militia auxiliary to the active army. Its theoretical responsibilities included defense of fortified places, coasts, and borders and maintaining public order. A special law had to be passed to mobilize it. No funds had been allocated for training and no units had been formed when the Franco-Prussian War broke out in 1870.[19]

Events on the battlefields quickly revealed that the French army was overmatched.[20] On September 2, 1870, Napoleon surrendered at Sedan with tens of thousands of his troops. The professional army, made up of *vieux soldats* ("old soldiers"), had failed. Two days later, Léon Gambetta and Jules Favre proclaimed a republic—and a "government of national defense" under the leadership of General Trochu.[21] Gambetta himself, with Charles de Freycinet, directed the war effort. They sought to replicate the success of the Revolutionary *levée* and succeeded in raising more than a million soldiers in five months. The makeshift Army of National Defense, however, fared no better than the army of professionals. On January 28, 1871, the French agreed to an armistice, which required elections to ratify a peace treaty. In a country exhausted by war, the republicans' uncompromising bellicosity cost them dearly: monarchists won roughly four hundred of the 645 seats in the National Assembly.[22] On March 1, the new legislature reluctantly ratified a draconian preliminary peace agreement. To make matters worse, Paris erupted in insurrection in March 1871.[23]

Universal Conscription?

In the wake of the defeat, vital constitutional and political issues were up in the air. Should France be a monarchy or a republic? Should it have a unicameral or bicameral legislature? How would it pay its five-billion-franc indemnity? Yet in this turmoil, almost everyone in France recognized the urgent need to rebuild the army. Differences over the nature of the regime seemed to pale next to the need to build an army capable of repelling the Germans. The National Assembly's speed shows this: on May 17, 1871, even before the Paris Commune had been crushed, it created the "Commission of Forty-Five" to examine the army and propose new legislation.[24]

Over the next four years, three important laws emerged: a recruitment law, a law on the organization of the army, and a law on cadres and effectives.[25] Each would have an important effect on the reserves and the relationship between reserve duty and active duty. To varying degrees, the Prussian army would be the inspiration for all three.

The Prussian army was superior technically: it had made better use of modern transport, had developed and deployed better artillery, and had a large and competent general staff.[26] The most crucial difference between the armies was Prussia's reliance on short-term conscripts and well-trained reserves. Yet whether and how the French should adapt the Prussian system was the subject of fierce debate.[27]

The March 1872 report of the Commission of Forty-Five divided army reform into two categories, recruitment and organization.[28] Recruitment had wide-ranging political and social consequences and would take priority. The nature of the defeat in 1870–1871 narrowed the choices for reform. The rapid destruction of the long-service army seemingly demolished the notion that France could rely on a small army of professionals, but the failure of the Army of National Defense suggested that a hastily improvised *levée en masse*—no matter how enthusiastic its soldiers—could not compete with a well-trained, well-armed, and well-led army. (The experience of the Paris Commune was another warning about the dangers of arming the citizenry.)

Between the discredited extremes of pure citizen militias and pure professional armies, the territory of compromise included variations on broad conscription combined with a trained reserve. Republicans, both radical and moderate, made the most sweeping arguments in favor of universal male conscription and building up the reserves. The war forced republicans to rethink their hostility to standing armies and their attachment to citizen militias, as Jules Ferry ruefully admitted: "This country has seen the war of 1870: it has forever turned its back on these perilous and deceptive utopias."[29] Like almost everyone in France, they understood that the Prussian system had deployed more and better-trained troops in the initial campaigns. In 1871, Charles de Freycinet, who had served as Gambetta's chief of military cabinet, wrote, "France was defeated because she was weaker. This inferiority appeared in a triple aspect: by numbers, by armament, and by organization."[30] Now, republicans embraced universal military service for both pragmatic and ideological reasons.

For republicans, universal conscription would field as many trained men as possible—but just as important, it met republican demands for equality before the law and would help revitalize France. A truly *national* army, one that served the interests of the French people rather than the particular interests of the regime, could be reconciled with the Jacobin traditions that republicans claimed. An army of citizen-soldiers would be more likely to fight bravely in defense of the nation.

One of the most cogent—and uncompromising—republican explanations about the nature of the citizen-soldier was given by the deputy Jérôme Farcy, a member of Gambetta's *Union républicaine*.[31] In August 1871, Farcy proposed reducing the term of conscription to two years but eliminating exemptions. *All* men would serve two years, subsequently spending three years in the *garde mobile*.[32] Farcy explained that, according to well-informed generals, soldiers were at their peak after two years of service. Farcy claimed the duration of military instruction could be reduced dramatically: soldiers could be properly trained in as little as six months; the remainder of their service in the active army would be spent on maneuvers that genuinely replicated the conditions of war. The two-year soldier, Farcy declared in June 1872, "has not yet had the time to be led astray by the bad principles of the barracks; he is still supple, obedient, and devoted, or, at least, he is much more so than the 'old soldier.'"[33]

If long military service could be detrimental to the moral health of young soldiers, it also posed a larger threat: soldiers who served five years under the colors would constitute a standing army (*armée permanente*). This, Farcy declared to the consternation of deputies on the right, was "a praetorian army rather than a national army."[34] Farcy's approach came as close at possible to the Revolutionary *levée en masse* while still maintaining a trained army. Shortening active duty to the minimum necessary to train soldiers avoided the danger of troops separated from the concerns of civilians; they would retain their attachment to the virtues of civilian life and simultaneously be better soldiers. Soldiers who strongly identified with their countrymen would be unlikely to take part in military action against other citizens. (This was the mirror image of the conservatives' logic that the state might need the army to put down popular insurrections.) Thus, universal equal male conscription fit neatly into a democratic republican idea linking the rights and obligations of the citizen while simultaneously placing an institutional check on the arbitrary power of government.

Farcy's proposal suggested that the military *qualities* of the French soldier came from the French citizen. Military service gave the soldier the proper *instruction* in the use of arms and the ability to perform military tasks. While Farcy distinguished between soldiers of the active army and of the *garde mobile*, his logic suggested that the difference was minimal. It would take little effort to bring reservists into the fold, because the discipline and motivation of the soldier was *not* a function of active duty. Republicans were not, however, unanimous. Gambetta remained silent during most of the debates on recruitment, perhaps because he had been persuaded that in the short term, reconstituting an army took priority over the form of that army.[35] Or he may have believed that conditions in France were not yet ripe to create the bellicose citizen-soldier idealized in his speeches.

That bellicose citizen-soldier was characteristic of radical republican contributions to debates about the recruitment law. Radicals were clear about one thing: the identity between the citizen and the soldier. In a summer 1871 speech, Gambetta declared that the republican citizen must not only "think, read, and reason, I want him to be able to act and to fight." And, in the ringing phrases that were Gambetta's stock in trade, he added,

> Next to the schoolteacher we must everywhere place the athlete and the soldier, so that our soldiers, our fellow citizens, are all able to hold a sword, handle a rifle, complete long marches, spend the night under the open skies, valiantly endure every challenge for the patrie. We must push these two educations to the fore, otherwise you will create a work of *lettrés*; you will not create a work of patriots.[36]

In 1872, when the recruitment bill was debated and passed into law, republicans were a small legislative minority with little direct impact on the recruitment law. Yet the "dangers" of long service and the "merits" of short service would become increasingly important as republicans began to win seats in the late 1870s and early 1880s.

Military officers based their argument for universal military service on an assessment of military capability. Many high-ranking officers argued that the Prussian system was militarily superior to the French system.[37] Led by Marshal Mac-Mahon and the generals Chareton and Guillemaut, they urged the adoption of short-term universal male conscription for pragmatic reasons: in modern warfare, numbers mattered. They did acknowledge the failures of French military leadership and preparation. The Prussian army had been able to mobilize and concentrate many more men much faster than France. Prussia's system had clearly outperformed France's army of long-service conscripts.

Their idea was of universal service, but of longer duration than the republican nation-in-arms model: three or four years. The focus of this system was on numbers, but numbers of active-duty soldiers rather than reserves. Professionals concluded that numbers, materiel, discipline, and training were the keys to French defense. The war showed the need for larger forces, necessarily implying a broadening of conscription. To officers, universal military service was not primarily or even importantly about politics or social change: it solved the technical problem of improving French military capabilities. Universal conscription harnessed the human resources necessary to fight modern, large-scale warfare, but it inevitably represented a tradeoff between numbers and quality.

Alongside the need for greater numbers, though, was the conviction of many officers that the army needed intellectual reform. The man who would later command the *Ecole supérieure de guerre*, Colonel Jules Lewal, declared that the formula for a successful modern army was "Obedient masses, very intelligently led."[38] This aim also suggested the need for improved military education. The concern for a renewal of military education linked pragmatically minded officers with some conservative politicians.

These politicians argued that the French nation had been found wanting not just militarily but morally. Universal military service would furnish the troops to fight a modern war and also serve as a corrective to the decadence into which France had fallen. Discipline from the army would rebuild the patriotism that was lacking in soldiers—a notion diametrically opposed to that emanating from republicans. For some conservatives, the need to improve the civic-mindedness of the people of France justified the equalization of military service. The old system of purchased exemptions would eventually erode the public spirit: "If the *patrie* were endangered, even gravely threatened, hearts would no longer stir in the same way, a kind of selfishness would appear, and many individuals would no longer measure their misfortune by any standard other than what they had to bear personally."[39] This, rather than the republican belief in citizens' fundamental equality, was why the Commission of Forty-Five argued against the old system.

In the war, to be sure, French soldiers and volunteers had fought with enormous courage, but the principle of equal military service would reinforce this courage. It would also serve as a corrective to the possibly corrosive effects of democracy on order and liberty. "Let us proclaim it loudly, because it is true, gentlemen, the army is the great school of the nation!" the report trumpeted. That school would teach future generations about "patriotic sentiment, discipline, and honor," and the nation would receive "a virile education that will not be without influence on its destiny!" The school would nonetheless classify its students "in advance according to their aptitudes"—a reminder that the commission did not share the profoundly egalitarian sentiment of radical republican military reformers.[40]

The most formidable opponent of a Prussian-style system was Adolphe Thiers, who as "chief of the executive power of France" (monarchists had denied him the title of president of the republic) wielded enormous authority. Thiers believed the problem in 1870 primarily had been poor political leadership. Radically changing the army was therefore no answer. The "professional" army of very long-service soldiers best suited France's political and social condition. Long-term conscription had served France well; he felt that long-term soldiers were better able (despite recent evidence to the contrary) to fight wars than short-term soldiers and reserves. Thiers suggested that recruitment was inextricably bound up with the political, social, and historical character of a nation, so he made "little or no concession to the idea of universal conscription that had been the theoretical basis of the military reform of 1872."[41] France could not adopt the Prussian system of military recruitment because her social and political structure differed from Germany's. Nor would the French national budget, weighed down by the costs of the war and the peace settlement, permit the adoption of a Prussian-style regional system. Furthermore, the adoption by France of a regional system of reserves would be "a veritable counter-revolution."[42] Finally, a nation's army had to match its character, and the French were not temperamentally suited to military service. The key to France's past military glory and its future success lay in the fighting qualities of its soldiers, so the only possible way to instill those fighting qualities was by long service. Thiers would have made the reserves a simple auxiliary to back the real fighting force of France; their only function would have been to hold down fortifications in the rear and to maintain public order.

In the end, the 1872 recruitment law compromised between these views, creating a modified system of universal conscription. As its first article declared, "All French men owe military service." By extending military obligations to twenty years (five in the active army, four years in the reserves, five in the territorial army, and six in the territorial army reserve), it created the structure for a massive pool of trained reserves.[43] Yet the law was less egalitarian than its first article suggested. While all French men *owed* military service, the law did not impose *equal* military service on all men. Each annual "class" of young men who had turned twenty the preceding year would be divided into two portions: the first would serve a term of five years; the second would be released from the active army, having served a maximum of one year. The minister of war would decide, based on the need for men and budgetary limits, the size of each portion of the contingent, but the selection was by lottery. The one-year men, though not yet formally part of the reserves, had a status called *disponibilité*, or "availability," and could be recalled to active service if the need arose. They were also supposed to take part in military exercises.[44]

While the law abolished the hated system of replacements, it borrowed a provision from the Prussian system: the one-year volunteer. Article 55 stated that holders of the baccalaureate could preempt the lottery by volunteering for a year of service, provided they paid for their own uniforms, horse, equipment, and upkeep. At the end of their year of service, they could, if they wished, take an exam to become noncommissioned officers in the active army. Otherwise, they would remain on *disponibilité*, subject to recall. To critics, the provision was little more than a way of protecting the sons of the bourgeoisie from the rigors of full-blown active duty. The minister of war's power to waive the financial requirement for those who had demonstrated their merit and were unable to pay reinforced the sense that this provision was unjust.

Exemptions and deferments created further inequality. Some were plainly worse than others: while few complained about exemptions for men incapable of serving in any capacity, rules on the eldest sons of widows, orphans (the provision that orphans be legitimate seemed especially unfair and arbitrary), and the exemptions for students at certain of France's elite *grandes écoles* who committed to public service for ten years caused considerable friction. But it was the provision for the exemption of many ecclesiastical students that sent republicans into a white fury, and it was the broadening of this exemption that prompted Léon Gambetta to declare, "But I say that one must go further, and that it is the commission's system itself that must be condemned, on pain of committing a poignant injustice that nothing justifies, above all in light of the immense mutilations to which you have subjected the principle of compulsory military service."[45]

While Gambetta apparently gave his tacit assent to Thiers' demand for a five-year term, the manifest injustice of a system that required some men to serve up to five years and allowed others to defer their service continued to vex republicans. Until the passage of the two-year law in 1905, they would focus most of their attention in military matters on equalizing the burden of active-duty service. The "mutilation of universal service" meant, furthermore, that future debates would revolve around the time it took to properly train a soldier. Military officers, naturally enough, viewed the men on active duty as the key element in future wars; when republicans pushed to equalize and shorten military service for all conscripts, most officers evaluated these efforts on the basis of their impact on active-duty soldiers. As the historian Joseph Monteilhet observed, the assumption underlying the 1872 law was that universal conscription necessarily involved a compromise between quality (provided by long-service troops) and quantity (supplied by reserves).[46] The central focus of the law was the active army.

Ironically, though, the principle of equality was best reflected in the provisions for reserve service. For the first time, France had a system that incorporated a robust framework for reserve service. While many could defer or reduce their active-duty service, that was not true of the reserves and territorial army. All men shared this obligation; in theory, at least (and in contrast to the system produced by the Niel law), all reservists would have had some military training. The central tension in the law was between ideas about the nature of soldiers and the origin of their ability to fight effectively. On one side was the idea that republican citizens would be effective soldiers if only they got the basic instruction necessary to learn about marching, shooting, riding, and so forth; on the other, the idea that the military qualities of soldiers stemmed from submission to military hierarchy and discipline.

Organizing the Army

After the recruitment law, the army had four separate categories of soldier: the active army, reserves, territorials, and territorial reserves. Then there were the men of the *disponibilité*—men nominally within their period of active service but not actually under the colors. (These included the second half of the contingent, along with the volunteers who had completed their year of active duty and certain categories of exempt men.) But the distinctions among these men were not as clear cut. In peacetime, active army units always operated at reduced strength; in wartime, the *disponibilité* men would be assigned to active army units, along with the younger reserve classes, bringing them to full strength. The remaining reservists formed the reserve units.

The July 1873 law on army organization and the March 1875 law on the constitution of cadres and troops drew sharp distinctions between the active army and the territorial army.[47] The 1873 law established nineteen military regions: eighteen in metropolitan France and a "special" region in Algeria; each region would support an active army corps and a territorial army corps.

The active army corps, consisting of two infantry divisions, one cavalry brigade, one artillery brigade, and a logistics squadron (*escadron du train d'équipages*) was supposed to be ready for campaign. It always had a full complement of officers, administrative units, and materiel. The 1875 law detailed the composition of the army in meticulous detail, down to the number of buglers and drummers per company.[48] Reservists played a vital role in the active army: each infantry company had a legal minimum peacetime strength of sixty-six men; its wartime complement of 250 was reached by incorporating men of the army reserve.[49] Together, the active army and the reserves would total approximately 1.25 million men. The territorial army, with reserves, would double that number.[50]

The territorial army corps, however, was a shell. In peacetime, its staff consisted only of the personnel needed to perform the administration, accounting, and mobilization preparations.[51] Although it had a permanent roster of officers and NCOs, the men were not actually present except during annual maneuvers or mobilization. In principle, recruitment for the active army was national, but troops of the territorial corps were drawn exclusively from men domiciled in the region.[52] The major purpose of the territorial army was to function as a defensive second-line army (guarding fortifications, defending the coasts, and securing "strategic points"), but its members could also be formed into field units serving alongside the active army.[53]

Beyond the organizational differences between the active army and territorial army, there were important differences in the officer corps.[54] The active army obtained officers through a "dual recruitment" system set up by the 1818 Gouvion-Saint-Cyr law, which the military laws of the 1870s retained. To become an officer, a man either served two years as an NCO or spent two years at a special military school and passed a barrage of rigorous exams.[55] After the Franco-Prussian War, requirements became more stringent: the dismal performance in 1870–1871 highlighted the deficiencies of officers promoted from the ranks. They had negligible higher military education: they had never taken courses in strategy or tactics, topography, map reading, or logistics. An 1874 decree required NCOs seeking commissions to spend a year in special schools getting the general and technical education to make them better officers.[56] (Ironically, this made promotion more difficult for men from the "popular classes" just as a republic that preached equality was poised to take power.)

The active reserve and territorial army drew their officers from elsewhere. The 1875 law created a "reserve officer cadre" to furnish the "personnel necessary for the mobilization of the active army." These men were drawn from retired officers of the active army, graduates of the *Ecole polytechnique* and the *Ecole forestière*, one-year volunteers who had passed an exam, and doctors, pharmacists, and veterinarians. Finally, former NCOs of the active army who had not yet finished their nine-year obligation but who had been declared suitable for commissions by their commanders could also become officers.[57] Not only was their recruitment different; an 1878 decree stipulated that reserve officers were to serve as auxiliaries to regular army officers, not lead men into combat.[58] The requirements for territorial officers were even less stringent. One of the consequences was to inculcate a sense of qualitative difference—based, it must be said, on reality—among the different corps of officers. And this feeling got worse, rather than better, over time.[59]

Under the 1872 recruitment law, active reservists had to report for two maneuvers, each of twenty-eight days.[60] (Territorial army soldiers, by contrast, were not required to maneuver until the 1889 recruitment law, underscoring the low expectations of the territorial army. Members of the territorial reserve would never have an obligation to take part in peacetime maneuvers.) Annual maneuvers took place in autumn and were meant both to provide training to soldiers and to give commanders experience with full-strength units.[61] Dismissed by some as "theater organized in advance,"[62] maneuvers nonetheless helped create a sense of duty and obligation among reservists and revealed that soldiers of the active army and reservists alike "interiorized the values of courage, discipline, and duty."[63]

Although the basic organization of the French army was settled by the laws of the early 1870s, reserves were pushed in several different directions. Republicans sought to eliminate the inequalities of the 1872 recruitment law; conservative officers and politicians fought bitterly against republican efforts. The growing influence of offense-minded doctrines of warfare militated against the growth of the reserves. Finally, there were structural problems.

The Legacy of Inequality

In the early 1870s, a time of political turmoil and international uncertainty, republicans accepted a recruitment law that fell far short of their demand for equality for all male citizens. As they began to win power at the ballot box, they pushed to rectify what they saw as a manifest injustice. But because the inequality applied only to the active army, debates would focus on the duration of active duty—not the reserves. As early as 1876, republican deputies tried to reduce the official term from five to three years but made little headway.[64] After crushing republican victories in the 1881 elections, the question could no longer be deferred, but attempts were painfully slow and convoluted.[65] It was not until 1889 that the bill finally passed. Active-duty service was limited to three years, but to the chagrin of republican reformers, most of the exemptions survived, as did the division of each annual class into two parts and selection by lot. Some men would still escape a full term of military service.

While the 1889 law reduced the active-service obligation, the overall obligation rose from twenty years to twenty-five years: time in the reserves increased from four to seven years, in the territorial army from five to six years, and in the territorial reserve from six to nine years. Reserves continued to be obliged to take part in two maneuvers each lasting twenty-eight days, and now territorials had a two-week exercise. Rather than being subject to two twenty-eight-day periods of maneuver during four years of reserve service, reservists were now subject to those same periods over seven years. Because these were spread over more time, the average reservist was much further removed from active duty than under the 1872 system.[66] The age of the oldest reservists shot up: previously, with a nine-year period of service in the active army, units of the active army would consist of troops aged twenty-one to thirty; now French reservists would be as old as thirty-four—significantly older than their German counterparts.[67]

Little was done to make better use of reservists. This largely stemmed from a deeply rooted conviction in conservative circles that military service and democracy were antithetical. In 1885, Etienne Lamy and General Gaston Galliffet published the two-part "L'Armée et la démocratie" in the influential *Revue des deux mondes*. They witheringly attacked the premises of the republican reforms.[68] As they saw it, the problem in 1872 had been twofold: to equalize French and German numbers but also increase quality. Republicans, Lamy and Galliffet insisted, were not interested in combat readiness but in entrenching their particular political agenda, even at the cost of military readiness: "To an assembly that had organized everything in the nation for the development of the military force there succeeded an assembly that would do everything in the army for the triumph of democracy."[69]

While they acknowledged that soldiers could be *instructed* reasonably quickly, Lamy and Galliffet declared that proponents of short-term service "had forgotten one single thing, that his business [*métier*] confronts the soldier with death."[70] They insisted that the only way to conquer that fear was to spend long years absorbing military *education*, which to them was a constellation of values centered on self-abnegation: "Ignorance gives way to study, that is to say, to time."[71] Long service was particularly important in a democratic society, because democracy was not about a collective identity but individual advantage: "Men who think about it rarely find the occasion weighty enough to get themselves killed. Such a people will not contemplate victory, but will think of battle, of blood; even to reach the Promised Land, it will not wish to cross the Red Sea."[72]

Consequently, only soldiers who spent long years under the colors were fully ready for modern war; the unstated corollary to this was that reserves would lack the cohesion and solidarity of active army soldiers because they lacked the continual disciplinary framework of the army. These arguments were reprised in the National Assembly by such conservative stalwarts as Count Albert de Mun.[73] During debates in June 1887, a vehemently antirepublican deputy, Adrien Gaudin de Villaine, took the argument a step further. Three-year service was suitable to Germany because "The German army is a large family that is essentially aristocratic, authoritarian, and, if I might say so, feudal." Democratic France could not trust the nation in arms: "In a monarchy the principle of the nation in arms is a military truth, [but] in a democracy like ours, it is a heresy, and what is needed in a democracy, the past has proven to us—and history does not change in these matters—is a professional army, an army of 'old soldiers,' of veterans."[74] Although the three-year law passed, the alleged incompatibility of democracy and discipline became an increasing part of the rhetoric of military-civil relations.

That incompatibility, of course, would explode into the public arena with the arrest, trial, and conviction of Captain Alfred Dreyfus.[75] Well before that affair, however, the groundwork for suspicion between republicans and army officers had been laid—based in large part on very different ideas about the nature of French citizens. Conservatives suggested that the soldiers had to be controlled and disciplined continually; discipline was difficult to instill and easy to lose. Republicans, for their part, did not deny that war entailed risk but asserted that the citizen-soldier, grounded in republican virtues and republican patriotism, would accept the dangers of war in order to save his nation.

David Ralston has noted that the conscription law of 1889 "did not represent a significant or important new departure in French military affairs, as had the 1872 law."[76] Practically, three-year service was a concession to reality: already, under the 1872 law, members of the active army were almost invariably released before the end of their service period—usually less than forty-six months.[77] Yet the tenor of the debates around the three-year law suggests that attitudes toward conscripts and reservists had significantly shifted.

In 1871 and 1872, there were serious differences over the shape of French military institutions, but the National Assembly was working toward a common goal: resurrecting the French army. In the 1880s, this was no longer the case.

For the reserves, the notion that the discipline necessary for modern warfare was slow to acquire and easy to lose meant that the most solid troops would be those of the active army.

The Impact of the Offensive

Fears about citizen soldiers' self-interest were compounded by the revival of interest in offense in the 1880s. An offensive strategy had proven disastrous in 1870, so the French high command had initially adopted a defensive strategy to give time to concentrate behind fortifications instead of launching a headlong attack with unprepared forces.[78] Reservists would have time to mobilize; if not immediately serving in front-line units, they would provide the necessary backup.

While the defensive posture was a nod to reality, it was nonetheless deeply unpopular among French officers.[79] As the memory of the war receded, officers began to develop a powerful set of arguments in favor of the offensive. An important contribution was the 1880 republication of Colonel Charles Ardant du Picq's *Étude du combat d'après l'antique*,[80] which asserted that material factors alone could not account for victory either in ancient or modern times. He concluded that two kinds of forces were involved in battle: a unit's "material action," which he defined as its "destructive power," and its "moral action," defined as "the fear it inspires."[81] The notion that morale was crucial found increasing support among writers on military affairs and professional military officers. A constellation of influential officers—Colonel Louis Maillard, General Henri Bonnal, and Lieutenant Colonel Ferdinand Foch, among others—tirelessly trumpeted the virtues of the offensive.[82]

The evolution of the army's attitude toward the offensive can be gauged by army regulations, which disseminated official doctrine. The 1875 infantry regulations, noting the devastating firepower of modern arms, required cautious and dispersed advances. By 1884, infantry regulations proclaimed the "principle of the decisive attack, head held high without concern for losses" and insisted that courageous and well-led infantry could advance under heavy fire and capture even well-defended enemy positions.[83] Certainly, the Second

Boer War and the Russo-Japanese War caused temporary pauses. The interim regulations of 1902, along with those of 1904, returned to dispersed advances.[84] Yet advocates of the offensive soon regained the upper hand, proclaiming that critics of the offensive had simply misunderstood the lessons of the Boer War.[85] The apotheosis of the offensive was reached in the infamous 1913 regulations: "The lessons of the past have borne fruit: the French army, returning to its traditions, recognizes no law in the conduct of its operations save the offensive."[86]

Mobilization plans likewise reflected an increasing skepticism about reserve troops and, over time, deemphasized territorials and reserves. Until 1884, the concentration of forces would take place far from the northeast, the region likely to be the source of conflict. The army would have time to gather its forces, including its territorial and reserve units, and thus avoid the calamity of having to go to war piecemeal.[87] Even as the shift toward more aggressive plans began in the late 1880s, large numbers of territorials were still included.

Mobilization plans were developed in rapid succession; the role that would be made of territorial and reserve soldiers shifted just as rapidly, underscoring the uncertain place of reservists and territorials in French military thinking. Plan IX, developed in 1888, envisioned "mixed" regiments, that is to say, regiments composed of companies of both active and territorial soldiers. Plan X anticipated eighteen new army corps (designated *bis*) to match the eighteen active army corps of metropolitan France; in 1891, Plan XI halved that number to nine army corps *bis* but boosted six active army corps with a reserve division.[88] In January 1895, Plan XIII created one new reserve division per active army corps, four army corps *bis* (of two reserve divisions and two territorial brigades each), and a fifth army corps *bis* of one active army infantry division, one reserve infantry division, and one territorial brigade.[89] Plan XIV of 1898 entirely eliminated the reserve army corps and relegated territorial troops to garrison duty.[90]

Between Plan XIV and the Great War, though, several attempts were made to give reserves a more significant role in French military organization. Most notable was the 1911 attempt by General Michel, vice president of the *Conseil supérieure de la guerre* and one of the few ardent advocates of reserves in the army, to create "demi-brigades." On mobilization, each active regiment would be joined with a newly created reserve regiment, doubling the number of wartime soldiers. Without any support from his colleagues on the *Conseil supérieure de la guerre*, Michel was forced to resign.[91]

Because the 1889 law had failed to redress their grievances about exemptions, republican reformers always viewed it as a compromise and came increasingly to see it as a bad one. Though the three-year law made more young men liable for the full term of military service and reduced the inequality between the long- and short-service components of the contingent, by the turn of the century almost a third of conscripts served only one year. This also compounded the shortage of NCOs: those most suited by ability and by education to take leadership roles in the army found ways to escape their full military obligations by pursuing liberal professions.

An Army of Reserves?

A new recruitment law in 1905 finally enacted what republicans had sought for decades: abolishing exemptions and reducing service to two years. Debates over the law repeated the themes that had been raised before: two years was insufficient to form real soldiers, democracy demanded equality, and so on. However, while the outcome was hardly in question (especially given the discredit into which many senior officers had fallen during the Dreyfus Affair), one fact stood out: senior military officers opposed the reduction. An offensive strategy, which they believed was the only way to win a modern war, could not be carried out with reservists.

The military problem facing French army commanders was to obtain a sufficient number of soldiers who would be disciplined enough to advance against withering fire, to train and retain a sufficient number of noncommissioned officers who would provide that disciplined "framework," and to recruit and educate officers who could lead their soldiers into battle. In the first decade of the twentieth century, the balance sheet was decidedly mixed.

There were serious efforts to improve the quality of the reserve officers. A series of changes in the promotion rules helped ensure that officers were qualified. Requirements to earn a commission were tightened: the 1889 law, for instance, finally abolished the one-year volunteers, whose qualifications were shaky and who did not, in any case, furnish very many officers. Now, reserve officers had to have served a full year as a NCO.[92] Nevertheless, in the early 1900s, the reserve officer corps was in full-blown crisis. Many would-be officers had been driven away by the crushing burden of an 1894 regulation demanding they attend weekly courses; by the time the regulations were eased in 1897, the Dreyfus Affair was in full swing, further discouraging potential reserve officers. In 1900, the army faced a shortfall of 4,300 reserve officers; by 1903, that shortfall had risen to seven thousand.[93]

The 1905 law was a turning point.[94] Military instruction became an integral part of the curriculum, not just at the *Ecole polytechnique, Ecole normale supérieure*, and the *Ecole forestière*, which already were supposed to provide military instruction, but also at the other *grandes écoles*. Their students had to perform a year of service as ordinary soldiers, either before or after their studies. After passing examinations, their second year of active duty was as reserve sublieutenants. The law also provided an alternative route: those willing to sign up for three additional periods of instruction during their years as reservists could take an exam at the end of their first year of active service. Those who passed became "reserve student-officers" (*élèves-officiers de réserve*) who took special courses ending with yet more exams. Those who passed these exams would be ranked in order of merit; the army would commission as many sublieutenants of the reserves at it needed. As Jean Doise notes, these reforms meant that by 1914, the French army had nine classes of reasonably well-trained reserve officers, though it would have taken another ten or twelve years for the territorial army to have benefited.[95] NCOs posed a similar problem, which only worsened after the 1905 law. Reenlistment rates dropped, probably because of poor incentives, and NCOs had little authority over reservists during periods of annual maneuvers.[96]

The biggest issue, however, remained ordinary soldiers. Unsurprisingly, conservatives remained steadfast in their conviction that two-year service would gut the army for the decisive initial battles of the next war. Nothing in the 1905 law did anything to assuage long-standing conservative fears. As David Ralston points out, "The official republican view on military matters had always laid great stress on the importance of the reserves, but there was no coherent body of theory indicating how they should be organized in time of peace or utilized in time of war."[97]

Republicans were hardly above reproach. Apart from morale-sapping crises over promotions and church-state separation, their position on reserves was inconsistent. Even as they proclaimed that the two-year law would create a true nation in arms, the republican Chamber of Deputies voted (to the consternation of even the radical republican minister of war, General Louis André) to reduce the periods of reserve duty from twenty-eight days to fifteen and to abolish the period for territorials outright. The Senate held fast, and the periods of reserve duty stayed at their previous level until 1908.[98] Arguing for this change, President of the Council of Ministers Georges Clemenceau declared that the issue was "to adjust the burdens of citizens according to their faculties."[99] Reservists saw their obligations shrink from two periods of twenty-eight days to one period of twenty-three days and one of seventeen days; territorials no longer owed thirteen days but merely nine.[100] In defense of the republicans, however, it should be noted that part of the purpose was to allow younger reservists to train with their active units and to bring the older classes in separately to train with their mobilization units.[101]

As conservatives (in and outside the army) saw it, reducing the term of service was not about equalizing the burdens of active duty but instead part of a concerted effort to undermine the army. It was the logical culmination of various insults, scandals, and attacks, both real and perceived, on the integrity of the army and the officer corps. They remained disgruntled about the Dreyfus Affair, were scandalized by government attempts to ensure the political loyalty of army officers,[102] and were offended by the government's use of the army to take church inventories in the wake of church-state separation.[103] Hostility to republican reforms was sometimes extreme. To cite just one of the many irate voices: the retired General Léon-Frédéric Metzinger maintained that radical governments had destroyed the harmony between army and republic that had existed from the end of the Franco-Prussian War. Until the turn of the century, the republic had wanted a "national army," an army "removed from the agitation of [political] parties, so that it would in no way be distracted from its professional duties."[104] Radical reforms, Metzinger insisted, had dramatically altered the situation. The French Republic had turned its back on the army; its reforms were not even inspired by "the love of equality and democracy." Instead, "it seems more plausible that the party that governs does not want an educated army, an army that is aware and that reasons; above all, it wants blind and deaf servants."[105] Metzinger, himself an avowed anti-Semite and anti-Dreyfusard, took no notice that army officers might have contributed to this breakdown during the Dreyfus Affair.[106]

In the meantime, though, a very different critique of France's military institutions emerged, this one from Jean Jaurès, the leader of the French Socialist Party (*Section française de l'international ouvrière*, or SFIO). In 1910, Jaurès introduced a bill to completely revamp the army. The accompanying report, published in 1911 as *L'Armée nouvelle*, was a work of marvelous erudition.[107] Jaurès had read widely in the military literature of the day and brought the mind of a philosopher and historian to the task of overturning the dogmatism he found in that corpus. He rejected the prevailing notion that war was inevitable and sought instead to create an army that would reduce the chances of war. Still, he recognized the risk of war would never entirely fade away, particularly if Germany remained a military monarchy.

While the 1905 law created an army that, on paper, seemed formidable, Jaurès insisted that it produced the "appearance of being the nation in arms when in fact it is not." In a withering critique, Jaurès pointed out that even the language used to describe the components of the army implied the inferiority of reserve troops: the initial two-year period of service was called "active duty," suggesting that the army command saw reserves as passive. Jaurès refused to accept this view, suggesting that since soldiers' motivation came from their attachment to the *patrie*, reserves would fight as well as active-duty troops. He rejected the premises on which the doctrine of the offensive was built. Wars would not be won by an initial battle, so an initial defeat would not doom France. Because under his plan the army would renounce the offensive (which he derided as "impotent and disastrous plagiarism" of German strategy), the need to maintain large numbers on active duty disappeared. In wartime, the nation would marshal all of the classes of men who had completed their military training. This system, Jaurès insisted, would increase the number of men available for national defense by one million.[108]

Where the military leaders of France looked to Napoleon for inspiration and Germany for a model, Jaurès turned instead to the Revolution for inspiration and Switzerland as a model. Jaurès argued that the Revolutionary armies of 1792 and 1793 had triumphed because they were motivated by the idea of liberating themselves and others from despotism. This idea of the republic created the "moral community of the army, of soldiers and leaders." The force of this idea not only "exalted the [soldiers'] souls to make the supreme sacrifice, but, by a deeper and more difficult effect, regulated the will, organized the institutions, and created discipline."[109]

The Swiss system eliminated the nefarious distinction between active and reserve troops. The Swiss maintained a small cadre of professional soldiers on active duty only to instruct recruits and deemed three months' training sufficient. Jaurès admitted that France had not yet developed the habit of premilitary training, so training in France might stretch to six months. By adopting a system of premilitary training, including physical education and shooting, France could eventually reduce that period.[110]

The Apotheosis of the Active Army

Jaurès' proposal was the logical extension of republican rhetoric on the army, but the political landscape had changed dramatically. Nationalism was in the air, fueled in part by the Moroccan crises of 1905 and 1911. Jaurès, of course, lost his battle, despite the grudging respect that many military officers granted his work.[111] The army and its officers regained much of the status they had lost in the last decade of the nineteenth century.[112]

This return to prominence and legitimacy was fueled by increases in Germany's active army in 1911 and 1912.[113] In 1913, the National Assembly increased the term of active duty to three years.[114] Although the law retained the basic structure of the 1905 law, its justification was diametrically opposed. Where the 1905 law placed faith (but little else) in a massive reserve force, the 1913 law sought to ensure that the active army was equal to Germany's. The effect on the active army was important. The strength of an infantry company was boosted from roughly one hundred to 140 soldiers; active soldiers made up roughly three-fifths of wartime strength. Front-line companies would have approximately two hundred active soldiers and only fifty reservists.[115]

The three-year law went hand in glove with Joffre's Plan XVII, the mobilization plan with which France went to war in August 1914. In July 1911, Joffre had been named chief of the general staff;[116] he immediately began revising mobilization plans toward a more offensive posture. The focus of Plan XVII, presented to the *Conseil supérieure de la guerre* in April 1913, was on the active army.[117] Territorials were not organized into army corps; instead, divisions, regiments, and battalions were parceled out to fortifications. Active units would be brought to full strength by an infusion of the youngest classes of reservists; surplus reservists were organized into reserve regiments of two battalions each. Each army corps received two such regiments. The remaining reserve regiments were assembled into twenty-five reserve divisions. A great weakness of this system was that reserve units had little of the cohesion of active army units. The men had spent little (if any) time in their units in peacetime. If the individual qualities of reservists—and their motivation—were often on par with those of the active army, their sense of unity and familiarity with one another was not. A further problem was a shortage of officers to train the influx of reservists.[118] The shortage of officers and cadres would be serious. The army of 1913 was, for all intents and purposes, an active army designed to carry out an offensive strategy with the maximum use of active soldiers.

The War

On August 1, 1914, France started mobilization. In two weeks, the 817,000 men of the active army were joined by 1,787,000 active reservists and 1,100,000 men of the territorial army and reserve.[119] Rather than the anticipated 10 to 13 percent no-show rate, less than 1.5 percent of mobilized reservists failed to turn up.[120]

How did they perform? In the early stages of the war, the French high command continued to express doubts. Joffre's General Order no. 8 of August 18, 1914, blasted noncombatant troops for their lack of military discipline and slovenly appearance: "The men appear intolerably negligent and disorderly [and] some leave their columns without authorization. . . . Finally, certain reserve units, while marching and while stationary, give the impression that they are not well commanded."[121] But France had to use her reserve and territorial units. The staggering casualties of the opening months (329,000 French troops were killed, taken prisoner, or missing in action in August and September 1914),[122] combined with the speed of the German advance, forced the quick use of reserve units, and three territorial divisions were even thrown into battle at Le Cateau on August 25 to give British II Corps some breathing room. While these "gray-haired men" helped save the British Expeditionary Force from encirclement, that they were needed at all shocked French commanders.[123]

By October, the French high command was already breaching the wall separating territorial and active units. Territorial divisions began to be assigned to the front lines.[124] Joffre still specifically warned against using them in attacks:

> These troops do not have the cadres [*encadrement*], the training, or the cohesion necessary to successfully conclude such operations. Incapable of organizing themselves on the terrain that they sometimes manage to conquer, they are at the mercy of the least

counterattack and give the enemy the opportunity to take prisoners easily.[125]

The distinctions between active, reserve, and territorial units quickly
blurred. In late November, Joffre requested that mobilizing territorials be trained alongside the new recruits and the men of the active
reserve.[126] Active units would draw upon the class of 1914 and all of
the reservists; territorials and territorial reserves would flow into
reserve units. By April 1915, the army was creating new battalions
composed not only of active and reserve troops but also younger
classes of territorials. The peacetime distinctions essentially disappeared.[127] Tacitly, by April 1915 the French high command acknowledged what it had resisted for decades: men could be trained for
warfare rapidly.

Conclusion

Like the German army described by Dennis Showalter in the previous chapter, the French army was the wrong tool for the conflict that
erupted. In part, this was the almost inevitable outcome of deeply
held prejudices against reserve troops. Because the French high
command had never been fully convinced that reservists would be
up to the task of modern offensive warfare, reserve units were not
as well organized, equipped, or led as active army units. Prophesies
of reservist deficiencies were self-fulfilling. Little surprise, then, that
Joffre remained reluctant to use reserve units offensively.

The irony of this prophecy was that while reserve *units* were
hamstrung by their relegation to second-class status because of
doubts about the motives of reservists, *individual* reservists and
territorials performed better in the aggregate than the high command had expected. They filled the gaps torn in the ranks of the
active army by modern artillery and machineguns. By turning up
and remaining steadfast in the face of a conflict longer, more violent, relentless, and lethal than anyone had predicted, French reservists underscored another grim irony of the Third Republic: France
had become far more militarized than the professional soldiers and
conservative politicians had thought possible.

4

"Each One a Pocket Hercules": The Bantam Experiment and the Case of the Thirty-fifth Division

Peter Simkins

Few episodes in the massive expansion of the British Army in 1914–1915 more graphically illustrate the haphazard, improvised, and often reactive nature of that process than the story of the "Bantam" experiment and, in particular, the experience of the Thirty-fifth (Bantam) Division.[1] It began as a well-intentioned attempt to harness the patriotic spirit of men who, because of their diminutive stature, would otherwise have been denied the chance to serve their country. However, it led to disappointment and tragedy, principally because no one at the outset appears to have carefully considered the full implications of the scheme they had initiated.

Recruitment

In August 1914, Field Marshal Lord Kitchener, the newly appointed secretary of state for war, began creating a series of "New Armies"— each duplicating the six infantry divisions of the Regular British Expeditionary Force (BEF)—but as yet he had no clear idea of the ultimate size of those forces. His first appeal for recruits, on August 7, invited men aged between nineteen and thirty to enlist for general service "for the duration," the stipulated physical minimums being five feet, three inches in height and thirty-four inches chest expansion.[2] The popular response, however, exceeded all expectations. In the absence of any prewar blueprint for mobilizing Britain's manpower resources, Kitchener's initial failure to impose a ceiling on enlistments and regulate the flow of volunteers overwhelmed the existing recruiting machinery. On September 3, less than a month after Kitchener's first appeal, 33,204 men joined the army—more than the prewar average *annual* intake.[3] Many regimental depots, designed for two hundred and fifty to five hundred men, had to cope with five or ten times that number. Most recruits immediately faced severe shortages of accommodation, uniforms, weapons, personal equipment, bedding, and rations. Criticism in Parliament and elsewhere grew, and Kitchener and the War Office were forced to find rapid solutions to these problems. One answer was to allow civilian committees to raise new local battalions and house, feed, and clothe them until the War Office was ready to take them over and refund the costs involved. A second solution was to slow enlistments by altering the physical standards. Accordingly, on September 11, they were raised (to five feet, six inches in height and a chest of 35.5 inches).[4] In late October, with enlistments sharply declining and depot congestion easing, the height standard was reduced to five feet, four inches. On November 5, it was reduced again to five feet, three inches.[5] Nevertheless, this relatively low minimum still excluded many potential recruits, such as many miners, who were small in stature but sturdy and physically fit. As the autumn wore on and enlistment returns continued to fall, civilian committees in various parts of the country began to seek ways to recruit such men.

The most widely accepted version of the birth of the first Bantam battalions recounts how, in October 1914, an unidentified miner had walked all the way from Durham to Birkenhead in Cheshire in a vain attempt to enlist. Rejected yet again in Birkenhead as being too small at five feet, two inches, he offered to fight anyone in the room and was only removed from the recruiting office with great difficulty. On hearing of the incident from Alfred Mansfield, the secretary of the Birkenhead Recruiting Committee, Alfred Bigland, the local member of Parliament, sought and obtained permission to raise a special "Bantam" battalion of medically fit men between five feet and five feet, three inches. On November 18, Bigland announced that the committee was "now ready to receive the names of men who are willing to join what it has been decided to call the 'Bantam Battalion,' believing that a man is as good a soldier and as plucky a fighter at 5ft. 2ins., as at 5ft. 6ins." Potential volunteers were told to send their particulars on a postcard, with the understanding that such postal applications would be given priority when recruiting commenced in the normal fashion. Details of the new battalion were circulated to recruiting offices throughout the country, and if prospective Bantams passed a local medical examination, they would be issued with a rail ticket to Birkenhead to join Bigland's unit. To avoid enrolling weaklings incapable of carrying full infantry equipment, men between five feet, two inches and five feet, three inches in height needed a minimum chest measurement of thirty-four inches.

By November 27, 1,098 applications had been received, and recruits arrived from all quarters as soon as the attestation process got under way, on November 30. Although a stringent medical examination saw some forty men rejected for inadequate chest measurements in the first hour, far more were accepted, and the initial target of 1,100 was reached in just two days. A similar number had enlisted by the evening of December 3, thus providing sufficient men for *two* Bantam units—subsequently designated the Fifteenth and Sixteenth (Service) Battalions, the Cheshire Regiment (First and Second Birkenhead).[6] It is plain that a large proportion of the early Bantams were robust individuals who certainly did not represent the "bottom of the barrel" for manpower. Bantam J. J. Hutchinson found himself among miners, shipyard men, dockers from Liverpool and Birkenhead, workers from the lead industry who carried heavy metal all day, and bakery workers accustomed to lifting weighty sacks of flour: "None of these men were exactly weak."[7]

A Bantam battalion was concurrently being recruited in Manchester, where six city battalions of normal-sized men had been raised by late November and a seventh was being recruited. On November 21, the mayor of Manchester sought permission to raise an eighth city battalion, this time of Bantams, and received approval the next day. Manchester's city fathers may well have been influenced by Bigland's activities, but some historians point out that a Mr. D. E. Anderson (from the Manchester branch of the National Service League) had for some time been compiling a list of undersized men, possibly hoping to spur the War Office into accepting volunteers below the normal standard. Advertisements for the unit appeared in local newspapers, including the *Manchester Guardian*, on November 26. Eventually designated the Twenty-third Battalion, Manchester Regiment (Eighth City), the Manchester Bantams attracted a large number of miners from the Wigan area as well as businessmen and office workers.[8]

Other British cities were also in the forefront of the Bantam movement. In Edinburgh, a prominent Rotarian, I. P. Dobbie, appears to have proposed a "Short Stature" battalion as early as

December 4. Enlistment soon began for what became the Seventeenth Battalion, Royal Scots (Rosebery)—the subtitle recognizing Lord Rosebery's leading role in local recruiting. In Glasgow, the Lord Provost (also backed by the Rotary Club) raised the Eighteenth Highland Light Infantry (Fourth Glasgow)—quickly nicknamed "The Devil Dwarfs." Not until early March, following parliamentary pressure, did the War Office officially confirm its approval of these Scottish Bantam units.[9] Meanwhile, in December 1914, the mayor and corporation of Leeds had raised the Seventeenth Battalion, West Yorkshire Regiment (Second Leeds). Three more Bantam battalions were raised in Lancashire in the first quarter of 1915—the Seventeenth and Eighteenth Lancashire Fusiliers (First and Second South East Lancashire) and the Twentieth Lancashire Fusiliers (Fourth Salford). The reservoir of potential volunteers was clearly not unlimited, as the Salford Bantam battalion was still only three hundred strong in early June 1915 and only attained the required numbers by the end of July. The Fifteenth Sherwood Foresters (Nottinghamshire and Derbyshire Regiment) were raised in Nottingham in February; the Nineteenth Durham Light Infantry (Second County) in January and February; and the Fourteenth Battalion, Gloucestershire Regiment (West of England) in April 1915. The Nineteenth Durham Light Infantry (DLI) contained a strong element of colliery workers and also men from the Tyneside and Wearside shipyards, and the West of England Bantams included miners from the Forest of Dean alongside recruits from Bristol and Birmingham.[10]

Together, these battalions formed the infantry of the Thirty-fifth (Bantam) Division. The divisional Pioneer battalion was the Nineteenth Northumberland Fusiliers (Second Tyneside Pioneers), and the artillery brigades were raised around England and Scotland. The Pioneers, artillery, and engineers were all non-Bantams. When the division assembled in camps in June and July 1915, the Seventeenth, Eighteenth, and Twentieth Lancashire Fusiliers and the Twenty-third Manchesters made up the 104th Infantry Brigade under Brigadier General G. M. Mackenzie; the 105th Brigade, commanded by Brigadier General J. G. Hunter, comprised the Fifteenth and Sixteenth Cheshires, Fourteenth Gloucesters, and Fifteenth Sherwood Foresters; and the 106th Brigade, under Brigadier General H. O'Donnell, contained the Seventeenth Royal Scots, Eighteenth HLI, Nineteenth DLI, and Seventeenth West Yorkshires. The divisional commander was Major General Reginald Pinney, a teetotal officer who would become notorious in the BEF for denying his troops their rum ration.[11]

A dozen more Bantam battalions were recruited, mostly in the spring and summer of 1915, enabling the War Office to form a second Bantam division, the Fortieth. Four of its original battalions were from Wales, two from Scotland, two from Lancashire, and one each from Yorkshire, Middlesex, East Anglia, and Derby. However, by the time it assembled at Aldershot in the autumn, it was obvious that many of the later Bantam recruits were unfit even for training at home. As George Cunningham, a Glaswegian in the Fourteenth HLI, observed: "We had a lot of wee lads who never should have been accepted. . . . I was fair disgusted at the medics for taking them in at all. We youngsters with a bit of heft to us could see there wasn't much chance for a fighting battalion until they got rid of the runts." Medical rejections cut one battalion from over one thousand to barely two hundred men. Four battalions were disbanded and—to avoid delaying the division's deployment—were replaced by non-Bantam battalions from Thirty-ninth Division, seriously diluting the Fortieth Division's Bantam character before it left for the Western Front.[12] Canadian Bantam units—the 143rd and 216th Battalions, from British Columbia and Toronto respectively—were raised in 1916, but both were broken up on reaching England the following year.[13] Thus, since it was the only division to cross to the Western Front with its original Bantam infantry component relatively intact, a survey of the performance of the Thirty-fifth Division in the field perhaps offers the best means of assessing the validity of the whole Bantam experiment.

Having completed its training on Salisbury Plain, the Thirty-fifth Division crossed to France by early February 1916, joining Lieutenant General Haking's XI Corps in General Sir Charles Monro's First Army. For the next five months, the division was engaged in routine trench warfare in what was then a comparatively quiet "nursery" sector in the flat Flanders countryside between La Bassée and Armentieres. The division sparked mixed reactions among the British units that it encountered. For example, the taller men of the Guards Division seem to have viewed the Bantams with affectionate amusement. One, Alec Thomas, wrote: "After we finished telling the Bants they had duck's disease, we had to take a lot of very funny insults in turn. Very sharp tongues they have, and we've taken to the little chaps right away." Others were less kind. On relieving a

Bantam battalion at the front, Captain Richard Peirson of the Northumberland Fusiliers was approached by his agitated company sergeant major, who protested: "Sir, them bloody little dwarfs have built up the fire steps so they could see over. Now when my lads stand up, half their bodies are above the parapet."[14] In an effort to eliminate such complaints, the Bantams were ordered to take two sandbags each into the line to be filled and placed on the fire step so that the men could see without raising the fire step or lowering the parapet.[15] Some sources indicate that the Germans would greet arriving Bantams with crowing noises or calls of "Cock-a-doodle-do."[16]

Throughout these first months of trench warfare, there were few signs of problems to come and, in fact, the men of the division were praised for their behavior in the line and for the manner in which they adapted to conditions at the front. Harrison Johnston, an officer in the Fifteenth Cheshires, wrote in his diary after a German bombardment: "The men were fine and none of them left their posts. . . . I was very proud of the lads." He remarked with equal pride how well his men had reacted to the miserable conditions at the front: "Lads who'll stand last night will stand anything. Up to their knees in snow water, most had been nearly up to their middles."[17] The troops were also congratulated by Haig, Monro, Haking, and Pinney for their response to a German raid on May 30 and for their actions during a successful raid by the Fourteenth Gloucesters on June 8.[18] Harrison Johnston noted on May 31 that there had been a "lack of any sort of 'wind'" in his battalion, and the war correspondent Philip Gibbs declared that the Germans "don't crow now over the Bantams."[19] On the Thirty-fifth Division's transfer from XI Corps early in July, Haking told Pinney he appreciated the division's "fine fighting qualities."[20] There had been important command changes, Brigadier General J. W. Sandilands having taken over the 104th Brigade on April 14 and Brigadier General A. H. Marindin the 105th Brigade on May 6. Both officers would remain with the division until the end of the war.[21]

Reverses

It was when the Thirty-fifth Division moved south in July 1916 for the Somme offensive that serious misgivings began to emerge about its *collective* combat effectiveness, fighting spirit, and physical fitness. To be fair, its prospects of success were limited from the start by a combination of factors beyond its control. First, it was never committed to an attack on the Somme as a complete division, its infantry operating always as individual battalions or brigades, often attached to other commands. Second, its infantry battalions were frequently employed on trench-digging duties or to provide carrying parties, thus suffering fatigue and casualties from almost constant shelling without being able to fight back. Third, the division was mainly deployed in the difficult Maltz Horn Farm–Arrow Head Copse–Guillemont sector, with the added complications of fighting alongside the French Sixth Army.[22] Fourth, it was serving under General Sir Henry Rawlinson in the Fourth Army during July and August, the very period when Rawlinson unfortunately tended to launch repeated small-scale and localized attacks with inadequate forces on narrow frontages, not least in the Guillemont area.[23] These extenuating factors notwithstanding, the division's performance on the Somme was unimpressive, and its morale and resilience apparently became increasingly and unexpectedly fragile in the latter half of 1916.

The Thirty-fifth Division *did* show some promise in its first serious engagement on the Somme. On July 18, the Sixteenth Cheshires (105th Brigade) played a key part in the defense of Waterlot Farm, near Delville Wood, against a determined German counterattack. Lieutenant H. D. Ryalls and the battalion commander, Lieutenant Colonel R. C. Browne-Clayton, both won the Distinguished Service Order in this successful but costly action.[24] However, on July 20, battalions of 104th and 105th Brigades had an equally painful but far less successful experience in a hastily prepared and ill-conceived attack typical of the Fourth Army's operations at this time. The Fifteenth Sherwood Foresters (105th Brigade) were ordered to capture one thousand yards of German trenches between Maltz Horn Farm and Arrow Head Copse, but the odds were stacked against them from the outset. The front to be attacked was far too much for a single battalion, the supporting artillery was unable to observe the objective, and attacking at 5 A.M. meant that the rising sun illuminated the advancing British troops. To make matters worse, the Sherwood Foresters were already exhausted and hungry, having been in the line under continuous artillery fire and gas since the night of July 16–17. A few hours before zero, Lieutenant Colonel R. N. S. Gordon reported that the men had been forced to wear respirators for some time, that they were badly shaken by shelling, and that only two of his companies were in a fit state to attack. Two companies of the Twenty-third Manchesters (104th Brigade) were accordingly sent up, just two hours before zero, to support the assault. When the attack went in, some parties on the right reached their objective but were driven back to their start line. A second attack later in the morning by the Manchesters, supported by the two remaining companies of that battalion, had a similar outcome. The combined casualties of the two battalions were over four hundred officers and men for no lasting gain of ground, with the Sherwood Foresters being temporarily reduced to one officer per company.[25]

Dismay at this setback was compounded by an incident involving an NCO and a ten-man section of the Sherwoods who had been instructed, in the early hours of July 19, to garrison a forward post near Arrow Head Copse and hold it at all costs for forty-eight hours. Under prolonged intense shelling and machine-gun fire, with no rations for three days and fearing an imminent German attack, the party returned to its own lines at 10 P.M. on July 20, some five hours earlier than ordered. The NCO, Corporal Jesse Wilton—who had enlisted in the battalion upon its formation in February 1915—was subsequently charged and found guilty of quitting his post, sentenced to death, and executed by firing squad on August 17, 1916. Recent historians of the Fifteenth Sherwood Foresters suggest that when Wilton's party returned from its isolated post, officers "drew revolvers to control some dreadful moments when a panicky retreat began to spread" and conclude that Lieutenant Colonel Gordon no doubt "feared for the steadiness of his battalion." However, with whole companies of the Sherwood Foresters and Manchesters having fallen back to their own lines several hours previously, it was perhaps not unreasonable for Wilton and his men to have followed suit later in the evening.[26]

Yet another battalion-strength attack was undertaken by the Eighteenth Lancashire Fusiliers (104th Brigade) on July 22. The assault was to be made in two columns against enemy trenches from a point southeast of Arrow Head Copse to Maltz Horn Farm, and it was intended, in the process, to demolish German wire entanglements invisible to artillery observers. Although company commanders only received their orders around 9 P.M. on July 21, the attack proceeded a few hours later, at 1:30 A.M. The right column reached the objective but was compelled to retire, while the left column did not even reach the German trenches. In his report, Brigadier General Sandilands noted that continuous shelling had probably prevented the battalion's officers from making all the necessary preparations, but he also revealingly commented that the time allowed for such preparations had been too short for an attack by New Army troops.[27] On July 30, the Seventeenth West Yorkshires and Seventeenth Royal Scots (106th Brigade) were scheduled to support the Thirtieth Division's attack in the Guillemont–Falfemont Farm sector. Congested trenches ahead of them blocked the progress of both battalions, and only one Royal Scots platoon could meaningfully contribute.[28]

The division's infantry got a welcome break from front-line duties until August 9, but, as the divisional historian underlines, the work involved in absorbing new drafts—now apparently containing many men of poor physique—and making them fit for the line "demanded a considerable amount of attention from the officers concerned, and left little time for rest or recreation." The replacements were sorely needed: the Sixteenth Cheshires, for example, mustered barely six hundred men by late July and received a draft of 150 before returning to the front.[29]

After the next serious action, senior officers of the division expressed mounting concern about its fighting efficiency and the low standards of recent drafts. The Sixteenth Cheshires were detailed to capture a German strongpoint some ninety yards east of Arrow Head Copse. Heavy artillery would bombard it and the field artillery would surround it with a box barrage once the heavier guns ceased fire. Zero hour was fixed for 9 P.M. on August 20, but, with only a few minutes to go, Lieutenant Colonel Browne-Clayton informed his superiors that he could not get the men ready to attack: the heavy artillery was not only still firing but firing short, the trenches were blown in, and most of the Stokes mortar ammunition was buried. Browne-Clayton was permitted to postpone the attack for one hour, but he insisted that any further enterprise that night was unwise. In a disturbing admission to his brigade commander, Browne-Clayton wrote that he was "ashamed to say that the battalion is quite demoralised. I do not think that they would stand up against anything, and I honestly think it would be safer to get them relieved if possible. Company commanders tell me that very few men would follow their officers over. They are quite hopeless." In the end, a compromise was reached, with a small party reconnoitering the strongpoint. The party got close to the objective and was joined at 4:30 A.M. by a patrol from the Fourteenth Gloucesters, but the German barbed wire proved impenetrable, and both groups withdrew under machine-gun fire. Brigadier General Marindin attributed the failure partly to the heavy artillery's mistakes, yet he too raised grave doubts about the quality of recent recruits: "The class of men we are now getting . . . are no longer the 'Bantam' proper, but are either half-grown lads, or are degenerates. Col. Clayton's and the Brigade Major's reports show the state of affairs among the men."[30]

Soon after this failure, on August 24, the division was due to cooperate with the French I Corps by attacking near Falfemont Farm. The 104th Brigade would assault 350 yards of the German front immediately southeast of the farm, with strong patrols followed by two infantry companies, which were expected to hold and consolidate the objective—no easy task for a relatively small number of men. Moreover, as no troops would be advancing on the left, that flank was exposed to German fire from Falfemont Farm itself. Representations to divisional headquarters that the attack had poor prospects were overruled, and the Seventeenth Lancashire Fusiliers were given the task. Preparations went further awry; artillery fire prevented the Pioneers from digging assembly trenches the evening before the attack. The rest of the division had suffered similarly from shelling, and Major General Pinney, after visiting the front line, had to report that, yet again, its infantry were in no condition to assault. Although other planned British attacks were canceled, the Lancashire Fusiliers were ordered to attack with the French at 5:45 P.M. on August 24 and to hold a line between Falfemont Farm and Angle Wood. The battalion managed to advance some three hundred yards and dig in on the southern slopes of the Falfemont Farm spur—a moderate success when measured against earlier attacks—but, for the third time in five weeks, officers at the divisional and brigade levels had registered severe doubts about the ability of their troops to mount an effective assault.[31]

There were other disciplinary problems during the division's service on the Somme. Private Hugh Flynn of the Eighteenth HLI was charged with desertion after going missing on July 26, when the battalion was about to return to the trenches. Private John McQuade (also of the Eighteenth HLI) committed a similar offence on July 29, while attached to the 106th Trench Mortar Battery. Both men were tried, sentenced to death, and executed. Given the growing criticism of the more recent drafts in the late summer of 1916, it should perhaps be noted that Flynn and McQuade were early recruits, enlisting in April and May 1915 respectively.[32]

By the last week of August, many officers were seriously concerned about the division's morale. Captain B. L. Montgomery (the future field marshal, then the brigade major of the 104th Brigade) wrote on August 27 that the brigade would probably not be committed to the battle again, as "the men could hardly stand three helpings of that sort of thing." Pinney had already received a "very bad account" of morale in the 106th Brigade and, on August 27, personally inspected the recent drafts for the 104th and 106th Brigades. His comments were damning: "Manchesters bad . . . HLI passable. West Yorks bad. DLI fair." He observed in addition: "It is no good putting large numbers of such men straight into a battle. Some degenerates quickly demoralise the lot. They have to be broken in to be brave but it takes time." Later that day, Rawlinson conceded that it was "rather hard" on Pinney "to have to command poor material." After preparing a report on "indifferent" drafts, on August 31 Pinney instructed all medical officers that "Men found medically unfit or men who are obviously deficient in physique or mind are to be returned to the Base forthwith." GHQ decided the weeding should not start until after the formation left the Fourth Army, but the process clearly began before the Thirty-fifth Division departed at the end of August.[33]

Any objective analysis of the division's performance on the Somme will confirm it was ill-used and that command shortcomings, especially at the army and corps levels, contributed to its woes. But how far can its own internal weaknesses and tactical failures fairly be attributed to the low physical and mental standards of recent drafts, as most sources maintain? In this connection, it is instructive to look at the casualties suffered by individual battalions *before* July 1916 and their participation in the Somme battle. The figures in the divisional history contain some obvious inconsistencies and points of confusion but nevertheless suggest that *no* infantry battalion suffered more than ninety-one battle casualties in all during those months and that the *average* number of killed, wounded, and missing per battalion from February to June was sixty-nine. Even allowing for sickness, accidents, and transfers to other units, these losses of personnel could scarcely be described as overwhelming, and it seems reasonable to conclude that the division began its service on the Somme with a fair proportion of original or early Bantam recruits still in its ranks.[34] In short, although half of its battalions would incur battle losses of between three hundred and four hundred in July and August, its failures cannot be wholly attributed to the poor standards of the latest drafts. Thus *some* of the blame for the division's apparently shaky morale and fighting spirit in the summer of 1916 should be laid at the door of the original Bantams, who may not all have been so "sturdy" in body and mind as their early supporters had claimed. Certainly, there were several New Army divisions that suffered equal or heavier casualties and that, in comparison with the Thirty-fifth, carried out many more assaults on the Somme over a longer period yet still achieved a success rate of 60 percent or more in their attacks.[35]

Patience with the Thirty-fifth Division's performance finally ran out in late November. By then, Pinney had been transferred to the Thirty-third Division, exchanging commands on September 23 with Major General H. J. S. Landon, an officer apparently less tolerant of the Bantams than his predecessor. The division had moved to the Third Army at the beginning of September and was serving in Lieutenant General J. A. L. Haldane's VI Corps, holding a three-brigade front immediately east and northeast of Arras. After a few weeks of routine trench warfare, the Germans opposite the division became noticeably more aggressive. Matters came to a head on the night of November 25–26, when a raid by over fifty officers and men of the Nineteenth DLI was due to take place. Following heavy trench mortar bombardments between 2 A.M. and 2:30 A.M. on November 26, the Germans launched three separate raids on the division's sentry posts and trenches, penetrating those of the Seventeenth Lancashire Fusiliers and Nineteenth DLI. The only appreciable resistance was offered by the Fifteenth Sherwoods, who counterattacked and drove the Germans out. The DLI's situation was exacerbated by the fact that a number of NCOs and men had left their posts around King's Crater, and another NCO—Lance Sergeant J. W. Stones, who had been visiting these posts on patrol with an officer, Lieutenant Mundy—had also left the front line when Mundy was shot and seriously wounded. Stones and a second NCO, Lance Corporal E. Hopkinson, were later intercepted, without their rifles, by battle police well to the rear, while the garrison of a sentry post south of King's Crater, including two NCOs (Lance Corporals J. McDonald and P. Goggins), had been stopped in the support line. Meanwhile, the scheduled raid by the Durhams had gone ahead at 3 A.M. Two small groups had entered the German trenches, but the remainder of the raiders, two officers and forty-five men, failed to follow, stopped by their own barrage, which fell short in No Man's Land and around the point of entry into the German line. As the 106th Brigade's war diary records, the raiders suffered several casualties from it, "becoming so demoralised that it was impossible to collect the men and make them return."[36]

The night's events reflected badly upon the whole division, not least the Nineteenth DLI, and retribution was swift and savage. From the Durhams alone, Lance Sergeant Stones was charged with casting away his arms in the presence of the enemy; Hopkinson, Goggins, McDonald, and four privates were charged with quitting their posts; and a sergeant, a lance corporal, and sixteen privates of the raiding party were accused of cowardice. In all, between December 24, 1916, and January 1, 1917, twenty-six members of the Nineteenth Durhams were tried and sentenced to death, although only three—Stones, Goggins, and McDonald—were ultimately executed. The other twenty-three had their sentences commuted to penal servitude for ten to fifteen years. Furthermore, the sentences passed on the men of the unsuccessful raiding party were then also suspended, so that they could return to duty in various forms, and some stayed with the battalion. One of them, Lance Corporal Michael Dempsey, actually won the Military Medal in 1918.[37] When his opinion was sought on the sentences handed out to the six who had abandoned their sentry posts, Brigadier General O'Donnell of 106th Brigade commented that the "battalion . . . has not done well in the fighting line. They suffered somewhat severely from heavy shelling while in the Somme fighting in July and were very shaky in the advanced trenches before Guillemont in August." Landon, the divisional commander, was clearly convinced that an example should be made of Goggins and McDonald and their death sentences confirmed:

> The NCOs must be held as having especially failed in their soldierly duties, and responsibilities. There are, however, some 400 men in the Division of whom 334 are in the Durham L.I. who are recommended for transfer as being unsuitable mentally and physically for Infantry Soldiers and it is possible that any of them would have behaved similarly under the circumstances described. . . . In view of the mental and physical degeneracy of these men I consider that although the sentence passed on all six is a proper one, the extreme penalty might be carried out in the case of the two NCOs only and the sentence of the four privates be commuted to a long term of penal servitude, and this I recommend.[38]

The divisional historian argues that the German raids again "brought forcibly to notice that which commanding officers had been reporting for some time, namely that the major part of the recently received reinforcements could not be trusted to hold the line." However, it seems pertinent to observe that most, if not all, of the twenty-six men of the DLI who were sentenced to death at this time were original or early recruits to the battalion. A number, including Stones and Goggins, were miners, while McDonald had been a laborer.[39] The fact that some of the first Bantams to join up—who had been judged, at the time, to meet the required physical and mental criteria—had been found wanting tends to reinforce the conclusion that it was not just the later drafts who were substandard. It also reveals serious flaws in the whole Bantam concept and raises additional doubts about the thoroughness of the medical examinations that individual Bantams had undergone.

Reorganization

Apart from its disciplinary ramifications, the November 26 episode also precipitated a radical overhaul of the division, which effectively ended the Bantam experiment. There seems to have been general agreement among officers from battalion commanders upward that drastic action could no longer be deferred. Haldane, of VI Corps, reported that he could not be responsible for the security of his front while the Thirty-fifth Division "continued to be constituted as it was," suggesting that a thorough combing out was essential. "In anticipation of that measure," he wrote, "I ordered the divisional commander to withdraw undesirables, and from the remainder whom I saw myself I extracted many more."[40]

As early as November 27, the division's assistant director of medical services (ADMS) inspected men of the 104th Brigade, who had been reported on by their officers with regard to their "military efficiency" and "physical and mental disabilities." The process accelerated in December, when the division was relieved from the front line and moved west of Arras. Spurred by Landon, the ADMS inspected all the infantry battalions in the first half of December, rejecting 1,439 men. Some units—such as the Seventeenth West Yorkshires, Fourteenth Gloucesters, and Sixteenth Cheshires—lost over 180 men, a substantial proportion of their strength.[41] Ernest Sheard, who had enlisted in December 1914 and served as a stretcher-bearer with the Leeds Bantams, noted, "there was a lot of dodging going on," with men faking all sorts of complaints in an attempt to avoid front-line service. However, he praised the spirit of others: "Some of the men when they stripped looked absolute wrecks, [and] how they had managed to carry full packs was simply wonderful. . . . I am sure that nothing else but bigness of heart had got them through." Harrison Johnston of the Fifteenth Cheshires viewed the dilution of his battalion with some regret: "I'm sorry as the little men had done so well, but I suppose there are no more, as all regiments now take small men."[42]

By December 21, Haldane himself had twice inspected those recommended for rejection, and the number of men deemed physically or mentally substandard had risen to 2,784. Brigade commanders were informed that no more Bantams were to be accepted and that, given the current reorganization of the division, the Bantam standard "must be disregarded for good and all." The divisional sign, previously a Bantam cock, was changed to seven interlocked 5s. To gain the high-level support necessary for the rejection of such a high proportion of the division's fighting strength, Haldane arranged for the "combed-out" soldiers to be inspected by Allenby, the Third Army commander. Haldane confessed that he stage managed the occasion to ensure that Allenby would sanction a ruthless purge of undesirables:

> The men who had been combed out were therefore drawn up in a line by company along some steeply sloping ground and care was taken that the army commander, who was not lacking in inches, should view them from above and not below. On the flank of certain companies were disposed a few files of tall cavalrymen . . . who had been sent to fill vacancies. Thus, when the inspection took place, the Bantams looked at from above seemed more of the dimensions of young chickens than dwarf poultry.

In spite of these precautions, one brigade commander, when asked by Allenby for his opinion of the Bantams, began to praise them. "Before he had committed himself too deeply," Haldane wrote, "he got a gentle reminder by a kick on the shins that he was spoiling sport, and the situation was saved."[43]

The division's infantry stayed out of the line for over two months, affording welcome breathing space to absorb large drafts. Several sources suggest that these replacements came chiefly from Yeomanry regiments and cavalry depots and, to help train them as infantry, a Depot Battalion briefly existed.[44] The evacuation of previously rejected Bantams continued well into March, temporarily reducing battalion rifle strengths—that of the Fifteenth Cheshires being only four hundred on March 12.[45] Many of the discarded men were transferred to the newly created Labour Companies or—particularly in the case of former miners—to Tunnelling Companies. John Sheen identifies over 150 original Bantams of the Nineteenth DLI posted to the Labour Corps and a further sixteen known to have served with Tunnelling Companies. He also shows that, although battalion commanders were told to guard against the possibility of discarded Bantams returning as reinforcements, some men *did* find their way back to their former units. Of the sixteen known transfers to Tunnelling Companies, eleven subsequently returned to the Nineteenth DLI.[46]

Recovery

The division's shaky reputation in early 1917 was reflected by the fact that it was not selected as an assault formation for any major offensive until October. It played only a small part in pursuing the Germans to the newly constructed Hindenburg Line, mainly repairing roads and railways. After three weeks, however, the division relieved the Sixty-first Division, entering the line between Fresnoy le Petit and the River Omignon, northwest of St. Quentin. On April 14–15, the three Fusilier battalions of the 104th Brigade between them cleared Gricourt, seized a large farm—Les Trois Sauvages—and established positions on Pontruet Ridge. The *Official History* noted these as the first operations "of any importance to be carried out by the division since its reorganisation," though they cost around four hundred casualties.[47]

On May 10, IV Corps ordered that, while the farm might be raided, its retention was not sufficiently important to justify ongoing losses. Raids duly continued, an example being that made by two companies of the Fifteenth Sherwood Foresters on May 15–16, under a barrage provided by artillery, Stokes mortars, and machine guns. Despite this support, the attackers encountered unsuspected wire and abandoned the raid after three vain attempts to cut their way through, having lost forty-one officers and men.[48] In July, the division relieved the Cavalry Corps at Epéhy, opposite Bony and Vendhuile on the St. Quentin Canal, in a sector destined to witness intense fighting twice the following year. In mid-1917, the line here comprised a series of detached posts on the high ground east of Epéhy. During that summer, attempts by the Thirty-fifth Division to gain better observation over the ground toward the canal led to a succession of sometimes fierce actions for possession of the ridges, spurs, and farms that formed the outlying defenses of the Hindenburg Line itself. Two features in particular—Gillemont Farm and the Knoll—rose some thirty-five to forty feet above the nearest British posts. The area around the former was disputed, but the Knoll was in German hands, offering a good view of the British positions. In front of Vendhuile was the Birdcage, a network of trenches jutting into the German positions to the east. The Thirty-fifth Division spent three months in the sector under a new commander, Major General G. McK. Franks having replaced Landon on July 9. As the MGRA of Second Army, Franks had masterminded much of the artillery plan for the recent outstanding victory at Messines Ridge.[49]

From July 12 onward, all three brigades saw action, as both sides strove to improve their tactical situation across the hotly contested ground. Serious planning began for a large raid in the Gillemont Farm sector to prevent the Germans from gaining complete possession of that spur. As more artillery and ammunition became available—possibly thanks to the influence of Franks—the plan was expanded to encompass an assault on, and possible capture of, the Knoll as well as a subsequent raid on trenches between Ossus Wood and Canal Wood. The Gillemont Farm attack was also enlarged, now including a scheme to capture the German front line opposite the farm. Rehearsals took place over full-scale replicas of the objectives to be assaulted, with the Fifteenth Cheshires and Fifteenth Sherwood Foresters, for instance, practicing almost continuously from August 6 to the eve of the operation itself.[50]

On August 19, the Cheshires and Sherwood Foresters (105th Brigade), attacking at 4 A.M., took the German trenches on the Knoll in just fifteen minutes. Elsewhere, the Eighteenth HLI (106th Brigade) cleared a semicircular trench east of Gillemont Farm after hand-to-hand fighting. The three battalions lost a combined total of seventy-four killed or died of wounds, 238 wounded, and sixteen missing in achieving these successes. The divisional historian noted that the spirit of the troops at the Knoll had been "excellent." Heavy fire support (nearly twenty-three thousand heavy artillery rounds, almost seventy thousand field artillery and trench mortar shells, and over one million machine-gun bullets) between August 19 and 23 helped the attacks and consolidation. However, the division was not allowed much time to settle into its new positions. On August 25, a German advance, after an intense bombardment, robbed the Eighteenth HLI of their gains at Gillemont Farm, and a gallant evening counterattack by the Nineteenth DLI could do little more than reestablish the original British front line. Six days later, a similarly violent German assault overwhelmed two companies of the Seventeenth West Yorkshires at the Knoll, and this position too was lost.

Although the division's tenure of these positions was brief, it had enabled British observers to obtain vital, if short-lived, observation over the German defenses, and elements of six German regiments were drawn into a sector previously held by a single battalion.[51] These actions were certainly tiny in scale when compared with other operations in 1917, but the methodical preparations were illustrative of the improvements in the BEF's planning, training, and tactics that had been wrought by the summer of 1917. Without taking part in a major offensive, the twelve infantry battalions of the division had, according to the divisional historian, lost 2,264 all ranks killed, wounded, and missing from February to August 1917—an average of 188 per battalion—but it can be argued that the occasional successes achieved in these minor actions did a great deal to restore the self-confidence and esprit de corps of the division after a rocky few months.[52]

The division moved north to the infamous Ypres Salient in mid-October and had only a brief supporting role in the Third Battle of Ypres.[53] For its officers and men, however, the division's attack at Houthulst Forest on October 22, 1917, was far from insignificant. It was not only the division's first large-scale operation since its reorganization but also its first attack on a two-brigade front since crossing to France in 1916.

The subsidiary operations by XIV Corps of the Fifth Army on October 22 (carried out in conjunction with the French First Army on the left) were to distract the Germans from preparations for the Second Army's planned thrust toward Passchendaele on October 26 while simultaneously providing a strong left flank for that main advance. The Thirty-fifth Division was to attack with the 104th and 105th Brigades in the front line, the 106th Brigade being judged numerically too weak for the initial assault.[54] When the attack was launched at 5:35 A.M., the Twenty-third Manchesters of 104th Brigade, on the extreme right, could not link up with the neighboring Thirty-fourth Division, so exposing the Thirty-fifth Division's flank to enfilade fire and obliging the survivors of the leading waves to fall back to their original line after tantalizingly reaching the first objective. The Seventeenth Lancashire Fusiliers were more fortunate and, by 6:45 A.M., reports were received that three companies were upon the final objective around Marechal Farm. Here they were joined by a company of the Sixteenth Cheshires (105th Brigade), while the remainder of that battalion established a line, for the time being, a little short of the final objective. The greatest success was achieved by the Fourteenth Gloucesters on the far left, the whole battalion having taken all objectives by 7:45 A.M. The inevitable German counterattacks began in the afternoon and continued on October 23 and 24, forcing the Sixteenth Cheshires and supporting troops of the Fifteenth Sherwood Foresters back, leaving the Fourteenth Gloucesters as the only battalion to retain a hold on the final objective.[55]

This disappointing overall result should not be attributed to the officers and men of the Thirty-fifth Division, who had displayed courage, determination, and tactical initiative at all levels during the fighting. The division's losses in the sector between October 18 and 29 totaled 2,564 all ranks, including 368 killed and 1,734 wounded. Stephen McGreal states that the Sixteenth Cheshires alone sustained losses of nine officers and 327 other ranks in under thirty hours. Despite good initial artillery support, appalling weather and poor conditions underfoot caused many troops to fall behind a deliberately slow barrage, particularly when struggling through undergrowth and over fallen trees in the forest, where snipers also lurked. Yet, in the words of the divisional historian, morale "was of a high standard throughout the operations."[56] A more detailed analysis of the casualties incurred by two of the battalions involved suggests that they still contained a fair proportion of original Bantams and other early recruits. For example, the Nineteenth DLI appears to have lost thirty-three other ranks dead in this period, of whom six (or 18.18 percent) were "originals," according to their serial numbers. Of fifty-two dead in the Fifteenth Sherwoods, nineteen (36.35 percent) were original or early recruits.[57]

On September 23, 1917, the Eighteenth HLI had received a draft of four officers and 146 other ranks from the Glasgow Yeomanry, and the unit's official designation became the Eighteenth (Glasgow Yeomanry) Battalion, Highland Light Infantry.[58] After the Houthulst Forest action, the infantry was again reorganized, further diluting its surviving Bantam elements. On November 15, while the division was still near Ypres, the Fourth North Staffordshires—a non-Bantam battalion—joined the 106th Brigade in place of the Seventeenth West Yorkshires, the latter recently having been reduced to the strength of a single company.[59] In February 1918, the cumulative effects of casualties and continuing manpower problems necessitated even more fundamental changes in the majority of the BEF's infantry divisions, which saw the number of infantry battalions in a division cut from twelve to nine and brigades correspondingly reduced from four battalions to three. Consequently, in many formations, new bonds had to be forged with unfamiliar battalions, fresh methods of command and control and tactical handling of units had to be devised, and esprit de corps had to be rebuilt.

The Thirty-fifth Division did not escape this painful process, most of the changes taking place in the first half of February. The Twentieth Lancashire Fusiliers, Twenty-third Manchesters, and Fourteenth Gloucesters were all disbanded, and other battalions were moved among brigades. Most men were posted to other battalions in the division, some to battalions of their regiments in other divisions, and any surplus men were posted to the newly created Twelfth Entrenching Battalion. Another non-Bantam battalion, the Twelfth HLI, came from the Fifteenth (Scottish) Division to join the 106th Brigade. Henceforth, until the Armistice in November, the 104th Brigade comprised the Seventeenth and Eighteenth Lancashire Fusiliers and the Nineteenth DLI (previously in the 106th Brigade); the 105th Brigade included the Fifteenth Cheshires, Fifteenth Sherwood Foresters, and Fourth North Staffordshires; and the 106th Brigade consisted of the Seventeenth Royal Scots and the Twelfth and Eighteenth HLI.

Redemption

True redemption for the Thirty-fifth Division as a fighting formation came with the great German offensive in Picardy in March 1918. When the storm broke on March 21, the division was hurried south from Ypres to join Lieutenant General Sir Walter Congreve's VII Corps on the left flank of the Fifth Army. On the morning of March 24 (after a twelve-hour rail journey and a trying seventeen-mile approach march), battalions of the 105th and 106th Brigades were thrust into the firing line in the Cléry–Hem–Maurepas area, on the north bank of the Somme near Péronne. Major General Franks was soon placed in temporary overall command of the VII Corps battle front, including detachments from the Ninth, Twelfth, and Twenty-first Divisions, while Brigadier General J. H. W. Pollard (who had led the 106th Brigade since May 20, 1917) assumed temporary command of the infantry of the Thirty-fifth Division. The Fifteenth Cheshires and Fifteenth Sherwood Foresters, in particular, resisted repeated German attacks throughout the day until, at 5 P.M., orders were issued for a withdrawal to a line from Curlu to Hardecourt, a mile or two to the rear. Though they had inflicted severe casualties upon the Germans, the Thirty-fifth had also suffered—the Fifteenth Cheshires, for example, losing their CO, thirteen other officers, and over three hundred men.[60] The next day, March 25, the division gradually fell back upon the old 1916 British zone of operations between Maricourt and Montauban, where it put up what the British official historian describes as "a magnificent fight against at least five German divisions." From early morning until mid-evening, when Army orders for a further withdrawal to the Bray-Albert road were confirmed by VII Corps, the Thirty-fifth Division largely checked repeated German attacks in this important sector. With outstanding local leadership at the brigade and battalion levels, several units—but especially the Twelfth HLI and Nineteenth DLI—organized or supported forceful counterattacks at critical stages in the fighting. When the withdrawal commenced after dark, it was carried out in a "perfectly orderly manner."[61] The Thirty-fifth Division had fought skillfully and courageously for two consecutive days, slowing the German advance appreciably and mounting effective counterattacks when necessary.

Early on March 25, all VII Corps troops under Franks north of the Somme had been transferred to General Byng's Third Army. Judging from the successive orders coming from its headquarters between 6 P.M. and midnight on March 25, the Third Army intended VII Corps to hold the Bray-Albert position as long as possible, then retire beyond the Ancre. At 2:20 A.M. on March 26, the Third Army reemphasized the need to dispute ground, stating that a retirement should occur only if "the tactical situation imperatively demands it." These guidelines were broadly echoed in an order sent by Congreve, at VII Corps headquarters, to Franks at 2:15 A.M., stating that Franks should delay the Germans on the Bray-Albert line as long as he could, "without being so involved as to make retirement impossible." Once the Ancre was crossed, all bridges were to be destroyed. In a lengthy telephone conversation, Congreve firmly impressed upon Franks that he was expected to remain on the Bray-Albert position until 10 A.M. but that the retirement to the west bank of the Ancre would definitely take place that afternoon. Not unreasonably, given the instructions he had received and the latitude apparently allowed to him, Franks therefore subsequently issued his own orders for a withdrawal in echelon from the right across the Ancre and identified the positions to be occupied on the far bank.

Although virtually the whole line was engaged by 1 P.M., several battalions held their ground until mid-afternoon, over four hours longer than anticipated. Nevertheless, under growing pressure, a general retirement of the 104th and 105th Brigades through Morlancourt toward the Ancre commenced between 2:15 and 3:15 P.M. As the troops pulled back, the Third Army—its resolve no doubt greatly stiffened by the positive messages emanating from that day's crucial conference at Doullens (where General Foch was empowered to coordinate Allied operations on the Western Front)—significantly changed its orders. First, at 2:35 P.M., the Third Army declared that "it must be distinctly understood that no voluntary retirement from our present line is intended." Congreve telephoned Franks to stop the withdrawal and restore the line. At 3:40 P.M., the Third Army issued a formal written order: the position at Bray was to be "maintained with the utmost determination." Franks was away from his headquarters when this arrived; having conferred with Pollard and Marindin at Morlancourt, he decided, at about 4 P.M., that it was too late to halt the retirement. With Franks still absent, his staff did their best, at 4:25 P.M., to inform his key subordinates, by written messages, that the Third Army had canceled all orders for withdrawal and, if the line were driven back, the retirement was *not* to be carried beyond the Ancre. By just after 7 P.M., when these messages reached their destinations, they were redundant, as the bulk of the Thirty-fifth Division and attached infantry had crossed the river to take up positions around Buire and Dernancourt, southwest of Albert. Marindin of the 105th Brigade tried to comply with the spirit of the Third Army's amended instructions by ordering his battalions to recross the Ancre and reoccupy Morlancourt, although he made it clear to his superiors that he thought the movement stood little chance of success, owing to his troops' exhaustion and ammunition shortages. Fortunately for all concerned, the orders to reoccupy the Bray line were canceled soon afterward. The retirement had opened a dangerous six-mile gap along the Somme, between the left of the Fifth Army and the right of the Third Army, and it was Franks who was made the scapegoat for this development. He was relieved from command late in the evening, perhaps somewhat unfairly, considering the ambiguous and contradictory orders he had received over the past twenty-four hours. His successor, Marindin, was at least a trusted officer from within the division; he had been with the 105th Brigade since May 1916.[62] One might add that the division's retirement on March 26 stemmed mainly from command-and-control failures and misunderstandings at the army, corps, and divisional levels and was *not* directly attributable to any serious shortfall in the performance of the front-line troops.

The Germans entered Dernancourt on the night of March 27–28, but the Thirty-fifth Division, with the Fourth Australian on its left, repulsed all further attacks on its positions along the Ancre until relieved on March 30, even maintaining outposts on the eastern bank at Treux and Marett Wood. In particular, the division fought hard to hold the embankment of the Amiens-Albert railway, which looped around the foot of the heights immediately opposite the western exits from Dernancourt. One German attack here on March 29 was driven back by a bayonet charge by one hundred men of the Nineteenth Northumberland Fusiliers, the divisional Pioneers. According to the *Official History*, the division sustained more than three thousand casualties in a week of severe fighting, but it had undeniably done much to halt the German offensive in its sector. The officers and men had little rest or food for eight days but, as the divisional historian remarks with justifiable pride, every retirement "which had been made had been ordered as part of a general plan and was not because the troops had been forced to relinquish positions." The fine performance of the division in the last week of March may well have helped it avoid the fate of nine other British divisions that were reduced to cadre and reconstituted that spring and summer.[63]

During the final and victorious Allied advance in 1918, the Thirty-fifth Division was at last given a real opportunity to prove itself in an offensive role. Between September 28 and the Armistice it was frequently in action, serving with the XIX Corps (under Lieutenant General Sir Herbert Watts) in General Sir Herbert Plumer's Second Army, which, for most of this period, was, in turn, part of the *Groupe d'Armées des Flandres* (GAF) under the overall command of the Belgian king. For the first time since it crossed to France—February 1916, over thirty-one months before—the division was allowed to participate in a *series* of major attacks as a complete formation rather than being committed to battle piecemeal, as on the Somme.

This undoubtedly helped the Thirty-fifth Division to achieve its commendable success rate of 60 percent in its attacks against meaningful opposition during the "Hundred Days"; only 20 percent of its attacks were outright failures. Its performance in these last months of the war compared favorably with the *average* success rate of 55.7 percent registered by the ten British divisions in the Second Army, was higher than that achieved by the Fourteenth, Twenty-ninth, Thirty-first, Fortieth, and Forty-first Divisions, and was only equaled or bettered by the Thirtieth, Thirty-fourth, and Thirty-sixth Divisions and by the outstanding Ninth (Scottish) Division.[64]

Its reputation restored, the division was among the assault formations chosen to lead the breakout from the old Ypres Salient on September 28, 1918. Attacking with all three infantry brigades in line—for the first time in the war—the division advanced some six thousand yards through Zillebeke toward Zandvoorde, recapturing such long-contested locations as the Caterpillar, Hill 60, Mount Sorrel, and Shrewsbury Forest and collecting around eight hundred prisoners in the process. It continued to battle its way forward over the following four days, with stiff fighting around Zandvoorde and Tenbrielen on September 29 and then in front of Wervicq and the Gheluwe Switch line on October 1–2. These operations were by no means an unqualified triumph. Bad weather and the poor state of the roads and tracks hampered the movement of field guns and heavier weapons and seriously limited the amount of artillery support that could be provided for some attacks. Casualties inevitably mounted. For example, in three days the trench strength of the 106th Brigade fell from 2,050 to only five hundred men. Even with these problems, however, the division advanced approximately eight miles in five days, seizing 1,100 prisoners, forty-two guns, and numerous machine guns and trench mortars.[65]

The Allies suspended the Flanders attack for ten days, from October 4 to 13, because of deteriorating roads and the need to reorganize the supply services, particularly behind the French and Belgian sectors of the front. When the advance resumed, the Thirty-fifth Division was involved in a week-long spell of active operations, which included crossing the Lys near Marcke and Bisseghem on October 18–19. On the latter morning, patrols of the Nineteenth DLI penetrated into Courtrai, thus claiming the honor of being the first British troops to enter the town. This was a hugely rewarding moment for a battalion that, less than two years before, had reached the nadir of its fortunes. The division's role in the Battle of Courtrai culminated in an action lasting some twenty-three hours on October 20–21. Partly attributable to Major General Marindin's shrewd order for a flank march and evening attack by the 106th Brigade, the Kreupel and Hoogstraatje ridges were secured and the defensive position known as the Courtrai Switch breached. Though its losses of forty-nine killed, two hundred wounded, and twenty-seven missing were relatively light considering its notable achievements, these operations, conducted over cultivated countryside full of glutinous mud, nevertheless were a strenuous physical ordeal for all ranks and, when relieved, the troops were cold, soaked, and exhausted.[66]

After another short rest, the division was called upon for a further series of operations in the advance to the Schelde between October 27 and 31. The 104th Brigade's capture of Eeuwhoek and numerous other villages on October 31—albeit at a cost of 428 casualties—helped the Second Army clear the western banks of the Schelde and earned widespread praise, including the personal congratulations of Plumer himself. The infantry of the 104th Brigade quickly acknowledged the contribution of the artillery in this attack, with one battalion describing the barrage as the best it had witnessed. As the divisional historian comments, this was a fitting conclusion to three-and-a-half years of cooperation, since it was destined to be the divisional artillery's last set-piece barrage.[67] The final period in the line was from November 4 to 11, a week that saw the division cross the Schelde. When the Armistice came into effect, the division's advanced guards were at Grammont on the River Dendre, some fifteen miles beyond the Schelde.

Reflection

An examination of the casualties listed for the latter half of 1918 in *Soldiers Died in the Great War* suggests that original or early Bantam recruits—those with relatively low serial numbers—were still present in sufficient numbers to make a genuine contribution to the final victory. In a sample of four battalions—the Fifteenth Cheshires, Fifteenth Sherwood Foresters, Seventeenth Lancashire Fusiliers, and Nineteenth DLI—an average of 20.6 percent of those who died during or as a direct result of the "Hundred Days" are known to have been born in the battalion's own recruiting area and to have been original or early recruits—that is, genuine Bantams. Similarly, an average of 17.8 percent of the dead of these battalions during the second half of 1918 were original or early Bantams known to have enlisted or resided in their home recruiting area. Bearing in mind all the trials, tribulations, and changes that the division had experienced in its short history, these averages are surprisingly high. They *do* indicate, however, that there was little essentially wrong with the fighting spirit of *individual* Bantams, even if the overall Bantam concept, in a *collective* sense, was flawed and unsustainable. Moreover, the Bantam experiment in 1914–1915 did not represent an attempt to "scrape the bottom of the barrel" but rather an effort to inject fresh impetus into a flagging recruiting campaign by offering a chance to enlist to patriotic men who would otherwise have been barred from joining the ranks of Kitchener's Army merely because of their small stature. It should not be forgotten that the original Bantams were all volunteers, many keen to serve their king and country. That a comparatively large proportion of the "originals" appear to have been still doing their duty in the last months of the war testifies to their courage and endurance, not to physical failings. It might therefore be more fitting to remember the Bantam experiment for the qualities of those individual Bantams who fought to the end than to overemphasize the inherent weaknesses of the experiment itself.

5   Scraping the Barrel: African American Troops and World War I

Steven Short

African Americans have served in U.S. military institutions since the colonial period, in many cases playing very prominent and gallant roles in fighting the enemies of the United States. Although the army did not offer complete equality, it did offer many blacks the opportunity to prove their worth to themselves and their country. Many hoped that loyal service in the U.S. Army would help bring about social improvements and equality in the nation. Opportunities in the army did not always present themselves, however, with African Americans finding themselves facing many obstacles, including poor assignments, a lack of job choices, and limitations in rank, if they were even accepted for service.

Consideration for service seemed to be a constant issue for blacks. They were often the last to be called for service and the first to be discharged once the war ended. Viewed by many political and military leaders as the "bottom of the barrel," black men willing to fight for the United States faced a long, hard struggle to earn a place of equality and honor among America's defenders.

Long-standing attitudes in the army limited the possibilities for blacks. Many whites believed that black men could make adequate soldiers but not capable leaders. Service for many blacks began during the various colonial wars and the French and Indian War (1754–1763), when colonists accepted blacks for military duty, and they often served in integrated units.[1] This opportunity did not last long. During the American Revolution, George Washington decided to "reject negroes altogether," even though black men such as Salem Poor and Prince Estabrook had already distinguished themselves in combat. Washington later reversed his decision and allowed blacks to serve, but that did not change the nation's demeaning attitude toward blacks, whether free or enslaved.[2]

After independence, white attitudes toward black military service continued to be negative. In the Militia Act of 1792, Congress specifically barred blacks from service and opened it only for white citizens. In spite of this act, some states did allow black men to serve in noncombat positions such as laborers or porters. This attitude reflected the white view that black men represented less-than-desirable manpower. Not until the Civil War was the issue of black service seriously reexamined.

When the Civil War began in April 1861, militia duty still did not include blacks for service. There appeared to be no need or desire by the federal government to utilize black manpower for the war. Of course, many black men viewed the opening of hostilities as a war to end slavery, and they wanted to fight. But racial attitudes prevailed; as one white New York volunteer stated, "We think we are far too superior a race" to fight alongside blacks.[3]

As the Civil War continued, the urgent need to utilize available manpower prevailed. Bottom of the barrel or not, the army needed men, and blacks were willing to fight. Through several government measures, the creation of black units took shape primarily in occupied portions of the South in 1862. Not until after the announcement of the Emancipation Proclamation in September 1862 did the door open for the more widespread recruitment and utilization of black troops.[4]

With emancipation as a war aim, fewer whites offered resistance to the recruitment and arming of African Americans. Black units performed with distinction in many engagements, such as the attack on Fort Wagner and the Vicksburg Campaign at Port Hudson and Milliken's Bend, but the troops served under the leadership of white officers. Racial prejudices still existed, but by the fall of 1863, over fifty black regiments had been formed, and 166 regiments would serve by the end of the war.[5] During the Civil War, few blacks received commissions as officers. Regimental surgeons and chaplains held rank, but outside of those "fewer than 100 . . . became officers."[6] While the illiteracy of many blacks played a role, "the reluctance to promote capable black men from the ranks was clearly a result of race prejudice."[7]

After the Civil War, the fortunes of black troops received a boost when Congress ordered that the army should contain six African American regiments, four of infantry and two of cavalry. In actuality, only two infantry regiments and two cavalry regiments survived budget cuts. These troops did not receive warm welcomes by the military or in the communities in which they served, primarily in the American Southwest and Great Plains. White officers still commanded these regiments, as the officer examination committees "rejected every black veteran of the Civil War who sought to be commissioned."[8]

The social inequality of blacks translated into military inequality and the prevailing fear that blacks could not function in leadership positions. In spite of this racism, twelve black men attended the United States Military Academy at West Point between 1870 and 1889. Of those twelve, however, only three graduated. By the turn of the century, only one of the three, Charles Young, still held an active commission.[9]

The focus of this chapter is on the effort of African American men not simply to enlist in the army and participate in World War I but to have the same opportunities afforded white men of becoming army officers and see combat. This struggle for equality in the army did not begin with World War I, but the war is the culmination of the effort by blacks to climb up from the bottom of the barrel and prove themselves as capable soldiers and officers.

Many black men had served in both the army and navy in noncombatant roles for decades and would continue to do so into the twentieth century. It was common for blacks to serve as stevedores, cooks, and attendants. This study, however, will center on the enlistment of blacks for active-duty combat roles and on how the U.S. government ultimately moved to utilize black troops and commission black men as officers.

The Spanish-American War

The extent of the roadblocks African Americans faced in the army depended on the severity of the crisis the nation currently faced. In times of peace, great discrimination occurred, while in wartime the ranks often expanded to include more black enlisted men (but very few officers). Even in the wake of black military successes, racism and discrimination remained commonplace.

Many African Americans took the opportunity to serve in their state militias and were activated for federal duty during the Spanish-American War, but not until there were protests from the black community did President William McKinley issue a second call for volunteers, one that included black volunteers. On this second call, volunteers from Alabama, Illinois, Kansas, North Carolina, and

Virginia helped fill the ranks. Overall, approximately 13,000 African Americans served in the Spanish-American War, including the existing four black Regular Army regiments.[10]

Command issues also played a role for African Americans in the Spanish-American War. Who would command the new volunteer units, white men or black men? The War Department largely avoided the issue by leaving it up to the states that provided the volunteers. Most state militia units, white or black, elected their own officers based on popularity, community influence, or political patronage. Additionally, some black enlisted men from the Regular Army received commissions as officers in the new volunteer state regiments. Major Charles Young did not receive orders for overseas duty.

The black volunteer regiments began to receive white officers (who often showed distaste for the assignment) as their commanders. A white regular officer took command of Virginia's African American troops and "promptly rid himself of every black officer he had inherited."[11] Racism and generally negative views toward African American troops came from northern states also. Black volunteers from Indiana were stripped of African American officers above the grade of lieutenant, an action that the War Department found acceptable.[12]

African Americans saw combat in the Spanish-American War and the subsequent war in the Philippines. The four existing black army regiments all sailed to Cuba and fought under white command, often side by side with white regiments, in the battles of El Caney, Kettle Hill, and San Juan Hill. Black troops performed well during the war, but any aspirations of equality within the army or desires that loyal service would bring about social improvements were short lived. After the war, all of the black units were demobilized except for the regular regiments; the number of black troops (approximately five thousand) did not increase, and equality in the army did not happen.

In some states, political movements to limit or eliminate black military service gained strength. Tennessee, Pennsylvania, and Iowa refused to allow any black National Guard regiments. The desire to limit African American military service also gathered momentum throughout the Spanish-American War and into the twentieth century as several southern states, such as Georgia and Mississippi, took measures to cut black National Guard units.[13] African American appeals to the War Department went unanswered, and only two regiments of African American militia survived, in Illinois and New York, along with various smaller units in other northern states, totaling five to ten thousand men.[14]

From Brownsville to World War I

In 1906, the Brownsville, Texas, raid further complicated and damaged the reputation of African American troops. White citizens of Brownsville did not want African Americans in their town, a place where Jim Crow reigned, and greeted the transfer of the 1st Battalion, 25th Infantry, with prejudice. After several skirmishes and confrontations between black soldiers and white citizens, a "riot" occurred after midnight on August 14, 1906, when shots were fired on the streets of Brownsville. White citizens claimed that rampaging black soldiers had fired over one hundred rounds into Brownsville, with one man killed and others wounded. Actual witness testimony proved dubious, and much of the evidence did not place blame on the 1st Battalion. Yet President Theodore Roosevelt punished the entire battalion with dishonorable discharges and a ban on future government employment.[15]

In spite of the repercussions of Brownsville, African Americans continued to serve in the army. Another opportunity for distinction came when tension between the United States and Mexico boiled over. By 1916, the United States had ordered several thousand troops (including the black 10th Cavalry) to Texas for a punitive expedition against Pancho Villa. General John J. Pershing commanded the troops.

On June 3, 1916, during the sporadic fighting along the border and into Mexico, Congress passed a National Defense Act, which expanded the Regular Army and increased the National Guard.[16] The conflict with Pancho Villa may have been the immediate motivation for this legislation, but many Americans were also keeping a close watch on the war in Europe, which threatened to engulf the United States.

The National Defense Act planned to increase the Regular Army by approximately 42,000 officers and men over a five-year period; it also continued summer training camps for students and other citizens as a means of preparedness. Another major aspect of the act increased the National Guard from one hundred thousand to four hundred thousand over the same five-year period.[17] Despite the act's passage, the army had only 5,791 officers and 121,797 enlisted men within U.S. borders by April 1, 1917.[18]

Whether there were to be additional black regiments was uncertain. Questions arose regarding African American capabilities and whether African Americans should be included for military service, or if they would even be needed. Some whites opposed allowing blacks to serve in the military at all, whether as officers or enlisted men. Some members of Congress and the military did not believe African Americans could be good soldiers or be capable of handling the duties of an officer. These attitudes reflect not only contemporary racist views but also long-held views toward African American military service as undesirable and incapable.

In 1914, Congressman Frank Park (D-Ga.) introduced a bill that forbade "persons of the Negro race to be designated, elected or appointed commissioned or non-commissioned officers in the Army or Navy of the United States." The House Committee on Military Affairs reviewed the proposal but would not accept it.[19] Shortly after Park's proposal became public, many of the leading black newspapers throughout the United States voiced their outrage. The Baltimore *Afro American Ledger* condemned the bill in several editorials and pointed out that blacks had fought in most of America's wars. The paper also stated that both the French and the British utilized "colored" troops and that it was "too late to draw the color line in war."[20]

The Preparedness Movement

The Crisis, the official organ of the National Association for the Advancement of Colored People, published a copy of a letter sent to President Woodrow Wilson. The letter asked President Wilson to form four new African American regiments. *The Crisis* addressed official fears that few blacks would even volunteer for service by arguing "there is no difficulty in recruiting colored regiments," then took the offensive by stating that not providing for more African American regiments was a decided lack of preparedness.[21]

Demands for more black regiments continued, but some supporters shifted direction as the United States drew closer to entering the conflict. The new effort centered on the Preparedness or Plattsburg Movement, begun in 1913 by General Leonard Wood and former president Theodore Roosevelt. Named for a training camp at

Plattsburg, New York, the movement sought to expose civilians to rudimentary military training in a series of summer camps. There, citizens (mostly professional men) engaged in limited military study, drilled and marched, and participated in calisthenics. The camps were initially funded by private citizens but received some federal money as part of the 1916 National Defense Act.[22] The original Plattsburg Camp was a state training facility, but new camps would be federal facilities.

The Plattsburg camp only catered to whites, and no provision existed for admitting African Americans. Throughout the country, several more Plattsburg-styled camps emerged, all efforts to provide some military training in case of war. Although the camp functioned more as a social retreat, the trainees hoped that they would provide a new core of army officers, if such became necessary. The fact that the camps were opened only to whites is indicative of the views toward African Americans as being less-than-desirable manpower. Once the Plattsburg camp received official government sanction and funding, however, the African American community rallied to the cause of including blacks.

Dr. Joel E. Spingarn, the chairman of the NAACP, tried unsuccessfully to get blacks admitted to the camp. Spingarn wrote Secretary of War Newton Baker, asking him to permit African Americans to attend. Baker declined, telling Spingarn "he could never persuade the bureaucracy to agree."[23] Rather than continue to challenge Baker and the War Department, Spingarn instead changed tactics and began lobbying for a separate training camp for African Americans. Although some black leaders felt that a separate camp accommodated racism, Spingarn held firm: "I could not forgive myself if I saw black millions serving in the ranks and had not lifted a finger to help them to positions of leadership."[24]

Supporters still had concerns. George Austin, of St. Paul's College in Virginia, worried that "business and professional men of color will be poorly provided for," believing that the solution to recruiting would be to wage immediately a "campaign of education and arousement [sic]." He was "willing to do whatever I can to secure a large attendance to this camp."[25] With support, Spingarn pushed ahead to make black men aware of the camp. In an open letter published in the New York *Age*, he encouraged African American men to apply directly to him. The brief application included such things as birthplace, education, occupation, present health, and two references.

Reprinted in different newspapers and later in campus advertisements, the applications slowly began to come in, and support for the separate camp grew.[26]

During this period, Spingarn apparently became worried he might lose his friends and questioned himself. In a handwritten note sometime in early March 1917, Spingarn scribbled several points he considered important for the movement. "Don't volunteer? Nation doesn't want you to volunteer—South afraid of war for this reason. (a) if negro goes, he'll return trained (b) if any whites go, negro left alone in South."[27] Spingarn clearly recognized that Senator James K. Vardaman of Mississippi and others would view arming and training blacks as a threat to white supremacy and Jim Crowism in the South.

In March 1917, Spingarn received an invitation to speak at Howard University about the proposed training camp. George Brice, the president of the student body, wrote Spingarn "you are very popular with the student body" and "your proposition would surely materialize if you could come here" to discuss it. Brice requested application forms for several presentations at the university fraternities to gain support and applicants.[28] Support also came from men such as Dean Pickens of Morgan College, Professor Cook of Howard, and R. R. Wright of Georgia State Normal and Industrial College, all of whom proved essential in developing the movement and providing volunteers.

Eight days after Spingarn's speech at Howard, the *Afro American* reported that Lieutenant Colonel Charles Young, still the highest-ranking African American in the military, supported Spingarn's movement for a segregated training camp. Young believed there would be a need for African American officers and leaders and that the four existing black regiments would indeed be expanded and new ones created. He wrote, "THIS PLAN OF DR. SPINGARN'S IS CONSTRUCTIVE, AND I HOPE IT WILL MEET WITH THE BEST OF RESULTS."[29] With support from prominent black leaders growing, it seemed that movement must certainly be successful.

The Question of Black Officers

The situation abruptly shifted on April 6, 1917, when the United States declared war on Germany. With the country now in the war, establishing more Plattsburg camps, segregated or not, became unimportant. The army would now rapidly expand, and a draft would have to be implemented to fill the ranks. Matters relating to the army and training shifted to Washington, D.C., from the individual regional commanders throughout the United States. Thus Wood's agreement for a Plattsburg-style segregated camp was overtaken by events.[30]

Under the National Defense Act of 1916, the Secretary of War and the War Department had authority over "camps for the military instruction and training."[31] Utilizing this provision, on April 17 the War Department called for Officer Training Camps (OTC) to begin on May 15, 1917. The first series of sixteen camps ran for three months and commissioned 27,341 officers of various ranks from colonel to second lieutenant.[32]

A few days after the start of the white OTCs, the long-awaited announcement from the War Department came. Ralph Hayes, private secretary to Newton Baker, wrote Howard University President Stephen Newman with the good news.[33] The Central Committee of Negro College Men (CCNCM), a group of Howard University students and graduates, then spread the news among blacks. Their letter cautioned the prospective officers: "there is a terrible responsibility resting upon us . . . the government has challenged the Negro race to prove its worth." Likely written by Thomas M. Gregory and George Brice, the letter outlined the pay structure, addressed questions about transportation and uniforms, and called for enthusiasm and energy in taking on the new challenge of becoming army officers.[34]

The War Department determined that 1,250 candidates would be admitted to the Fort Des Moines camp.[35] Several factors played a role in determining the number of candidates, and the General Staff debated the matter with Secretary Baker. Initially, members of the General Staff such as General Joseph E. Kuhn of the Army War College and Quartermaster General Henry G. Sharpe decided that two training camps for African American officers would be established. Some consideration had been given for creating two training camps, with approximately 2,500 men at each camp, but the Quartermaster Department was not confident of being able to supply two camps.[36]

General Sharpe told Chief of Staff General Hugh Scott that providing clothing and equipment for approximately five thousand trainees "would encroach to that extent upon the supply provided for the Regular Army."[37] Although Sharpe apparently did not object to training black men to become officers, his memo of May 8, 1917, certainly leaves him open to some criticism by implying that blacks were a tradeoff for more valuable whites.

General Kuhn, meanwhile, proposed that the second camp be put on hold until supply and logistics were determined and the actual enlistment numbers became apparent. Kuhn did not want to waste energy and resources establishing two separate training camps when only one might be needed.[38] Secretary Baker ultimately decided to accept the recommendations of the General Staff and establish one training camp at Fort Des Moines, with the enrollment set at 1,250, far below the estimated five thousand.[39]

General Tasker Bliss of the General Staff suggested that the black draft be delayed until later in 1917 and possibly even held separately from the white draft.[40] His motivation was using the black draftees as labor troops and not for combat. Although not official policy at the time, the idea of using black troops only for labor and supply must certainly have been in many white officers' minds, and it would likely play a role in determining how many OTCs to establish and how many candidates to accept.

Fort Des Moines

The Fort Des Moines Officer Training Camp would train the 1,250 men stipulated by the army. Two hundred and fifty came from within the ranks of the four existing African American regiments, the remaining thousand men from a pool of applicants from across the nation. Although no record of the exact number of applicants remains, Spingarn had retained many applications he had received for the earlier preparedness camp. Spingarn shared those records with the CCNCM to facilitate the OTC application process.

Applicants listed their age, profession, the college or university attended, and whether or not they had any military training or experience. Training or experience could include National Guard duty, service in the Regular Army, or simply drill in college or high school.[41] Of the 162 applicants who held college degrees, teachers comprised the largest portion at 24 percent, physicians comprised 10.5 percent, and lawyers 7.4 percent. An additional 13.6 percent did not list their occupation and offered no explanation. Other professions with at least two listings included minister, dentist, government employee, pharmacist, editor, and principal, commandant, or school administrator. From this sample, it can be determined that the applicants generally worked in skilled professions and not in manual labor or blue-collar jobs.[42]

The Central Committee utilized its connections with other black colleges and the fraternity system to gather the necessary applicants. Ultimately the CCNCM recruited many of the one thousand "general public" candidates.[43] Each approved applicant was then required to be "examined physically and as to general suitability by an officer of the Army" before an assignment to Fort Des Moines and officer training.[44] After the war, Jerome Dowd, a white journalist, wrote that although the future for African American soldiers appeared bright, not many African Americans could be found "who are qualified for positions of command."[45] In 1917, however, at least 1,250 black men were found to be acceptable for training.

Charles Ballou, a white colonel from the 24th Infantry, was appointed to command the 17th Provisional Training Regiment at Fort Des Moines. Ballou, a West Point graduate, was promoted to general, and the rest of the OTC's white instructors were pulled from stations within the Army's Central Department.[46] In spite of the skeptics and critics who regarded having African Americans in the army as undesirable, Colonel Ballou treated the men as if the camp would provide the foundation of military training required to lead troops into combat.

When the men assembled for their training, Ballou told them that he did not know "whatever may have been in the minds of those who made this decision [to have a black training camp]." But he promised that anyone who failed to meet military requirements "would be eliminated" and that no extra considerations would be extended to the trainees based upon race. Only men with "strong bodies, keen intelligence, [and] absolute obedience to orders" would be successful.[47]

Training started immediately, and the program varied only slightly from week to week over the fifteen-week course. The training regimen was the same as at other camps; the army issued general training guidelines and memorandums for infantry, artillery, or engineering troops but not for specific divisions, regiments, or races. Each week required a certain amount of training in different areas. While members of the General Staff and the training camp staff may have viewed African American troops as undesirable, the training they received did not reflect that view.

Over the course of training, several small incidents occurred among some residents of Des Moines and the visiting African

American troops. One incident of note occurred at the Empress Theater, when two trainees refused to sit in a segregated "Jim Crow" section of the theater. A police officer on duty at the theater removed the two men by force and took them into custody. Once at the police station, the authorities determined that the two trainees had not done anything wrong and released them. Local newspapers covered the story and sided with the actions of the trainees. In a telling editorial, the Des Moines *News* stated that "The United States is fighting for equality and democracy of other peoples—what about at home?"[48]

Colonel Ballou wished to avoid any further incidents, and he did so by "impressing the candidates with the fact that bumptious arrogance" would only "defeat the object they were working for." He told the candidates that they could not force others to accept social equality: it must be won by "modesty, patience, forbearance and character."[49] In this case, Ballou seems accepting and welcoming of the potential of breaking down barriers of racism and segregation, but later actions on his part cloud the picture.

Upon receiving his appointment at Fort Des Moines, Ballou had been told to file reports on the progress of the black candidates. The War Department wanted to know if the "character of the personnel" would make it possible to create a "complete colored division."[50] This hints at official interest in forming an African American division, but no decision would be made until October, when Secretary Baker and the War Department decided to organize black troops and officers into the 92nd Infantry Division.

Ballou filed his report on July 10, 1917, and quickly made the point that "many experienced officers" either expected the Fort Des Moines camp to fail or held serious doubts about African Americans developing into competent army officers. "There is no available means of comparing the results of . . . these negroes with that obtained in the white camps," Ballou wrote. He believed the 1,250 candidates were too few to provide a quality source of manpower from which to select officers; only half would graduate, and the number of African American candidates was half what the white OTCs had.[51] At first look, this suggests Ballou was unhappy with his trainees, but his criticism is directed more at the War Department for setting the number of candidates so low. Ballou's argument supported the idea that a larger training camp should have been established.[52]

Ballou noted various drawbacks within the training regiment. By highlighting the drawbacks, and especially doing so early in his report, Ballou did a disservice to the men of Fort Des Moines. A more productive approach would have been to emphasize the strengths and accomplishments of the men and their potential for becoming good officers. Comments such as this cast doubt upon whether Ballou wanted the camp to succeed in producing black officers. Colonel Ballou did praise his candidates by stating that they "are a remarkably strong, earnest, well-educated body of men" who maintained exemplary conduct.

To support his claim of good conduct, Ballou reported that "five cases of venereal disease" among the nearly 1,250 candidates had been reported. While it may seem strange to mention the five cases of venereal disease, Ballou meant that the low incidence of venereal disease was a testament to the "morality" of the men; however, it merely emphasized that some of the men were infected, no matter how that number compared to other camps.[53]

After voicing some initial concerns, throughout the report Ballou praised the trainees' conduct, noting that "no friction" existed with the white troops at Fort Des Moines and that the candidates exhibited great enthusiasm and resourcefulness, "all that could be desired and more than could be expected." Meanwhile, training progressed at the established pace, and "the prescribed work is up to the minute." Based on conversations with instructors, Ballou estimated that between 30 and 60 percent of the men would be capable of "development into useful officers."[54]

Yet Fort Des Moines could not fully staff a division, and Ballou advocated temporarily using white officers for artillery and engineering regiments. The white officers would be needed only "until experience and training have developed colored men to replace them."[55] The War Department took the report to heart, and the 92nd Division (Colored) would receive a large complement of white officers.

As the men of the 17th Provisional Training Regiment continued their training, unaware of Colonel Ballou's report, the War Department began seriously considering how to use the black officers. Even before the OTC began, the General Staff made the decision that "colored officers should not be assigned to white organizations."[56] Given this, it could be assumed that the African American officers would be assigned to a new division, but confirmation remained weeks ahead.

The Chief of the War College Division, General P. D. Lochridge, stated that since black draftees were not yet organized, there existed no need for black officers, although Lochridge did not rule out their use in the near future. Based on the fear of white soldiers coming under the command of African American officers and the fact that no large body of black enlisted men had taken form, General Lochridge declared "the graduates of the Des Moines Training Camp can not be employed with advantage at present."[57]

The commissioning took place on October 15, 1917. Emmett J. Scott attended the ceremony in his capacity as a newly appointed special assistant to the secretary of war. Formerly an aide to the late Booker T. Washington at the Tuskegee Institute, Scott now advised Secretary Baker on race relations. Scott spoke to the men, encouraging them to take advantage of their opportunities and to "remember always that you are on trial."[58] The graduating class at Fort Des Moines comprised 624 officers, 106 captains, 321 first lieutenants, and 199 second lieutenants.[59] (The War College Division instructed that the new officers be commissioned with ranks as determined by Ballou and his staff.)

It should also be noted that the War College called for 1,250 men to attend the training camp, yet only 624 men, approximately 50 percent, received commissions. Studies have not yet sufficiently examined why half of the men failed to graduate. Another report has the number of graduates at 624, with the number of candidates "who are not so recommended" at 316; this would mean a 66 percent graduation rate.[60] It is not clear why there is such a deviation in the reports. Likely, while 1,250 men attended the camp, some washed out before graduation, leaving only 940 who actually completed the entire program. While the latter numbers indicate a substantially higher success rate, the initial 50 percent success rate likely contributed to the War Department's decision not to open a second training camp for black men.

Upon earning their commissions, the men had no troops to command, and they received a brief furlough before reporting to their duty stations. The furloughs became necessary because the army did not have a plan to utilize the new officers, did not want to pay them for active duty, and no large body of black draftees existed for the new officers to command.[61] Ultimately, the new officers helped staff seven different camps, where they continued learning and awaited the black draftees they would command.[62]

Questions remained on how to utilize the new officers. While many in the army believed the new officers and coming draftees should be placed in service battalions, the issue was not resolved.

Secretary Baker faced public pressure from the black community to use black troops in combat roles. Additionally, the chief of engineers reported that it would "impracticable" to use black officers for service battalions, because their duties would lead to the frequent intermingling of units in which black officers might come in command of white troops.[63] Secretary of War Baker ultimately decided to put the Fort Des Moines graduates in command positions for combat units.[64]

African American National Guardsmen

There were already many black officers ready to serve their country. While many Fort Des Moines graduates went to the newly organized 92nd Division, National Guard units already had several black regiments. During the mobilization, National Guard units from New York, Illinois, Connecticut, Massachusetts, Tennessee, Ohio, Maryland, and Washington, D.C., were organized into the 93rd Division (Provisional).[65] The new division became the second such fighting force in U.S. history that included a substantial amount of African American officers.

Most the National Guard units were federalized "between 25 March 1917 and the declaration of war on 6 April 1917."[66] The total strength of all National Guard units numbered 3,733 officers and 76,713 troops.[67] Of this total, approximately 5,500 were African Americans, with about 125 African American officers.[68] Only the 8th Illinois enjoyed a full complement of black officers, led by Colonel Franklin Dennison; other units had all white officers or a mix of black and white.

The two largest African American National Guard units were the 8th Illinois and the 15th New York Infantry. The 15th New York formed in June 1916 under authorization of New York Governor Charles S. Whitman. The governor appointed his friend William Hayward as the white colonel of the regiment and charged him with organizing and filling it. Hayward commented of his soldiers: "There is no better soldier material in the world. Given the proper training, these men will be the equal of any soldiers in the world."[69] The 15th New York included more white officers than the 8th Illinois, but many African Americans filled the roster, including many of its first officers.

While the 8th Illinois had participated in actions along the border with Mexico and the Mexican Punitive Expedition, the 15th

New York was still organizing. After the declaration of war, the War Department ordered National Guard units be expanded to wartime strength; the 15th New York had roughly two officers per company but needed six. The 15th also received a number of white volunteers, many apparently not trained as officers but willing to serve in the African American regiment.[70] It is not clear why Colonel Hayward did not utilize more African Americans to fill the vacant officer positions rather than choosing whites. It is likely that Hayward believed, as other white commanders of African American regiments did, that many blacks "were incapable of passing an examination" to become officers. These assumptions led to the dismissal of many African American officers and their replacement by whites.[71]

The 15th New York and 8th Illinois easily transitioned into their new federal designations as the 369th and 370th Infantry Regiments; both functioned as regiments prior to receiving their federal orders and did so afterward.[72] Other African American National Guard units were not regimental size and, upon federalization, were merged into one regiment, the new 372nd Infantry. The 372nd formed from various smaller National Guard units: the Massachusetts 1st Separate Company, the District of Columbia 1st Separate Battalion, the 9th Ohio Infantry Battalion, Company G of the 1st Tennessee National Guard, the 1st Separate Company of Maryland, and the 1st Separate Company of Connecticut.[73] The regiment organized at Camp Stuart, Virginia, receiving its federal designation in December 1917.[74]

The Draft

While the National Guard was mustering, another plan existed to supplement the guard units and Regular Army. President Wilson wanted a plan for conscription ready even before a declaration of war, "so that, if I should be obliged to go to the Congress, I can refer to it in my message as a law ready to be presented for their consideration." A conscription program was formulated in February 1916 and presented to President Wilson shortly after the break in diplomatic relations with Germany. After the declaration of war, Wilson sent the Selective Service bill before Congress, and it became law in May 1917.[75]

The selection process would provide manpower to fill the newly organized regiments of the 92nd and the National Guard regiments of the 93rd that had not yet met wartime strength. Additionally, draftees filled the ranks of the 371st Infantry Regiment of the

93rd Division. African American draftees, many poorly educated, became the troops that most African American officers commanded.

The Selective Service Act did not distinguish between white or black men, citizens or aliens. All males between the ages of twenty-one and thirty-one were required to register. Adjustments to the act the following August included registering men in the 18–20 and 32–45 age brackets. The initial registration took place on June 5, 1917, and included 9,780,535 men, approximately 40.4 percent of the U.S. male population in the 21–31 age grouping.[76] Approximately 737,626 were African Americans, 7.5 percent of the total number of registrants, but only 75,697, or 10.3 percent, actually passed the examinations and were "certified" for service.[77] Two more registrations took place during the war, bringing the total number of draft-eligible men to 23,908,576. Of that number, 2,290,527 registrants were African Americans, constituting approximately 9.58 percent of all men registered for Selective Service.[78]

It is important to understand that the number of registrants greatly outweighed the number of men actually drafted and then those subsequently accepted for service. The process of Selective Service can be broken down into three distinct phases: registration, selection, and acceptance.

The first draft took place on July 20, and the states began to fill population-based quotas. A sparsely populated state such as Arizona had a quota of only 4,478 men; New York faced a quota of 122,424. A state also received credit toward its quota for men already in military service.[79]

The Selective Service boards in certain locations (especially the South) began exhibiting bias against African Americans. Local draft boards, mostly all white, handled examining and classifying men within their district. A draft board existed in every city or county with a population of thirty thousand people or more, for a total of 4,648 local boards.[80] Trouble arose when some local draft boards began to accept for service what seemed to be an alarming percentage of African Americans compared to whites and their respective population totals in society.

All men received a Class I draft status upon their registration, signifying eligibility to be drafted. Exemptions only came after an examination by their local draft boards. On the first call of the draft in July 1917, 1,078,331 blacks were selected and examined for service. Of that number, approximately 556,917 men retained their Class I status, while the rest were designated to lesser classes of eligibility. This amounted to 51.6 percent of black registrants accepted as fit for service. In contrast, the number of white registrants totaled 9,652,515, of which 3,110,659 received Class I status upon examination. Although almost six times as many whites as blacks were put into Class I, the percentage is very lopsided: 51.6 percent of blacks were accepted versus only 32.2 percent of the white registrants.[81]

Provost Marshal General Enoch Crowder tried to explain the numbers by heaping praise on the black community for providing "its quota, and uncomplainingly, yes, cheerfully." Crowder stated that blacks were full of "patriotism" and a "martial spirit" on par with that of whites. He avoided the deferments issue by arguing that both the African American draftees and the draft boards were fair in their dealings with one another. "There appears to have been no racial discrimination," General Crowder reported.[82]

Even Secretary Baker became involved. Baker publicly "made it clear that it [the War Department] will tolerate no discrimination against colored draftees." Allegations of discrimination would be investigated, "and any wrong done will be righted."[83] The secretary wrote Emmett J. Scott to explain that the department had "no intention . . . to settle the so-called Race Question" and stated that blacks and whites needed to work together throughout the war.[84] Shortly thereafter, the secretary commended African American draftees on the "relatively low percentage of exemption claims filed by them."[85] While the black officers possessed some education, many black draftees did not. It is possible that African Americans filed fewer exemption claims because of illiteracy and lack of education: they simply did not understand the system well enough to take advantage of it. This, of course, would reflect the lack of educational opportunities for Southern blacks during this period.

A total of 367,710 African Americans entered service, whether volunteers or draftees, between June 5, 1917, and November 11, 1918. The number of white men inducted during the same period numbered 2,442,586. In spite of the disparity in the percentage of Class I certifications between white men and black men, the ultimate percentage of white men who served totaled 86.92 percent to 13.08 percent for African American men.[86] The final percentages do not reflect the discriminatory pattern that initially alarmed African Americans.

Utilization of Blacks

As the National Guard units federalized, the black draft began, and the officer candidates at Fort Des Moines trained, plans for utilization slowly took shape. General Tasker Bliss ordered that each divisional training area should have space for one regiment (approximately two thousand officers and men) "to be composed of colored drafted men and colored company officers." Bliss wanted the African American regiments established in addition to the normal four infantry regiments in a division.[87]

Once the various regiments were established, Bliss estimated that approximately thirty thousand African Americans would remain for assignment. These extra troops would be held "subject to the demands of the various staff departments" and likely put into service as communication troops or as stevedore units at ports.[88] Thus although Bliss and Baker did indeed plan to utilize black troops for combat in France, some black draftees would find themselves in noncombat roles. Whether those regiments would be used in an African American division or attached to white divisions remained to be seen.

The plan for sixteen infantry regiments and placement of only the surplus of men in "special units" showed potential for African American recruits. Combat duty seemed possible for many, which offered a chance, as it had in the past, for blacks to prove themselves to doubting white Americans and escape the stigma of being the "bottom of the barrel." Discrimination continued, however, and some branches of the service did not open for African American soldiers. The Ordnance Department never opened its doors to blacks. Chief of Ordnance General William Crozier flatly told the adjutant general that "drafted colored men cannot be utilized by the Ordnance Department." Crozier stated that "it will be impracticable to have organizations part white and part black."[89]

As the plan to utilize African American troops in combat developed, the War Department began to assemble draftees for organization and training. Many southern states did not welcome the prospect of an influx of black draftees, but the War Department had already decided. At one point, South Carolina Governor Richard Manning traveled to Washington, D.C., to lobby against sending troops to his state. The War Department did not change its plans.[90] The War Department also formed white divisions from a state or region to construct a "definite geographical locality" for each division as best it could. Blacks were not handled this way either as divisions or as regiments.[91]

South Carolina received 5,900 African American draftees along with the black 15th New York National Guard. Both groups trained at Camp Jackson, near Spartanburg. This decision to send draftees and National Guard units, both white and black, to some of the same camps developed as part of the plan to bring the guard regiments up to full strength. Once the National Guard units reached full strength, the remaining draftees would be used to create new divisions.[92]

There were concerns about assembling the whole 92nd Division at one camp. Placing so many black men in one area would be an "impracticability," according to the War Department. Colonel Joseph Leitch of the General Staff suggested that African American troops be stationed at camps "where the proportion of white troops to colored will be at least three to one." The camps chosen were all in the north, to reduce "the chance of friction between the civil population and the colored troops."[93] Dispersal might have hurt the development of the 92nd Division; it would never train together as a division while in the United States, and its African American officers would not learn to coordinate movements within a system of larger battlefield units. Many historians have cited the 92nd's lack of large-scale training for its initially poor performance on the battlefield. While there may be some substance to that argument, many other American divisions also did not train together before embarking for France.

The chief of staff approved Leitch's suggestions, which included many limitations on black officers. For many positions in the division, the War Department believed "white officers are . . . essential." Leitch provided a list of spots reserved for white officers, including the rank of general, medical officers and veterinarians, supply officers, captains of field artillery and engineering regiments, "aides to Brigade commanders," and "all officers attached to Division Headquarters." The War Department accepted Leitch's recommendations, feeling that any reduction in the number of white officers would greatly lower the efficiency of the division.[94]

Despite that the black draftees assembled at different camps, their training was similar to OTC training. They devoted a certain number of hours each week to marching, drill, rifle marksmanship, signaling, and regulations. Troops trained approximately forty hours each week, with a minimum of thirty-six hours prescribed; there were some open hours for rest or additional drill "for backward men."[95] The army kept the barracks and mess areas segregated, and headquarters troops were all white. War Department policy maintained separate organizations for whites and blacks because of the "difficulties" they believed would arise with integrated barracks, mess halls, and administration. Each cantonment enforced this policy.

The 93rd also did not train together as a division in the United States. It consisted only of four infantry regiments, lacking support units such as artillery, engineers, sanitary trains, or machine-gun battalions, but even the four infantry regiments did not train together. The elements of the 93rd sailed for France at different times, with the old 15th New York departing from Hoboken, New Jersey, in December 1917, and the 8th Illinois and additional black troops departing Newport News, Virginia, in April 1918. On arrival in France, some parts of the division remained in Brest, briefly serving as stevedores, while other parts of the division began the train ride into the country.

Service in France

The African American combat troops from the 92nd and 93rd Divisions have been well chronicled. There are various chapters and books devoted to their stories and exploits in France. Since these resources are readily available, the description provided here will be only an overview of their combat experience.[96]

Once the United States formally entered the war in April 1917, the British and French pressured it to immediately send any available troops to help fill the lines. Despite this pressure to have U.S. troops "amalgamated" into Allied armies, the United States remained unwilling to place Americans under foreign command. Pershing wanted to build a separate army under American command and to have that army fight as a unit. Hoping that this American army would strike the decisive blow against Germany, President Wilson supported Pershing in the decision.[97]

However much Pershing and Wilson wanted to avoid amalgamating U.S. troops, their allies needed manpower and needed it quickly. French demands increased during the period, and Pershing wrestled with the issue of sending the 15th New York into combat. Soon after a meeting with Colonel Hayward, General Pershing informed the War Department that he had ordered the 15th New York to serve with French forces. Pershing also expected the other three regiments of the 93rd Division to serve under French command once they arrived.[98] In March 1918, during the process of attaching the 15th New York to the French 16th Division, the Americans officially received their new designation as the 369th Infantry Regiment.

As the remaining regiments of the 93rd joined French divisions, the U.S. Army often initiated personnel changes within the regiments, replacing several of the higher ranking black officers with white officers. Colonel Denison of the 370th Infantry was replaced by Colonel T. A. Roberts, a white officer previously assigned to the regiment as an observer for the American Expeditionary Force (AEF). William S. Braddan, a chaplain in the regiment, believed that Roberts intended to replace all the black officers with whites, but that did not happen.[99]

The division's African American officers faced racism from within their own units and from outside, yet they did not lose heart in their cause. Although black officers experienced segregated facilities and some were removed from command, as a whole they acquired experience and prepared for their role in the French army. The leadership and bravery of the officers and men of the 93rd Division would be tested, but they would ultimately come through in fine fashion.

The 93rd adjusted to the French command structure and its different weapons without many issues, and the black units of the 93rd integrated into the white French units. After a period of training, the regiments of the 93rd performed well under French command and participated in the Meuse-Argonne offensive, beginning on September 26, 1918. The regiments stayed in the front lines of the Champagne sector until relieved on October 8. They had achieved their objectives, capturing the town of Séchault and moving through the woods of Petit Rosiere.[100] The French were glad to have the American troops and cited the combat units for several awards, including the French Croix de Guerre and their "superb spirit and an admirable disregard of danger."[101]

Some criticisms emerged, and at one point Major R. L. Fredendall, assigned by General Pershing to investigate the criticisms, suggested that the 93rd be removed from French command. However, Pershing did not reclaim the 93rd, and it remained under French command until the end of the war. Some of the charges of inefficiency against the 93rd may have stemmed from a lack of translators.[102]

The 92nd began to sail for France in June and July 1918. Officers were required to distinguish between white and black on their luggage so that "proper" (that is, segregated) berths could be assigned. During the voyage, men of the 92nd and other divisions ate their meals in shifts, with separate mess facilities provided for officers. The mess facilities of the ships could only accommodate a certain number of men, so various sittings occurred. In the case of the USS *Mt. Vernon* and the 92nd Division, with both whites and blacks onboard, reports criticized the "mixture of Races at every Sitting in the Mess Hall" and that such mixtures "should be avoided if possible." This point was reemphasized at the end of the report.[103]

Throughout the voyage to France, some of the white officers of the 92nd Division expressed the concern that white and black troops were on the same ship. Memorandums suggested that in future "Colored troops and White troops be placed on separate vessels."[104] Segregation reflected War Department policy and was indicative of the unwillingness of some white officers to recognize the service or importance of African American soldiers and officers. Similar complaints by white officers occurred on other ships, reinforcing the idea that black troops and officers were widely viewed as substandard in the army.

Upon arriving in France, General Pershing planned to send the 92nd Division to the British sector for training, although it would be returned to Pershing and the U.S. Army for combat. However, the British protested against the black division, arguing that the 92nd did not appear on the list of divisions to train with them. As a result, Pershing assigned the 92nd to the French for training.[105]

The schedule of training in France was similar to what they had previously experienced. The infantry regiments trained six days per week under the supervision of their Fort Des Moines graduates. On Sundays, there were inspections instead of training; on Fridays, the main activity was a march "of at least 10 miles" rather than training or drills.[106]

The 92nd Division trained and functioned around St. Dié, in Lorraine. It worked in conjunction with the French Seventh Army, replacing the U.S. 5th Infantry Division in the lines in August 1918. There were several engagements and skirmishes, and although labeled a quiet sector, the division conducted patrols and reconnaissance missions on a daily basis. Averaging thirteen patrols daily, the division captured eight prisoners and turned back eleven German attacks and raids during approximately thirty-seven days in the lines.[107]

On September 21, 1918, the 92nd moved to the U.S. First Army, taking a position about ten kilometers north of Triaucourt and about twenty kilometers west of the Meuse River, near the small town of Clermont. Few of the officers and men of the division could know it, but the move was preparation for the upcoming Meuse-Argonne offensive.[108]

The Meuse-Argonne campaign was a disaster for the 92nd Division. In its five days of battle, the 368th Infantry Regiment experienced conflicting orders and confusion, and some men retreated without orders under heavy German fire. The regiment and division were quickly withdrawn from the lines and ultimately sent to a quiet sector to finish out the war. The division suffered eighty fatalities and over three hundred wounded and gassed.[109] However, after that opportunity to come together as a unit and gain combat experience, the 92nd performed very well for the remainder of the war.

The performance of the 368th Infantry did not affect the outcome of the offensive, but it did influence the army to take action against some African American officers. Commendable records of African American units in France quickly vanished, and the only memory of significance became the poor performance of the 368th. Although its 1st Battalion performed well, all of its achievements and successes did not matter after the 2nd and 3rd Battalions "disintegrated and . . . ran from the enemy."[110]

As a result of the 368th's collapse, General Ballou, now commanding the division, quickly relieved thirty black officers as unfit for duty and command. Major B. F. Norris, the 3rd Battalion commander (reported as "gone to bed" during the first night of the offensive and unreachable to confirm the retreat orders) pushed for stronger action against his black officers. Norris brought formal charges against five of his African American officers; all were convicted, and four received death penalties. However, a special investigation by Secretary Baker and the War Department cleared the men of charges.[111]

The attention paid to the performance of black troops was clearly intentional. Viewed as undesirable and substandard manpower, these troops faced intense scrutiny and suffered for even the slightest misstep. Whether that meant breaking a Jim Crow law in the United States or crumbling under heavy enemy fire overseas did not matter. The army watched and took notes, judging these men by their actions. Despite being exonerated of cowardice during the Meuse-Argonne offensive, the reputations of all black soldiers suffered from the hasty charges and trial conducted by the army.

In the case of the 92nd Division, the army's extreme prejudice against African American officers dominated thinking. The heroics of the 1st Battalion of the 368th Infantry in the Meuse-Argonne were effectively ignored, despite that several officers and men of the battalion had earned Distinguished Service Crosses in that battle while advancing some four kilometers into German territory. It must also be noted that during the same offensive, the white 35th Division, serving in the same sector as the 92nd, broke in combat under enemy fire. Suffering from many of the same conditions as the 92nd (lack of food, poor communications, and no combat experience), the 35th retreated three kilometers.[112]

The plight of African American men and officers in the 92nd did not end with the dismissals, courts-martial, or relief from the Meuse-Argonne offensive. Despite African American officers later being exonerated by the War Department, the stigma remained. General Robert Bullard, commanding the U.S. Second Army, which included the 92nd Division for a period, believed the division a failure. He stated that African American officers "have an inadequate idea of what is expected of soldiers, and their white officers are too few to leaven the hump." Bullard continuously berated the 92nd and its officers, chastising them for not fighting and for a lack of military qualities.[113]

Racial stereotypes dominated the views of senior officers and commanders. Even in the face of complimentary combat reports regarding black soldiers and officers, divisional and army commanders ignored the achievements and failed to mention them in their own reports. More members of the 92nd earned Distinguished Service Crosses than the 6th, 35th, 81st, or 88th Divisions, all of which saw combat, including one, the 35th, which served under General Bullard.[114] These accomplishments were ignored and the record of the African American officers in the 92nd and 93rd Divisions tarnished. The November 11 armistice ended battlefield hostilities, and the officers and men awaited their orders. With the war in Europe over, what would become of the African Americans of the U.S. Army?

After the War

African American troops in the 92nd and 93rd were soon transferred to the French coast in preparation for returning to the United States. These troops, accepted into service under political pressure, would be some of the first troops sent home and discharged. While men of the 92nd Division worked on the docks awaiting transport, they did not take part in the various victory parades in France, and they continued to train and drill, submitted to hourly roll calls, and suffered from constant monitoring and restrictions of liberty.[115] All of these limitations and restrictions seem to stem from the War

Department's desire to keep black troops away from the French population, which was putatively more liberal and progressive than American society. Additionally, support for isolating the black troops may have also come from long-held white assumptions of African American men as sexual aggressors toward white women.

In the weeks after the Armistice, a rape hysteria spread throughout the army, directed against black troops. Dozens of allegations against black officers and men resulted in hourly roster checks and a close watch over which men received travel passes. General Ballou believed the crime of rape to be "very prevalent" among black troops.[116] It is difficult to determine just how prevalent rape was, but the army took steps to ensure that "undue social mingling of these two [races and sexes], be circumspectly prevented."[117] In fact, according to Major Adam E. Patterson, the judge advocate of the 92nd Division, only nine cases of rape involved that division, and only two of the nine were found guilty.[118] These numbers certainly do not justify an actual "hysteria" regarding rape, instead demonstrating the inherent fears and racism which existed in the army.

Certainly, barriers existed for the black troops of the 92nd and 93rd Divisions. The institutionalized racism of the U.S. Army hindered their development as military units and destroyed any sense of equality and value they might have gained. In many regards, it appears the army desired to keep black troops relegated to the ranks of less-than-desirable manpower through the use of segregation and discrimination.

While awaiting transport back to the United States, W. E. B. Du Bois joined the black troops to interview and observe their treatment and facilities. Du Bois came to believe that black servicemen were experiencing a great injustice. He wrote that "prejudice was rampant . . . and the officers were particularly subjected to all sorts of discrimination."[119] The officers and men suffered from a lack of respect by their white counterparts, surveillance by military intelligence, the stigma of being labeled "failures," and the hysteria of the rape scandals. All of these things served to create the hostile environment in which African American officers functioned.

African American troops began embarking for the United States on February 1, 1919. On February 2, 1919, the 369th and 370th Infantry sailed. Parts of each division followed over the next month; all of the black combat troops were en route for home by March 6.[120] Some of the black troops returned home to parades and vibrant welcomes; others simply received orders to report to various cantonments in preparation for demobilization.

Even as the peace treaty was being negotiated, the army was demobilizing. Secretary Baker and Chief of Staff General Peyton March appeared before Congress in January 1919 and pushed for a new bill to reorganize the army. The proposal would have maintained five hundred thousand officers and men, but the House Military Affairs Committee did not approve the bill. Instead, in 1919–1920, the House of Representatives passed several amendments to the 1916 National Defense Act, almost immediately lowering the number of army officers from 77,966 in 1919 to only 15,451 in 1920.[121]

In 1920, the War College surveyed white officers regarding the effectiveness of black men and officers. The reports did little to build a better reputation for those men, although some, including Ballou, softened their positions. A few officers criticized the way the army handled African American officers and men. Colonel Vernon Caldwell, a white officer, suggested that black officers would have performed better if the troops had been integrated to some extent, much in the manner that the French used the 93rd Division. Another white officer, Colonel James Parsons, believed that no black units should exist; instead, companies and regiments should be fully integrated.[122]

In the midst of the War College survey and House of Representatives discussions over the strength of the military, the War Department took steps to limit the enlistment of blacks in the army. The army retained the four black regiments in existence before World War I but added no additional units. African Americans would continue in limited roles in the U.S. Army, still viewed and utilized as undesirable manpower, until the nation once again needed their help in defending freedom and liberty, once again attempting to make the world safe for democracy. As in World War I, thousands of black Americans would answer the call to serve in World War II, with hopes that their service would this time open doors.[123]

6

Below the Bar: The U.S. Army and Limited Service Manpower

Sanders Marble

In 1918, the U.S. Army adopted Limited Service (LS) as an efficient way to use men with physical shortcomings. The United States was not in World War I long enough for problems to develop, and LS was written into future mobilization plans. The World War II mobilization started without using LS, and when the policy was implemented, it overlapped other developments in the army and became an administrative problem. In 1944, the army abolished the LS category in favor of a more sophisticated system of physical standards, trying but largely failing to implement that in wartime.

The Pre-1917 Background

The army had long had physical standards, and they changed as medicine changed. Starting from purely physical requirements (having all four limbs and enough teeth to chew hardtack) in the early days, the army gradually added more, such as not being obviously insane or addicted to drugs. In the 1890s, major changes were implemented. Volunteers had to be citizens (or immigrants who had declared they wanted to become citizens), and they had to be literate in English. Standards were high; only 44 percent of applicants were accepted in peacetime.[1] The army had a one-size-fits-all mentality, with only one physical standard regardless of a man's future assignment, be it charging with rifle and bayonet, to driving wagons, to sitting behind a desk. Upon entering the army, men were minimally trained and received the rest of their training (technical or not) on the job.

In 1917, the army only had about two hundred thousand men. The declaration of war triggered the question of what the American strategy would be, and that was quickly answered: "send large forces to France." That meant raising the forces, and a draft was implemented for men, with the age range set at twenty-one to thirty. (When Newton Baker asked Congress to pass a draft, he pledged exemptions for the physically, mentally, and morally unfit.)[2] Even before the draft was operational, the secretary of war lowered some of the standards: National Guardsmen no longer had to be able to read and write English, although they did have to speak it.[3] As the draft was starting, the very first Regulations Governing Physical Examinations allowed examiners to dip below normal height/weight standards if the man was "active, has firm muscles, and is evidently vigorous and healthy."[4] By late August, there were several further loosenings of standards, including that infamous military bugbear, flat feet.[5]

The first draft call was for around one million men, and this would be the army's first experience in memory of getting vast numbers of men who all needed processing quickly. The army lacked both time to train slowly and the cadre to continue the small-group instruction implied by on-the-job training. It needed a way to mass produce soldiers and ways to speed technical training, since for the first time a majority of soldiers would be in noncombat units and about 30 percent of the army would be technical or administrative personnel.[6]

In early 1918, Pershing more than doubled the projected size of the AEF, from thirty divisions to eighty and then one hundred.[7] The War Department was left to find the required manpower, which led to Congress revising the draft law and drafting from the ages of eighteen to forty-five.[8]

There were other pressures as well. First was the political pressure to draft as few men as possible. That would disrupt as few families as possible and would also reduce any disruption of the economy (and war production) by pulling fewer men from their jobs. But to square having a larger army with drafting fewer men, there had to be a higher acceptance rate, and that led to two things. First were remedial units to improve the physically marginal; they would also be tasked with teaching enough English for recruits to be acceptable. The larger program would be Limited Service: matching men with physical limitations to the jobs they could adequately perform.

Development Battalions

In late 1917, as data became available from the first draft, the public (or at least the politically active middle-class whites) were shocked at how few men were actually fully fit. Almost half the draftees had defects, often more than one—and these were men who were presumably in the prime of life. Not all defects warranted rejection (only 29 percent of men were turned down, and 40 percent of accepted men had a defect),[9] but the public was amazed. Much of the problem was attributable to poverty and a lack of access to health care: tenement dwellers and sharecroppers were often in poor health and could not do much about it. Another problem was the rejection of immigrants because they did not understand English; they were of no use to the army if they could not follow an order. The middle classes had a more selfish reason to worry about these problems: for every tenement dweller or immigrant rejected for service, an "all-American boy" had to be drafted.

In November 1917, an Ohio doctor, John Quayle, enthusiastically proposed "reclamation camps for the physically unfit," where exercise, better diet, and minor surgery would make up to 90 percent of rejects fit for duty.[10] He also thought that discipline and what he called "mass psychology" would inculcate patriotism and somehow overcome neuroses and even psychoses. Quayle got the ear of Senator Atlee Pomerene, who trumpeted[11] a "Man-Reclamation Act," and the idea rattled around some mass-market magazines and journals.[12]

In many ways, Quayle was right: hernias, hemorrhoids, and varicose veins could be repaired; teeth could be replaced with dentures; and exercise could bulk up weedy specimens and slim the overweight. He reflected a Progressive Era mindset that man is perfectible (although recognizing that hereditary problems could not be remediated) and probably tapped into the middle-class concerns about the "melting pot," using the military as a way to Americanize the working class. By April 1918, there was still enthusiasm, but it was tempered with the recognition that many individuals would not welcome army doctors performing surgery on them in order to put them in the trenches and that certain religious groups (especially Christian Scientists) would complain.

While Pomerene's bill faded, the draft was amended from an either/or, accept/reject standard to include Class B, that is, men who were remediable when cured of (fill in the blank) condition. Yet the bottleneck of lack of capacity in military hospitals precluded putting more than 89,000 men (2.76 percent of the second draft) into Class B. With the creation of Class C (about which more later), Class B was reserved for drug addicts the military was willing to dry out, men with a deformity that might interfere with wearing the uniform, and "a few other special conditions."[13] It would also be combined with a dumping ground for "all unfit men," including enemy aliens, conscientious objectors, and the morally degenerate.

The army may not have been responding directly to Quayle's idea, but there were already Development Battalions afoot.[14] These took men with remediable problems (including venereal cases) and convalescents who needed a gradual return to full duty, but with "all unfit men" they were as much an administrative convenience for other units as actually developing men. Begun locally as early as December 1917, the War Department issued General Order 45 in May 1918 to spread them around camps in the United States.[15] Men were to receive appropriate care and training for up to two months (although four months were allowed for English-language training) and then be assessed for transfer. If they could serve, they would serve, otherwise they were discharged. Ultimately, over 209,000 men went through Development Battalions, with almost 20 percent going on to full duty, 42 percent to limited duty, 17.4 percent discharged, and 19.4 percent still in the battalions when the fighting ended.[16]

Limited Service

Four medical groups were potentially involved in setting manpower standards, and their roles in the wartime background of Limited Service have to be considered.

First, physicians evaluated draftees against the army's standards and treated soldiers once they had been accepted into the army. They were busy enough doing that that they played essentially no role in creating the LS policy that focused on job skills rather than physical standards. Once LS was created, physicians used their judgment for that different yardstick much as they had previously, when there was only one yardstick.

Second, neuropsychiatrists were involved in both screening draftees and treating patients.[17] In the early twentieth century, neurology and psychiatry were not yet fully split, because there was much less certainty as to where the diseases of the nervous system ended and the disorders of the mind began. Perhaps because neuropsychiatrists were already physicians, and perhaps because of the prominent shell-shock problems, the Medical Department had no hesitation in utilizing them: Surgeon General William Gorgas commissioned a few and sent them over to Europe to gather information and make recommendations, which appeared in a lengthy report saying the army should utilize neuropsychiatrists: they could help screen manpower, they could help treat diseases, and they could help the war-shattered recover. They believed that screening out unstable personalities was not only highly desirable but possible; the report stated, "the most important recommendation to be made is that of rigidly excluding insane, feebleminded, psychopathic, and neuropathic individuals from the forces which are to be sent to France and exposed to the terrific stresses of modern war."[18] Yet despite being the "most important recommendation," that statement was buried in the middle of a lengthy report—and was the only mention. Neuropsychiatrists were far more interested in treating patients, and that was where their activities focused.

Five hundred and sixty-four neuropsychiatrists served in the army, and they did screen out around seventy thousand men, 2 percent of the draftees.[19] As physicians, their signatures could formally eject men from the army, and they were used to examine men who had raised concerns during the assembly-line medical examinations. Interestingly, almost 22,000 of the men were rejected for mental deficiency.

Third, academic psychologists actively sought to serve in the army. At that time, psychology had only weak professional acceptance; it was stuck between being a science and being a part of philosophy departments. The American Psychological Association, which was largely the academics, was interested in gaining more prestige in the universities, since psychology was not going to be granted equality with the physician psychiatrists. The army offered a path to such credibility, and the president of the APA, Robert Yerkes of Harvard, moved to join the patriotic bandwagon. He quickly wrote Gorgas, offering the services of psychologists to test the intelligence of recruits so the army could weed out the low-scoring ones and thereby increase efficiency.

Yerkes' first effort, one-on-one testing of each recruit, was ludicrous; wiser heads prevailed, and mass tests were introduced.[20] These were products of the misunderstandings of the age and in good measure mistook knowledge for intelligence. Without going into details, the results were skewed too low, partly from the design of the test and partly from the way they were administered and interpreted.[21] Mental testing, which had been intended to help the army weed out the "mentally incompetent," caught only 0.5 percent—fewer than the amount weeded out by the neuropsychiatrists, who were not interested in the work.[22] The army also used the psychological tests to sort men for Officer Candidate School and as an additional piece of data on the personnel cards (of which more later), so there was little harm done during the war: while the tests produced faulty readings, they were fairly consistent faulty ratings and would generally reveal who was the most intelligent in a group.

Fourth were a group of self-described applied psychologists, headed by Walter Scott (of the Carnegie Institute of Technology), who had drifted into human-resources work. The Committee for the Classification of Personnel was formed by practical-minded men from the National Association of Employment Managers who were happy to throw away part of their own tests if the client (in this case the army) found no value in it. Scott and his colleague Walter Bingham had walked out of the April 1917 APA meeting where Yerkes had wanted to test everyone in the army; Scott realized how utterly impractical that proposal was. Through contacts, he got in touch with the assistant secretary of war and was accepted at Plattsburgh to devise a test that would help sort the better officer candidates. In August 1917, another more important direction was taken: classifying enlisted men according to skills and coding their first-, second-, and third-best skills on a compact but detailed card. The army had a great number of technical jobs and wanted to find the men with at least roughly the right skills to speed up training.

The CCP ultimately sorted over six hundred thousand men for the technical branches plus almost a million for technical units. Its work was embraced by the army because it had clear application and it clearly used real-world methods: to assess whether a man was a master, journeyman, or apprentice carpenter, the CCP looked at his wages rather than the length of experience—wages reflected his skills, not how long he'd tried. Late in 1918, the CCP had trade tests ready to more accurately assess skills, and building those tests was the only psychological work they did. The CCP happily accepted Yerkes's test scores for entry onto the classification card, but they presented it as one piece of information to be considered along with a man's skills—and later his physical ability.

The "Limited Service" Category Created

While Class B was remediable men, Class C was Limited Service men, those not fully fit for every possibility but useful for something.

It was an outgrowth of a December 11, 1917, proposal by Major Edgar King[23] that men need only meet the requirements of their job, whether it was a strong back or the right skills. This proposal pointedly ignored the intelligence testing being done. Instead, this approach saw the military as a factory with many specialty jobs where skills were the key factors.[24] King's motivations are unclear, but his memo (approved by the surgeon general and forwarded to the General Staff) arrived at the right time. It would help the War Department by raising the percentage of men judged fit for service. This would reduce both draft calls and the turmoil the draft was causing in the workforce, where it called men away from work even if they were not ultimately drafted. Matching the man and the job dovetailed neatly with what the CCP had accomplished in the Adjutant General's Office. Moreover, it bothered neither the neuropsychiatrists nor the academic psychologists: they could still render their professional judgments.

Approval from interest groups was immaterial; the question was how the army would take it, and the army loved it. It was practical, helping solve a tremendous need for fit manpower at the front while not interfering with skilled manpower in the rear. The General Staff did show its bias toward a fully fit army, with men all of hardy, eagle-eyed, pioneer stock: the subject-index card[25] for LS men reads "See—Defectives," but that did not stop utilization. (LS officers also existed, but in far smaller numbers and raised no policy questions; apparently the Adjutant General's Office could manage the numbers without trouble.) In April 1918, the secretary of war ordered implementation. Initially, the men could be utilized in administration (including army-run factories), the Coast Artillery, and for camp staff.[26] Even before the plan was generally approved, it was being locally implemented. Those "physically unfitted for active combatant duties" were transferred to places such as quartermaster units, cooks and bakers school, or medical detachments.[27] Men could be assigned to the paramilitary U.S. Guards (an organization that handled some security duties in the United States) or even used as sergeants major.[28] Even the Historical Branch of the General Staff took LS men, although in this case it was physically limited men, not the mentally limited ones.[29]

So pressing were the needs of the AEF that the army's default position changed: all jobs in the United States were coded for limited-service men unless otherwise justified. On September 9, the clear edict went forth:

The following War Department Policy is announced. In order to conserve the man power of the nation it is essential that every man who is physically fit for combatant service overseas be used solely for such service. Limited service men must be used to the maximum extent for service both in this country and abroad. No general service man will be used in this country for duty whatsoever which can be performed by limited service men.[30]

Again, reality had preceded official policy, and there were special draft calls for LS men with particular skills (such as chemists or stenographers), and there were also large calls for men without specific skills. Plans were made for a camp to take ten thousand LS men for three weeks' training in firefighting.[31] The army considered them barely soldiers, and they would only get inoculations and elementary training in the School of the Soldier before being posted to duty at ports of embarkation. At the same time, the army retained some discretion. Where it was sensible to hire day laborers instead of getting a labor battalion of LS men, that was ordered; similarly, the War Department wanted to use women before using LS men where "the duties are not injurious [to women's] physical well-being or manifestly inappropriate for women employees."[32]

So persuasive was the logic of LS personnel that they were soon assigned overseas; their technical skills were just as useful there, or they could free up a General Service (GS) man in France as much as at home. The General Staff considered it from July 13, and in August a group in the AG's office began overhauling unit organizations to see where LS men could be used even in field units.[33] They redefined the army into combatant, administrative, and technical-vocational categories, creating tremendous opportunities for coding a position for a LS man and thus freeing up GS men to fight.

World War I burned itself out before the AEF needed anything like all the GS men the army had, and the army put the brakes on recruiting the week the war ended. Just as the draft was ending, the General Staff stopped weeding out GS men for the front.[34] However, demobilization allowed enough time to codify the CCP skills-classification system (which had expanded to cover LS men) for a future draft.[35] It was recognized that "limited service" was not an adequately defined category, since it did not differentiate between "physical condition, illiteracy, low intelligence, or low morality,"[36] but it had helped the United States mobilize quickly, it had reduced the inefficiency of that haste, and it probably helped win the war.

Ultimately 112,000 LS men served; the largest groups were in spruce production (for the Air Service), quartermaster (that is, labor), medical, and the draft office itself.[37]

However, 112,000 LS men still only composed 3 percent of the 3,685,000 men who served overall. Some LS men were scarce specialists, but others were simple laborers, and it is likely that the CCP's skills-based sorting was more important for the army than were the actual men sorted. In addition, the principle of LS had been wholly accepted; in a major war, not every soldier needed to be top-notch.

The Interwar Period

After World War I, the army retained its new system, but in cold storage. The National Defense Act of 1920, the fundamental legislation for the army, did not mention Limited Service, probably because of politics. The debate about national service and a peacetime draft had generated much heat, the NDA had fallen back on traditional volunteering, and there were large numbers of Great War veterans who were now in the reserves. Thus there was no mention of a draft, and since there was no need for a large military, there was presumably no need for substandard troops. Physical standards apparently went back to prewar levels,[38] but LS remained an option from the early 1920s.[39]

During the 1920s and 1930s, with no wars to fight, the army focused on mobilization planning for industry (the Industrial Mobilization Plans) and personnel. There were Protective Mobilization Plans, dealing with how to deploy paper forces, but they were never used. LS fit the industrial plans by efficiently mobilizing men, reducing the personnel turnover in industry; fewer men would be drafted or even called up for examination if a higher percentage were useful.[40] LS also retained its skills element. Enlisted men would be classified using CCP procedures (including the World War I master/journeyman/apprentice ranking); this would apply to early-mobilization volunteers and draftees alike.[41] While early-mobilization volunteers might be patriotic, they were not expected to be the cream of the physical crop, and thus the army would not only "secure the maximum number of enlistments for limited as for general service" but would also resurrect the Development Battalions, now called Special Training Battalions.[42] The published Mobilization

Regulations provided a framework, but of course there was no draft, and in the 1930s (especially during the Great Depression), the army was able to attract plenty of men.

By 1931, the Army War College was teaching students about LS. The adjutant general told students that the topic had received a "great deal of thought" in recent years and would be used in the Zone of the Interior, that is, within the United States.[43] This was formalized by regulations in 1934 and would remain the main place to use LS men.[44] In 1934, the industrial part of LS was made explicit, along with firm guidance on the use of LS men in the United States.[45] The starting position was that all positions in the United States were for LS men unless proved otherwise, and planners were told to expect that one-ninth of the whole army could be LS men. This could be a far higher percentage in some areas; in 1929, the surgeon general remarked that half of the Medical Department's men both in the United States and in the rear areas overseas could be LS men.[46] In 1936, the G-1 was still committed to LS, even calling for better plans.[47] In 1937, there was a slight backing off, with civilian employees to be used before soldiers, but LS soldiers still to be the standard within the United States.[48]

Another wrinkle was added in 1939 with the consideration of men already in the military who, through wounds, injury, or disease, no longer met GS standards.[49] Since they might already be overseas, they could be retained overseas and used there. This would reduce the draft by retaining trained personnel, it would reduce personnel movements by not calling for GS men from the United States, and it would economize on shipping space and decrease the time needed to fill positions behind the fighting line. As the war in Europe grew more intense, and after the Congress authorized a limited draft, the army was steady in its thinking on LS as a useful method of utilizing manpower.[50]

The Mobilization for World War II

Although the use of LS men—including being called up early to run the installations in the United States that would train the combat units for overseas—was written into mobilization plans, it was not implemented.[51] Partly, this was the result of mobilization plans being ignored; they foresaw a clear-cut mobilization day (M-day) apparently simultaneous with a declaration of war. Instead, there was a gradual mobilization as tensions grew and American public opinion shifted. The IMP and PMP were both scrapped, and President Roosevelt gradually mobilized the country.

The Selective Service and Training Act, passed in September 1940 as part of the move to war, did not mention LS, but it did not have to.[52] It authorized the draft but left most details of implementation to the executive, and LS was a policy, never a law. Instead, the draft maintained standards so high that almost half of the men were rejected; the United States was classifying men as unfit for military service who would have been considered fully fit in most European armies.[53] With half of the men rejected, it is clear that the army was getting GS men rather than LS ones. There was a mismatch between the policy of drafting LS men early to staff the base camps and the army not having LS men until the War Department specifically authorized it, different provisions in the same regulations.[54]

Several reasons can be advanced for why the War Department did not start out using LS men. It likely would have been politically embarrassing to start "scraping the barrel" long before a war started. The mobilization was meant to deter war, making combat units the priority; not only were LS men not for combat units, but with shortages of equipment, supplies, and trained soldiers, there was little to spare for training LS men. With the economy still very weak at the end of the Great Depression, the nation had plenty of GS men available and unemployed. The army probably did not want LS men when there were plenty of GS ones available.[55]

The 50 percent rejection rate caused consternation, although much of it was attributable to high standards and the poor health of many men who during the Depression lacked money for food, let alone health care. There were several responses, drawing on various ideas from World War I and ones that would be important in World War II. In May 1941, the Selective Service tried "prehabilitation," whereby individuals would pay for their own medical care to remedy defects.[56] That did not last, and five months later Roosevelt personally announced a program to rehabilitate two hundred thousand men at the federal government's expense—although they were to be GS men, and there was still no mention of LS men.[57] The goal was to fix 20 percent of the rejected men, filling their teeth, operating on hernias, issuing eyeglasses, treating VD, and handling "other minor defects." In addition to raising men above the standards, the standards were also lowered for things like being under-weight, dental problems, correctable vision, and having VD.[58]

With "prehabilitation," there was apparently no need for the Special Training Battalions, at least for physical cases, although they were used to teach English.[59]

After Pearl Harbor, the floodgates opened. Volunteers sprang forward; the draft increased dramatically. The army also lowered its physical standards to the point of taking toothless men and issuing dentures.[60] Yet still there was little use of LS men.

Assignment Policies: Skills and the AGCT

In World War I, the Committee on Classification of Personnel had largely matched the job with the man, whether the key requirement was a strong back or specialized skills. There were also special draft calls to obtain special skills. Skills and testing took two different paths during World War II. First, skills were used to build the army back to front. Second, the Army General Classification Test was used as the other main indicator of a man's quality, although it was only intended to indicate his practical intelligence (not his IQ or "mental age") as a rough guide to his ease of training. These may have supplanted LS as the main way to sort manpower.

The World War II army was largely built back to front, with rear-area units getting the first pick of manpower and the front-line infantry getting the leftovers, both physically and mentally. This was the reverse of the planners' intentions, but it was the predictable outcome of several policies. The army recognized that many military assignments had civilian equivalents or that at least there were civilian jobs that approximated the military ones and thus would make training easier and faster. In the spring of 1940, before the draft was authorized, the adjutant general established a Classification Division run by the same sorts of "applied" psychologists that had worked for the surgeon general in World War I.[61] (Walter Bingham himself was brought back as an adviser.) Soldiers would be classified at induction and again after training and could be reclassified (either physically or occupationally) as needed, to get them the military occupation closest to their civilian one.[62] Unfortunately, the regulation that was drafted included both "limited assignment" men for noncombatant duties and "limited service" men who might be mentally or physically limited.[63] While it had implications in pulling intelligent men away from combat units (they were likely to have skilled civilian jobs and thus a military job in the rear areas),[64] classification by skills should have intersected with LS, especially since military positions in the United States were supposed to be filled by LS men where possible.

The AGCT also reflected and affected how the army thought of manpower quality. A combination of IQ test and knowledge test, men were divided into five categories. Men in I and II could be officers; those in V were marginal, with only a limited percentage accepted. The army intended intelligence to act as a practical surrogate for how quickly men could be trained and also assumed that more intelligent men would have fewer psychiatric problems.[65] Much of the discussion at the time and since has focused on allocations by AGCT category without looking at other factors, either physical standards or occupational sorting.[66] All other factors being equal, smarter is better, but the army was giving it undue weight and paying too little attention to physical condition.

1942–1944: Limited Service Implemented and Abolished

In the second half of 1942, the army began using LS men because it was expanding rapidly and the manpower pool was being drained.[67] They were to be assigned "where their limited abilities and convictions can be used to advantage without retarding the training of combat troops."[68] (The comment about "convictions" was because the army was now lumping conscientious objectors along with the physically limited and emotionally unstable; anyone who would cause the personnel officer any problems was being labeled LS.) The door was opened wide in mid-July. There was no particular quota, but each induction site was allowed up to 10 percent of its total per day as LS; if more LS-qualified men turned up in that day's batch, they were rated unfit for service but might be again sent for examination by their draft board; this sort of uncertain future was one of the things that LS was intended to avoid.[69] Ten percent was also the educated guess about how many LS men the army could use, which would store up trouble, because if the GS quota was filled before men were downgraded to LS (through accidents, disease, or wounds), the army would have to judge whom to keep or whether to increase the LS quota.

Receiving the men was relatively straightforward, but utilizing them proved more troublesome for the army. An early experiment on replacing GS men with LS was instead turned around: 5 or 6 percent of LS soldiers could be reclassified for GS, and the army changed (lowered) the GS physical standards.[70] In July 1942, the Army Service

Forces installations (rather than units) were required to take 60 percent of their strength in LS men, although for some time these men could be supernumerary. Even Army Ground Forces units (not installations) had to take LS men in September, when the army was short 330,000 men and a limited man seemed better than no man at all.[71] It took the army until late September to spread the word on how to use LS men, first explaining to officers what LS was and then decentralizing how the men should be used.[72]

That would lead to problems. Commanders proved unwilling to make much use of LS men, likely for several reasons. First, they were evaluated on their unit's performance, and it was more trouble to handle LS men than GS ones, especially when transferring or discharging LS men would bring in a batch of GS men.[73] Second, "limited service" seemed a derogatory term not only to the men labeled as such but to their commanders.[74] While there was no cross-reference card for "defectives," contemporary society used terms such as "handicapped" or "substandard," which if not necessarily demoralizing to the men would certainly not enhance morale. Even a proponent of using LS manpower recognized he "caused my people a great deal of grief by insisting that they utilize I-Bs."[75]

LS men appear to have been a particular problem for the Medical Department. Since it was a noncombatant organization, there were no possible claims of needing GS men for combat. (Combat medics were screened out by the provisions against LS men in AGF units.) In early and mid-1942, the Medical Department was so under strength that getting even LS men was an improvement, but by October medical field units (such as medical battalions and field hospitals) for overseas deployment had to accept LS men. The Medical Department's complaints were rebuffed with the bland comment, "the key to the efficient utilization of limited-service personnel is careful assignment on the part of the unit commander."[76] Trying to make the best of it, the surgeon general asked that 10 percent of his LS men at least be of high quality (another example of AGCT scores being equated with quality), but even that was rejected.[77] It is a sidelight on the World War II army that the Medical Department then contemplated using uniformed women. The year 1942 would end for the Medical Department as for the whole army, with the first authorization to discharge LS men who were not smart enough (having skills already or being smart enough to train) or robust enough for hard daily labor.[78]

In 1943, the army could not make LS work. In February, the adjutant general proposed distributing 65 percent of LS men to the Army Service Forces, 20 percent to the Army Air Forces, and 15 percent to the Army Ground Forces. There were arguments over the quotas until April, but the decision essentially stood.[79] ASF responded by requiring installations to take 80 percent of their numbers as LS; at the same time, the army cut the intake limit to 5 percent of any particular day.[80]

That trimmed the numbers coming in, but other moves caused more dramatic changes. On July 1, 1943, a new Troop Basis cut the overall size of the army, thus reducing the overall need for manpower.[81] Two weeks later, War Department Circular 161 authorized the discharge of LS men if they were below the current (albeit lowered) induction standards unless their commander wanted to retain them.[82] But even now the army would continue to draft men who were below the physical standards "predicated on their ability, skill, intelligence, and aptitude." Finally, the term "limited service" was abolished. The results were chaotic. First was the inability to utilize former LS men now that the term was abolished, although the abolition had to be repeated in November, and apparently individuals continued to use it (and "limited assignment") because it was useful.[83] From August to November 1943, the army discharged around 55,000 LS men (tripling the discharge rate) but—because the manpower standards had been lowered—it was often taking in men of lower physique than it was discharging.[84] During this period, it took one hundred draftees to actually raise the strength of the army by five men. Realizing the problem, in late August a memo went out explaining there was no intent to examine all LS men, let alone discharge them. Unfortunately, this reminded commanders that they could administratively discharge LS men, and the administrative discharge rate increased.[85] With one hand the army was purging the ranks, and on the other it was trying to get more men. The personnel system took months to respond, but in November things swung the other way.[86] Now men would not be discharged if they could "render effective service," and the tone was to waste neither manpower nor skills; all men would be used according to their physical ability. In consequence, the disability discharge rate plummeted two-thirds, to the rate it had been before the summer.[87]

From another angle, Circular 312 created adjutant general teams that would render "such aid as may be required to achieve the classification and assignment objective," including making reports to commanding generals where units were wasting manpower.[88]

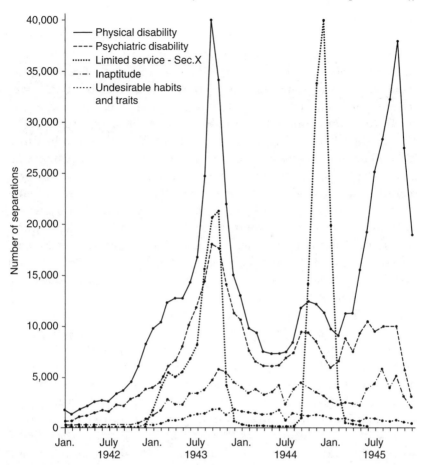

Figure 1. Premature Separations of Army Enlisted Men, by selected cause, 1942–1945. From Eli Ginzberg et al., *The Lost Divisions* (New York: Columbia University Press, 1959), 73. Original sources: unpublished data from the adjutant general and the surgeon general.

In late 1943, the military sought alternative sources of manpower, and it made the most sense to look at draft-deferred or -exempt groups. One of the largest but also most contentious groups was the pre–Pearl Harbor fathers. Before drafting them, Congress demanded a more thorough investigation of whether the military was actually using its available manpower efficiently. President Roosevelt established a committee of eminent physicians and the service surgeons general to examine physical standards. Their report[89] accepted the Navy and Marine Corps' position against them using LS men, said the army was "saturated" with physically limited men, noted the army would no longer be forming noncombat units so new men would mainly be combat replacements, and argued that the forthcoming combat would generate enough LS men. They slightly reduced physical standards, but now Congress had political cover from experts that it was necessary to draft the older fathers.

At the same time, other proposals were moving around. The Army Ground Forces had long been dissatisfied with both the physical and mental quality of its recruits and was pushing a system that made the physical qualities of a man the primary basis for his assignment.[90] It wanted a front-to-back army, with combat troops being the first priority. From December 1943 through the end of January 1944, the proposal advanced through the Pentagon bureaucracy and was somewhat watered down (constitution would not be the sole criteria), and in February 1944 tests started, with new draftees and men leaving hospitals and training centers being classified according to the new PULHES system.

PULHES was adapted from a Canadian system and considered the duty a man could render broken down into six categories: P (physical capacity or stamina), U (upper extremities), L (lower extremities), H (hearing), E (eyes), and S (stability, or neuropsychiatry), with four levels in each.[91] Rather than looking at defects, it looked at what could be achieved for the military. The February tests were positive, and physical "profiling" was in full swing by June 1944, with most assignments by physical profile rather than AGCT score.[92] It could sound extremely bland: "Men with assignment limitations will be assigned where they can best be utilized, in accordance with the actual requirements of the job."[93] At first, the system had to be simplified to only three layers, A (fit for combat or strenuous work), B (close combat support), and C (the lines of communication, base areas, or in the United States).[94] This seems to have been a recognition of the problems in implementing a wholly new system during a war; it would simplify coding each position on the thousands of Tables of Organization so that it could be appropriately filled. Yet while the profile system was gathering early approval, it was probably too late for it to show its full effect during World War II: half the combat divisions were already overseas, and the rest were in intensive preparations to ship out, and since they were in final training, they were off limits for physical profiling.[95]

As the profiling was developing, the army still had to manage the men it had. In April, Circular 164 reiterated the efficient use of men, getting the man to the right job, and prohibited discharging men if there was a job they could do.[96] This was the same line but a tougher tone than Circular 293, and it would be reiterated in still tougher language in May: "The discharge of men who can render effective service is prohibited."[97] The summer's casualties in Normandy did not shake the army's confidence that there would be enough high-quality men. On August 23, the decision was reached that there were too many marginal men in the army and that they were wasteful to both the army and the economy; now anyone below induction standards would be discharged.[98] The decision was published as Circular 370 and can be summed up as a shift from "find a job for the man" to "keep him if there's a job available."[99] There is no clear reason for why this shift occurred in late August, although Allied forces were advancing on all fronts against the Germans and Japanese; perhaps senior officers in the Pentagon were growing confident again. Whatever the reasons, the discharge numbers spiked again, as shown on the chart, above.

Early in 1945, the policy was changed again: the discharge of men below induction standards was stopped.[100] Presumably enough men had been discharged, and the army may have wanted to hold onto trained soldiers in light of casualties during the Battle of the Bulge. Fortunately, 1945 saw less fighting in Europe, and otherwise policy was little changed. One provision in Circular 164 was for combat-wounded men to opt for discharge instead of staying in the army, and that was apparently stopped in June 1945 during the confusion of demobilizing some men, sending some to the Pacific for an invasion of Japan, and keeping others as an occupation force in Germany.[101] June also saw an article reach *Military Review*, a major army publication, explaining what the physical profile was and that "brain and brawn" were both elements in classification.[102] The PULHES system had been operational for over a year, but the delay in publishing an article suggests it had not spread as quickly as intended.

Classification teams, manpower professionals from G-1, continued to pull GS (now profile A and B) men out of rear areas and send them forward.[103] Apparently, commanders in 1944 and 1945 were no happier about losing GS men and getting LS ones in return than their predecessors had been in 1943: they listed only highly skilled positions as suitable for conversion when there were no men available to fill them. The classification work could be urgent, as on Okinawa, when unexpected casualties meant combing around two thousand GS men out of the rear areas and replacing them with LS ones.[104]

Postwar Developments

The postwar army was left with a manpower shortage in peacetime, even though the Soviets were soon perceived as a threat and the possibility of a war continuing after a nuclear exchange meant considering a long war. Late in 1946, an unprecedented policy was tried: "physically handicapped" men with critical skills were judged "not so disabled" and could serve in peacetime.[105] Their numbers were limited to five thousand, but in the midst of a hasty and dramatic demobilization, the army was desperate for trained manpower. While that program gradually grew,[106] there was talk about how high manpower standards needed to be, what percentage of lower-quality men could be tolerated, how close to the front lower-quality men could be used, and the effects of national service on manpower standards.[107] But LS never came back as a manpower category: the draft calls from 1948 were so low that physical standards could be kept high, and there was time to assess both the men and the positions, solving the administrative problems of 1944–1945.

Conclusions

"Limited Service" was a mixed bag for the army. It had worked in World War I, partly because the draft was used to call men with particular skills and partly because there was not enough time for flaws to become apparent. Between the wars, the LS system was written into regulations but never implemented, not even during the pre–Pearl Harbor mobilization, thanks to politics and equipment shortages. During World War II, the policy proved to be extremely problematic, partly because of attitudes about "handicapped" men and partly because of other policies that caused their own problems, such as an overreliance on the AGCT to grade manpower. The solution was the PULHES physical profile, but it was developed too late for effective implementation. Over time, appropriate profiles could be assigned to every man and every slot, and with time officers would grow accustomed to having good-enough men in their units.

Soviet Use of "Substandard" Manpower in the Red Army, 1941–1945

David Glantz

Manning the Force, 1935–1945

The size, nature, and composition of the Soviet Union's Red Army changed fundamentally in the mid-1930s, as the clouds of war began forming across Europe. The worsening international situation, characterized by increasingly dangerous crises in Europe and the Far East, increased the perceived threats to the Soviet Union. In early 1935, this prompted Soviet leaders to alter the way they raised and organized their military forces and made the transition from peace to war. Ten years before, Soviet People's Commissar of Military and Naval Affairs M. V. Frunze had implemented the so-called territorial/cadre system for manning the Red Army. Frunze's system established an army whose nucleus was an active cadre/regular component backed up in times of war by a mobilized component consisting of "territorial/militia" troops. When mobilized, this territorial force of trained conscripts and reservists was designed to at least triple the size of the Red Army.[1]

Thanks to Frunze's reforms, by 1928 the Red Army consisted of a cadre/regular force of twenty-eight rifle and eleven cavalry divisions, all formed on an all-union (national) basis and manned at two levels of fill, supplemented by a territorial force of roughly forty-five divisions deployed on a regional basis and capable of rapidly mobilizing in time of war. In effect, this system expanded the Red Army's peacetime force of twenty corps into a wartime force of more than forty corps.[2] Under this system, the Red Army expanded to a total force of one hundred divisions (twenty-six cadre rifle, sixteen cadre cavalry, and fifty-eight territorial rifle) and a small number of national (ethnic) divisions and regiments by early 1935.

However, the crises of the late 1930s and the perception of increased threats to the country convinced Stalin that Frunze's force-generation system did not expand the army sufficiently to defend the country in time of war.[3] As a result, in May 1935, the Politburo decided to convert the territorial/militia system into a new regular/cadre system. This system abolished territorial forces and converted them into regular forces, which were manned at various levels of cadre strength in peacetime but could be filled out rapidly with reservists and conscripts as war approached. Under this system, the Red Army was to consist of 106 divisions, seventy-one of them cadre by January 1, 1938, and all of them to be cadre by early 1939.[4] This transformation occurred from 1937 to 1939, while Stalin was purging the Soviet military leadership. Although the transformation did not significantly increase the number of divisions in the Red Army, it did fundamentally alter how the army was configured and how it would expand during the transition from peace to war (see Table 1).

During the crises and local wars that plagued Europe and the Far East between early 1938 and June 1941, the Soviet Union used the regular/cadre system to expand the size of the Red Army drastically. Table 2 charts the progress and results.

The Red Army's dramatic expansion continued unabated after June 22, 1941, when Hitler's Germany launched Operation Barbarossa, its invasion of the Soviet Union. In addition to maintaining a large force capable of contending with the formidable German Wehrmacht, the Soviet Union had to compensate for the immense losses the Red Army incurred during the Barbarossa campaign. These losses

Table 1. The conversion of the Red Army from a territorial/militia to regular/cadre force, 1937-1939

Formations and Units	January 1, 1937	January 1, 1938	January 1, 1939
Cadre rifle divisions	49	50	84
Mixed rifle divisions	4	2	0
Territorial divisions	35	34	0
Cadre mountain rifle divisions	9	10	14
Separate brigades	0	0	5
Separate territorial regiments	2	2	0
Total divisions	97	96	98
Total regiments/brigades	2	2	5

Source: I. G. Pavlovsky, *Sukhoputnye voisk SSSR* [The ground forces of the USSR] (Moscow: Voenizdat, 1985), 65.

Table 2. The expansion of the Red Army, 1939-1941

Formations and Units	January 1, 1938	September 1, 1939	December 31, 1940	June 22, 1941
Armies	1	2	20	27
Rifle corps	27	25	30	62
Rifle divisions	71 regular, 35 territorial	96	152	198
Motorized (mechanized) divisions	—	1	10	31
Cavalry corps	7	7	4	4
Cavalry divisions	32	30	26	13
Rifle brigades	—	5	5	5
Mechanized (tank) corps	4	4	9	29
Tank divisions	—	—	18	61
Fortified regions	13	21	21	57
Airborne corps	—	—	—	5
Airborne brigades	6	6	12	16
Strength	1,513,000	1,520,000	4,207,000	5,373,000

Sources: I. Kh. Bagramian, ed., *Istorii voin i voennogo iskusstva* [A history of wars and military art] (Moscow: Voenizdat, 1970); A. Ryzhakov, "K voprusu o stroitel'tsve bronetankovykh voisk Krasnoi Armii v 30-e gody [Concerning the question of the formation of the Red Army's armored forces in the 1930s]," *VIZh* 8 (August 1968); and *Boevoi sostav Sovetskoi Armii, chast' 1 (iiun'-dekabr' 1941 goda)* [The combat composition of the Soviet Army, part 1 (June–December 1941)] (Moscow: Voroshilov General Staff Academy, 1963).

amounted to more than five million men in the first year of the war and many millions more before the Red Army was able to halt the German onslaught and resume major offensive operations of its own after the German defeat at Stalingrad in November 1942. In fact, the ferocity of the war right up to Germany's final defeat at Berlin in May 1945 required the Soviet Union to mobilize immense numbers of soldiers and, while doing so, resort to mobilizing classes of Soviet citizens previously deemed unfit or unsuited for military service.

By war's end, the Red Army had raised, manned, and fielded an immense armed force totaling as many as 661 divisions (490 rifle, eighteen airborne, ninety-one cavalry, one motorized, thirteen NKVD, eleven tank, and thirty-seven people's militia), which, on an annualized basis, included 419 divisions in 1941, 126 in 1942, ninety-two in 1943, twenty-two in 1944, and two in 1945. In addition, it formed 666 brigades (313 rifle, twenty-two airborne, forty-eight motorized, thirty-two mechanized, 251 tank, and 128 other types) primarily in 1941 and 1942. Therefore, in terms of division equivalents, the Red Army began the war with 303 divisions and formed another 981 by war's end. In terms of combat attrition, however, particularly during the war's first eighteen months, the Germans and their Axis allies destroyed 297 Red Army divisions and eighty-five brigades.[5]

These enormous personnel losses in 1941 and early 1942, coupled with the strenuous mobilization efforts of the Soviet State Defense Committee (GKO) and the Stavka (Headquarters of the High Command) strained Soviet manpower resources to the breaking point. In addition to replacing the Red Army's staggering losses, the People's Commissariat of Defense (NKO) had to mobilize huge numbers of soldiers to man hundreds of new military formations of every type. To satisfy these demands, with Stalin's approval, the GKO, Stavka, and NKO, albeit gradually and reluctantly, had no choice but to conscript into the army's ranks personnel previously considered unfit for military service. While in 1941 and early 1942 this involved older reservists, ethnic minorities, and women, ultimately it also encompassed troops found guilty of disciplinary violations, criminals, and convict labor. In fact, this process of progressively lowering the standard for military service continued unabated throughout the end of the war, as the NKO lifted restrictions on the combat and noncombat service of younger, older, and less-fit reservists and conscripts, women, imprisoned criminals, convict labor, and, in 1944 and 1945, even non-Russian inhabitants of territories liberated by the Red Army. As a result, many wartime divisions in the Red Army took on a multinational, polyglot nature (see Table 3).

Ethnic (Non-Slavic) Formations and Soldiers

By law and custom, prior to June 22, 1941, the Soviet Union severely restricted the employment of ethnic and religious minorities and women in the armed forces, and, once war began, it intended to adhere to those laws and customs. Under the territorial/militia system prior to 1935, separate and distinct national formations existed in the Red Army. However, because Stalin questioned the reliability of national (ethnic) formations, the regular/cadre system, which transformed the Red Army into an all-union force under firm Great Russian control, abolished these formations and integrated members of non-Slavic minorities into the Red Army on an all-union basis, meaning that they were embedded in largely Slavic (Russian, Belorussian, and Ukrainian) military formations. Furthermore, most non-Slavic personnel served primarily in noncombat forces such as construction or railroad troops. The same general restrictions applied to women, who were permitted to serve only in such traditional roles as nurses, clerical work, and chauffeurs. Thus, on March 7, 1938, the NKO ended all "extraterritorial" recruitment and, soon after, disbanded all existing national formations and schools, incorporating their troops into the Red Army as a whole. This abolished thirteen divisions, one brigade, and ten regiments hitherto formed from ethnic-minority soldiers.[6]

However, as the international situation worsened in the late 1930s and as Stalin began expanding the Red Army, the increased demands for fresh manpower forced Soviet authorities to pass new laws pertaining to the military service of its citizens, Slavic and non-Slavic alike. For example, a new Law on Universal Military Service, approved by the Supreme Soviet on September 1, 1939, increased the term of military service of enlisted men and noncommissioned officers to three years, improved Red Army training, and "required the creation of a many-multi-million-man cadre army based on a unified extraterritorial principle of formation independent of ethnic nationality."[7]

While this law implied a greater use of non-Slavic manpower resources, it was the war itself and its huge demands on manpower that swept away most of the prewar restrictions on the employment of non-Slavic soldiers as well as similar restrictions on the use of religious minorities such as Jews and fundamentalist Muslim sects. In short, by 1943 the Red Army's insatiable requirements for additional manpower converted the Red Army into a thoroughly multiethnic force manned by both men and women.

The integration of non-Slavic minorities into the Red Army and their employment in combat took place in two ways: first, once war began, the NKO began forming new national military formations outright; and, second, it began integrating non-Slavic-minority soldiers into the armed forces in far greater numbers. Subsequently, the NKO created numerous national military formations, most of them in late 1941 and 1942, and these forces fought with distinction throughout the remainder of the war (see Tables 3 and 4).

Despite this loosening on constraints on the employment of non-Slavic soldiers, some biases against these soldiers continued to exist through war's end. For example, during the struggle for the Caucasus in the fall of 1942, on several occasions the Stavka and its operating *fronts* directed subordinate headquarters to remove ethnic soldiers from specific divisions and replace them with more reliable "Russian" soldiers.[8]

The greatest influx of non-Slavic minority soldiers into the Red Army occurred from late 1941 to early 1943. In addition, when the front lines began moving inexorably westward in late summer 1943, particularly after the Battle of Kursk, the Red Army began impressing into its ranks vast numbers of men of military age, Russians and non-Russians alike, from the territories the Red Army had liberated from German control. By this time, one of the most important missions fulfilled by the field forces of the Soviet security services (the NKVD) was to accompany the advancing Red Army and impress men of military age into the Red Army's ranks.

Stalin first raised the possibility of conscripting forces in territories liberated by the Red Army in an order he issued on February 9, 1942, which declared it would be expedient to "Conscript into the ranks of the Red Army . . . citizens in the liberated territories between the ages of 17 to 45 who have not been conscripted into the Red Army during the previous months of the war," since they were "Burning with hatred for the invader and a desire to participate in the subsequent liberation of their Soviet Motherland with weapons in their hands."[9] Although the German offensive toward Stalingrad in the summer of 1942 rendered this order irrelevant, when the Red Army resumed its westward advance, Stalin returned to this theme. For example, on March 25, 1943, the Central Front's 121st Rifle Division reported it had a strength of 7,025 men, "of which 5,573 joined as replacements by means of a mobilization on the territory of the Kursk region, which was just liberated from the German invaders."[10] Likewise, the 248th Student Rifle Brigade reported its strength as of March 25 at 2,389 men, "of which 774 joined as replacements by means of a mobilization conducted in the Kursk region, which was now liberated from the fascist invaders, and from the disbanded Drozdov Partisan Detachment."[11]

Table 3. The composition of selected Red Army Divisions, 1941–1945.
N.B.: There were over nine hundred divisions in the Red Army; available
information on the composition of manpower shows that over three
hundred had substantial percentages of nonstandard manpower. These
tables show only a few of the units formed each year and do not show
some manpower categories, such as women soldiers and penal units.

Formed 1941

45th RD	95% Uzbek (October 1942—50% Uzbek, 20% Kazakh, 15% Tartar, 15% Russian) (90% year groups 1897–1922, 10% year groups 1923–1924) (became 74th GRD)
157th RD	77% Russian, Belorussian, and Ukrainian, and 23% Armenian and Georgian (replaced by Russians and Ukrainians, January–March 1942) (became 76th GRD)
183rd RD	50% Latvian (July 1943—60% Turkmen, 15% Russian, 25% mixed)
204th RD	95% Kazakh and Uzbek (became 78th GRD)
208th RD	60% Azerbaijani, 40% Russian and Far Easterners (disbanded August 1942)
326th RD	60% Russian, 40% Tartar
345th RD	38% Russian, 62% Central Asian and Caucasian (disbanded July 1942)
402nd RD	90% Azerbaijani (January 1944—50% Azerbaijani)
408th RD	31% Russian and Ukrainian, 25% Georgian, 23% Azerbaijani, 21% Armenian (disbanded November 1942)
8th GRD	95% Kirghiz and Kazakh (June 1942—70% Kirghiz and Kazakh, 30% Uzbek)

Formed 1942

103rd RD (2nd formation)	50–60% Russian, 20–30% Kirghiz, 20% Uzbek (90% year groups 1901–1905, 10% year groups 1920–1923)
109th RD	2,534 Russians (43%), 1,613 Ukrainians (28%), 459 Georgians (8%), 309 Azerbaijanis (5%), 301 Armenians (5%), 249 Jews (4%), 141 Tartars (2%), 63 Lezgins, 58 Ossetians, 50 Belorussians, 23 Moldavians, 21 Kalmuks, 20 Uzbeks (total 5,841)

(Continued)

Table 3. Cont'd

112th RD (2nd formation)	Mostly Siberian Russians (year group 1923), with many penal troops (February 1943—60% Turkmen, 30% Russian, 10% Ukrainian, year groups 1925–1927)
175th RD (2nd formation)	95% Siberian, Bashkir, and Tartar (mostly year groups 1900–1909) 30% penal troops (disbanded September 1942)
175th RD (3rd formation)	70% Russian, 25% Ukrainian (mostly year groups 1913–1923) (October 1944—90% recently conscripted Ukrainians and Belorussians)
181st RD (2nd formation)	(12,719 men, including 2,271 Communists (18%), 297 veterans (2%), 1,530 Kulak penal troops (12%), 8,864 Russians (70%), 2,616 Ukrainians (21%), 298 Jews (2%), 182 Belorussians (1%), 168 Kazakhs (1%), 139 Tartars (1%), 89 Armenians (ages: 2,602 under 20 years, 1,515 20–25 years, 2,043 26–30 years, 2,178 31–35 years, 2,280 36–40 years, 2,043 41–45 years, 81 over 45 years)
193rd RD (2nd formation)	50% Russian, 50% Azerbaijan, Kirghiz, Siberian, and Cossack (September 1942—50% Russian, 30% Uzbek and Kazakh, 20% Communist [NKVD])
226th RD	80% Uzbek, Bashkir, Tadjik, and Ukrainian, 20% Russian (95th GRD in May 1943)
258th RD (2nd formation)	50% Russian, 50% Turkmen, 20% penal troops (96th GRD in May 1943)
316th RD (2nd formation)	95% Kirghiz and Kazakh, few spoke Russian, and most were age 35–50 (disbanded November 1942)

Formed 1943

16th RD (2nd formation)	36.5% Lithuanian and 75% Jewish (October 1943: 10% year group before 1908, 40% year groups 1908–1924, 50% year group 1925).
127th RD (3rd formation)	90% Russian, 8% Ukrainian, 1% Belorussian and Jewish (April 1944—60% Ukrainian, 30% Russian)

Table 3. Cont'd

180th RD (2nd formation)	50% recently conscripted Ukrainians (year groups 1894–1926)
2nd Guards Airborne Division (GAbnD)	60% Russian, 40% Turkmen (year groups 1923–1925) (March 1945—33% Russian, 33% Bessarabian, 33% Lithuanian)
6th GAbnD	40% Russian, 35% Ukrainian, 25% non-Slavic (May 1944—60% recently conscripted Ukrainian, 40% Russian, plus 300 penal troops)
7th GAbnD	50% Ukrainian, 40% Russian, 10% Uzbek (70% year groups 1918–1932, 20% year groups 1901–1913, 10% year groups 1910–1913) (January 1944—80% Ukrainian)
47th GRD	60% Russian (December 1943—30% Tartar) (November 1944—50% Russian, 30% Ukrainian, 20% mixed nationalities)
66th GRD	80% Ukrainian (year groups 1895–1926) (February 1944—90% recently conscripted Ukrainians, year groups 1897–1907, 10% year group 1925)
97th GRD	75% Russian and Ukrainian, 25% Turkmen (November 1944—67% Ukrainian, 50% year groups 1900–1914)
110th GRD	70% Asian, 30% Russian (June 1944—85% recently conscripted Ukrainian) (March 1945—67% Russian year groups 1926–1937, 33% Ukrainian)
Formed 1944	
70th RD (2nd formation)	80% Asian, 80% year groups 1900–1909
121st RD	80% recently conscripted Ukrainians
136th RD (3rd formation)	70% Uzbek, 15% Russian, 15% Ukrainian (60% from year groups 1904 or older)
147th RD (2nd formation)	90% recently conscripted Ukrainians
152nd RD (2nd formation)	60% Bukovinian, 30% Ukrainian, 10% Russian

(Continued)

Table 3. Cont'd

162nd RD (3rd formation)	35% Ukrainian, 35% Kazakh, 20% Russian, 10% mixed (50% from year group 1923) (July 1944—80% Ukrainian (mostly year group 1904)
172nd RD (2nd formation)	65% Ukrainian, 35% Russian (70% year groups 1900–1914 and 30% year groups 1914–1925)
6th Guards Rifle Division (GRD)	40% Russian, 50% Ukrainian, 10% Asian (25% year group 1925, 40% year groups 1904–1924, 35% year groups prior to 1904)
14th GRD	50% Russian, 50% Asian (August 1944—25% Russian, 50% Ukrainian, 15% Moldavian, 10% Asian (50% from year group 1914)
117th GRD	20% Russian, 45% Ukrainian, 35% Armenian (40% year groups 1924–1925, 35% year groups 1903–1908, 35% older year groups)
Formed 1945	
92nd RD (2nd formation)	67% Russian, 33% Ukrainian
9th GAbnD	70% Russian and eastern Ukrainian, 30% western Ukrainian (year groups 1896–1926)
39th GRD	40% Russian, 50% Ukrainian, 10% Uzbek

Table 4. The composition of selected Red Army cavalry divisions, 1941-1945. Most cavalry divisions formed before 1943 were heavily non-Russian, typically 95 percent non-Russian. Many were Cossacks from the Kuban, Kuban-Terek, Don, and Crimea; others were Bessarabian, Kazakh, Uzbek, or mixed Caucasian or Central Asian. This did not stop them being retitled as Guards Cavalry Divisions when they performed well. Cavalry divisions with a substantial percentage of Russians were generally only formed later in the war.

Unit	Formed	Composition
1st Mountain Cavalry Division	July 1941	95% Kuban Cossack
2nd CD	June 1941	95% Kuban Cossack
3rd CD	June 1941	95% Bessarabian (5th Guards Cavalry Division in December 1941)

Table 4. Cont'd

Unit	Formed	Composition
31st CD	July 1941	95% Russian (7th GCD in January 1942)
44th CD	July 1941	95% Uzbek (merged into 17th CD in April 1942)
50th CD	July 1941	95% Don Cossack (3rd GCD in November 1941)
1st Guards Cavalry Division	October 1943	Mostly Russian (February 1944—60% Russian, 30% Ukrainian, 10% mixed nationalities) (August 1944—50% Ukrainian)
3rd GCD	November 1941	95% Don Cossack (formed from 50th CD)
7th GCD	February 1944	50% Russian, 50% non-Slavic (70% year groups 1918–1926, 30% year groups 1913–1917) (January 1945—60% Russian, 20% Asian, 15% Ukrainian, 5% mixed nationalities from year groups 1920–1924) (formed from 31st CD)
11th GCD	May 1943	30% Kalmyk, 30% Cossack, 40% Russian (year groups 1898–1923) (formed from 15th CD)

Year group means soldiers who reached eighteen years of age in the given year.
2nd and 3rd formation units replaced those destroyed in previous combat.
Disbanded units were generally destroyed by German forces.
Sources: Robert G. Poirier and Albert Z. Conner, *Red Army Order of Battle in the Great Patriotic War*, 2nd ed. (unpublished manuscript, 1985). This data is derived from German *Fremde Heere Ost* [Foreign Army's East] reports, 1941–1945; and Aleksander A. Maslov, *Captured Soviet Generals: The Fate of Soviet Generals Captured by the Germans, 1941–1945* (London: Frank Cass, 2001).

On the negative side of the ledger, a report by the same *front*'s Thirteenth Army noted that although "Replacements are joining the ranks of the Red Army from regions liberated from the enemy's forces," it was necessary to use stronger blocking detachments in the struggle against possible instances of desertion and the avoidance of military service. Specifically, the detachments were "systematically" to "conduct universal inspections of the entire male population in all population points," "comb all forests and orchards thoroughly and examine all haystacks, uninhabited buildings, and especially dugouts situated along the lines of the old defenses," and "strengthen the inspection of documents of those passing through the populated points and [other] suspicious persons."[12]

Later in 1943, this time while Red Army forces were liberating eastern Belorussia and central Ukraine, the Stavka had to spell out what must be done, stating: "The military councils of operating armies were granted the right to conscript Soviet citizens who are living in territories liberated from the German occupiers into military service by means of mobilization," but "Serious violations of established laws concerning the conduct of mobilization were being tolerated while fulfilling this order."[13] On November 16, 1943, the Stavka again underscored its determination to raise fresh troops by conscription, spelling out the numbers of conscripts it expected to be raised.

> 1. During November the *fronts* listed below are authorized to mobilize the following quantities of soldiers in territories liberated from German occupation to reinforce the *fronts*' forces:
>
> First Baltic Front: 15,000 men
> Western Front: 30,000 men
> Belorussian Front: 30,000 men
> First Ukrainian Front: 30,000 men
> Second Ukrainian Front: 30,000 men
> Third Ukrainian Front: 20,000 men
> Fourth Ukrainian Front: 30,000 men
> Total: 185,000 men[14]

These and many other Stavka directives underscored the vast scope of the Red Army's mobilization efforts while it advanced westward. Although these orders have yet to be released for publication, the Red Army presumably conscripted at least two hundred thousand soldiers per month, and perhaps more, into its ranks from the liberated regions. Some Red Army divisional histories vividly describe the process of combing haystacks and cellars for potential recruits, who were immediately assigned to the division's training battalion. Based upon the remaining months of 1943 and 1944, this translates into a figure of as many as 2.8 million additional soldiers conscripted into the Red Army, primarily from the Ukraine, Belorussia, the Baltic region, and Moldavia, and perhaps as many as one million conscripted in the same fashion during 1945.

The Red Army's ability to tap into this fresh and ever-expanding pool of manpower resources certainly lessened the necessity for it to rely on ethnic minorities within the Soviet Union as a source of conscripts. As Table 5 indicates, the percentage of Red Army troops conscripted from Ukrainians, Belorussians, Moldavians, and other ethnic groups living in former Soviet territory liberated by the Red Army in 1944 and 1945 increased dramatically, while the percentage of non-Slavic troops fell precipitously during the same period.

Table 5. The Red Army's wartime ethnic composition and death rate by nationality

	Soldiers	Dead
Mobilized	29,574,900	—
Total served	34,476,700	8,668,400
Russian Rep.	21,187,600 (67%)	5,756,000
Tartar		187,700
Mordvian		63,300
Chuvash		63,300
Bashkir		31,700
Udmurt		23,200
Mariitsy		20,900
Buriat		13,000
Komi		11,600
Dagestani		11,100
Ossetian		10,700
Polish		10,100
Karelian		9,500
Kalmyk		4,000
Kabardino/Balkar		3,400

(Continued)

Table 5. Cont'd

Greeks		2,400
Chechen/Ingush		2,300
Finns		1,600
Bulgars		1,100
Czechs/Slovaks		400
Chinese		400
Yugoslavians		100
Others		33,700
Ukrainian	5,300,000	1,376,500
Belorussian	1,100,000	252,900
Kazakh	1,000,000	125,500
Uzbek	1,200,000	117,900
	(6,000 women)	
Armenian	600,000	83,700
Georgian	800,000	79,500
	(16,000 women)	
Azerbaijani	600,000	58,400
Moldavian	300,000	53,900
Kirghiz	400,000	26,600
Tadjik	400,000	22,900
Turkmen	400,000	21,300
Estonian	270,000	21,200
Latvian	90,000	11,600
Lithuanian	70,000	11,600
Jews	800,000	142,500
Union Republics	13,289,100 (Total)	

Sources: *Liudskie poteri SSSR v Velikoi Otechestvennoi voine* [Personnel losses of the USSR in the Great Patriotic War] (St. Petersburg: Insititut rossiiskoi istorii, 1995), 75–81; G. F. Krivosheev, ed., *Rossiia i SSSR v voinakh XX veka, Poteri vooruzhennykh sil: Statisticheskoe issledovanie* [Russia and the USSR in twentieth-century wars, the losses of the armed forces: A statistical investigation] (Moscow: Olma Press, 2001), 238; V. A. Zolotarev, ed., *Velikoi Otechestvennoi voina 1941–1945 v chetyrekh knigakh* [The Great Patriotic War, 1941–1945, in four books] (Moscow: Nauka, 1999), book 4, 13–14, 290; and S. Enders Windbush and Alexander Alexiev, *Ethnic Minorities in the Red Army: Asset or Liability* (Boulder, Colo.: Westview Press, 1988), 55.

As Table 6 suggests, by the end of 1943, the Red Army was a multiethnic army manned by soldiers ranging in age from seventeen to fifty-five years and representing virtually every ethnic and religious group in the Soviet Union. In fact, when the need arose, the Red Army also conscripted forces from other ethnic groups, such as Galicians, that were living outside the prewar Soviet Union. For example, one officer's description of the composition of his rifle division typified the Red Army as a whole. Created at Stavropol' in the North Caucasus in August 1941, the 343rd Rifle Division initially consisted of "40 years old, 38 years old, *kolkhoz* [collective farm] chairmen, *raiispolkom* [district executive committee] chairmen, *raikom* [district committee] secretaries, and so forth, but they were

Table 6. National military formations in the Red Army, 1941-1945

Nationality	Rifle/mountain divisions	Cavalry Divisions	Regiments, brigades, and and battalions	Total
Azerbaijani	5	—	—	5
Armenian	4	—	—	4
Georgian	10	—	1	11
Tadjik	—	2	2	4
Turkmen	2	4	2	8
Uzbek	—	6	9	15
Kazakh	—	2	3	5
Kirgiz	—	3	—	3
Estonian	2	—	—	2
Lithuanian	1	—	—	1
Latvian	2	—	—	2
Kalmuk	—	2	—	2
Bashkir	—	2	—	2
Chechen-Ingush	—	1	—	1
Kabardino-Balkar	—	1	—	1
Chinese	—	—	1	1
Total	26	23	18	67

Sources: Boevoi sostav Sovetskoi armii, 1941–1945 gg. v piatikh chastiakh [The combat composition of the Soviet Army, 1941–1945, in five parts] (Voroshilov General Staff Academy and Voenizdat, 1963–1990), and V. V. Gradosel'sky, "Natsional'nye voinskie formirovaniia v Velikoi Otechestvennoi voine [National military formation in the Great Patriotic War]," *Voenno-istoricheskii zhurnal* [Military-historical journal] 1 (January 2001): 18–24.

not young." Thereafter, however, "Our regiment traveled through 7,500 kilometers of combat, and only 16 veterans who had joined up in Stavropol' remained." Most of those who remained "were guys 40 and 45 [years of age]," and "the composition varied . . . with all kinds—Kazakhs, Uzbeks, Tatars, Armenians, Georgians, and Azerbaijanis." In short, "There were up to 25 nationalities in the regiment," but "no problems arose. It was one big friendly family—a regimental family," and "there were always 10–15 women in the regiment."[15]

While this testimony underscores the remarkable degree of ethnic diversity among soldiers serving and fighting in the ranks the Red Army divisions, it also emphasizes the role women played in the Red Army's wartime victory.

Women in the Red Army

One of the most controversial issues regarding the manning of the Red Army during the war has been the extent to which the GKO and NKO exploited women as soldiers, either in combat or more traditional noncombat roles. Although Soviet historians later played down the role women played in the Red Army's war effort, that role was indeed significant. One Red Army veteran typified the traditional Russian attitude toward women serving in the Red Army in his assertion that there were no women in his units. Instead, "some signaler girls appeared, but eventually all of the officers married them."[16] More recently, however, historians have lifted the veil of secrecy and, together with newly released archival materials, have exposed the major contributions women made to victory.[17]

Recently published official accounts of the war now grudgingly note:

> Women entered the ranks of the Soviet Army from the first days of the war, voluntarily, in the people's militia divisions. A massive mobilization of women began on the basis of GKO decrees dated 25 March and 13 and 23 April 1942. On the basis of the conscription of Komsomol members alone, more than 550,000 [women] patriots—representatives of all nationalities in the country, became soldiers. More than 300,000 women were called up into the PVO [air defense] forces (more than one quarter of all of the soldiers in that branch), and hundreds of thousands [more] entered service in the military-medical facilities of the Soviet Army's medical service, in the signal forces, in road units, and in other services.

In May 1942 the GKO issued a decree concerning the mobilization of 25,000 women into the Navy. Communist women conducted 5 mobilizations. Along the line of the Red Cross, 300,000 women received the specialty of nurse, 300,000 as medical orderlies, and more than 500,000 as medical helpers in MPVO and 220,000 young girl-snipers, communicators, and others were trained in youth sub-units of *Vsevobuch* [Universal Military Education].

Three aviation regiments, one of which was commanded by Hero of the Soviet Union M. M. Raskova, were formed from women. Hero of the Soviet Union V. S. Grizodubova commanded the 101st Long-Range Aviation Regiment. The 1st Separate Women's Volunteer Rifle Brigade [based in Moscow], the 1st Women's Reserve Rifle Regiment, and the Central Women's School for Sniper Training were formed, and other women participated in decisive operations of the Red Army. In addition, more than 100,000 women fought in the partisan movement and in the Party and Komsomol underground.

More than 150,000 women were awarded with combat orders and medals for bravery in the struggle against the German-Fascist invaders. More than 200 persons received the Order of Glory 2nd and 3rd degree, and N. A. Zhirkina, N. P. Petrova, D. Iu. Staniliene, and M. S. Necheporchukova became full cavaliers of the Order of Glory. Eighty-six Soviet women were awarded with the rank of Hero of the Soviet Union, including 29 pilots, 26 partisans, and 17 medical service workers, 18 of whom received the reward posthumously.[18]

Recently published Russian statistics reveal that a total of about 220,000 women received military training through *Vsevobuch*, including at a minimum:

Mortar operators: 6,097
Heavy machine gunners: 4,522
Light machine gunners: 7,796
Submachine gunners: 15,290
Snipers: 102,333
Communications specialists: 49,509
Total: 185,547[19]

The first orders to employ women in a combat role occurred on October 8, 1941, shortly before the desperate defense of Moscow.

Under Stalin's signature, the NKO ordered the Red Army Air Force to form three all-female aviation regiments by December 1, 1941. These were the 586th Fighter, 587th Close Bomber, and 588th Night Bomber Aviation Regiments.[20]

In addition, in early spring 1942 (while locally conscripting manpower from liberated regions), the GKO and NKO implemented a number of new policies designed to free up additional precious manpower for combat forces. Collectively, these measures increased the number of military women, expanding the pool of manpower that could reinforce the Red Army struggling at the front.

The first of these decrees, issued by the GKO on March 25, 1942, authorized the NKO to mobilize one hundred thousand "girl-Komsomol members" to replace male soldiers. These women were to serve in antiaircraft artillery, machine-gun, and searchlight units, barrage-balloon units, air-warning units, and other PVO Strany (national air defense) units, primarily as instrument operators, telephone operators, range finders, radio operators, air scout observers, antiaircraft-gun crews, machine gunners, medical personnel, warehouse personnel, and chauffeurs.[21] The main purpose of this decree was to "free up Red Army male soldiers to fill out those rifle divisions and rifle brigades that have been withdrawn from the front in accordance with the *Glavupraform*'s plans." Several weeks later, on April 5, 1942, the NKO ordered the Red Army to reinforce front-line forces by systematically replacing many male soldiers in rear-service units and facilities with 80,828 fit women by April 15, 1942.[22]

This accelerated on April 14, 1942, when the NKO ordered the Red Army to conscript thirty thousand women into the signal services, replacing men who would go to the front. In this case, the women were to become BODO (encoded telegraph), ST-35, and Morse code operators, telephone and radio operators, telegraph operators and technicians, radio technicians, film-radio mechanics and technicians, field postal workers and clerks, draughtsman, clerks, secretaries, cooks, warehouse clerks, medical assistants, librarians, tailors, metalworkers, and lathe operators.[23] Once again, the NKO justified its replacement of males with females by citing the critical need for additional manpower at the front, particularly regarding "signalmen in rifle divisions and rifle brigades, and artillery, tank, and mortar units that are situated at the front."[24] The NKO issued similar decrees on April 18 and 19, covering women in rear-service organizations and forty thousand women in the Red Army Air Forces, still primarily in noncombat positions.[25]

The NKO completed this round in the process of replacing males with females on April 25, 1942, when it issued a final order entitled "An order concerning the truncation of the *shtats* of the NKO's main and central directorates and military district headquarters and also concerning the replacement of command and management cadre fit for line service with older soldiers, who are limited in fitness or unfit for line service, and women." Without providing the exact number of male and female personnel affected by this order, the NKO formed a special commission to scour the Red Army to determine what additional positions female soldiers might occupy. Headed by Major General A. D. Rumiantsev, the chief of the Red Army's Main Cadre Directorate, this commission also included all of the other involved NKO directorate chiefs. Its specific task was to screen all personnel covered by the order and provide a list of all replacements to the People's Commissar of Defense by May 5, 1942.[26] Although no documentary evidence has yet been released regarding the work of this commission, presumably it added thousands more women soldiers to the Red Army.

After mounting a prolonged and arduous defense during the summer and early fall of 1942, during which it suffered significant personnel losses, the Red Army resumed large-scale offensive operations across major portions of the front during the second half of November. As in 1941, as the Stavka expanded these offensive operations, it also drastically increased the manpower requirements of the Red Army, particularly its tank and mechanized spearheads. As a result, on January 3, 1943, the NKO truncated the size of the Red Army's tank brigades, tank training regiments, and field army automotive-tank warehouses and directed that many male soldiers be replaced with older soldiers and female soldiers by January 15, 1943. Once again, the NKO's stated purpose was "to use the freed-up personnel to fill out tank and mechanized units and formations at the direction of the commander of the Red Army's Tank and Mechanized Forces."[27] The order directed the latter to report the precise number of freed-up personnel every three days, beginning on January 10, 1943. Although the attachment to this order, which supposedly listed the precise duty positions subject to the order and the quantity of female soldiers involved, has yet to be published, it is clear the NKO did assign some female soldiers to the Red Army's tank and mechanized forces. As was the case with other types of forces, however, the women soldiers were designated to occupy primarily noncombat positions.

Recently released archival documents also reveal one interesting byproduct of the increasing number of women serving in the Red Army: the necessity for improved sanitary conditions in the forward area. For example, on April 11, 1943, the NKO ordered the soap ration for female personnel be increased by 50 percent, to one hundred grams per month.[28]

Collectively, NKO orders issued between March 1942 and January 1943 conscripted a total of over 250,000 women into the Red Army, and more general directives probably added tens of thousands more women to the Red Army's ranks. Official sources now claim that a total of 490,000 female soldiers and eighty thousand female officers served in the Red Army and Navy in wartime, for a total of 570,000 women in uniform, and a total of 463,503 women were serving in the army and navy's ranks on January 1, 1945.[29]

While the roughly three hundred thousand female soldiers who served in the local air defense constituted the bulk of these women in uniform, more than 150,000 women also served in primarily non-combat positions in the rear services, the air force, and the signal forces, and lesser numbers served in aviation, tank, and mechanized forces—at least a few of these in combat positions. However, this figure of well over five hundred thousand female soldiers does not include those who served as nurses, medical assistants, and helpers in the Red Army's many medical facilities and organizations. Counting these auxiliaries, it is likely that more than one million women in uniform served their country during the war. These included the aviation regiments and, most notably, the 1st Women's Rifle Brigade stationed in Moscow, which trained women snipers for assignment throughout the Red Army's operating forces.

Numerous sources, some of them anecdotal but others archival and genuine, indicate that an as yet undetermined number of female soldiers did indeed perform combat duties in Red Army combat forces. However, improved access to Soviet (Russian) archival materials is necessary before we can properly answer the questions of how many women served in combat and how long they served.

The Use of Penal Troops, Convict Soldiers, and Labor Deportees

One of the most astonishing phenomena during World War II was the fact, that, unlike its Tsarist predecessor, which crumbled as a viable combat force in 1917, the Red Army managed to survive its ordeal by fire and fought on to emerge victorious over Hitler's

Wehrmacht despite its immense and unprecedented combat losses. The Tsarist Army had faltered and crumbled during World War I because its staggering defeats, its appallingly heavy loss of life, its participation in an increasingly unpopular war, and skillful and relentless political agitation all undermined the morale of its soldiers. The results were numerous mutinies, wholesale desertion, and finally the army's utter collapse under the hammer blows of the enemy combined with a welter of revolutionary agitation.

Like the Tsarist Army, the Red Army also suffered severe military defeats during the first few weeks of war, only to see these defeats mount to catastrophic proportions later in 1941 and during most of 1942. The Tsarist Army lost two armies and 245,000 men in the battles of Tannenberg and the Masurian Lakes in the late summer of 1914; the Red Army lost three armies and 748,850 men during the first two weeks of Operation Barbarossa alone. Subsequently, the Tsarist Army lost 2,254,369 men throughout the entire war (1,890,369 in combat) out of a force whose total strength ranged from 2,711,253 on October 1, 1914, to 6,752,700 on May 1, 1917.[30] Not to be outdone, the Red Army lost at least 6,155,000 soldiers during the first period of the war (June 22, 1941, through November 18, 1942) and another 2,553,400 soldiers during the second period (November 19, 1942, through December 31, 1943), for a gruesome total of 8,708,400 soldiers. This in an army that began the war with just over five million men and ultimately mobilized over twenty-nine million soldiers throughout the remainder of the war.[31]

There were many reasons why the Red Army was able to survive its many defeats yet remain a coherent, viable, and reliable military force throughout the war. It is difficult, if not impossible, to assign relative importance to any of the many factors that fostered cohesion with the Red Army. At a minimum, these factors included stringent political controls exercised by commissars and political workers through the Red Army's entire chain of command, ruthless and effective discipline enforced by military tribunals, and the harsh punitive measures the Soviet state employed to ensure discipline within its military forces, such as the widespread use of penal units and blocking detachments. For the standpoint of this chapter, this political control structure and its associated military tribunals and penal units permitted the Soviet Union to employ as soldiers persons deemed unfit for duty based on their presumed disloyalty to the state, inappropriate combat performance, or other acts deemed criminal. In essence, the elaborate system of military tribunals established by the Red Army provided it with necessary personnel at a time when manpower was running short, and it became the primary vehicle for the formation and manning of an equally pervasive system of penal units throughout the Red Army.

The legal basis for penal and disciplinary service was a series of decrees issued from August 1941 through the first half of 1942. These established so-called penal (*shtrafnye*) units made up of soldiers and officers sentenced for breach of military disciplinary codes. While this system was at first haphazard, the devastating defeats the Red Army experienced during the German Operation Blau in the summer of 1942 prompted Stalin to systematize the penal structure throughout the entire Red Army. In conjunction with the infamous Order No. 227 (the "Not a Step Back" order) of July 28, 1942, Stalin mandated the widespread formation and use of penal troops and, soon thereafter, criminals (both common and political) appeared in the Red Army's ranks.

As defined by the NKO on September 28, 1942, penal battalions were "to provide an opportunity to individuals among the mid-level and senior command, political, and command cadre personnel who have violated discipline by cowardice or unsteadiness, to redeem their honor before the Motherland with their blood by virtue of courageous struggle with the enemy in the most difficult sectors of combat operations."[32] Accordingly, the NKO authorized all *fronts* to form from one to three penal battalions and each army from five to ten penal companies. The *fronts* and armies then attached the penal battalions and companies to their subordinate combat units. As far as the convicts (*shtrafniki*) themselves were concerned, each served a sentence of from one to three months. If they survived, they then returned to regular Red Army service. In the wake of Stalin's initial order, the NKO broadened the legal basis of penal service throughout the remainder of 1942.

In addition to penal troops, in 1943 the Soviet Union decided to exploit convicts and political prisoners as soldiers in the Red Army. On April 6, 1943, for example, the GKO ordered the conscription of many civilians of military age so far exempted because of their legal problems. In essence, this order provided for early release into Red Army service of criminals and some political prisoners who had already served a portion of their sentences.[33] Thus, the search for new sources of military manpower by this time included former convicts and political prisoners and men of up to fifty-five years of age. Although this clearing out of the prisons and labor camps could not have had a salutary effect on Red Army discipline, never-theless, in August 1943, the NKO issued another directive drastically expanding the number of officers who could assign soldiers to penal units.[34]

Individually and collectively, these decrees and orders formed the legal basis for the formation and employment of hundreds of penal units as well as for the wholesale call-up of thousands if not millions of former criminals and political prisoners from the infamous labor camp system, the Gulag. While ostensibly impelled by the need to enforce strict discipline, these policies were also driven by the burgeoning manpower requirements of the Red Army. Thus, they formed but a small portion of an immense mosaic of massive call-ups to military service of numerous ethic and religious minorities, many citizens above the normal age of military service, and millions of women.

As a result, penal units became ubiquitous throughout the Red Army, particularly after July 1942. Although the Red Army formed over one hundred penal battalions and about three hundred battalions and companies, Russian authorities have yet to release a comprehensive list of these units. Allowing for some local varia-tions, penal battalions consisted of roughly eight hundred men organized in two to three rifle companies, heavy and light machine-gun companies, an antitank rifle company, and antitank, mortar, sapper, and signal platoons. Separate penal companies (normally 150 to two hundred men but sometimes as many as seven hundred) had from three to six rifle platoons and supporting machine-gun, mortar, and antitank platoons.

As was the case with regular Red Army forces, as the war pro-gressed, their parent *fronts* and armies increased the fire support allocated to penal units, primarily by reinforcing them with addi-tional antitank and submachine guns, and also improved their reconnaissance capability by adding a reconnaissance platoon to them. By virtue of these reinforcements, average penal companies had over two hundred soldiers by mid-1943 and sometimes many more. In part, this increased strength reflected the widespread employment of penal forces as virtual "holding areas" for the condemned. Quite naturally, these forces experienced appallingly high attrition rates while they were fulfilling their routinely hazard-ous missions. In return for performing their hazardous duties, conscripted prisoners who were fortunate enough to survive their ordeal had their sentences remitted in accordance with the NKO's implementing instructions. The normal reference on the form releasing the convicted from their captivity in penal units was the notation, "Expiated his guilt with his own blood."[35]

Penal units existed on a legal basis from September 1942 through May 1945. Excluding their permanent cadre of nonconvicts, the total number of convict-soldiers (*shtrafniki*) who served in penal units included 24,993 in 1942, 177,694 in 1943, 143,694 in 1944, and 81,766 in 1945, for a total of 427,910 men by war's end.[36] These figures, however, do not include those who served in "unofficial" penal units prior to September 1942.

While the Russian government has yet to reveal the precise number of penal units that operated in other years, it has released accurate data concerning penal units that operated in 1944. The number of penal battalions in the Red Army's operating *fronts* ranged from eight in May to fifteen in January, with a monthly average strength of 227 *shtrafniki* per battalion. The number of penal companies ranged from 199 in April to 310 in September, at an average of 243 per month, with each company averaging 102 soldiers. For the year, 170,298 *shtrafniki* were killed, wounded, or fell ill, for an average monthly loss rate of 14,191 soldiers, or 52 percent of their average monthly strength of 27,326 soldiers. The casualty rate in penal units was three to six times greater than the casualty rates of other regular army units.[37]

As required by Stalin's initial guidance, most *fronts* and armies employed penal units in "dangerous" sectors. Missions included leading assaults on fortified positions (a Red Army version of the British Army's concept of the "Forlorn Hope" during the Napoleonic Wars), attacking bypassed strong points, and "manually" clearing mines before and during offensive operations. For obvious reasons, few commanders employed penal units during the exploitation phase of operations, when opportunities for desertion individually or en masse were more likely.

In addition to the hundreds of penal units formed from Red Army officers and soldiers convicted of various crimes, beginning in early 1942, the GKO authorized the call up into Red Army service of what ultimately became hundreds of thousands of men from what one author termed "the last reserve of the Empire," specifically, the over two million men and women exiled to Soviet labor camps for a variety of political and criminal offenses. Most of these persons had either fallen victim to Stalin's forced collectivization program of the late 1920s and 1930s or were members of ethnic groups that demonstrated even the slightest receptivity to German propaganda or disloyalty to Stalin and the Soviet authorities. As of March 1940, the NKVD's Gulag system consisted of fifty-three separate labor camps and work projects manned by 1,668,200 prisoners and 107,000 guards. By June 22, 1941, the number of prisoners had risen to between two and 2.3 million souls. Many of these prisoners were the product of either outright political repression or the mass resettlement of "unreliable elements" of Soviet society, meaning ethnic or religious groups that Soviet authorities perceived as a threat to the Soviet state. Between 1941 and 1944, the authorities forcibly exiled tens of thousands to camps in remote regions of the Soviet Union such as Kazakhstan or Siberia. Those transplanted included Germans living in the Volga region and other localities, Crimean Tartars, Chechens, and other nationalities.

By June 1, 1944, however, the number of prisoners in the Gulag had decreased significantly, to about 1.2 million persons. Discounting the number of prisoners who perished in captivity, it is reasonably certain that as many as 420,000 of these prisoners were impressed into the Red Army in 1941 and over one hundred thousand more in 1942. In addition, the GKO and Presidium of the Supreme Soviet of the USSR freed more than 157,000 "politicals" by special resolutions during 1941 and early 1942 and sent them to the Red Army. The most recent estimate is that 975,000 of these prisoners were "freed" and ultimately served in the Red Army before war's end.[38] However, how many of these prisoners returned to the Gulag after the war remains unknown.

The first recorded employment of these prisoners on a large scale reportedly occurred in the late summer of 1941, when the "Polar" Rifle Division, which "was, on the whole, made up of prisoners, including its command cadre," took part in the defense of Murmansk in the Soviet far north. These troops "wore the numerical designations of the Vorkuta camps instead of swords and diamonds," and "even now they basically remain anonymous."[39]

The motive force behind the Stalin's decision to employ camp prisoners as Red Army soldiers, or more properly as "canon fodder," was the Red Army's catastrophic personnel losses during the first six months of the war, amounting to more than 2.8 million soldiers. The Red Army absolutely had to find additional manpower. Accordingly, on April 11, 1942, a GKO decree directed the NKVD to "draft 500,000 men who were fit for line service from its work settlements." Another GKO decree, this one dated July 26, 1942, mandated the conscription of five hundred thousand more men from the same category of conscripts.[40] Most of these prisoners were exiled *kulaks* (landed peasants). They had been called "special migrants" (*spetsperelentsy*) before 1934, "labor deportees" (*trud-poselentsy*) from 1934 to March 1944, and "special migrants from the former kulak contingent" (*spetspereselentsy kontingenta "byvshie kulaki"*) after March 1944. The GKO intended to remove the names of labor deportees who were impressed into the army (and their family members) from the official lists of deportees after a year's military service.

Despite the GKO's careful plans, the release program developed painfully slowly, largely because it had not been anticipated. Only 47,116 labor deportees were released to the army by December 10, 1942 (including 17,775 draftees and 29,341 family members), and another 102,250 were released in 1943. Overall, and in part as a result of this conscription, the total number of labor deportees still in camps and at various work projects fell from 911,716 on January 1, 1942, to 69,687 by January 1, 1944.[41]

The most accurate data concerning how this release program worked and generated forces for the Red Army is found in an examination of the formation of military forces in Siberia. For example, in July 1942 the NKO, the Siberian Communist Party, and the Siberian Military District headquarters formed the 6th Volunteer Rifle Corps, which adopted the name "Stalin." The nucleus was the 1st Siberian Volunteer Rifle Division, formed on July 8, 1942, by the Novosibirsk Regional Communist Party Committee and the Siberian Military District. On July 17, the Separate "Stalin" Omsk Siberian Rifle Brigade formed at Omsk, manned in part by 1,200 Siberian labor deportees. Soon after, the 1st Special Siberian Altai Volunteer Brigade joined the corps and was redesignated the 74th Separate "Stalin" Altai Siberian Brigade on August 24.[42] Finally, the 78th Krasnoiarsk Siberian Volunteer Rifle Brigade and the 91st "Stalin" Special Siberian Volunteer Rifle Brigade joined in September and October. The latter was formed in the Kuzbas region in July 1942 and consisted primarily of "special volunteers," that is, prisoners from NKVD camps and labor colonies. In fact, a large proportion of the soldiers throughout the corps were former labor deportees, leavened by a sizeable command cadre of Communist Party and Komsomol members to ensure the force's reliability. For example, every third man in the 6,720-man 91st Rifle Brigade was a Party or

Komsomol member. Local records indicate that of the 6th Rifle Corps' total strength of 37,500 men, 44 percent were industrial workers or miners, 26.6 percent were peasants, and 29.4 percent were white-collar workers, while 38.6 percent of the corps were Party or Komsomol members and up to 40 percent "special volunteers."[43]

Despite being subject to harsh discipline, near constant fear, and often outright intimidation, most of the Red Army's soldiers endured their service, lived, fought, and either perished or survived without their army collapsing, first and foremost, because they were accustomed to doing so. Millions of Soviet citizens—subjected to repression, confinement, punishment, or other restrictions during the prewar years—would find the Red Army's wartime discipline different only by a matter of degree. Unlike the soldiers in Western armies, the Red Army's soldiers were products of a political system and a society whose innate harshness replicated life in the military in many ways. While the quality of life of Soviet citizens in peacetime was far better than that of the Red Army soldier in wartime, neither came close to Western standards.

In short, in the Soviet Union, the transition from civilian to military life was only a short step. Citizens accommodated themselves to internal passports, arbitrary arrests and confinements, punishment by imprisonment or death, or internal exile; soldiers coped with arbitrary arrest, summary trial, and perhaps execution on the spot, assignment to a penal unit, or death in the field at the hands of a blocking detachment.

Conversely, just as many civilians were accustomed to surviving in the harsh and often arbitrary Soviet society, Red Army soldiers became accustomed to coping with and surviving in the military. Of course, within the context of their military life, the soldiers' most formidable challenge was the fact that they had to endure and survive both the threat from the Wehrmacht and their own system. This is why recent memoirs are so replete with instances of soldiers enduring political control, circumventing the harsh disciplinary regime, traveling with relative ease to and from the front to rear and home, and engaging in other pursuits so characteristic of soldiers in any army, who bend the system to satisfy their needs.

Despite this somber existence, which seems depressing to those ignorant of Russian history, whether worker, peasant, or bureaucrat, Slav or non-Slav, man or woman, Orthodox, Muslim, Jew, or atheist, and whether motivated by "Soviet" patriotism,

"Great Russian nationalism," sheer love of the Motherland, or simple hatred of invaders, most Red Army soldiers endured unimaginable deprivations and survived the most terrible war of the twentieth century—and possibly ever. By doing so, collectively, they recorded the singularly remarkable feat of vanquishing Europe's most formidable military machine, albeit at tremendous cost, in an astonishingly brief period of just under four years of combat.

8   German Bodenstandig Divisions

Walter Dunn

Germany, Britain, and France all suffered heavy casualties in World War I. Between 1914 and 1918, millions of potential fathers were either killed, wounded, made prisoners of war, or kept at the front lines for long periods. The result was a low birth rate in all three nations from 1915 to 1919 and, as a result, the number of males reaching the age of eighteen from 1933 to 1937 was much lower than normal. The German military called those years the "white years," when the average number of potential recruits was smaller than usual. Although this trend ended in 1938, the cumulative impact of four years of small classes resulted in fewer men available for military service. Once Germany was involved in large-scale military operations, the army was forced to employ men who were considered unfit in other armies, until the higher birth rates provided larger classes of recruits.

Limited-service men were used by the German army to perform duties less strenuous than those assigned to panzer and infantry divisions. They were used in service units and in divisions assigned to defensive tasks (and with limited transport) called *bodenstandig* divisions. (Chapter 2, on the German reserve divisions in World War I, has some comments on how the German army had earlier handled less-fit manpower.) The bodenstandig divisions of the German Army were usually referred to as infantry divisions (bo), pointing up that these divisions were truly combat divisions but lacked mobility. During World War II, Allied intelligence referred to them as "static divisions," but given the several meanings of "static," this translation was not universal. The use of the term "occupation divisions" is misleading, because the divisions had no special capability for occupation duties and controlling the population in foreign countries.

The early bodenstandig divisions, created in 1939 to defend the German border with France while the bulk of the German Army invaded Poland, were filled with overage soldiers who were then discharged in 1940. Later in the war, the divisions contained limited-service men who were less able to withstand the rigors of mobile warfare, with its frequent marches and poor living conditions.

The Manpower Pool

To expand beyond the hundred-thousand-man army allowed by the Versailles Treaty, the Germans initiated universal compulsory military service on March 16, 1935. Men eligible for service were examined, and a system was established for inducting future draftees. Men twenty-one years of age were examined for immediate military service. Twenty-year-olds were examined for service in the RAD (German labor service), a paramilitary force that skirted the limitation of the Versailles Treaty. When the men turned twenty-one, they could be called for military duty. In addition, one hundred thousand volunteers were given physicals. The young men were eager to serve, and the lenient examining physicians passed a majority of them. Conscripts and volunteers were classified either as fit for the army or the RAD or unfit for service altogether.

When the recruit was mustered in, he was examined by two physicians, a chief and his assistant. The assistant made a preliminary examination; the chief passed judgment on fitness using data provided by the assistant. The physicians gathered additional information relevant to the recruit, obtaining information from government or private sources. The examination included a description of body types as slender, muscular, or rounded. Weight and height guides were used, but deviation from the table was permitted. The normal circumference of the chest was about half the height of the body, and expansion had to exceed 2.4 inches.

Physicians examined the recruits using a table listing disqualifying diseases and defects. Defects were grouped by body system; for instance, eye defects were eight of the seventy-eight listed problems. Each of the seventy-eight was divided into six levels: defects that did not impair fitness, defects acceptable for conditional fitness, remediable but temporarily unfitting, defects establishing limited service, defects permitting only work duty, and defects making the man unfit for any duty.

Given the 468 permutations, a few examples will have to suffice. Normal vision in one eye without glasses with limited vision in the other eye up to one-half was acceptable. Sixty percent vision in both eyes without glasses was acceptable, if normal vision could be achieved with glasses. Normal vision with one eye after correction was also accepted. Those with only one-fourth of normal vision for the better eye were not accepted. Those with slightly defective hearing in one ear were acceptable, but serious deafness in both ears was not. Conscripts with no teeth were acceptable, provided they had suitable dentures. Injuries to the jaws that hampered speech or eating were declared unfit for military service. Mental illness, such as being judged an imbecile or an idiot, made a man unfit. Standards regarding venereal disease were lax. The U.S. Army, at first, rejected all cases of venereal disease, but later gonorrhea and syphilis were accepted unless there were other symptoms. In general, American standards were much higher than the German ones. In 1939, the Germans dipped deeper into the manpower pool. While the American army was limiting itself to 1-A men, the Germans had further categories: fit, second class; conditionally fit; temporarily unfit; and limited fit.

Forming Divisions

During World War II, the German Army created new divisions in groups called waves. Generally, a wave was organized within a few months, and the divisions shared some characteristics with other divisions in the same wave. In December 1939, the Sixth Wave, consisting of four divisions, was formed with older men for defense duty; this was the first wave formed from substandard men. They were issued Czech arms and vehicles, and most of the men were older reservists. By January 1941, most of the older men were discharged and replaced with young recruits. The divisions remained in France until October 1941, when one by one they were transferred to the Russian front.

In late 1940, Hitler made plans to invade Russia during the summer of 1941. Most of the first-class German infantry divisions were transferred from the west to the east. In November 1940, seventeen bodenstandig divisions were formed to defend the Atlantic coast, nine (302, 304, 305, 306, 319, 320, 321, 323, and 327) in the Thirteenth Wave and eight (332, 333, 335, 336, 337, 339, 340, and 342) in the Fourteenth Wave. They had three infantry regiments and three artillery battalions but a minimum of service units. These divisions were equipped with captured French and Czech weapons, along with German artillery left over from World War I and enough trucks or horse-drawn wagons for coastal defense duty. Their mission was to protect the coastline from commando raids and to act as a delaying force in the event of a major invasion. They performed these duties well. They were not intended to take part in mobile warfare once an invading force had gained a foothold. The older and limited-service men were not able to withstand the rigors of prolonged combat, and supplies of ammunition for the captured weapons were limited, but this was duty they could do.

Anticipating the invasion of Russia, in the spring of 1941 more bodenstandig divisions were formed to release mobile divisions. In April 1941, the Fifteenth Wave, with seven divisions (708, 709, 711, 712, 715, 716, and 719), was formed and assigned to coastal defense duty in France in June and July. The had only two infantry regiments, one field artillery battalion, and minimum service components. The 302nd Division would repel the Allied raid on Dieppe (August 19, 1942), but 1942 would otherwise be a generally quiet year for German forces in the west. Operations in Russia continued, with German attacks inflicting punishment on the Red Army, but the offensive that headed to Stalingrad failed to knock out the Soviet Union.

In late 1942, Hitler continued to plan for a major attack in Russia in 1943. On November 1, 1942 (before the Stalingrad offensive), he ordered the rebuilding of forty-two divisions. Five new bodenstandig divisions were to be formed and filled with limited-service men. Previously, these divisions had employed older men, but that source had been exhausted.

By the end of March 1943, the German army was short 830,000 men. The losses suffered during the Stalingrad campaign exacerbated a shortage of manpower, prompting a variety of changes. (Losses between June 1941 and June 1943 would reach nearly four million killed and wounded, roughly half between July 1942 to June 1943. Most of the wounded eventually returned to duty, and new recruits would more than compensate for those that did not.) Frontline strength was cut, so that paper authorizations were closer to actual strength; rear-area units were culled for manpower; men were rushed to the front with less training; and manpower standards were lowered. Infantry divisions were reduced from nine battalions to seven. The average combat strength of the rifle company was reduced from 180 to eighty in 1943, primarily by reducing the number of riflemen and by providing more automatic weapons. The firepower of the new company was greater. Back on October 29, 1942, a 10 percent cut in manpower had already been made in all service units, the men being sent to combat units. To provide immediate replacements, the wounded were returned to active duty as soon as possible. Eighteen-year-old boys were drafted and, after a few weeks of training, were sent to France for further training and to replace men being sent to the Russian front.[1] Air force personnel were drafted to the army, occupational deferments were tightened, and other nationalities were employed as soldiers. (For the impact of these policies on the Waffen-SS, see Chapters 9 and 10.)

The resurgence of the Red Army scuttled German plans for building a reserve. The Wehrmacht had to replenish and expand by dipping deeper into manpower resources. A new plan for creating a reserve was issued on February 4, 1943, including the formation of eight further (343, 344, 346, 347, and 348, and 16, 17, and 18 Luftwaffe) bodenstandig divisions. The five army divisions were organized with fortress infantry units made up of both older and limited-service men.

As an example, the 346th Division had a cadre of men transferred from the 257th, 319th, 320th, 204th, and 332nd Divisions, mainly bodenstandig divisions. (Commanders in every army used such transfers to rid their units of undesirable men.) Other men came from Wehrkreise VI and IX, most likely all limited-service men who were not fit to be assigned to infantry divisions.[2] The 346th Division, despite the effort to scrape together a reasonable force, included only five fortress battalions, two artillery battalions, and minimal service elements. Total strength was only five thousand men.

The February 1943 plan also included creating two new infantry divisions with young men from the training battalions. However, in May 1943 those two divisions (326th and 338th) swapped their young men with other divisions for older men and limited-service men, which brought the divisions' average ages near thirty-six years. The divisions were reclassified as bodenstandig divisions, and the infantry regiments were renamed fortress regiments. In February 1943, the German commander in the west ordered that seven of the recently formed bodenstandig divisions be trained to form a mobile reserve by June 1, 1943. This program probably included the assignment of more horse-drawn vehicles and possibly better weapons. Some of the bodenstandig divisions formed mobile battle groups that saw action in Normandy.

The seriousness of Germany's manpower position in the spring of 1943 was obvious: divisions of old men and limited-service men were all there was to face any Allied landing in France. In April 1943, the force defending France consisted of nineteen bodenstandig divisions, ten reserve divisions training young recruits, twenty-three skeleton divisions that had been destroyed in the Stalingrad campaign, and three other divisions, none of which were combat ready. Thus the front-line defense of France was in the hands of the bodenstandig divisions assigned permanently to coastal sectors. They were familiar with their areas and, installed in permanent defenses, could defend their beaches in the most economical way in terms of equipment and manpower. Most of the officers and men were overage, and there were fewer weapons compared to other divisions. The divisions were spread very thin; there were only three to cover the three hundred miles from the Loire to the Spanish border. The German manpower shortage forced them to rely on bodenstandig divisions (and men in training for normal combat units) to garrison quiet sectors.

On July 25, 1943, Hitler issued an order to build up the army in France and the Low Countries. In July, twenty-five bodenstandig divisions and one reserve division guarded the coast, six infantry divisions and two motorized divisions were in reserve behind the coast, and nine reserve divisions were training men in the countryside. (A Bosnian SS division was also training in France, as part of the policy decisions covered in Chapter 9.) In September, the coast had twenty-seven infantry and bodenstandig divisions, and only twenty-three divisions were on the coast in October, seventeen of which were bodenstandig divisions. Each division had one or more *Ost* battalions, units made up of Russian prisoners that might or might not be willing to fight. The total ration strength of the forces in the west was 1,370,000 in the army, navy, and Luftwaffe, plus service troops and *hiwis*, for a total of 1,709,000.

Bodenstandig divisions were assigned to other theaters in 1943. The 210th Division was organized in Finland to guard the north coast. Three divisions were formed in Norway (230, 270, and 280), but they were divisions in name only; for instance, the 280th Division comprised only a headquarters, four fortress battalions, a signal company, and coast artillery batteries. The divisions only combined existing fortress units and coastal batteries and only marginally added to the defensive strength.[3] A fortress brigade was created in Crete. The 704th, 714th, 717th, and 718th bodenstandig divisions were in the Balkans.

The program in 1943 had some success. Between April 1 and June 30, 1943, a net 216,000 men were added to the army. On July 1, 1943, the German army had 4,484,000, men compared to four million on July 1, 1942. However, the quality of the German army had declined. Men who had been grooms for horses, supply clerks, and teamsters did not necessarily make good riflemen. These men were physically fit, but, as is common in all armies, less capable men were assigned to rear-area duties. If they had previously been conditionally fit, fit for limited service, or fit for work duty, changing the standards so that they were eligible for combat did not improve their constitution; it only testified to the manpower shortage of the Third Reich. There had been nearly a 100 percent turnover in the army, and the average soldier had less than two years of experience. Even the average American army soldier had two years' experience in 1943. German divisions were filled with inferior men and lacked offensive power.

After July 1943, the demand for replacements grew more intense, both to replace losses and to form new divisions. Three operations—the Battle of Kursk, the invasion of Sicily, and the Russian offensive—cost men who then had to be replaced. The armies in the east received men from not only the Replacement Army but also from divisions in France. Between September and November, ninety thousand men were sent from west to east. Selective transfers of men from divisions in France would have given commanders an opportunity to weed out incompetent men. To prevent this, divisions were ordered to transfer existing companies and battalions to Russia and to rebuild them with replacements. In consequence, on September 1, 1943, the total strength of the western army had decreased to 770,000, including the SS, Luftwaffe divisions, service units, and security troops.

During 1943, the Replacement Army maintained a healthy average of about a million men: instructors, recruits in training, men recuperating from wounds, and trained men awaiting movement to the front. From October 1942 to September 1943, it sent an average of one hundred thousand replacements per month to the eastern front; smaller numbers were sent to the Mediterranean and to the west. With a maximum of six months' training or recuperation for the average soldier, the Replacement Army could produce 1.5 million trained men yearly. At the rate of ten thousand men per year per division, 1.5 million replacements could maintain 150 divisions in active combat—and a substantially larger army, since divisions not actively engaged needed few replacements.

Yet to replace losses and form new divisions, the army requested the induction of seven hundred thousand additional men for the second half of 1943. A total of 1.5 million men were drafted in 1943 and processed through the replacement system. One expedient to find these men was to draft young men of the class of 1926 (seventeen years old) in the fall of 1943. Older men between fifty and sixty were also drafted; they would replace younger men in noncombat positions. Those with hearing and stomach ailments were drafted and formed into Ear and Stomach Battalions for defensive assignments on quiet fronts. In September 1943, in desperation, the exemption of the last or only son of a family was canceled, along with the exemption of fathers of five or more children. The railroad and the border service were also combed for additional men.

Men who were not fully fit for combat in Russia (mainly due to the climate) were sent back to their hometown replacement battalions after recovering from wounds or frostbite. These men were noted as unfit for duty in Russia, and the replacement battalion sent them to a division serving in France.

With low-quality men coming in, the Germans created more bodenstandig divisions to replace infantry divisions in France, Norway, and other theaters. An order of May 12, 1943, outlined a massive buildup program. In addition to the infantry divisions formed in waves, ten bodenstandig divisions were created and assigned to the west between July 1943 and January 1944 (47, 48, 49, 70, 242, 243, 244, 245, 265, and 266). In addition, the Germans reorganized seven divisions (319, 708, 709, 711, 712, 716, and 719) in France as bodenstandig divisions. These divisions would form much of the coastal defense force in northern France in June 1944. The new bodenstandig divisions consisted of seven battalions in three regiments, with reduced service elements. Because bodenstandig divisions were of little use other than in coastal defense, only four more were formed during the remaining months of the war. On the other hand, the rapid formation of bodenstandig divisions shows the ability of the Replacement Army to create divisions.

All of the measures taken to provide additional men on the firing line were critical. By the fall of 1943, there were only a few trained front-line divisions left in France. Most of the remaining divisions were either reserve divisions, made up of recruits in training, or bodenstandig divisions of older men in fortifications with little transport.

The divisions being reformed were shipped from France to either Russia or Italy as soon as they reached a state of combat readiness.

Hitler knew from deciphered and unscrambled transatlantic telephone conversations between Roosevelt and Churchill that the Allies had no intention of invading France in 1943. With no need to fear the invasion of France, he could use those troops in the east and south. Between May and August 1943, the Germans sent thirteen divisions into Italy, twelve from France and Belgium and one from Denmark. Most of these units were still in the process of reforming, but immediate action was not anticipated. The units sent to Italy disarmed the Italian army after its surrender and fought a delaying action after the Allies landed.

The Germans had other fronts that required resources but had relatively low threats. The Scandinavian countries were a source of divisions for other theaters during 1943. Denmark was a link in the communication to Norway and a potential landing site for the Allies, but the naval situation meant that the garrison could mainly be second-rate units not ready for combat. The garrison comprised three divisions training replacements and the 416th Infantry Division, which was a bodenstandig division formed in December 1941 with two regiments of Luftwaffe men and guard units supported by only a single artillery battalion.

In Norway, the 230th, 270th, and 280th had been organized. The 702nd was at Narvik and the 710th at Oslo, although neither was trusted to be the sole garrison of the area. They may not have had the numbers or the quality to be adequate garrisons; no information has been found. From September 1943, there was a steady exodus of front-line forces from Norway, leaving its defense to existing bodenstandig divisions.

Additional divisions were needed in the Balkans in 1943 to fight the partisans. Equipment for Tito's communists was supplied by British airdrops of German arms captured in North Africa, and the Italian collapse also gave the Partisans much equipment. The well-armed Partisans caused the Germans increasing difficulty. In Croatia were the 714th, 717th, and 718th Infantry Divisions and the 187th Reserve, 7th SS Mountain, and two divisions (369th and 373rd) with German cadre and Croatian junior personnel, plus Croatian national units. Greece and Serbia were occupied by the 704th Infantry Division and three Bulgarian divisions. Eight Italian divisions completed the garrison in Albania and Greece until September 1943. Holding Crete was necessary because it could have become an airbase threatening anywhere in the Balkans, especially the oilfields at Ploesti. It was occupied by the Crete Fortress Brigade of bodenstandig men and later reinforced by the 11th Luftwaffe Division and the 22nd Infantry Division.

Increasing resistance meant that the occupation troops had to be upgraded. In April 1943, four bodenstandig divisions (the 704th, 714th, 717th, and 718th) were reorganized into Jäger (light infantry) divisions. The older men were replaced by young men, although some of the older men may have been used to form service elements previously lacking. Existing infantry regiments were redesignated Jäger regiments, artillery battalions were reinforced into regiments, engineer and signal companies became battalions, and new reconnaissance and antitank battalions were formed. All these accomplishments were completed within a few weeks in 1943, showing what could be done when there was enough fully fit manpower available. The older men were transferred and replaced with new recruits and recovered wounded from Germany.

Hitler issued a directive on November 27, 1943, for the army and the SS to produce a million new combat soldiers. New recruits from the class of 1926 and a few limited-service men would provide 440,000. The remaining 560,000 came from cutting divisional service units by a quarter. Some independent service and headquarters organizations were abolished. The 560,000 men were apportioned: 120,000 from 150 infantry divisions, twenty thousand from panzer and panzergrenadier divisions, 120,000 from service units, 260,000 through substituting Russian volunteers for German troops in service units, twenty thousand from various headquarters, and an additional twenty thousand from miscellaneous sources. Special control commissions were organized to ensure that unit commanders implemented the cuts. The program succeeded, and by the spring of 1944 the Replacement Army had more than a million trained men, some of whom were organized in four hundred march battalions, each with a thousand trained men.

The Stomach Division

Under the order, many men previously considered unfit for duty were reclassified as fit for limited service. However, by regulation, those who were physically and mentally inferior could be used only for duty in the rear areas. These limited-service men replaced combat-fit men in service, communications, and headquarters units. Those with stomach disorders were formed into battalions and even into a coastal division in Holland that received special food.

Similarly, deaf men were formed into "ear battalions" and assigned to defensive positions.

The number of men with stomach diseases in Germany was unusually high during World War II for reasons that have not been determined. Although there were different causes and symptoms, all of the afflicted men suffered from stomach and intestinal pains. Medical examination determined the severity of the case. The Germans considered the best treatment of gastric diseases to include nursing care of the stomach, rest, heat, and diet. Slight cases were cured by change in diet; bed rest and treatment were prescribed for serious cases. In severe cases, surgery was required. Stomach disease related to nerves was more difficult to treat, because the patient did not know if the stomach problem was causing bad nerves or the reverse; medical examinations might not be conclusive. Men constantly reporting sick were a burden to a unit. They were placed in special wards, given a special diet, forbidden to smoke, and observed. Many recovered. Others were treated in hospitals. They did not need medical treatment but did not want any training or work duty. They were gathered in special wards and hospitals, and each Wehrkreis had a special hospital for gastric diseases. Every gastric patient had to be examined in these hospitals, which were the only ones authorized to make a decision as to the fitness for service. A report was attached to the soldier's pay book, which he always carried, to prevent gastric patients from going to a hospital of their choice and repeatedly requesting x-ray examinations. Replacement units had special companies and battalions because of the need for specialized physicians and treatment equipment.

In May 1944, the 70th Infantry Division was formed, consisting entirely of stomach battalions. Intended as a bodenstandig division, the "stomach" division was at the confluence of a large number of men suffering from stomach diseases and the great demand for more troops. Holland offered favorable circumstances for obtaining special food and was a front expected to remain quiet. On the negative side, the Dutch climate (moist air, fog, and a high water table) and the location of defense positions close to the beach were considered very unfavorable for people suffering from stomach diseases. The number of stomach cases increased, because the troops constructing beach obstacles often had to work in water up to their waist.

The 70th was hatched from the 165th Reserve Division, which already had a dual role. Its primary assignment had been to defend the Antwerp estuary (specifically the islands of Walcheren and North and South Beveland) while providing a ninety-day training course for replacements, some of whom would be sent to the eastern front. The division was subordinated to two different commands, the 89th Army Corps (of the Fifteenth Army) for its defense duty and to the 64th Reserve Corps (and the Commander of the Replacement Army) for its training mission.

As a reserve division, the 165th Reserve Division included a division staff, three infantry regiments of two battalions each, and an artillery regiment. Each infantry battalion consisted of three rifle companies and one machine-gun company. The artillery regiment had two light battalions, each with three batteries. The division had extra personnel and material for training with heavy infantry weapons. For its defensive mission, it was reinforced with a fusilier battalion, which was usually attached to an infantry regiment. The division also received an artillery battalion of three heavy 150mm batteries. An engineer battalion of three companies and a light bridge-building column were also assigned to the division, along with a signal battalion of two companies, a motorized reconnaissance detachment, and a military police detachment. A thirteenth (infantry gun) company and a fourteenth (antitank) company were added to each infantry regiment. In addition, the division received a battalion of fortress troops, an Armenian battalion, and a Russian battalion. Some officers were old, and others were recovering from their wounds, but they had combat experience. The noncommissioned officers of the 165th Reserve Division had been selected to train replacements and were excellent. In April 1944, the cadre of the 165th Reserve Division and the replacements, who had completed their three months of training, were given additional instruction in defensive weapons and defense techniques.

In May 1944, the 165th Reserve Division received new orders. Its commander, Generalleutnant Wilhelm Daser, had requested that his division be converted from a reserve and training division into a bodenstandig division with the strength and equipment of a normal division. It would lose the training mission as a reserve division and become the 70th Infantry Division. The process of creating the new division began in mid-May 1944, when men with stomach problems were assembled in companies and battalions in three military districts in Germany after completing their normal ninety-day training program. These battalions and companies were transferred to the 70th Division in May and June. Henceforth, new recruits suffering from stomach problems were assigned to the 70th Division, gradually replacing the fitter men who had completed their training. The potential 70th Infantry Division men were examined by a commission consisting of the division commander for special employment, the regimental and battalion commanders, and the doctors of the 165th Reserve Division, working with medical specialists. Men who were considered unfit for combat were assigned to a battalion employed with the 89th Army Corps in the Antwerp area.

The first units arrived from mid-May to mid-June and were billeted in the villages. They were placed under the command of a small division staff for special employment formed by the 165th Reserve Division and located at De Donck, five kilometers north of Antwerp. Daser commanded not only the 165th as it converted but the 70th as it formed.

The new 70th Division units were organized into three infantry regiments of two battalions each and two artillery battalions. Most of the batteries were assigned to guns emplaced in fortifications, although one battery was horse drawn. The infantry was issued Italian rifles. The training of the engineer and signal units was conducted by the division commander for special employment. The troops also constructed defensive positions and obstacles to prevent aircraft from landing in the rear. Training the infantry in the use of the heavy weapons began after the "stomach" men had replaced the fitter ones.

The 70th Division received special rations, including white bread, vermicelli, and greens instead of peas and beans, to supplement the meat rations. Only mashed potatoes and stewed fruit or jam was provided. The doctors urged that smoking be prohibited, but preventing the soldiers from smoking was impossible. Cigarettes could be obtained from the civilian population and other German units.

Most of the fit men were removed in June, and the remnants of the 165th Division moved to Antwerp. Some healthy officers and men of the 165th Reserve Division were retained by the 70th Bodenstandig Division. The company and battery commanders' positions in the 70th Division were filled with healthy officers, and the engineer battalion was formed with sound and well-educated people. The new "stomach" battalions of the 70th Division trained as infantry and prepared defensive positions and obstacles against glider landing. On July 1, 1944, "stomach" men composed about half the regimental and battalion staffs, 90 percent of the infantry,

75 percent of the artillery, 10 percent of the engineers, and 30 percent of the signal company.

In July and August 1944, the division improved the coast fortifications and dug obstacles on the shoreline; the engineers planted mines. The division continued combat training and marching. The reserve units constructed pillboxes and air-landing obstacles. Output, discipline, and spirit were excellent.

At the beginning of September, the division was committed at Ghent, except for the 1019th Infantry Regiment, which remained in the fortress area of Vlissingen, on Walcheren Island.[4] During the march to the new positions, about sixty to eighty kilometers, there were a few casualties owing to sickness. However, action against numerically superior motorized and tank forces caused heavy losses, and sickness also climbed. The Fusilier Battalion alone lost three hundred men. The division had only a few antitank guns, most of them drawn by teams of Dutch horses, and the moral effect on the men of fighting without enough support weapons was great. They had spent several years in hospitals or on light duty; the engagement was their baptism of fire.

During the retreat from the island of Walcheren in October 1944, the 70th Division did not do well in mobile warfare against a superior enemy and had only limited success in defending positions during the retreat. By mid-October, the 70th Division was able to create a defensive line at Ghent. The 64th Infantry Division (also a bodenstandig division) and the 70th Division repelled British attacks from October 20 to November 8, 1944, and the British suffered heavy losses during the battle. The main body of the 70th Division fought better than could be expected, under most unfavorable conditions. Its stubborn defense of the coast was attributable to the self-sacrifice of the individual soldiers. The bodenstandig divisions were formed to fight in established positions, and the 70th Division succeeded. The recruits' integration into the 70th Division in nearly complete companies may have preserved some internal cohesion from the training process and help explain how these marginal men gave a fairly solid performance in combat.

However, after the war, Daser had second thoughts and questioned the value of activating a division consisting exclusively of men with stomach ailments. Certainly, soldiers with stomach ailments could be formed in companies and battalions and assigned for service in the rear area. Yet Daser believed that a whole division of soldiers with stomach ailments was unworkable even for position warfare; the demands of fortification work, training, and combat were too much.

Additional battalions and companies of unfit men had been formed in the Replacement Army, and finding a use for these units was a problem. In 1943, a *Landesschutzen* Battalion consisting of men suffering from stomach diseases was successfully employed by the military government headquarters at Lille, France, as railroad guards. Later, stomach battalions were assigned to infantry divisions on both the Russian Front and in France in quiet sectors. These battalions did not meet front-line requirements of marching, digging, and fighting in unfavorable weather conditions. They complained of cold, rain, hunger, and thirst.

As an example, on October 15, 1944, the chief medical officer of Army Group B was ordered to visit Stomach Battalion 276, a unit of the 347th Infantry Division, itself a bodenstandig division that had been destroyed in Normandy and the retreat to Germany but was reformed on the German frontier. The battalion was on the front line and housed in the underground West Wall shelters in an extremely muddy area. Except for the medical officer, the entire staff consisted of officers suffering from gastric diseases. The battalion commander said he had only half a stomach left, which caused him constant troubles. Having been informed of the combat tasks assigned to this battalion, the medical officer was surprised that it still functioned. Stomach Battalion 276 was engaged in position warfare, and the enemy was aware of its physical condition, sending over leaflets listing the names and diseases of the officers. The battalion commander asked for immediate relief of his unit, but no replacement was available. Ultimately, after several weeks the battalion was withdrawn to a rear position.

Conclusions

The bodenstandig concept did work well when not seriously attacked. In 1939, Hitler was able to concentrate his entire army for the Polish invasion while bodenstandig divisions held the Siegfried Line. Despite probing attacks, the French were able to take only minor pieces of territory. Then bodenstandig divisions provided an adequate covering force for the Atlantic coastline. From 1941 until June 1944, bodenstandig divisions guarded the coastline from the Spanish border to the Arctic Circle. Commando raids were repulsed with little impact on the war. The 302nd Division repulsed the

Canadian raid on Dieppe, inflicting heavy losses on the attackers for minimal losses, and it did it without substantial help from higher-quality units.

The success of the bodenstandig divisions was the result of two factors. Most of the men who had served in World War I were born between 1878 and 1900, making them between eighteen and forty-one during the war. The youngest veterans of World War I were thirty-nine in 1939, well over the ideal age for an infantryman, but these veterans had combat experience and excellent morale. They had lived through terrible economic times in the 1920s and early 1930s. Hitler had improved their economic situation and made them proud to be Germans. They were eager to serve. These older men were perfectly adequate for the mission of the bodenstandig divisions, waiting endless months for the attack that finally came in June 1944. They were serving their country in combat units with little physical stress or danger. Younger men could become impatient for more action. The lack of service elements made good sense. Rations were delivered directly to the divisions by commercial railroads. Fortifications were either already available or constructed by the RAD. Practically no ammunition was used. The divisions seldom moved, so there was no need for motorized or horse-drawn vehicles.

Once a major landing took place, it was expected that the bodenstandig divisions would perform a delaying action and quickly be replaced by infantry divisions, as was planned in Normandy in June 1944. The plan failed because Allied air power and the French underground interdicted all of the railroads leading to Normandy in the weeks following the invasion. Although the damage was repaired within a week or so, the expected reinforcements did not arrive on time, and the Allied armies were able to establish a bridgehead. Bodenstandig divisions were not able to react to the invasion; their lack of transportation meant they had to use the damaged railroads for the bulk of their equipment, while the limited-fitness men would have been less able to endure the twenty-plus miles of marching day after day.

The bodenstandig divisions could then have been rebuilt as infantry divisions, as was done by the four divisions in the Balkans earlier. However, the Replacement Army, with more than four hundred trained combat battalions, refused to release them, pending the uprising planned after Hitler was assassinated. Instead, these battalions remained in their barracks in Germany until the plot against

Hitler failed and Germany's disastrous defeats in Belarus and France. The four hundred battalions were then used to rebuild battered infantry divisions along with the remnants of the bodenstandig divisions. The bodenstandig divisions were used as cadres for new divisions, with the older men usually assuming positions in the service elements.

Sources

Daser, Wilhelm. Manuscript #B-274, *165th Infantry Division and 70th Infantry Division*. Historical Division, Headquarters, United States Army, Europe.

Dunn, Walter S., *Second Front Now, 1943*. Tuscaloosa: University of Alabama Press, 1981.

Heroes or Traitors: The German Replacement Army, the July Plot, and Adolf Hitler. Westport, Conn.: Praeger, 2003.

Mueller-Hillebrand, Burkhart. *Das Heer, 1933–1945*. 3 vols. Frankfurt am Main: E. S. Mittler and Sohn, 1959–1969.

Scharf. Manuscript #B-275, *Medical Commentary on Special Organizations Such as Stomach Battalions and Stomach Divisions*.

Tessin, George. *Verbande und Truppen der Deutschen Wehrmacht und Waffen SS in Zweiten Weltkrieg, 1939–1945*. 14 vols. Osnabruck: Biblio Verlag, 1965–1980.

World War II Standards in Allied and Enemy Armies. The Historical Unit, U.S. Army Medical Service, Forest Glen Section, Walter Reed Army Medical Center, Washington, D.C.

Editor's Note

In addition, W. Victor Madej's *German Army Order of Battle: The Replacement Army, 1939–1945* (Allentown, Penn.: Game Publishing Company, 1984) reprints U.S. Army reports and studies on German manpower and describes the Ersatz Heer.

Samuel W. Mitcham Jr., *Hitler's Legions: The German Army Order of Battle, World War II* (New York: Dorset Press, 1985), describes the "waves" of divisions and in places has information on particular bodenstandig divisions and their combat performance. "A Study of the Employment of German Manpower, 1933–1945" (alternately known as German Manpower MS) was written from German sources by a combined Canadian-British-American research team in 1945–1947; it covers many personnel topics. Copies are available at the U.S. Army Center of Military History, Washington, D.C., and the U.S. Army Military History Institute, Carlisle, Penn. Microfilm copies are available at the National Archives in College Park, Md.

German manpower, including industrial and military manpower, with consideration of the declining quality of Wehrmacht manpower and efforts to make do, is considered at length in the Militär-geschichtliches Forschungamt's magisterial *Germany and the Second World War*, English trans., vol. 5, pts. 1–2 (Oxford: Oxford University Press, 2000–2003).

9 Recruiting *Volksdeutsche* for the Waffen-SS: From Skimming the Cream to Scraping the Dregs

Valdis O. Lumans

By all appearances, Franzfeld was a small farming town somewhere in southwestern Germany. Its cobblestone town square centered on a weathered statue of a local hero of long ago, the clock outside the Rathaus chimed time as it had for some two hundred years, and the buildings around the square had the traditional German half-timbered look, painted in pastels and colorful murals. Horses and wagons from outlying farms stood hitched to watering troughs. A larger-than-normal crowd had assembled; perhaps it was a market day, or some celebration, though the muted atmosphere presaged nothing festive. Those gathered were overwhelmingly women, along with children, and only a few men, mostly elderly. They were waiting for something, apparently something unpleasant. The year was 1943, a troubling time when more and more Germans began to sense that the fate of the German *Volk* stood in a precarious balance.

A ruckus from the direction of the town's sports field hushed the murmur. The assembled turned to see marching around a corner several armed men in field-gray German military uniforms, others in partial uniforms. Behind them trudged an indistinguishable human mass, tightly squeezed in a rough circle, accompanied by more armed men, both in gray uniforms and the mixed-and-matched attire. As the procession drew closer, one could discern at least fifty forms in the pack, men of varying ages, from teenagers to the middle aged, of all shapes and sizes. Visible to the onlookers, chains and ropes bound them tightly into the ring, which the guards derisively called the *Feigenkranz*, the "coward's wreath." Hanging around some of their necks were hastily scratched signs mocking them as "the shame of Franzfeld."[1]

Obviously the captives had been roughed up, with bruised and bloodied faces. As the human bundle shuffled through the square, women wept and wailed, the more defiant of the older men in the crowd cursed and raised fists—but it was not altogether clear whether they spewed their invective at those in charge or those inside the "ring of shame." Several of the bound managed to raise their shackled hands and shouted: "This is our volunteering!" Some of the spectators, who had come to see their fathers, brothers, husbands, and sons—perhaps for the last time—lurched forward, some pleading, others menacingly. Eager to avoid confrontation, the officer in charge chose not to linger too long with this public humiliation and hurried the parade of "cowards and traitors to their *Volk* and Fatherland" to the train station.

This spectacle illustrates the metaphor of "scraping the barrel" as applied to Adolf Hitler's war effort by late 1942, when the Reich's military, starting to run critically short on manpower and sensing defeat, increasingly applied press-gang measures to meet recruitment quotas. With the help of local Nazis, recruiters had rounded up those men of Franzfeld and its environs who so far had evaded military service. They seized and shackled them, humiliated them before their families and fellow townspeople, packed them off to military training, and then assigned them to one of Germany's many battlefronts.

This scene abounds in ironies and incongruities. Although Franzfeld was a German town, it was not located in Germany but rather hundreds of miles to the southeast in a region of occupied Yugoslavia known as the Banat. The people of Franzfeld were indeed Germans, but not Reich Germans, not citizens of Germany. They were the so-called *Volksdeutsche*, or ethnic Germans, living outside the Reich as cultural Germans but citizens of non-German states—in this case, erstwhile citizens of Yugoslavia. They had, as had millions of ethnic Germans throughout Europe—particularly in Eastern Europe—preserved their ethnic German identity and heritage while living amidst a majority of non-Germans, in some instances for centuries. These Volksdeutsche of Franzfeld were called Donauschwaben: their eighteenth-century ancestors had emigrated from Swabia in southwestern Germany to the fertile farmlands of the Danube plain as wards of the Habsburgs, who were colonizing Germans in lands reconquered from the Turks.

Another oddity at Franzfeld was the branch of the German soldiers leading the press gang. As their collar emblems indicated, the men in gray belonged to the Waffen-SS, the segment of the German military that by 1942 had become its elite fighting force and prided itself on its "voluntary" nature.[2] Originating in 1933 as the "armed SS," these militarized units of the Nazi Schutzstaffel SS officially became the Waffen-SS in 1940—though in the interest of simplicity, "Waffen-SS" will also refer to the armed SS in its earlier stages. Not only does this episode in Franzfeld parody the notion of voluntarism—which the Waffen-SS proudly but deceptively claimed to the very end of the war—but one could reasonably conclude that treating recruits in this manner would hardly net soldiers with the morale and the physical attributes required for an elite military force. Few if any metaphors are as apropos for describing what transpired in Franzfeld as "scraping the barrel." Scholars, including the historian George H. Stein, an expert on the Waffen-SS, have characterized the procurement of German manpower in World War II in precisely these terms.[3] As Germany's military fortunes declined from 1942 onward, the SS "scraped" for recruits throughout Eastern Europe, not only in the Banat. A Slovak witnessing a similar sight remarked: "Hitler has lost his mind to make these 15 to 16 year old boys report for military service! . . . Germany must be pretty bad off to have to draft its soldiers from Slovakia."[4]

Once the forced inductions began, even the chief Waffen-SS recruiter Gottlob Berger confessed that this pool of ethnic German manpower, though numerous, lacked in bodily and moral quality. Often physically deficient, short on education, and with inadequate use of the German language, Volksdeutsche recruits allegedly brought down the overall quality of the SS and evoked contempt from Reich comrades as being cowardly and untrustworthy. An incorrigible critic was Theodore Eicke, commander of the elite SS Division *Totenkopf*, who by late 1941 complained about the shortcomings of his Volksdeutsche replacements: These recruits were "undernourished and less suited for physical strain" as well as "spiritually weak." They tended to be "disobedient and evasive," often excusing themselves from difficult assignments by claiming a poor grasp of German. Eicke disdained these "undisciplined and dishonest scoundrels and criminals."[5]

The Volksdeutsche nonetheless had their advocates. Felix Steiner, commander of the elite 5th SS Panzer Division *Wiking*, praised a young officer from the Italian South Tyrol for leading a breakthrough of Russian lines.[6] Another *Wiking* officer observed how a farmer's son from Romania, even though his German was not too good, always accepted the most demanding tasks, such as carrying ammunition. Regrettably, as he was lifting some ammo cases, he was shot in the head and killed.[7] Since these few anecdotal examples challenge the premise that "scraping the barrel" resulted only in inferior soldiers, the recruiting process that sent off virtual prisoners in manacles to fight as "volunteers" in the Waffen-SS warrants closer scrutiny. Were they indeed mostly "dregs," or did the bottom of the barrel yield enough "gems," such as the ammo carrier from Romania, to challenge the standard image?

The essential issue this prologue raises is whether the "scraping" process had an effect on the reputation and the combat effectiveness of the Waffen-SS, the branch of the Reich's armed forces ranking first in the esteem of Adolf Hitler himself.[8] After all, could "barrel scraping" meet the high standards espoused in the Waffen-SS myth and justify the Führer's confidence? Did a causal link exist between the recruitment of ethnic Germans (both nature and results) and Waffen-SS combat performance? Scrutinizing the recruitment of Volksdeutsche cannot resolve this issue conclusively, but it should help in understanding relevant wartime circumstances, thus enabling those interested to arrive at more enlightened appraisals of their own.

The Volksdeutsche

The two main protagonists of this study are the Volksdeutsche, or ethnic Germans, the commodity to be scraped from the metaphorical barrel, and the Waffen-SS, the elite German military branch doing the dredging. At least numerically, the prospects of utilizing Volksdeutsche as soldiers boded well. As a consequence of World War I, in 1935 an estimated ninety-five million Germans lived throughout the world, most residing in predominantly German states; the new German Republic, shorn of territory and population, still contained some sixty-five million Reich Germans. Several neighboring states also possessed German majorities, including the reconstituted Austria, a fellow loser in the war, which accounted for 6.5 million; Switzerland, 2,950,000; Danzig, 400,000; Luxemburg, 285,000; and Liechtenstein, 10,000.[9] Although the Germans living in these states comprised ethnic majorities, the fact that they were not Reich citizens designated them Volksdeutsche. Approximately ten million more Volksdeutsche resided as national minorities in European states ruled by non-German majorities. These included the 3,318,500 Germans of Czechoslovakia; Poland, 1,190,000; Alsace-Lorraine (France), 1,500,000; Belgium, 70,000; Lithuania-Memelland, 100,000; Denmark, 30,000; Italy, over 200,000; Yugoslavia, 700,000; Hungary, 500,000; Romania, 750,000; Latvia, 60,000; Estonia, 20,000; and the Soviet Union, 1,240,000. Thousands more lived scattered across the globe as Übersee Germans.[10]

The most telling distinction differentiating specific minorities, or Volksgruppen, was their historic relationship to either the Reich or pre–World War I Habsburg Austria. Although after 1933 Hitler and the Third Reich claimed the allegiances of all Germans everywhere, Volksdeutsche residing in territories that had belonged to Imperial Germany attracted the most attention: the Memelland in Lithuania; Hültschinerland of Czechoslovakia; Danzig; West Prussia, Pomerania, and parts of East Prussia and Silesia of Poland; North Schleswig in Denmark; Eupen-Malmedy in Belgium; and Alsace-Lorraine in France. The erstwhile Habsburg subjects of Austria-Hungary stood nearly equal with former Reich Germans. These included the Sudeten Germans of Bohemia and Moravia and the Karpathen Germans of Slovakia; the Donauschwaben of the Hungarian plain, divided among postwar Hungary, Romania, and Yugoslavia; the Transylvania Sachsen, split between Hungary and Romania; the South Tyroleans of Italy; Austrians living in parts of Carinthia, Carniola, and Styria in Yugoslavia; and the Germans of Croatia and Bosnia-Herzegovina, also attached to Yugoslavia. Postwar Poland received Austrian Galicia, and Romania took Austrian Bukovina, both with local German communities. Several Volksgruppen had never belonged to a German state, including those living in the non-Habsburg Balkans, formerly Russian parts of Poland, the Baltic States, Bessarabia in Romania, and the Soviet Union. Although initially many ethnic Germans accepted their post–World War I minority status, others found fulfilling responsibilities to non-German regimes onerous and in their personal priorities ranked their "Germanness" ahead of their duties as citizens of their states—particularly so after Hitler came to power in 1933.[11]

Prewar Volunteers and the Waffen-SS

With the advent of Hitler, even more Volksdeutsche readjusted their loyalties toward the Reich. One crucial issue of allegiance was military service: whether to serve in the ranks of their non-German nation or in those of the Third Reich. The branch most interested in their service was the Waffen-SS, which, beginning in 1933 expanded its military role, much to the discomfiture of the Wehrmacht, Germany's official armed forces. With the reintroduction of a universal obligation in 1935, one of the most contentious issues became whether or not service in the Waffen-SS satisfied the Reich military obligation, which the Wehrmacht adamantly refused to recognize. Step by step, nonetheless, the SS succeeded in legitimizing service in these armed SS units. Himmler may have won the dispute, but the Wehrmacht still obstructed his access to the Reich's manpower pool. Given the ambiguous status of the armed SS—a Nazi Party organization performing state service—and its annoyance with an impertinent upstart, the Wehrmacht denied the SS the right to draft Reich citizens. Indeed, it would only permit the SS to recruit volunteers and restricted those to 10 percent of draft-eligible Reich German men annually. Undeterred, Himmler envisioned greater things for his Waffen-SS, but not until the outbreak of war in 1939 could he take his ambitions further. This is when the Volksdeutsche came up for serious consideration as SS manpower.

The paths of the Volksdeutsche and the armed SS had converged earlier, however, when in the mid-1930s Himmler tendered his claim as the chief Reich authority in racial matters, including the affairs of all Volksdeutsche. His efforts culminated in early 1937 with the appointment of a trusted SS officer, Werner Lorenz, as head of the Volksdeutsche Mittelstelle (Ethnic German Liaison Office, VoMi), the Nazi Party center Hitler created to coordinate all Reich and Party involvement with the Volksdeutsche. Lorenz soon centralized all related activities under his authority, and, by manipulating the political strings attached to Reich monies destined for the minorities, guided them in the interest of Reich policy.[12] As VoMi "nazified" the ethnic Germans, it prepared them to do Hitler's wartime bidding, including providing soldiers for the Waffen-SS.

Prior to the war, some Volksdeutsche had already found their way to the Waffen-SS, exclusively as volunteers. A few youths from abroad envisioned an exciting rejuvenation in Hitler's new Germany and enthusiastically (but illegally) fled to the Reich to sign up with its armed forces. However, the Wehrmacht (both before and after the 1935 military legislation providing for German rearmament and a concomitant universal Reich military obligation) strictly limited military service to Reich citizens. Himmler and others in the SS saw things differently and welcomed these young, foreign zealots. The SS perceived in them a potential treasure trove of racially and ethnically acceptable manpower—and without the restrictive Reich citizenship. Inside the Reich, the SS could sign up as many non-Reich citizens as it pleased, and abroad it was limited only by the vigilance of foreign authorities. Recruiting foreign citizens would have to remain surreptitious, since such activities violated state sovereignty and affronted national sensitivities. Brushing aside the Wehrmacht's legal compunctions, the SS began to enlist racially and physically qualified Volksdeutsche volunteers. Once the practice began, the Waffen-SS appetite grew insatiable.

Prewar Volksdeutsche volunteers often arrived as runaways, deserters from other armies, or as political fugitives whose pro-German or pro-Nazi activities had provoked their governments. One common SS ploy was to arrange for seemingly innocuous athletic training or advertise education or employment opportunities in the Reich, and only after the Volksdeutsche arrived did they realize the true purpose. Once inside the Reich and exposed to inducements and under duress, some of the visitors "volunteered" for the SS. Willing recruits, however, knew from the start the reason for their Reich journey and found an accomplice in the VoMi.[13] Once enlisted, little distinguished these early Volksdeutsche recruits from their Reich comrades, since at this point the SS applied the same stringent requirements to all its recruits, both domestic and imported.

Several prewar events improved the SS's chances to enlist men from abroad. One such incident was the failed Austrian Nazi coup of July 1934, which prompted a flight of Austrian Nazis to Germany. Refugee camps housing these fugitives became prime SS recruiting grounds.[14] Four years later, the Austrian Anschluss of March 1938 spurred further SS growth, though the annexation was a mixed blessing. Since the Reich bestowed citizenship on all racially qualified Austrians, the Wehrmacht's restrictions on the SS recruiting citizens henceforth applied to Austrians. Only partly stymied, the Waffen-SS continued to accept Austrian volunteers, whose response was so enthusiastic Himmler created a new, mostly Austrian SS Verfügungstruppe regiment named *Das Führer*. In the coming war years, Austrians constituted a disproportionately high ratio of Waffen-SS soldiers.[15] The prominent SS wartime hero Otto Skorzeny, who became the Reich's commando par excellence and the famed rescuer of Mussolini, was one such Austrian volunteer.[16]

Another fortuitous development for the Waffen-SS came with the Sudetenland dispute in 1938 and the final dismantlement of

Czechoslovakia as a state in March 1939. Volksdeutsche were multi-ethnic Czechoslovakia's second largest nationality, divided in two distinct groups: the more than three million Sudeten Germans of Bohemia and Moravia and the 130,000 Carpathian (Karpathen) Germans of Slovakia.[17] Prior to 1938, a small but steady stream of Sudeten German activists had crossed into Germany and joined the SS, including Fritz von Scholz of Pilsen. He had served in the prewar Habsburg army, fled to Germany, signed with the SS in 1935, and ultimately commanded several elite Waffen-SS regiments and a division.[18] Although the Germans of the annexed Sudetenland and the occupied Protectorate of Bohemia-Moravia received Reich citizenship and came under the induction authority of the Wehrmacht, many still volunteered for the SS. As enlistments climbed, the SS dispersed this latest wave of recruits across extant SS units.[19]

The situation in Slovakia was different. In the fall of 1938, disgruntled Slovak nationalists had negotiated autonomy with the Czechs in Prague, and in March 1939, while the Reich subjugated Bohemia and Moravia, they arranged for national independence under the auspices of the Reich. Though nominally sovereign, Slovakia became Hitler's first Axis client state. Thanks to the Reich's preponderant influence, Slovakia's Karpathen Germans, 4 percent of a population of 3,284,000, formed an autonomous state within a state. Since they remained citizens of Slovakia, the Wehrmacht had no military jurisdiction over them, but the Waffen-SS immediately began to meddle and assert its influence.[20]

An extension of SS influence was the ET-Sturmbann, a Carpathian German paramilitary force with ties to the Waffen-SS. Even before the destruction of Czechoslovakia, it had secretly supplied the SS with recruits. The Slovaks demonstrated their commitment to Germany by granting generous military concessions to their Germans, including sanctioning service with the ET-Sturmbann—but not with the Waffen-SS—as fulfilling their military duty. Slovakia also offered its Karpathen citizens the option of performing their duty in exclusively German units in the Slovak army. Although young Germans could choose either the army or the ET-Sturmbann, they felt considerable pressure from the German community and even their own families to enlist with the SS. Shortly afterward, Bratislava added the option to enlist directly into the Reich's armed forces, specifically the Waffen-SS. The response, however, was disappointing, and by January 1940 only 109 recruits had been examined; the SS deemed only fifty-eight as qualified. By the end of 1941, only six hundred Karpathen Germans had volunteered for the Waffen-SS.[21]

One reason for the poor SS harvest of Carpathian Germans was Slovak generosity and being able to serve alongside friends and neighbors. Unlike most non-German states in the region, Slovakia assigned its Germans to ethnically exclusive units. For instance, an entire Volksdeutsche battalion of the Slovak army joined in the September 1939 invasion of Poland.[22] These units even had German officers, altogether some thirty serving in the Slovak army, including Col. Rudolf Pilfousek, who commanded one of two Slovak divisions in the invasion of the Soviet Union. Pilfousek served Slovakia until August 1944, when its army rebelled against the German "allies"—only then did he switch to the SS.[23]

Early Wartime Waffen-SS Recruitment: 1939–1941

The Waffen-SS joined Germany's attack on Poland on September 1, 1939. Its original units, both the elite Verfügungstruppe and the TK-Verbänden of concentration camp personnel, received their "baptism under fire." Both initially consisted of volunteers, but on the eve of the invasion the SS abandoned the principle of pure voluntarism for the duration of the war. For one, as the TK-Verbänden went off to war, Himmler reorganized the remaining concentration camp guards into TK-Standarten, which were to assume domestic police duties, but as the war dragged on he designated them armed SS formations as well—essentially an involuntary induction.[24] The men of the TK-Standarten, in units or individually, were transferred to the TK-Verbänden, which after the conquest of Poland became the SS *Totenkopf* Division.[25] The elitism of the Waffen-SS, based on voluntarism and selectivity, had begun its downward slide.

Along with these new TK formations, Himmler introduced another type of Waffen-SS formation, the armed police. By 1939, he had mixed the police and other Reich security agencies with the SS, and just prior to the attack on Poland he armed policemen from across the Reich and grouped them in military-like SS units—tantamount to another a mass induction. Thus many of the Reich's police and KZ guards—already paid servants of the state, and with their units designated armed SS and sent into combat—in essence had been drafted, thereby discarding elite voluntarism except as a fictitious propaganda ruse. Though one's volition henceforth counted for little, volunteers still signed up, such as the Baltic German Harry

Phönix of Latvia, who was on a sports junket in Berlin when the war broke out and on a whim joined the SS regiment *Das Reich*.[26]

Just as Austria and Czechoslovakia had produced some prewar Volksdeutsche volunteers for the SS, so had Poland. And just as Austrians and most Sudeten Germans had received Reich citizenship after annexation and occupation, so did the 1,250,000 Germans of conquered Poland. The Reich incorporated former Imperial German lands and granted their ethnic Germans Reich citizenship. It also bestowed citizenship on those residing in central Poland, which the Reich occupied under the ambiguous moniker of "the General Government," which was similar to the Protectorate in status. These new Reich citizens became subject to induction, but they could opt to enlist with the Waffen-SS.

Following the Polish campaign, a diplomatic turn offered the SS a further opportunity for growth and access to Volksdeutsche as soldiers. In early October, Hitler publicly declared that Poland was the last of his territorial demands and hence Germany would seek only peace. In that spirit, he announced the resettlement of Volksdeutsche from across Eastern Europe to the Reich and its occupied territories—thereby reducing potential for strife with neighbors. But general peace was not Hitler's goal. Instead, he schemed to preempt pitfalls in his alliance with Stalin by evacuating Volksdeutsche from lands he allotted to the Soviets in secret agreements of August and September 1939—Latvia, Estonia, and Lithuania, the Volhynia and Galicia regions of eastern Poland, and the Romanian provinces of Bessarabia and Bukovina. Since it was just a matter of time before Stalin claimed these territories, Hitler sought to preserve his Soviet alliance by getting these Germans out of his partner's way. This operation added an unexpected bonus for the SS—access to a half-million ethnic German evacuees.[27]

Himmler soon persuaded the Führer to grant him command over the resettlement, adding the title Reichskommissar für die Festigung Deutsches Volkskstums (RKFDV, Reich Commissioner for the Strengthening of Germandom). As RKFDV, Himmler and the SS assumed full authority over this project.[28] The SS office in charge of the evacuation aspect was VoMi. VoMi dispatched SS commandos abroad, registered eligible and willing Volksdeutsche and their property, organized their transportation, and then cared for the evacuees along the way. Back in the Reich and conquered Poland, VoMi constructed "resettler camps" where the SS processed the new arrivals and ascertained their "Germanness" family by family.[29]

SS control at every stage offered the Waffen-SS the pick of young Volksdeutsche. Although resettlers received Reich citizenship and became eligible for the Wehrmacht draft, the SS first selected the choicest recruits.[30] Since many spent months, even years, confined in VoMi camps waiting for a final placement, the SS frustrated Wehrmacht efforts to reach them. The earliest resettlements, in the fall of 1939, brought 61,858 Baltic Germans from Latvia and Estonia "home to the Reich." The Volhyinia, Galicia, and the Narew actions from Soviet eastern Poland in early 1940 exposed 134,950 more resettlers to SS recruiters, and the Bessarabia and Bukovina operations from Romania added another 137,116. Subsequent resettlements from the Baltic and parts of the Balkans netted 139,293 more.[31]

The military occupation of Scandinavia and victories in the West in the spring and summer of 1940 opened yet another source of recruits. As in earlier instances, the Germans of Alsace-Lorraine, Luxemburg, and Eupen-Malmedy in Belgium received Reich citizenship and draft eligibility; they also gained the "privilege" of volunteering for the Waffen-SS.[32] Since the defeated states retained their identities under German occupation and their residents kept their citizenships, the latter were off limits to Wehrmacht induction. But in the west, Himmler, not burdened with racial reservations as in the Slav-dominated east and lacking the Wehrmacht's legalistic scruples, eagerly exploited the ethnic German as well as racially acceptable non-German manpower—above all Scandinavians, whom Nazis regarded as the font of Nordic, Germanic racial purity. The Germanic Dutch and the Flemings of Belgium racially ranked close behind. Racially inspired SS ideologues, led by Himmler, and pragmatists such as Chief Recruiter Gottlob Berger perceived in these "racially kindred" peoples a treasure trove of potential SS soldiers.

A handful of Germanics had found their way into the Waffen-SS earlier, but with the invasion of Denmark in April several hundred Danish volunteers (along with some of their Volksdeutsche neighbors from North Schleswig, the southernmost Danish borderland) entered the ranks of the SS.[33] In late April, the SS established SS Regiment *Nordland*, the first formation designated for Germanic volunteers, to entice even more Scandinavian volunteers. Far fewer showed up than expected, forcing the SS to augment "exclusively" Germanic formations with Reich Germans and Volksdeutsche, setting a precedent for the rest of the war. One early supplement for *Nordland* included some four hundred Baltic Germans.[34] As the dust of battle settled in the Low Countries and France, SS Regiment *Westland* was established to lure Dutch, Flemish, and even Walloon volunteers.[35] Then in December 1940, the SS assembled its first "Germanic" division, SS *Germania*, by combining the regiments *Nordland* and *Westland* and transferring the all-German regiment *Germania* from the SS Verfügungstruppe Division—which changed its name to *Deutschland*, then to *Reich*, and finally to *Das Reich*.[36]

The commander of the *Germania* regiment, Felix Steiner, took over the new creation and, so as not to confuse the *Germania* regiment and the division then also named *Germania*, the SS renamed the Germanic division *Wiking*—eventually assuming the title 5th SS Panzer Division *Wiking*, the fifth of the "classic" Waffen-SS divisions. Although *Wiking* retained the reputation of being a Germanic division, Germans, including numbers of Volksdeutsche, constituted the ethnic majority.[37] On the eve of Operation Barbarossa in June 1941, of the 19,000 men assigned to *Wiking*, only 1,500 were Germanic volunteers; the rest were Reich Germans or Volksdeutsche.[38] The most illustrious was the aforementioned Fritz von Scholz, the Bohemian commander of *Nordland* and a recipient of the Reich's highest decoration, the Knight's Cross of the Iron Cross.[39]

Going into the crucial year of 1941, the numbers of Volksdeutsche in the Waffen-SS grew, usually assigned as replacements to the classic divisions. Most had volunteered as recently nationalized Reich citizens, but a trickle continued to enlist from abroad, including Karl Nicolussi-Leck—a South Tyrolean who quit his studies at the University of Padua and volunteered for the Waffen-SS, ending up with SS Division *Wiking*.[40] Berger, however, still chafed at being limited to volunteers from Reich Germans and available Volksdeutsche inside the Reich. He therefore broached recruiting from the largest reserve of German manpower left in Europe, the Volksdeutsche of Romania, Yugoslavia, and Hungary. Fortuitously for him, the fortunes of war had shifted decidedly in the Reich's favor in 1940, and the states of southeastern Europe preferred to flow with the current of German success rather than resist. Their dependency on the Reich deepened, in turn opening access to the two million Volksdeutsche of the region. The SS drooled at the prospects.

Recruitment in the Southeast: 1941–1943

Given Germany's escalating needs in 1941, the handfuls of surreptitious Balkan volunteers would be inadequate to replenish anticipated losses, and Berger concluded that only diplomatically approved campaigns could net the needed recruits. Two developments in 1940 had opened up access to Balkan Volksdeutsche: one affected Romania, the other Romania and Hungary together. After World War I, Romania had expanded its territory, thereby adding over seven hundred thousand new Volksdeutsche citizens. In 1940, this much-enlarged national minority had come under the leadership of Andreas Schmidt, a Transylvanian Saxon and Gottlob Berger's son-in-law.[41] Schmidt, an ardent SS officer, placed Volksdeutsche interests behind those of the SS, which he interpreted as those of his father-in-law Berger and the Waffen-SS. Schmidt played a shadowy role in the so-called thousand-man operation of 1940, when Reich diplomats wrangled the release of one thousand young Volksdeutsche from Romania for work in the Reich—where the Waffen-SS "employed" them by training and dispersing them across its ranks.[42]

An even more critical point in the evolving relationship between Romania and Germany came later, in June 1940, when Stalin demanded that the Romanians cede Bessarabia, which Hitler had secretly promised Stalin in their August 1939 pact. After consulting Hitler, Romanian statesmen surrendered the territory in question, but Hungary and Bulgaria tendered claims as well. Hitler counseled Romania to accommodate them too, and the Vienna Award of August 30 surrendered lands to Hungary and Bulgaria. Consequently, Hungary and Romania, though at bitter odds with each other, assumed close bilateral relations with Germany and recognized its special relationship with their respective German minorities. With an enhanced Reich presence in both states, their regimes were more willing to overlook questionable SS practices, and the numbers of illegal recruits climbed. Although prospects for enhanced recruitment looked promising in Romania and Hungary, the same was not true in neighboring Yugoslavia, where the vigilance of the Belgrade authorities prevented enlisting their Volksdeutsche.

Yugoslavia, consisting of pre–World War I Serbia and Montenegro and lands formerly belonging to the defunct Habsburg Empire of Austria-Hungary, was the quintessential multiethnic state, home not only to Serbs, Croats, and Slovenes but other national groups as well, including over seven hundred thousand ethnic Germans. Hitler had courted Yugoslavia as a cog in a German-dominated southeastern Europe, and his efforts bore fruit in late March 1941, when Yugoslavia joined the Axis. But the alliance was short lived, with a military coup overthrowing the Belgrade government. The plotters professed loyalty to the Axis but tilted Yugoslavia toward the West. A furious Hitler ordered an impromptu invasion, adding this objective to an attack on Greece that bailed out his militarily inept ally, Mussolini. The operation, launched on April 6, included two Waffen-SS units, the Leibstandarte SS *Adolf Hitler* (LSSAH) and SS Division *Das Reich*, which attacked the Vojvodina from the Romanian Banat, regions having substantial ethnic German populations.[43]

Yugoslavia's military resistance quickly collapsed, and the government sued for an armistice on April 17. Young Volksdeutsche that had either gone into hiding to avoid mobilization or had deserted from the Yugoslav army surfaced to join invading Wehrmacht and Waffen-SS columns.[44] *Das Reich* was the prime beneficiary of this enthusiasm, gathering hundreds of Yugoslav Volksdeutsche. On its return route through the Romanian Banat, *Das Reich* smuggled out some six hundred young Romanian Volksdeutsche as well.[45] With the subsequent breakup of Yugoslavia, the Reich annexed the northern parts of (formerly Austrian) Slovenia, bestowing Reich citizenship on its Germans. It then imposed military rule over Serbia, and for strategic purposes also over a piece of Bosnia and a large part of the Banat (Vojvodina) adjacent to Belgrade. The occupation regime for Serbia-Banat functioned not unlike Reich military rule in the Protectorate and the General Government. In Croatia, however, the ultranationalistic Ustasha declared independence, recognized by both the Germans and Italians. Croatia, henceforth an Axis ally, became a puppet state of the Third Reich, and as a reward received much of Bosnia. Italy seized parts of Slovenia, the Dalmatian islands, a strip of the Adriatic coast, and occupied Montenegro. Another accomplice, Hungary, claimed the western Vojvodina, thereby restoring some of its pre–World War I territories—including the town of Franzfeld. Even Bulgaria took a bite, Serbian Macedonia.

The breakup of Yugoslavia partitioned its German minority. Although the Germans of Serbia and the Banat welcomed freedom from non-German rule, they soon discovered that satisfying the Reich outweighed the benefits. The Reich and the SS could do with them as they pleased, and many ended up as the nucleus of the soon-to-be-created 7th SS Gebirgs Division *Prinz Eugen*. Germans living in the parts of the Vojvodina ceded to Hungary disappointedly joined its extant German minority. Hoping for territorial autonomy, they came instead under a regime in Budapest that jealously clutched

every bit of its sovereignty.[46] As for "independent" Croatia, it surrendered much of its authority over its German subjects with little
fuss, but since it was also in the Reich's interest to preserve a modi-
cum of this client's sovereignty, getting what it wanted from Croatia
usually meant "asking" permission. Its ethnic Germans remained a
national minority but a privileged one, a virtual German state within
the Croatian state.

Imposing a Military Obligation: 1941–1943

Though the SS officially referred to enlistments in the southeast as
"voluntary," under the occupation the process became tantamount
to a draft, through propaganda, intimidation, and even outright
police coercion. Over the next few years, "voluntarism" became no
more than a misleading euphemism to assuage the national sensitivities of allied governments and to bolster the esprit de corps of
the Waffen-SS. A corollary to the issue of voluntarism in the southeast was a military obligation. Were Volksdeutsche obligated to
"volunteer"? Chief recruiter Berger boasted that if a Volkgruppe was
properly led, then its Volksdeutsche "would report voluntarily."[47]
Occupied Serbia-Banat and "independent" Croatia were the first to
have Reich military obligations imposed. As early as 1941 the SS had
set up recruitment centers in Serbia-Banat to handle the flood of
enthusiastic young Volksdeutsche. But the initial luster dimmed
later that year, and the Waffen-SS initiated the southeast's first
major recruitment drive in 1942, pronouncing a *völkisch* obligation
for ethnic Germans in indisputably binding terms. Step by step,
with one minority group and then another, "voluntary" enlistment
with the Waffen-SS became mandatory.[48]

Unlike the Wehrmacht, SS leaders had no qualms interpreting
the Military Law of May 21, 1935, to include the Volksdeutsche among
those obligated. Construing the law as applying to all Germans,
even though it failed to mention the Volksdeutsche and explicitly
applied the term *Deutscher* to a Reich citizen, in early March 1942
Himmler ordered the Germans of Serbia-Banat to enlist with the
Waffen-SS, instructing men aged seventeen to forty-five to report
to their local minority officials. He deceptively informed minority
leaders that a military obligation did exist—presumably sanctioned by
the Führer—but for diplomatic reasons he could not broach the issue
publicly.[49] The outspoken minority leader Sepp Janko brashly protested, but an unsympathetic Himmler ordered VoMi chief Werner

Lorenz to Serbia to take Janko "by the tie" and impress on him the Reichsführer's displeasure. A chastised Janko obediently decreed an induction for the duration of the war, which no "healthy man" could avoid.[50] Behind the pretense of voluntarism, the SS began drafting Balkan recruits.

Thus the scraping of the Balkan Volksdeutsche barrel commenced. Into 1942, local minority officials delivered induction notices to eligible ethnic Germans, warning that failure to comply would be punished severely. As sentiments turned against the mandatory enlistments, SS dispatches from the Banat reported growing resistance. One German who dared speak out against the induction was beaten severely. In Belkerek, the SS security service, the SD, built a detention camp for Volksdeutsche refusing to heed the call.[51] A confident Berger blustered: "The SS could do with the *Volksdeutsche* as it pleased."[52] The majority of those passing muster in the occupied territories went directly to *Prinz Eugen* as its first "volunteers."

The first foreign regime the SS approached regarding a military obligation was Croatia's. Its independence was flimsy, but the Reich still had to negotiate over the status of its Volksdeutsche. Since Croatian sovereignty, like Slovakian, rested upon the goodwill of the Reich, Zagreb conceded generous terms. The Croats designated special ethnic German units within their armed forces and granted the local German paramilitary organization the "privilege" of joining the Ustasha. The two Axis partners formalized the specifics of their arrangement in a treaty in September. A crucial provision allowed 10 percent of each annual levy of Volksdeutsche to volunteer with either the Wehrmacht or the Waffen-SS, with service satisfying the Croatian military obligation.[53] A Reich Foreign Ministry memo used the term *verpflichtet*, or "obligated," in reference to volunteering for service. The individual, however, would be spared the trouble of volunteering; the minority leadership's collective declaration on behalf of all ethnic Germans was binding. The generosity of the Croats and the ruthless determination of the SS to reach its "voluntary" enlistment goals made Reich military service for the Volksdeutsche of Croatia compulsory in fact, if not yet in law.[54] By late 1941, the SS had enlisted numerous Croatian Volksdeutsche, many ending up as replacements in Russia.

Going into 1942, Berger was still dissatisfied, begrudging the option of service in the Croatian army. He equally, if not more, resented their service in the Wehrmacht—which the Croats also allowed.

Above all, Berger smarted at the Wehrmacht training and providing cadres for the Croatian army's Volksdeutsche units.

Anxious about further infringements on his authority, Himmler schemed to exclude the Wehrmacht entirely from the military affairs of these ethnic Germans. His efforts paid off in May 1942, when the Führer decided in his favor, ordering the OKW (Oberkommando der Wehrmacht) to stop its involvement with Croatian Volksdeutsche—but even more importantly for all of southeastern Europe.[55] With the Wehrmacht no longer an interloper, the SS asserted total control over Croatia's Volksdeutsche.

By mid-summer 1942, many of Croatia's previously enthusiastic Volksdeutsche had soured on the SS and its recruitment methods. Dissatisfied with fewer volunteers and facing growing replacement needs, Berger and Himmler, with the intervention of the Reich Foreign Ministry, demanded the Croats transfer en masse the German units serving in the Croat army to *Prinz Eugen*. The Croats balked at such a transfer but offered to place all Germans not yet in uniform at the disposal of the SS. Berger, ignoring Croat wishes, continued to recruit and enlist any and all Volksdeutsche, even those in the Croat military. Resignedly yielding to the Reich's badgering, Zagreb conceded that its Volksdeutsche would henceforth fulfill their military duty in the Waffen-SS. Although nominally still "voluntary," the SS had replaced an individual declaration of volunteering with a collective declaration. The process became an overt induction, with summons reaching the "volunteer" both in writing and by public announcements, including a medieval-like drummer summoning recruits in the village of Neu Pasua to report.[56] Volksgruppenführer Branimir Altgayer, probably aware of Janko's scolding, threatened those who did not report with the severest consequences, including declaring them deserters.[57] Altgayer and local SS authorities applied intimidation, physical abuse, and even the trashing of homes and the like to enforce individual compliance. Whole groups of mustered men, mostly ignorant farmers under orders from both SS and local minority officials, accepted their collective enlistment without fully understanding the consequences.[58] By mid-November 1942, the SS had inducted some four thousand Volksdeutsche from Croatia, but it craved even more, especially after Stalingrad.[59]

With a Reich military obligation for Volksdeutsche securely in place in Serbia-Banat and an almost finalized one in Croatia, Berger extended his plans. Although Reich diplomats dithered over pressuring the states in question (regarding this as yet another infringement on their fragile sovereignty), Himmler scoffed at their caution and insisted that the entire *Volk* shared in a *völkisch* military obligation. When several minority leaders still objected, Himmler submitted the issue to the SS legal office for clarification. As could be expected, SS jurists decided in his favor, arguing that a military obligation indeed existed, but because of potential diplomatic repercussions, it could not be formally declared. In early August 1942, Himmler informed all minority leaders that a *völkisch* military obligation toward the Reich was in effect and had to be performed in the Waffen-SS. As a sop to the sensitivities of the host governments and to appease the Foreign Ministry, these operations nominally would remain "voluntary." This confidential order set the stage for recruitment campaigns across the Balkans.[60]

The declaration of mandatory military service for the Germans of former Yugoslavia resonated in neighboring Hungary and Romania. Excited by the German presence just across their border, draft-age ethnic Germans as well as German deserters from the Romanian army surreptitiously crossed the frontier to enlist. These defections only hardened the Romanians against German requests to allow Romanian Volksdeutsche to enlist with the Reich military. Even before the invasion of Yugoslavia the Reich had found Marshal Antonescu evasive when confronted with a second "thousand-man" recruiting operation.[61] With the Romanians still brooding over the territorial losses in the Vienna agreements, Reich diplomats advised the SS to back off, sensing the timing was wrong for further concessions. What mattered most in 1942 was Romania's continued military involvement in Russia, and Reich diplomats feared alienating the Romanians over the Volksdeutsche issue. As a result, the first major SS recruitment campaign in the summer of 1942 bypassed Romania.[62]

Hungarian attitudes were more flexible. After all, their association with the Reich had brought them territorial additions, mostly at the expense of Romania. Further, in the dismemberment of Yugoslavia, Hungary had gained large numbers of Volksdeutsche from the Vojvodina. On the one hand, the Magyars felt obligated to demonstrate good treatment of their Germans and to acknowledge the special relationship between these Germans and the Reich, but on the other hand the Volksdeutsche of the new territories were flocking to the SS by the hundreds, and by late 1941 the Magyars were losing patience. Bowing to diplomatic pressure, Himmler suspended further recruitment in Hungary, but as the SS launched its campaign for 1942, it was evident that access to the Volksdeutsche of Hungary was critical.[63]

In January 1942, Reich diplomats brazenly demanded the Hungarians surrender to the Reich some twenty thousand Volksdeutsche. Budapest emphatically refused, though agreeing to a voluntary enlistment through the Honved, the Hungarian army. In February, the two Axis partners signed an agreement whereby Hungarian ethnic Germans could opt for the Waffen-SS. Consequently, Hungarian Volksdeutsche, mostly from former Yugoslav areas, along with thousands from Serbia-Banat and Croatia, constituted the bulk of the first major SS recruitment in the region.[64] Most Germans from Hungary ended up at the eastern front as replacements, though with the start of Waffen-SS expansion, many were assigned to new formations, particularly the SS Kavallerie Division. As it evolved into the 8th SS Kavallerie Division *Florian Geyer*, Hungarian Volksdeutsche eventually constituted an ethnic majority.

Reports and eyewitness accounts from Hungary relate the same SS ruthlessness in recruitment as elsewhere. As early as the fall of 1941, Germans living in the Hungarian Banat had been summoned to report to the authorities, where they were first told that they belonged to the SS. After six weeks of training in the German-occupied Banat, they took the SS oath. In one instance, the officer in charge, playing a charade of voluntarism, asked anyone who could not take the oath to raise his hand. About sixty did, but each one had to give an excuse, and as he did, the officer rejected it; every recruit signed the oath. Most did not want to sign but were berated until they did.[65] Since the minority leadership was entrusted with the induction, those who did not report were kicked out of the German community and were no longer recognized as Germans. Though the act of reporting supposedly was voluntary, only the bravest dared stay home.[66]

Slovakia's Karpathen Germans also contributed to the 1942 campaign. The Reich expected no problems from this quarter, since Bratislava already allowed Volksdeutsche preferring to serve with the Waffen-SS to do so. But what the SS had in mind exceeded recruitment from the civilian population. Not only did Berger covetously eye the large numbers of Germans still serving in the Slovak army as prospective SS men, but he also sought approval for service in the Waffen-SS as satisfying the Slovak military obligation. The Slovaks yielded on both counts in September, and by the end of

1942 Slovakia no longer enjoyed military authority over its German population: these Volksdeutsche had no option but to join the SS— a de facto Reich military obligation if not entirely de jure.[67]

Implementing a mandatory military obligation under the ruse of "voluntarism" was no easy matter.[68] The SS itself characterized the 1942 action in this way: "This entire operation stimulated considerable unrest within the ethnic group, since for now a number of ethnic Germans do not seem inclined to heed this call for mandatory volunteering."[69] Another dispatch noted, "It is not surprising that as a result of incidents like this, that nightly demonstrations occurred, in which the windows of the minority's *Deutsche Partei* office were shattered. On the other hand, depending on the political composition of the communities, terror was visited upon those who refused to volunteer as well as their families."[70]

Whereas the Volksdeutsche recruited in 1941 and 1942 from all across the southeast replaced SS losses and filled out the ranks of new divisions on all German fronts, one new unit turned exclusively to homegrown German manpower. In mid-summer 1942, the SS organized the Volksdeutsche living in the junction of the Italian South Tyrol, Istria, and Slovenia first into a company and then a battalion of mountain troops known as the *Karstjäger* (Karst Hunters), named for the chalky limestone or karst mountains of the region. These erstwhile Austrians knew their homeland well and effectively fought Partisans both Italian and Yugoslav. They, like their Balkan counterparts in *Prinz Eugen*, organized at about the same time, earned a reputation as hard and cruel anti-Partisan combatants in their familiar, rugged mountain terrain. In the late summer of 1944, they received the designation 24th SS Gebirgs Division *Karstjäger*, though it never exceeded the strength of a brigade.[71]

After Stalingrad: The Bottom Comes into Sight, 1943–1944

The shocking defeat at Stalingrad and the subsequent reversal of German military fortunes sent seismic waves through the Waffen-SS recruitment system. From early 1943 until the end of the war, the Reich pressed its Axis allies ever harder for concessions regarding the military service of their Volksdeutsche. As Germany's prospects deteriorated, the Reich expected its allies to make even more of their Volksdeutsche available for the Waffen-SS—and if the allies were reluctant to do so, the Reich was prepared to bypass these regimes as intermediaries between the Reich and the Volksdeutsche.

Himmler bragged in April 1943 that the "sons of the Volksdeutsche" enlist as true volunteers, even though the SS had the authority to force a man to serve without official state sanction.[72]

Although the SS continued to refer to enlistments as voluntary—mostly to bolster its esprit de corps and perpetuate its elitist image—it unapologetically resorted to inducting its soldiers, from both within the Reich and abroad, particularly from the southeast. As the Volksdeutsche manpower barrel emptied, scraping became the order of the day, with the SS-declared and -enforced mandatory military obligation weighing heavily in the process. For instance, in the spring of 1943 the Reich demanded the Croats approve obligatory military service in the Waffen-SS for all Volksdeutsche, including those in the armed forces. In late April, Zagreb complied, and by the year's end, 17,538 Croatian Volksdeutsche served in the Waffen-SS, the majority in *Prinz Eugen*. Technically "volunteers," they had been coerced to enlist and certified their "voluntarism" in writing.[73] The Volksdeutsche of Serbia-Banat, already facing compulsory military obligation, could increase their quota only by inducting older and younger age groups.

Since most eligible Volksdeutsche from the former Yugoslavia already were or were about to be placed at the Reich's disposal, the SS principally targeted Romania and Hungary and their still sizeable reservoirs of German manpower. As the war continued, the Reich wore down Romanian resistance, the devious machinations of the minority leader Andreas Schmidt leading the way. But it was not until after the disaster at Stalingrad (in which Romanian troops had shared fully) that the Reich leaned more firmly on Romania. Genuine sympathies for the German cause had dissipated, and Bucharest searched for ways out. Although anti-German feelings pervaded the Romanian public, an increased German military presence in Romania made it harder for Antonescu to defy the Germans. The Romanians finally relented in May and signed a treaty extending SS recruitment to Romania. Antonescu also begrudgingly approved service in the SS as fulfilling the Romanian military obligation and ordered the release of all Volksdeutsche in the Romanian army—estimated at around forty thousand—making them eligible for enlistment in the Waffen-SS as "volunteers." By then the Romanians did not care what the Reich did with the ethnic Germans, though they still refused to sanction an official induction.[74]

The mustering in Romania had begun even before the treaty was signed, though afterward all *Volksdeutsche* between the ages of eighteen and thirty-five were ordered to report. Some responded to the summons freely, but for many the "voluntarism" clearly was forced, resulting from both social and physical duress.[75] Purportedly, many Volksdeutsche abhorred service in Romania's army and pre-ferred service with fellow Germans, but not everyone welcomed a transfer to SS units. Those delaying or refusing to obey orders to enlist were declared cowards and traitors to the *Volk*. Local German officials harshly rebuked the unwilling and those not enthusiastic enough. One reluctant recruit whom a local official had slapped around went home and hanged himself. The SS even dragged German inmates out of Romanian prisons to serve—an irrefutable instance of scraping the dregs. By the end of July 1943, the SS had inducted 41,560 recruits from Romania, but many of them proved unreliable, especially those of the Romanian Banat, who, when sens-ing an opportunity, deserted. Some found their way back home, but local authorities (both German and Romanian) routinely returned these fugitives to the SS for certain and severe punishment.[76] A wit-ness referring to "so-called volunteers" and "forced voluntarism" when recalling the situation in 1943 in the Romanian Banat observed that orders to volunteer used the term *muss* (must)—"*Muss-Freiwillige*." At one center, recruiters wrote on a chalkboard that volunteers "*muss*" report and enlist.

As the Romanian army released its German soldiers in 1943, SS recruiters often waited for them at home, signed them up, and sent them back to war. One example of this is Josef Wittje, a Volksdeutscher drafted into the Romanian army in February 1942 and sent to the Russian front in August. Wounded near Stalingrad in late 1942, Wittje returned home, along with other surviving and retreating Romanian soldiers. Although in the chaos of retreat many Volksdeutsche deserted to nearby German units, Wittje remained loyally in the Romanian army until late July. At that point the SS seized him and pressed him into its ranks.[77] Local minority officials even assisted in house-to-house searches. Berger noted that "If a *Volksgruppe* is halfway appropriately led, everyone will report vol-untarily, and those who do not report freely, they will find their house broken up." A witness recalled that "house-busting" was a method commonly used to enforce the *völkisch* military obligation.[78] As ruthless and brutal as the campaign may have been, it yielded results. By the year's end, a total of 54,000 *Volksdeutsche* from Romania were serving in the Waffen-SS. Until the collapse of the Reich-Romanian alliance in August 1944, the recruitment in Romania nominally remained "voluntary," but the process was anything but that.

In February 1943, the SS proposed another round of recruitment for Hungary. Again the SS sought not only civilian Volksdeutsche but also members of the Hungarian army. Hungary's wartime leader, Admiral Miklos Horthy, rebuffed these latest demands, but after a scolding by Hitler in Salzburg, the admiral relented. He not only consented to open recruitment but also permitted Germans in the Honved to "volunteer" for the Waffen-SS.[79] The 1943 campaign unabashedly applied terror to prompt "voluntarism." A witness spoke of *Gewissensterror* extending to everyone close to the inductee.[80] In late 1943, all men suitable for combat and of draft age in the Hungarian Batschka were to be inducted and shipped off for training and assignments. Reports noted women screeching "like hyenas" when the SS tried to take away their men. Many of those dragooned from here, as was increasingly the case everywhere, deserted. One fugitive from *Florian Geyer* caught in Belgrade was sentenced to death by a firing squad; his unit was ordered to witness the execution.[81] As the recruitment continued, the SS turned the screws tighter. When three inducted Hungarian Volksdeutsche refused to take the SS oath, they were incarcerated for a year—not in a KZ but in a so-called SS punishment camp near Danzig, where they would "learn their duty toward their German Fatherland." They could then return to the front lines.[82]

Along with mustering the ethnic Germans of Romania and Hungary, in 1943 the SS still cast its nets in Slovakia. Well into 1943, the Slovaks had continued their generosity, allowing civilian ethnic Germans to volunteer for Reich military duty. Another example of Slovak cooperation was sending a flak regiment with a large German contingent under the command of Volksdeutscher Col. Dotzauer to the Reich. Later, the aforementioned Karpathen Col. Pilfousek supervised the transfer of German volunteers from the Slovak army to the SS.[83] But the SS did not respond in kind. In February 1943, the SS admitted its chicanery and intimidation:

> The fact that the attitude of the German population has seriously worsened can be attributed to the inductions of the ethnic Germans into the Waffen-SS a month ago. The ethnic Germans indeed reported voluntarily, but believed they would never be inducted into the armed services. Since the mustering commission has now mustered the people who reported and found 80% of them fit, the

ethnic Germans living in Slovakia were very surprised. The biggest
surprise for them was that the first transport of those found fit
occurred just one month later. . . . The next day [after departure
from Bratislava] I heard already that allegedly 17 members of the
departing transport had run off and were now being sought by the
police and gendarmerie . . . I heard from the political chief . . . who
is on friendly terms with me, that he was very unpleasantly surprised by the reactions of some ethnic Germans when the induction
notices were delivered.[84]

A traveler passing through Slovakia noted the lack of enthusiasm on the part of ethnic Germans for the Reich and its demands:
every ethnic German who could evade enlisting did so, especially
in the rural areas, and as inductions replaced voluntarism, many
resorted to excuses not to report, such as illness. He also reported
that the recruitment, which started out with some semblance of
voluntarism, soon resorted to "pressure," and those who could
evade it did so.[85] Another report referred to "massive pressure"
applied to recruits and mounting opposition. In some instances, the
Slovak police brought in reluctant "volunteers" to the Waffen-SS
office in Bratislava.[86] By the end of 1943, SS recruiters had brought
in 139,567 Volksdeutsche from southeastern Europe into the ranks
of the Waffen-SS—but more than 12,000 were already dead or
missing.[87]

The SS also tried mustering Volksdeutsche closer to the eastern
front. In the late spring of 1943, the SS gathered 12,600 Ukrainians
and local Volksdeutsche, willing or not, in the occupied Ukraine in
the environs of Lvov (formerly Lemberg in pre–World War I Austrian
Galicia) into what became 14th Waffen Grenadier Division der SS
(Galizien Nr. 1). Poorly trained, equipped, and led, the division suffered a calamitous defeat at Brody. Only three thousand escaped.[88]
Farther east, in so-called Transnistria, the territory north of the
Dniester River occupied by Romanian forces, the SS had discovered
large numbers of Volksdeutsche that the Soviets had failed to deport
in 1941. The SS trained them into a self-defense unit of eight to
nine thousand men but, although tempted, refrained from building
a more formal SS force and sending it far from home.[89] These men,
along with their dependents, later evacuated along with the retreating Germans; once removed from their home territory, they were
dispersed across Waffen-SS formations as replacements. Numerous
isolated pockets of ethnic Germans throughout the occupied Soviet

Union shared this fate—service in local militias and then evacuation westward, with the Waffen-SS waiting for them.[90]

The Final Scraping: 1944–1945

The Soviet invasion of southeastern Europe in the late summer of 1944 turned it into a major battlefront. From this point on, the Waffen-SS recruitment and manpower replenishment process in the region merged with the fluctuating military situation. Diplomatic niceties no longer mattered. Operating SS units, as they maneuvered, withdrew, or advanced, simply absorbed local German militias and self-defense forces and swept up any German men they found. Most of their training henceforth was on the job—with live ammunition. Likewise, SS police and military authorities throughout the region rounded up and repackaged survivors of destroyed and dispersed Waffen-SS units into new or refurbished formations as circumstances necessitated and permitted.

To the west, a new regime in Budapest, backed by Reich troops, came to power on March 15, 1944, and signed over full authority over their Volksdeutsche. Hungary's ethnic Germans no longer had a choice, and for the final year of the war they had to serve with the Waffen-SS.[91] By mid-1944, as Hungary was becoming a battlefront, SS gangs searched from house to house, dragging out the unwilling, placing them on wagons and driving them off, often directly to the closest combat. In one Hungarian village, the SS beat some resistors half to death and locked them up in huts where previously they had detained Jews. In one particularly difficult situation, the SS threatened the draft resisters with shooting. When several tried to flee, the SS shot two of them.[92]

In 1944, Romania was no more accommodating. Whereas the Reich had occupied Hungary, nothing comparable ensured compliance in Romania. Antonescu procrastinated and parried Reich demands until early August, when he finally agreed to permit further enlistments. By then the issue was moot. The Red Army had already invaded northern Romania, and shortly the coup of August 23 resulted in his overthrow and Romania's defection from the Axis camp to the Soviets.[93]

In Slovakia, relentless SS recruiters demanded the transfer of all Germans in the Slovak armed forces to the SS and untrammeled SS control of Slovakia's Germans. In June 1944, the browbeaten Slovaks finally relinquished all authority over the Carpathian Germans.

All local Germans became eligible for induction, and those still in the Slovak army would be transferred to the Waffen-SS. These moves occurred just in time for the Slovak uprising in late August, when units of the Slovak army (alongside Partisans and Soviet commandos) revolted against German forces and Slovak collaborators. After Gottlob Berger's grab-bag of SS units subdued the uprising in October and November, some remained behind as security, while most moved on to other assignments or joined newly founded SS formations in the region. One such October creation was 31st SS Freiwillige Grenadier Division *Böhmen-Mähren*, on paper eleven thousand strong, made up of local Carpathian German militiamen as well as SS men and other Germans from the Protectorate. Members of this predominantly Volksdeutsche division hailed from areas such as the South Tyrol and nearby Hungary. Much of its cadre came from the dissolved *Kama* Division, a recently aborted experiment in using Albanian Moslems as SS fighters for the Reich. Other SS men and Volksdeutsche ended up in the brand-new 32nd SS Panzer Grenadier Division *30 Januar*, including units of SS Kampfgruppe Schill from Hungary and irregulars from local ethnic German militias.[94] The ineffective performance of these final-hour SS creations reflected their composition: a haphazard collection of Volksdeutsche, including battle-hardened veterans but mostly untested, untrained inductees.

Yet another division formed in Hungary in May 1944 was 22nd Freiwillige Kavallerie Division *Maria Theresia*—named for the eighteenth-century Habsburg empress—which consisted almost entirely of Hungarian Volksdeutsche. Its nucleus was a regiment transferred from *Florian Geyer*, which already contained a large contingent of Hungarian Volksdeutsche. It was enlarged to division size with Germans recently transferred from the Honved and draftees rounded up locally. Most of its officers came from *Florian Geyer*.[95] A late arrival in the area was 16th SS Panzer Grenadier Division *Reichsführer SS* (*RFSS*). It received a large infusion of Volksdeutsche when *Totenkopf* transferred to it almost all its Hungarian ethnic Germans. Organized as a division in northern Italy and Slovenia, the *RFSS* joined *Horst Wessel* and *Maria Theresia*, all with sizeable Volksdeutsche contingents, in the 1944 occupation of Hungary.[96] In the winter of 1944–1945, these new SS creations, mostly filled with southeastern Volksdeutsche, fought alongside redeployed "classic" divisions from other fronts in a futile, last-ditch campaign to hold Budapest.

When the surviving battle-weary SS divisions abandoned Budapest in early 1945 and retreated, a few new ones appeared from the ashes of the old—one final, desperate "barrel scraping." The fodder for these eleventh-hour units drew mostly from Volksdeutsche survivors of the Budapest siege, combining veterans of defunct SS formations and freshly dragooned novices. By early 1945, most of these formations, both old and new, were divisions on paper and in Hitler's mind, certainly not in real numbers in the field. The SS had ordered all groups of at least battalion size or larger to be called "divisions," no longer using the previous terminology for reassembled survivors, the *Kampfgruppe* (battle group).[97] The numbering of Waffen-SS divisions, which reached thirty-eight by the end of the war, is grossly misleading; at no one time did the Waffen-SS field thirty-eight divisions. In 1945, divisions came and went, but no stretch of the imagination could construe any as true divisions.

One such deceptive last hour creation with a large number of Volksdeutsche was the 32nd Freiwillige Grenadier Division *30 Januar*. Combining SS men and units from the Slovak uprising with some Budapest survivors, *30 Januar* was reassembled and dispatched to the defense of Berlin, from where only a few returned alive.[98] The last few SS divisions to be formed had almost no Volksdeutsche unless there were some among the officers, cadets, or RAD workers caught up in this final "scraping of the barrel."[99]

Waffen-SS recruitment of Volksdeutsche in World War II evolved from enlisting volunteers meeting the same rigid standards as the best physically, racially, and politically qualified young Reich Germans in the prewar years and the early phases of conflict, to the "voluntary" inductions of minimally suitable ethnic Germans of the southeast by extending a mandatory obligation, and culminated in the eleventh hour helter-skelter, press-gang seizures of any and all available German men, of any age, who could walk and shoot. Critics attributing the post-Stalingrad decline of the Waffen-SS to the growing numbers of these foreign Germans in its ranks may have a point, at least in terms of a numerical correlation: By the end of 1943, nearly 122,000 Volksdeutsche fought in the armed SS: from Slovakia, 5,390; Hungary, 22,125; Romania, 54,000; Banat-Serbia, 21,516; Croatia, 17,538.[100] By mid-1944, more than 150,000 served, and by the end of 1944 approximately 310,000 Volksdeutsche served as compared to some 400,000 Reich Germans, out of a total strength of 950,000 for the Waffen-SS as a whole.[101] Although George Stein's assertion that "Long before the end of the war [Volksdeutsche] out-numbered native Germans in the Waffen-SS" may fall somewhat short of accuracy, their numbers and their performance were decid-edly significant.[102]

If numbers correlate with performance, then attributing the deterioration of SS combat prowess to the rising proportion of Volksdeutsche carries some merit—but only if one presumes these men were of low combat quality. Before concluding that the scrap-ings from the bottom of the barrel spoiled the Waffen-SS as a fight-ing force, one must examine the combat performance of the ethnic Germans and their units, which is the focus of a subsequent chapter. One should also consider the drafting of Reich Germans for the Waffen-SS starting in 1942—itself a form of "scraping." Furthermore, beginning in 1943 the SS increasingly relied on non-German sources, whose wartime record (except for the three Baltic divisions) was dismal. These late-hour manpower supplements surely played a role in compromising the Waffen-SS's abilities and reputation. But in the final analysis, the means of procuring Volksdeutsche manpower cannot be discounted as a determinant, in particular beginning in 1942 and by 1943, when even the pretense of voluntarism was discarded. Other fighting qualities aside, coerced, intimidated, demoralized, and even physically abused men do not make good soldiers—especially when they do not wholly accept the cause for fighting as theirs. As this study suggests, the nature of SS recruit-ment virtually guaranteed if not failure then at least a deficiency in the results. The final verdict lies at least partly in the "scraping" process and not entirely in what the scraping dredged out.

10 The Ethnic Germans of the Waffen-SS in Combat: Dregs or Gems?

Valdis O. Lumans

The armed formations of the Nazi Schutzstaffel SS, the Waffen-SS, earned a reputation as the toughest and most effective of all German forces in World War II. Its soldiers sported an esprit de corps comparable to that of elite American units such as the Marines and Army Airborne. The principles of voluntarism and elitism prevailed.[1] The most ardent promoter of Germany's Waffen-SS was the Führer himself, Adolf Hitler, who extolled its praises and nicknamed it his "fire brigade," capable of plugging holes in front lines, seizing impregnable targets, and halting enemy offensives. Hitler once confided to a group of generals: "I am proud when an army commander can tell me that his force is based essentially on an armored division and the SS *Reich* Division."[2]

Paradoxically, Hitler thought poorly of a portion of the Waffen-SS, the so-called *Volksdeutsche*, or ethnic Germans of non-Reich origin, though by the end of the war, according to some, they constituted its largest element. His opinion dropped so low that he used the ratio of *Volksdeutsche* to Reich Germans in an SS division as its measure of quality: the more *Volksdeutsche*, the lower the unit's combat proficiency. When in July 1944 he inquired about the composition of two new SS divisions, he was relieved that although *Volksdeutsche* constituted 40 percent in one and 70 percent in the other, at least the rest were Reich Germans.[3]

What accounts for the Führer's confidence in the Waffen-SS generally but contempt for one of its components? Was his disrespect justified by poor combat performance on the part of *Volksdeutsche* soldiers? At least a partial answer lies in their recruitment, the coerced inductions presented publicly as voluntarism (as discussed in Chapter 9). But if truth be told, by war's end the Führer's confidence in the Waffen-SS as a whole had waned, as he questioned the ability of even the "classic" SS divisions to halt the Allied tide.[4] Had the *Volksdeutsche* improved—or perhaps the elite had dropped in quality? By then, the entire Waffen-SS, including the elite units, stooped to what metaphorically is called "scraping the barrel"—whatever is left in the "barrel" will have to do. But did dredging up manpower remnants both inside and outside the Reich yield only human "dregs," or could one also discover "gems," competent, effective, or even exemplary soldiers to form effective units? As the Waffen-SS's wartime expansion and the need for replacements diluted its prewar quality, compromised its elitism, and negated claims of voluntarism, what role, if any, did the *Volksdeutsche* play in this deterioration?[5]

The Waffen-SS and *Volksdeutsche* at War: The Early Phase

This author assumes readers have some familiarity with the Schutzstaffel SS, its origins and nature, particularly of its early armed units, which Hitler officially designated as the Waffen-SS in 1940 in recognition of their metamorphosis in Poland from "asphalt soldiers"—good only for the parade ground—to the Reich's elite wartime combat force.[6] As for the *Volksdeutsche*, it suffices to say that they played a relatively small, indistinguishable role in the prewar armed SS. It is not until the outbreak of war that one can begin to evaluate these foreign Germans as SS soldiers, and even then their profile remained too low for meaningful comparisons. Nevertheless, the attack on Poland is an appropriate opening, since their anonymity in this stage of the war contrasts sharply with their much-enhanced role beginning in June 1941, with the invasion of the Soviet Union.

Although armed SS troops had participated in the incursion into the Rhineland, the Austrian Anschluss, and the occupations of the Sudetenland and Bohemia-Moravia, their first combat test came in Poland. Their numbers amounted to a drop in the overall Blitzkrieg manpower bucket, and SS units were dispersed among various Wehrmacht divisions and corps. As for postcombat reviews, Wehrmacht generals commanding SS units in the field found little to commend and plenty to criticize, particularly their high casualty rates—which became a regular combat feature of the armed SS.[7] As for the few *Volksdeutsche* scattered across the SS units, having enlisted as volunteers meeting the same strict qualifications as Reich Germans, little distinguished their collective performance.

Following the Polish campaign, the SS consolidated these units into three divisions: the SS Verfügungstruppe became the SS *Verfügungstruppe* Division, ultimately the 2nd SS-Panzer Division *Das Reich*; the SS Totenkopfverbände emerged as the SS *Totenkopf* Division, later the 3rd SS-Panzer Division *Totenkopf*; and the armed police units turned into the SS Polizei Division, eventually the 4th SS Polizei Panzer Grenadier Division.[8] The Leibstandarte SS *Adolf Hitler* (*LSSAH*), which originated as the elite-of-the-elite detachment guarding the Reich Chancellery, fought as a reinforced regiment until its 1942 upgrade to the 1st SS-Panzer Division Leibstandarte *Adolf Hitler*.[9] These elite (or "classic") divisions formed the core of the Waffen-SS.

In the spring of 1940, the reorganized Waffen-SS joined in the attack in the West. No Waffen-SS units occupied Norway and Denmark in April; all fought in the Low Countries and France in May as the unofficial "fourth branch of the Wehrmacht."[10] As in Poland, no separate appraisal of the *Volksdeutsche*—still dispersed across all units—is possible, and short of examining individual records, one may only assume that these soldiers did no better and no worse than their Reich counterparts. Following this campaign, the SS leaders constructed the first non-German SS division, ultimately the 5th SS Panzer Division *Wiking*, intended for Scandinavian and other Germanic volunteers, such as the Dutch and Flemish. Since disappointingly few stepped forward, the SS supplemented this nominally Germanic division with Reich Germans and some *Volksdeutsche*, resulting in a German majority.

The next phase of war came unexpectedly in early April 1941, after Yugoslavia defied Hitler with a regime change that tilted this briefly Axis ally away from Germany. The attack on Yugoslavia substantially enhanced the role of Europe's *Volksdeutsche* within the Waffen-SS for the remainder of the war, as a native armed insurgency soon appeared, challenging the Reich's occupation and threatening the civilian *Volksdeutsche* of the former Vojvodina, eastern Croatia, and much of mountainous Bosnia-Herzegovina. Insurgents targeted German communities as exponents of the ethnic arrogance and atrocious behavior of the Reich German conquerors. The most effective were the Partisans, a multiethnic movement united both against the invaders and by their communist ideology. From this initially inchoate movement coalesced the People's Liberation Army of Yugoslavia (PLA), whose leader was the Croatian communist Josip Broz, commonly known as Tito.[11] As guerilla action escalated, the Reich had no choice but to devote more troops than planned to pacifying and securing the land. Hitler regarded the Balkan theater as little more than a sideshow, an annoying digression delaying his main event, the invasion of Russia. As his first-line divisions left the Balkans for the main stage, inferior garrison divisions, police units, and the like replaced them, an Axis force including Italians, Croats, and Bulgarians of more than twenty divisions and at least one hundred autonomous smaller units.[12] It would be in the Balkans and southeastern Europe in general that ethnic Germans would play their most important military role in the war.

Operation Barbarossa and the *Volksdeutsche*

On June 22, 1941, Hitler launched his assault on the Soviet Union, codenamed Operation Barbarossa. The Waffen-SS would come of age on the eastern front and in Hitler's eyes would justify his praise and confidence. The operation stoked SS demands for manpower replacements and pushed expansion to unprecedented levels, raising the issue of a mandatory *Volksdeutsche* military obligation, especially as it became evident that Barbarossa would not be another swift Blitzkrieg success. The targeted *Volksdeutsche* would mainly be those of southeastern Europe. Ironically, dipping heavily into the ethnic German manpower pool of the region, which some critics claim compromised the overall quality of the Waffen-SS, paralleled the apotheosis of the wartime Waffen-SS to legendary status. Given increased SS reliance on *Volksdeutsche* and their pronounced concentration in certain units, for the first time their performance became distinguishable and observable.

Operation Barbarossa set in motion an estimated three million Germans and half a million allies, a force including 160,405 men of the Waffen-SS.[13] Early reports on SS performance were tentative but improving, although when the recently organized SS Kampfgruppe *Nord* took on the Red Army in Karelia, its men reportedly fled at first contact. Units of *Das Reich*, on the other hand, advanced within twenty kilometers of Moscow.[14] As for the *Volksdeutsche*, still mostly scattered across the Waffen-SS, little marked their performance one way or another in the elite divisions. *Nord*, however, with numerous *Volksdeutsche* from mountainous areas of Europe, was an exception. It attracted undesirable attention with its poor showing, which may have raised allegations about the inferior fighting qualities of its *Volksdeutsche*. Reports and rumors may have also reached the Führer and impressed on him an enduring, negative image of his non-Reich SS soldiers.[15]

As the 1941 campaign literally cooled down by late fall, it was clear the days of Blitzkrieg were over. The Waffen-SS had once more taken high casualties. By the end of 1941, of the original 160,405, the dead numbered 407 officers and 7,930 men; 816 officers and 26,299 men were wounded; thirteen officers and 923 men were missing. One may assume that *Volksdeutsche* casualties were proportional to their numbers. Although the Reich's forces thawed out and resumed their offensive in the spring of 1942, casualties continued to mount.[16] These losses had to be replaced, and *Volksdeutsche* from the southeast increasingly replenished the Waffen-SS.

The Southeast: Building SS Division *Prinz Eugen*

As the SS stepped up recruitment for replacements in 1942, it also created more divisions. For the *Volksdeutsche*, by far the most important of these new creations was the almost exclusively ethnic German 7th SS Freiwillige Gebirgs Division *Prinz Eugen*—named for the late seventeenth/early eighteenth-century Habsburg commander who rolled back the Turks in the Balkans. If any single Waffen-SS unit embodied and represented the *Volksdeutsche* wartime experience, for better or for worse, it was *Prinz Eugen*. The results of the "barrel scraping" from 1942 to 1945 manifest themselves in this unit more graphically than in any other.[17] With the growing insurgency in the Balkans, it made good sense to exploit local German familiarity with the terrain, peoples, and languages of the region. Henceforth, most *Volksdeutsche* from Serbia, Croatia, the Banat, and even far away as Transylvania—whether true volunteers, coerced draftees, transfers from non-German armies, German militias, or whatever—would serve in *Prinz Eugen*.[18] Formed in March 1942, it initially operated within the Balkans under General Alexander Löhr's Army Group E.[19]

For its division commander, Himmler turned to the most accomplished *Volksdeutscher* available, General Arthur Phleps of Romania, possessing both impressive credentials and experience for the task. Born in Transylvania in 1881, Phleps began his military career in the Habsburg Army, served throughout the Balkans, fought in World War I, continued his career in the Romanian army as a member of its General Staff, and even advised King Carol on military matters. He retired prior to World War II but in 1941 heeded the *völkisch* call and volunteered for the Waffen-SS. Assigned to *Wiking* in Russia, Phleps received a general's rank and fought to the Caucasus, and in January 1942 he returned to the Balkans to construct *Prinz Eugen*.[20]

Phleps set up headquarters in the occupied Banat, home to the largest number of accessible *Volksdeutsche* in the southeast, and started from scratch. He found plenty of enlisted men, thanks to nearby recruitment efforts in Croatia and Serbia-Banat, but qualified officers and NCOs (noncommissioned officers) were harder to procure. He gathered some from existing SS units, including *Wiking*, but throughout the war securing competent cadre remained a chronic problem. Phleps nevertheless collected several top-flight SS officers, including fellow *Volksdeutscher* Desiderius Hampel of Croatia, also a veteran of the Habsburg World War I armies.[21] Of the officers, most were *Volksdeutsche*, not Reich Germans. Otto Kumm, one of Phleps's eventual successors as commander, estimated that in 1942 the ratio of *Volksdeutsche* to Reich German company-grade officers in *Prinz Eugen* was three to one, the same for battalion commanders; for regimental commanders, the ratio was two to one. *Volksdeutsche* NCOs outnumbered Reich counterparts five to one.[22] Based on Hitler's yardstick, these proportions did not bode well.

Though bountiful in numbers, the rank and file left much to be desired—they were mostly simple farmers unaccustomed to military discipline and alien even to basic hygiene. An officer described one encampment as a "pig-sty"—indeed "the greatest pig-sty of all time." He also complained about transforming Banat peasants into "Prussian parade soldiers."[23] Otto Kumm recalled the division's low initial reputation and how most SS officers deemed an assignment to *Prinz Eugen* "no great honor," hardly above disciplinary action, even tantamount to a demotion. The word spread quickly that it did not belong with the elite. At Junkerschule Bad Tölz the image of *Prinz Eugen* was so dismal that graduating officers ordered to *Prinz Eugen* immediately requested transfers. An SS ditty caught on reviling the new division: "*Prinz Eugen*, the noble troop, it must scuffle with Serbs, our trash division."[24] Chief SS recruiter Gottlob Berger thought little of Phleps's leadership and believed rumors he was an Allied agent.[25]

A few sympathizers appreciated the simplicity of *Prinz Eugen*'s men: "Often stood father and son in the same formation. What these men lacked in peacetime education, they replaced with daring and toughness . . . through knowledge of the enemy's way of waging war."[26]

Kumm, a converted critic, eventually became the division's chief advocate: "Few divisions could boast such willing, unpretentious, persevering, self-sacrificing and extremely brave soldiers. In spite of such a difficult beginning, they fulfilled the high standards of an SS Division."[27] Two prominent wartime SS commanders, both post-war apologists, Paul Hausser and Felix Steiner, later praised *Prinz Eugen* for its prowess, usually under the most difficult circum-stances.[28] At least, according to some, these simple *Volksdeutsche* soldiers of *Prinz Eugen* loved their "Papa Phleps."[29]

The equipment allocated to *Prinz Eugen* was also substandard. Most weapons were captured and obsolete, an assortment of Czech, Yugoslav, and Polish issue—many left over from the previous war. As for transportation, horses, oxen, and mules were standard, and except for occasional railway rides, *Prinz Eugen* knew little of the mechanized Blitzkrieg way of war. All things considered, these primitive ways suited waging anti-Partisan warfare in the rugged Balkans—and "no-one, except for their adversaries, knew the terrain better."[30] As for preparation, after some basic instruction the train-ees practiced "on-the-job-training," patrolling as soon as they were armed.[31]

The issue of quality aside, *Prinz Eugen* left in its wake a legacy of rapine and a shameful record of atrocities. One of its major detrac-tors, the historian George H. Stein, notes that "the most shocking evidence against the Waffen SS" submitted at the postwar Nuremberg Tribunal came from Yugoslavia. He refers to *Prinz Eugen*'s "crimi-nal activities" coming to light, including "burning villages, massacre of inhabitants, torture and murder of captured partisans."[32] The critic Robert L. Koehl concurs that the division "gained a horrible reputation for cruelty."[33] For instance, though Otto Kumm denied ever following the infamous order requiring a "hundred to one" ratio of hostages to be shot in retaliation for the deaths of German soldiers, *Prinz Eugen* most assuredly did: "Bandits seized in battle are to be shot. All other bandit suspects, etc., are to be seized and deported for labor purposes to Germany."[34]

Blame for atrocities in this theater cannot be ascribed solely to *Prinz Eugen*, although as the war progressed, a strong case can be made for it being the chief perpetrator. As Robert Herzstein amply documents, the Wehrmacht also executed tens of thousands of Yugoslavs, including innocent civilians, in ruthless, cold-blooded reprisals.[35] Most SS apologists concede that the monstrous *Prinz Eugen* reputation exists, but they attribute it to the historically cruel and savage nature of Balkan warfare, the resumption of ethnic, tribal warfare—an allegation holding some truth, since the crimes of the Croatian Ustasha against Serbs were at least as terrible as those of the Germans. In 1941 alone, the Ustasha murdered some two hundred thousand Serbs.[36]

Others allude to the inherent barbarity of all guerilla warfare and indict both sides for perpetrating a ceaseless, unforgiving cycle of brutality.[37] Certainly no one can deny that the Partisans executed most enemies regardless of ethnicity and, in the case of *Volksdeutsche*, civilians as well as combatants.[38] Milovan Djilas, Tito's wartime right-hand man, acknowledged savagery on both sides, matter of factly and without remorse admitting to Partisans executing their prisoners. He also candidly compliments the local SS division as the "famous Seventh SS Prinz Eugene Division." When referring to an impenetrably dense stretch of forest, he notes, "Not even these SS men from the Seventh" were willing to enter.[39] Several postwar advocates for the SS tend to agree with Djilas on the fierce image of *Prinz Eugen* and proudly accept that its men were feared and hated by their enemy.[40]

By October 1942, enough of *Prinz Eugen* was combat ready to move out on its first operation, according to its motto, "*Vorwärts, Prinz Eugen!*" Its first assignment took the division to the mountainous Serbia-Montenegro border, where its men launched the first of many anti-Partisan actions. Through the rest of 1942 and into 1943, *Prinz Eugen* operated through, around, and over rivers, mountain ranges, cities, towns, and villages that became familiar names fifty years later during the Balkan warfare of the 1990s: Sarajevo, Mostar, Karlovac, Dubrovnik, Tuzla, Srbeniza, and many others—for the same reasons as before: indiscriminate bloodshed, widespread arson, mass murder, and repeated cruelties.[41] In this borderless conflict, the *Volksdeutsche* of *Prinz Eugen* devised an apropos second slogan: "Wherever we are, that is the front."[42]

The SS Cavalry Units and Antipartisan Warfare

The second Waffen-SS division formed in 1942, the SS Kavallerie Division, which evolved into the 8th SS Kavallerie Division *Florian Geyer*, was also known for its *Volksdeutsche* majority and its counterinsurgency mission. Originating in Poland in 1939 as a collection of SS riding units, it performed police duties, including protecting ethnic Germans, hunting Polish stragglers, and rounding up Jews.

In 1940, it helped evacuate *Volksdeutsche* resettlers from Volhynia, then evicted Poles from their farms to make room for these Germans. At one point Himmler augmented this formation with South Tyrolean *Volksdeutsche*, all cavalry veterans of the Italian campaign in Ethiopia.[43] Its first commander was the accomplished SS equestrian Hermann Fegelein, who later served as a special SS adjutant to Adolf Hitler.[44] In June 1941, the unit, now the SS Kavallerie Brigade, "mopped up" in the rear of Army Group Center.[45]

Although the SS primarily relied on Einsatzgruppen killing units for clean-up missions, it learned that cavalry could hunt suspects more effectively in rugged, "bandit"-infested terrain such as the forests and swamps of the Pripet Marshes. Since many *Volksdeutsche* hailed from rural backgrounds and working with animals and riding came as second nature to them, the cavalry was a fitting assignment. Under the pretense of counterinsurgency, they and their Reich comrades routinely perpetrated the most insidious SS duties, the shooting of women, children, the elderly, and even a few genuine partisans.[46] For example, in one week in November 1941 the SS Kavallerie Brigade shot 281 partisans and suspects, meaning civilians. These horsemen continued their bloody campaign in western Russia into 1942, shooting 239 prisoners and 6,504 more civilian "suspects."[47] The brigade received another supplement of *Volksdeutsche* in June 1942, several thousand recruits with equestrian experience from the Hungarian Batschka, expanding into the SS Kavallerie Division, ultimately the 8th SS Kavallerie Division *Florian Geyer*, named for a sixteenth-century Franconian defender of Martin Luther.[48] By late 1942, the new division had a strength of 161 officers, 677 NCOs, and 5,471 men (by another count 10,879), 80 percent of them *Volksdeutsche*, mostly from Hungary.[49]

Although Fegelein's successor Willi Bittrich complained about his ethnic German soldiers' poor German and inadequate military training, by February 1943 the unit had earned five Knight's Crosses, 115 Iron Crosses First Class, and 939 Iron Crosses Second Class—not a bad haul for a relatively new division away from the front, and one with mostly ethnic Germans.[50] Into 1943 it continued to patrol behind the eastern front. In August, the SS ordered raising a fourth cavalry regiment, to be filled by *Volksdeutsche* from occupied areas of the Soviet Union. When ordered to the front lines for conventional combat—where the enemy shoots back—the division suffered heavy casualties and in December had to be withdrawn and transferred closer to home—at least for its *Volksdeutsche*—to Croatia.

One regiment, however, remained in Russia fighting partisans until it too was later expanded into a division.[51]

One may reasonably conclude that since *Volksdeutsche* eventually comprised the majority of *Florian Geyer*, they must share complicity in the most heinous deeds of the SS, the murder of civilians, specifically Jews—after all, it was commonly understood in the SS that "partisan" was often synonymous with "Jew." But this indictment, though it mirrors a certain moral turpitude, does not necessarily reflect on soldierly qualities. One related development does, however, shed more light on the quality of antipartisan troops. A batch of trainees arrived at Bobruisk in Belarus (on the Minsk-Bobruisk railway line, a favorite target for saboteurs) in July 1943.[52] They were Transylvanians just released from the Romanian army. The cadre was appalled at their condition—pathetic! At least half were unfit for soldiering, crippled by an assortment of maladies, from hernias to dental problems requiring extraction of as many as sixteen teeth. Although most had combat experience, many were previously wounded and partly disabled. The majority were "farm laborers, dull-witted and inept in speaking standard German because of their local dialects. More than two-thirds suffered from bad teeth, which caused . . . stomach and bowel disease." The least capable were collected in one company and assigned the simplest chores, a unit of "useless men . . . intellectually deficient . . . failing basic cognitive tests . . . clumsy."[53] Truly dregs? Not so fast. After about three weeks, a few showed signs of becoming "useful soldiers."[54] Nonetheless, the Waffen-SS had sunk quite a distance, from the exemplary prewar "Praetorian guards" at the Reich Chancellery to the *Volksdeutsche* guards at Bobruisk.

After Stalingrad: The Manpower Crisis

The war continued for nearly two and a half more years after Stalingrad, but most combatants, on both sides—with the exception of the Führer and a few zealots—realized the tide of war had shifted. Germany's armed forces would still eke out some victories, but sooner or later all roads and military columns pointed toward the Reich. All the Germans could do was to continue fighting, trust their Führer, replenish themselves as they could, and hope for the best. This sentiment permeated the Waffen-SS fighting in Russia, seven divisions in all, with a total of 221,000 men. One solitary SS division, *Prinz Eugen* with its nearly twenty thousand ethnic Germans, carried on in the Balkans—albeit alongside several lower-quality Wehrmacht units.[55]

The elite SS had doggedly fought along the Russian front, earning accolades from SS superiors, begrudgingly from their Wehrmacht field commanders, and above all from their Führer. But glory had come at a heavy price in casualties. Replacements filled the gaps, including draftees from the Reich, but increasingly from the *Volksdeutsche* "barrel" of the southeast. Moreover, a planned expansion in 1943 would more than double the size of the Waffen-SS in the numbers of divisions and manpower—at least on paper, if not in the field.[56] Expansion drew heavily on the *Volksdeutsche*, but with one major exception, *Prinz Eugen*—and increasingly the Kavallerie Division—the SS still distributed recruits across divisions as needed. Another facet of enlargement was the creation of non-German, non-Germanic SS divisions of so-called Eastern peoples, as Hitler finally discarded his racial reservations about arming non-Germanics. The results were mixed, with outstanding performances from one Estonian and two Latvian divisions, but the rest were hopeless failures—far worse than the scoops from the dwindling *Volksdeutsche* barrel.[57] Indeed, in the Balkans *Prinz Eugen* experimented with building a Bosnian Moslem division, the 13th Waffen Gebirgs Division der SS *Handschar*, and providing its cadre, but these Bosnians proved unreliable and made ethnic Germans look like paragons of SS elitism.[58]

The price of expansion was dilution in quality of SS men and units. Most experts concur that by 1943 the Waffen-SS, except for the "classic elite" units, was no longer what it used to be.[59] Although some blame the decline on the increased use of *Volksdeutsche* after 1942 and the wholesale enlistment of non-Germanic "Eastern peoples" beginning in 1943, others point to the 1942 extension of Waffen-SS conscription to ordinary Reich Germans as a factor.[60] The practice of transferring entire units from the navy and the Luftwaffe to the Waffen-SS in the last two years of the war also diminished quality. The SS hoped to preserve its elitism and esprit de corps by spreading veterans throughout the new units, but this did little to correct the deterioration and further weakening the older formations.[61]

The Southeast Theater: *Prinz Eugen* in Action, 1943

Having examined the *Volksdeutsche* experience at the heights of German success, one turns to its slide downhill. As the Battle of Stalingrad reached its denouement, its repercussions rippled to the Balkans, where Tito's fighters, encouraged by Red Army victories, intensified their activity.[62] *Prinz Eugen* continued chasing them across the western Balkans, inflicting heavy casualties but doing nothing to discourage enlistments. By late 1942, PLA and Partisan strength had grown to around 150,000, organized into nine divisions and numerous local units.[63] Taking the matter more seriously, Hitler summoned the highest Reich and Italian diplomats and commanders to his Rastenburg headquarters in December to plan a strategy for wiping out this menace once and for all. He declared the "bandits" not only a tactical nuisance but also a strategic threat, possibly linking up with an Allied invasion of the Balkans.[64]

The result was Operation Weiss, *Prinz Eugen*'s first major offensive, launched in January 1943 in bitter winter weather. The Axis collected five German divisions (four Wehrmacht and *Prinz Eugen*), several Italian divisions, and the Croatian Ustasha. All prisoners and suspected accomplices were to be shot and some ninety thousand civilians deported to Italian and German camps.[65] But as would repeatedly be the case, instead of destroying the enemy, the Axis merely dislodged and scattered a few Partisan units.[66]

The Germans ordered yet another offensive, to be launched on May 15, labeled Operation Schwarz; if "White" failed, try "Black." They gathered another superior force, 120,000 troops in all, including 67,000 Germans, 43,000 Italians, and 11,000 Croats, against some 16,000 Partisans. By then, the Axis alliance showed strains, with Reich commanders deploring Italian reluctance to take the fight to the Partisans. The ruffled feelings were mutual, since Italians took umbrage at the Germans appropriating the name of Phleps's division's namesake, "Prince Eugene of Savoy," who, although a Habsburg general, ethnically was Italian. But there was more to the tension than Prince Eugene's birthplace. One of the most exasperated Germans was Arthur Phleps, who decried the lack of Italian cooperation in Operation Schwarz—for example, the Italians denied the Germans use of the Mostar airfield—and demanded the transfer of Herzegovina from Italian to German occupation.[67]

This Axis quarrel climaxed in a heated exchange during a meeting in Podgornica on May 22, where Phleps (never hesitant to speak his mind) appalled his Wehrmacht interpreter, Lt. Kurt Waldheim, by calling his Italian counterpart General Roncaglia a "lazy macaroni" and nearly coming to blows with his ally. After the encounter, Phleps scolded young Waldheim, whose translations evidently were toning down Phleps's vitriol: "Listen, Waldheim, I know some Italian and you are not translating what I am telling this so-and-so."[68]

Another time, Phleps, on his way to meet with an Italian general, threatened to shoot the Italian sentries that kept him waiting at a checkpoint.[69]

Despite Italian intransigence, the operation—especially the men of *Prinz Eugen*—blazed a swath of destruction through the central Balkans, destroying villages, shooting Partisans, but mostly murdering civilians—even burning buildings with live people locked inside. In one instance, they crammed locals into a church in Kniwaja Reka and then blew it up.[70] But as in Operation Weiss, Tito's forces slipped away to fight another day.[71] The Germans did manage to replace the Italians as the occupiers of Herzegovina, an act celebrated in German newsreels picturing Phleps ceremoniously riding into Mostar on horseback.[72] Shortly afterward, Phleps assumed command of the newly established 5th Mountain Corps and devoted most of his energies to organizing the Bosnian division *Handschar*, turning *Prinz Eugen* over to Carl von Oberkamp.[73] Following Operation Schwarz, *Prinz Eugen* continued skirmishing the Partisans, all the while terrorizing the civilian population, murdering, destroying, and burning.[74] In retaliation for an ambush on an SS patrol requisitioning cattle and food in the Bosnian countryside, men of *Prinz Eugen* ordered the people of nearby Popovaca from their homes and, unable to distinguish between the guilty and the innocent, shot one hundred civilians at random.[75] Would this behavior be that of dregs or gems?

Then, in early September 1943 *Prinz Eugen* received an unexpected duty—accepting the surrender of Italian troops along the Adriatic coast. Anticipating a total Italian collapse after Mussolini's overthrow on July 26, the Reich military had drawn up plans for disarming the Italians, Case Axis.[76] Following Italy's capitulation to the Anglo-Americans on September 8, Reich forces occupied Italy north of a line drawn across the peninsula south of Rome. *Prinz Eugen* disarmed Italians along the Dalmatian coast, from Split in the north to Dubrovnik in the south.[77] Not all of the seven hundred thousand Italians in the Balkans surrendered meekly. On the Greek island of Cephalonia alone the Germans killed some four thousand resisting Italians. For the *Volksdeutsche* of *Prinz Eugen*, however, rounding up Italian POWs in picturesque locations such as Dubrovnik, Split, and the Dalmatian islands amounted to a much-needed respite. The 18,000 Italians *Prinz Eugen* captured in Split alone undoubtedly were among the 426,000 Italians the Germans deported to labor camps.[78] It is also estimated that as many as twenty thousand Italians defected to the Partisans, accounting for the large numbers of Italians noted in subsequent German reports on captured "bandits."[79]

Following the roundup of Italians, *Prinz Eugen* returned to chasing Partisans and in mid-November 1943 launched yet another major offensive, Operation Kugelblitz. Phleps had personally met with Hitler to discuss the plan. The offensive got off to an ominous start when *Prinz Eugen's* new commander, Carl von Oberkamp, bowed out, claiming physical and emotional stress. His replacement, August Schneidhuber, was barely up to the task. After struggling across rugged terrain, fighting in ice and snow, and suffering a rash of foot maladies inflicted by the horrendous weather, Kugelblitz smoked the Partisans out of their winter lairs but accomplished little else.[80] The Germans regarded this action a success, since the Partisans discarded much equipment and suffered more losses, an estimated—by German count—two thousand killed, 2,280 wounded, and 2,330 captured, along with 1,900 Italians. German losses were much lower.[81]

In his postwar account of this action, Phleps's chief of staff Otto Kumm mentions no German wrongdoing. He never refers to the general order to shoot all captured "bandits," an action that surely followed. Instead, sensitive to postwar charges of SS misbehavior and in an attempt to exonerate *Prinz Eugen*, he recalls captured Partisans on their knees thanking their German captors for bread.[82] Kumm also cites seizing an American flier, whom *Prinz Eugen* purportedly turned over chivalrously to the Luftwaffe in Sarajevo as a POW.[83] From the perspective of the adversary, the Partisan commander Milovan Djilas saw things differently—captured Partisans, except for those important enough for prisoner exchanges, had virtually no chance of survival.[84]

1944: Replenishing the Two Major Fronts

The year 1944 heralded German reversals all along the eastern front. In the coming year, the Red Army would drive German forces off all Soviet territory except the Kurland pocket in western Latvia. The Reich's forces could only muster defensive delays and a few brief counteroffensives. More than ever before, the Führer called on the Waffen-SS to stem the Red surge. In this futile effort, the Waffen SS truly earned its sobriquet "fire brigade," as Hitler frantically shuffled its units back and forth all across the front, hoping that his elite SS could halt the enemy's advance once more. Both the Wehrmacht and the Waffen-SS endured horrific casualties, with entire divisions obliterated. It would be under these deteriorating circumstances that the proportion of *Volksdeutsche* to Reich Germans in Waffen-SS units jumped in leaps and bounds.

One after another, in early 1944 several Waffen-SS divisions, including the elite *Totenkopf* and *Wiking*, turned westward from the eastern front after suffering debilitating losses. Many SS units by then had been replenished with ethnic Germans from the southeast, such as the large group from Batschka retreating with *Wiking.* Other ethnic German remnants joined *Florian Geyer.*[85] Another division with a large ethnic German contingent was the 11th SS Panzer Grenadier Division *Nordland*, which withdrew along with Army Group North from Leningrad through the Baltic States.[86] One of its surviving brigades was upgraded in early 1945 as the 23rd SS Freiwillinge Panzer Division *Nederland*, with its 2,500 Dutchmen augmented by two thousand *Volksdeutsche.*[87] One more SS division to appear in 1944 with a heavy infusion of *Volksdeutsche*, mainly inductees from the German-occupied Banat, was the 18th SS Panzer Grenadier Division *Horst Wessel*, which had trained briefly in Croatia by scrimmaging partisans. In March 1944, both *Horst Wessel* and *Florian Geyer* arrived in Hungary to hold its wavering regime in the Axis alliance—an assignment much closer to home for their southeastern *Volksdeutsche.*[88]

As the eastern front receded westward, in June the Anglo-Americans landed in northern France at Normandy and opened up the long-awaited second major front. Hitler frantically dispatched Waffen-SS "fire brigades" to Normandy to do what they could not do in the east—stop the enemy. Most of the SS divisions rushed to France contained sizeable contingents of *Volksdeutsche*; some were veterans of earlier campaigns, but most were recent conscripts from the southeast.[89] Although *Volksdeutsche* continued to fight on the two major fronts, for the majority, their principal effort in the last year of the war would be expended closer to home, in the Balkans and Hungary. Beginning in late summer 1944, SS divisions converged on the region, all well below strength but hoping to glean local ethnic German replacements. Several altogether new divisions would also arise in the area from the refuse of destroyed units—nearer to home but also closer to the battlefields.

At the start of 1944, the most experienced SS division fighting in the Balkans, engaged mostly in anti-Partisan hunting, remained

Prinz Eugen, which had steadily improved its image up to the status of a reliable, if not quite elite, SS formation. George Stein wryly comments that *Prinz Eugen* becoming a centerpiece of German defenses in the southeast was a sad commentary on the level to which Reich armed forces had sunk.[90] But just as it was about to take center stage, *Prinz Eugen* faced a leadership crisis. Its most recent commanders, Carl von Oberkamp and August Schneidhuber, who had taken turns at leading the division, had allowed it to run down. After an inspection in January 1944, prompted by an encounter in which a battalion was overrun and had fled, Phleps, as commander of the 5th Mountain Corps, was appalled at the generally poor condition, low morale, and scruffy appearance of his former unit. Attributing the less than stellar outcome of Operation Schwarz and recent reversals to its commanders, he asked Himmler for a replacement. Meanwhile, Phleps ordered *Prinz Eugen* to the Adriatic coast for rest and refitting and to await its new commander. The replacement in February was none other than Otto Kumm, a sharp critic of the division and Phleps's chief of staff.[91] Kumm steadily came to appreciate his new unit and sought to set it on par with the SS elite, capable of facing any crisis or contingency.[92]

In April, *Prinz Eugen* and its new commander returned from the Adriatic beaches and resumed hunting Partisans. Tito meanwhile had secured Allied recognition as a co-combatant warranting a British military liaison. When German intelligence in Belgrade discovered the location of Tito's political and military headquarters in Drvar in western Bosnia, Field Marshall Alexander Weichs ordered an assault for May 25—Tito's birthday—under the code name of Rösselsprung, the tricky knight's jump in chess. The Wehrmacht again assembled a huge force, hoping to wipe out the Partisans. The SS contribution included *Prinz Eugen* as well as its elite 500th SS Airborne battalion. The plan envisioned surrounding Tito along with the British mission and his highest political and military officers and then annihilating them, along with several PLA divisions, all in one swoop. The assault would begin with the Luftwaffe bombing the base, followed by the SS airborne jumping right on top of Tito's camp.[93]

The attack unfolded as planned with the Luftwaffe raid and the airborne assault, but then all hell broke loose: the defenders resisted fiercely, and Tito managed to escape, though just barely—leaving behind some twenty British dead and hundreds of other casualties, including on the German side a nearly destroyed SS airborne battalion.

A wounded Tito and his entourage fled to Kupresko Polje—an arduous journey of about a week—with *Prinz Eugen* in close pursuit. On one occasion the fugitives barely escaped, leaving behind Tito's marshal's uniform draped over a chair. Another war souvenir was the rucksack of Randolph Churchill, the British prime minister's son and a member of the Allied mission. Along the way, *Prinz Eugen* destroyed an entire Partisan division in rear-guard skirmishes, but Tito flew the coop: on the night of June 3–4, a Soviet-flown DC-3 lifted Tito and his party from Kupresko Polje to an Allied airfield at Bari in southern Italy.[94]

Although *Prinz Eugen* and its German partners failed to snag Tito, they claimed success, at least in the body count and in dispersing enemy forces. Otto Kumm, who had criticized his predecessors and blamed them for recent *Prinz Eugen* failures, placed as positive a spin as possible on this latest exercise in futility—since the major Partisan breakout from the encirclement had come through his sector. He blamed anything and everything—except for his own leadership—for the failure to close the trap: disruptive Allied air support for Tito, hasty and incomplete planning from above, inadequate communications and coordination, insufficient weaponry.[95] On the other hand, Kumm discerned improved performance from his men. He boasted how the Army's 15th Mountain Corps, a partner in the assault, commended both the 5th SS Mountain Corps and above all *Prinz Eugen* for distinction. Kumm also cited a wounded Wehrmacht soldier: "We were lucky soldiers to have comrades from *Division Prinz Eugen*, who were mostly *Volksdeutsche*, come save us."[96]

While still pursuing Tito, Phleps threw a victory party along the way and declared "free hunting," which in the context and parlance of counterinsurgency could mean only one thing—shoot everything and everyone in sight.[97] Before the men of *Prinz Eugen* could get back to "free hunting," they enjoyed some more downtime near the coast. It was during this interlude in the first week of June that a dismayed Kumm informed his troops of disturbing events hundreds of miles away in France:

> The great decisive battle of this war has begun with the invasion . . . the combat we are conducting here is also important for the overall outcome of the war. Continue to fight courageously and decisively. These fateful weeks and months will decide whether Germany survives or perishes. If each of us bravely commits his

life, then victory will be ours. Long live Germany! Long live the Führer! Forward, Prinz Eugen![98]

Despite Kumm's optimism, the war was about to take a very different turn in southeastern Europe, especially for the men of *Prinz Eugen*. Having returned to the combat zone, they discovered new partners, no longer their old friends of the Army's elite 1st Mountain Division but rather the new *Handschar*, which, except for its mostly *Volksdeutsche* officers (including its Croatian *Volksdeutscher* commander, Desiderius Hampel), consisted of Bosnian Moslems.[99] The Bosnians, however, preferred getting even with ethnic enemies to fighting Partisans, and in combat they deserted at the first opportunity. In September, the SS dissolved *Handschar*, sent most of the Moslems home, and transferred the German cadre to other SS units.[100] The same fate soon befell a second Bosnian division, the 23rd Waffen Gebirgs Division der SS *Kama*, with most Moslems released and its *Volksdeutsche* officers, many from Hungarian Batschka, recycled as the cadre for the new 31st SS Freiwilligen Panzer Grenadier Division *Böhmen-Mähren*.[101]

One final attempt at employing Balkan Moslems alongside ethnic Germans was the 21st Waffen Gebirgs Division der SS *Skanderbeg*, formed of Kosovo Albanians whose only inclination was murdering Kosovo Serbs. As their desertion rate approached one-half, in December *Skanderbeg* went the way of the other two Moslem divisions, with its rank and file sent home and its mostly Austrian and *Volksdeutsche* officers reassigned—many in this case to the new 32nd SS Panzer Grenadier Division *30 Januar*.[102] The only redeeming consequence of this dismal experiment in Balkan Moslems fighting for the Reich was having a ready-made German cadre available for the new, heavily *Volksdeutsche* SS divisions appearing at this late stage in the war.

The Southeastern Front: The Soviet Invasion

As the Red Army fought westward in a two-pronged assault toward Germany, one force along the Baltic coast and a second farther south through Poland, starting in the summer of 1944 a third Soviet thrust pushed into the Balkans, threatening to engulf the region and ultimately setting its sights on the Reich from that direction. Consequently, *Prinz Eugen* abandoned counterinsurgency and adopted an unaccustomed style of combat—conventional warfare, engaging regular armed forces, including the massed Red Army. By mid-July 1944, the Red threat attracted Hitler's attention to the Balkans as never before. Although the prospects of an Allied invasion in the southern Balkans still obsessed him, the real threat came from the northeast, where on August 19 the Red Army cut loose its offensive, quickly crossing the Dniester into Romania with nearly one million troops.

As Soviet forces advanced deeper into Romania, disillusioned and war-weary officers in Bucharest overthrew the wartime leader Marshall Ion Antonescu on August 23. They denounced the German alliance and defected to the Soviet side, trapping some sixteen German divisions in Romania. Two days after the reversal, some seven thousand German troops in Bucharest surrendered. Others tried to fight their way out of Romania, which resulted in heavy German casualties. Conversely, the Romanians granted the Soviets free passage into the Carpathians and Transylvania, home to one of the largest *Volksdeutsche* communities—at a time when most of their men were elsewhere, fighting in the ranks of the Waffen-SS.[103] By the end of August, the Red Army had occupied most of historic Romania and much of Transylvania. In early September, the Axis partner Bulgaria also defected.[104]

As the Soviets occupied Romania, in late August Arthur Phleps bid farewell to the men of *Prinz Eugen* as well as to his 5th Corps cadre and left for his native Transylvania—parts of which were already controlled by the Soviets, others by Romanians—to rally any remaining ethnic German men into a viable self-defense force. He arrived at Brasov (Kronstadt), hoping to use his friendship with Romanian officers to his advantage. Although cordial, his former Romanian colleagues denied his requests for organizing a militia as well as for evacuating the civilian population. In early September, while on a reconnaissance mission with only his driver, he mistakenly ran into a Soviet patrol and was captured. Evidently, he was taken to a local Red Army command post and then shot—though the Soviets claim it was a misunderstanding and not their intent.[105]

As if two defecting Axis allies were not enough, on August 29 Slovakia, emboldened by Romania's reversal, staged a rebellion.[106] The uprising caught both the Reich military and the Carpathian *Volksdeutsche* unprepared. Thousands of ethnic German civilians suffered terrible atrocities at the hands of rebelling Slovaks, particularly in central Slovakia. It was at this point that Germans who had remained loyal to Slovakia and had not yet switched to the SS, such as Col. Rudolf Pilfousek, did so. The first line of German defense was the *Heimatschutz*, the local ethnic German paramilitary self-defense force, along with available odds and ends from the Wehrmacht and the Waffen-SS. Several SS replacement units were tossed into the battle, as were two SS panzer grenadier battalions, organized as SS Kampfgruppe *Schill*. Himmler appointed none other than the chief Waffen-SS recruiter Gottlob Berger to command these German forces. Berger, accustomed to mustering troops from the most unpromising sources, was the right man for the job.[107]

Berger pulled together the aforementioned units as well as three nearby SS formations, *Horst Wessel*, elements of the 14th Waffen Grenadier Division der SS *Galizien*, and the infamous *Dirlewanger* Brigade—none by reputation among the elite, far from it. *Horst Wessel* arrived from Hungary, where it had joined in the Reich's military occupation of March 1944. It consisted overwhelmingly of *Volksdeutsche* draftees from Hungary, some eight thousand in all, reluctant and desertion-prone soldiers—true military dregs, at least in spirit if not physically.[108] *Galizien* had been refitting in Silesia after a drubbing in the Ukraine, and its ethnic Ukrainians and Galician *Volksdeutsche* added numbers, if not much else, to the fray.[109] The lowest of the low the Waffen-SS mustered were the thugs of the *Dirlewanger* Brigade, mostly convicted criminals who had applied their antisocial experiences to antipartisan operations on the eastern front. Few of the gathered troops were Reich Germans; the majority comprised *Volksdeutsche* from nearby Hungary, the Protectorate, and Slovakia itself.[110]

By November, this motley assembly had quelled the Slovak revolt. Some remained behind as security forces; others moved on to more urgent assignments or to one of several SS divisions under construction. Hungary henceforth became a staging area from where SS divisions or component parts deployed throughout southeastern Europe as expediency dictated. For better or for worse, the majority of *Volksdeutsche* from the southeast were finally fighting closer to home, and once they realized the immediacy of the threat to one's family and homeland, even the "dregs" became respectable if not quite elite soldiers. The war had finally become their battle, not just the Reich's.

While Berger's forces were suppressing the Slovak uprising, nearby areas heated up. One source of volatility was the rejuvenated Partisan movement. Tito was back in Yugoslavia, eager to fight but no longer satisfied with waging guerilla war in remote mountains.

He anticipated finishing the war leading a national liberation army and claiming both postwar authority and recognition.[111] But the paramount determinant remained the Red Army, which held the initiative. The Reich military, stretched thin across the region, could only react, scurrying between crises. Hitler ordered more "fire brigades" to the region, but the SS discovered that its knack for success had fizzled. Furthermore, as more divisions arrived, expecting to replenish manpower needs by dipping into the "barrel" of local *Volksdeutsche*, the bottom had come into view, leaving little but offal to scoop.

Meanwhile, *Prinz Eugen* was about to try its hand at conventional warfare. In late September, Army Group F Commander Weichs summoned Otto Kumm to Belgrade and ordered his division to Nish, close to the Bulgarian border, to halt the Red Army and its new Bulgarian allies. Kumm glumly noted that *Prinz Eugen* was about "to begin its next, most difficult page in its history."[112] Unaccustomed to fighting conventional forces and grossly outnumbered, the division took extremely heavy casualties but held its ground into October.[113] Indeed, the Partisans reported that at Nish they and their Soviet and Bulgarian allies had destroyed the main body of *Prinz Eugen*.[114]

The reports of *Prinz Eugen*'s destruction were premature, and its mission to hold Nish led into another, even more demanding assignment—securing a bridgehead at Kraljevo on the Morava River until the end of November, long enough to allow for the evacuation of Löhr's Army Group E from Greece. This fiercely contested withdrawal of some 300,000 to 350,000 German troops across Macedonia and the central Balkans covered more than one thousand kilometers and took several weeks—a monumental accomplishment often referred to as a "German Dunkirk." Kumm's division disengaged at Nish in mid-October, and its remaining four thousand soldiers marched over rugged terrain to Kraljevo. Here, these ethnic German veterans held on until November 28, when the tail end of Army Group E crossed the Morava. Sappers blew up the bridges, and *Prinz Eugen*'s survivors covered the retreating German columns, engaging in rear-guard action all the way. Several times they foiled traps and escaped annihilation, but with losses so heavy that the pronouncements of their demise were approaching truth.[115] Kumm, who received the Knight's Cross with Oak Leaves and Swords, declared Kraljevo his division's most illustrious wartime accomplishment. Erich Schmidt-Richberg, chief of staff of Army Group E, acknowledged *Prinz Eugen*'s heroism: "If Kraljevo was lost, Army Group E would have been lost."[116] Having earned copious accolades and a trove of decorations, *Prinz Eugen* returned to Bosnia then withdrew into Croatia.[117]

Prinz Eugen's *Volksdeutsche* had fought a conventional operation against tremendous odds and fulfilled their mission. Whatever their record may have been in terms of hunting guerillas (with all the concomitant atrocities, cruelties, and inhumanities charged to them), at Kraljevo, whether dregs or not, they performed at the highest level anyone could have asked of German soldiers at this low point in the war. While entire Wehrmacht divisions were being obliterated and other Waffen-SS units rendered useless, these *Volksdeutsche* continued fighting, and effectively at that. *Prinz Eugen*'s determined resistance at Kraljevo raised its status within the Waffen-SS, at least for the moment on par with those of the elites fighting on the other fronts.

The men of *Prinz Eugen* were not the only ethnic Germans battling across the expanding southeastern theater. Earlier, *Florian Geyer* and its mostly Hungarian *Volksdeutsche* troops had retreated from southern Russia across Romania, westward through Transylvania, eventually to Hungary.[118] In September, units of *Horst Wessel* stationed in Hungary briefly moved into northern Transylvania, as did the newly formed Kavallerie Division *Maria Theresia*, also encamped in Hungary—only to be repulsed by the Soviets. Survivors of these three SS divisions, mostly *Volksdeutsche*, limped back to Hungary to defend Budapest.[119]

While *Prinz Eugen* briefly had deployed eastward and southward in the fall, Tito's forces occupied more of the central Balkans and much of the Dalmatian coast and islands. Meanwhile, the Soviets advanced, targeting Belgrade as their principal goal; by mid-October, they had nearly surrounded the city. Concluding that resistance was folly, the Germans evacuated on October 19 and relocated west to Sarajevo and toward Croatia.[120] The Soviet "liberation" of Belgrade on the following day was part of a choreographed act—not entirely to Tito's liking—with the main Partisan force arriving two days later. The Soviets, however, had agreed to leave Belgrade in Tito's hands and turned north into Hungary, reserving the final defeat of the Germans in Yugoslavia for his indigenous forces.[121] Actually, Tito's maneuvering worked to the German advantage, since the Partisans, once outside their familiar mountain environment, were not as adept at conventional combat.

The Germans far preferred fighting Tito's "conventional" forces to the Red Army.

The *Volksdeutsche* and the Siege of Budapest

With the Soviet decision to concentrate on Hungary, the defense of Budapest became the Reich's top priority in the southeast—arguably equal to that of the Reich itself on its western and eastern borders. The situation turned particularly alarming for the Germans when in early October Hungary's wartime leader, Admiral Miklos Horthy, sought an armistice with the Soviets. Hitler, getting wind of this potential treachery, ordered SS supercommando Otto Skorzeny, along with men from *Maria Theresia*, many of them local *Volksdeutsche*, to arrest Horthy and replace him with a more malleable puppet regime.[122] As of October 15, the Reich totally dominated its Axis partner.

Hitler determined to defend Budapest at all costs and transferred divisions, including several "classic" Waffen-SS divisions, from the defense of the Reich itself to Hungary to reinforce the two predominantly *Volksdeutsche* divisions already there, *Maria Theresia*, with an estimated strength of eleven thousand and *Florian Geyer*, with another eight to twelve thousand, and Kampfgruppe *Ney*, mostly ethnic Germans formerly of the Honved.[123] In addition, the SS "dredged" up local German civilians who so far had evaded the roundup. In early November, one more scrape of the barrel resulted in a Home Guard of mostly overage *Volksdeutsche*.

On the last day of October, the Red Army had crossed the Tisza in eastern Hungary in force, and by November 2, Soviet tanks rumbled through Budapest's suburbs. With the Soviets at the gates, Hitler and his generals knew that once Budapest fell, the road to Vienna and the Reich lay open. The Führer also realized time was running out on another wartime objective, the annihilation of Europe's Jews. With all haste, SS police authorities in Budapest deported the city's remaining thirty-eight thousand Jews to the Reich and certain death. When one assesses the eleventh-hour German defense of Budapest, including the exploits of the two doomed *Volksdeutsche*-laden divisions, *Maria Theresia* and *Florian Geyer*, one must weigh not only their stubborn stand but also the costs of their foolhardy defense: the destruction of this magnificent city and, above all, facilitating the eleventh-hour murder of the city's last Jews.

An estimated fifty thousand Germans defended "fortress" Budapest—first and foremost the two predominantly ethnic German SS cavalry divisions, which fought alongside local police units, three Wehrmacht divisions, various headquarters and supply units, and thirty thousand demoralized Magyars, whose devotion to the Axis cause was suspect at best. Complicating the effort was the presence of eight hundred thousand entrapped civilians. Through November, the besieging Soviet forces, as many as 250,000 organized into two *fronts*—the Soviet equivalent of a German army group—tightened the noose around Budapest and by Christmas closed it completely. The mobility of the two SS cavalry divisions could no longer be exploited, though the presence of horses ensured that hunger would not be a problem for some time to come.[124]

Hitler threw in one Waffen-SS division after another to relieve Budapest, but they all failed to break the siege. In December, he sent two crack divisions, *Totenkopf* and the rebuilt *Wiking*, followed in January by the "Phoenix" version of the Sixth Army, the one destroyed at Stalingrad but later resurrected.[125] Two more "classic" units arrived—*Das Reich* and eventually *LSSAH*, with Otto Kumm, the erstwhile commander of *Prinz Eugen*, at its helm. Also on the scene were two below-strength units with large *Volksdeutsche* contingents, *Nordland* and *Nederland*. Others converging on Budapest included the 16th SS Panzer Division *RFSS*, the 12th SS Panzer Division *Hitlerjugend*, the 9th SS Panzer Division *Hohenstaufen*, and *Horst Wessel*.[126] Despite repeated probes by these relief columns, the Soviets did not yield. By February, only some sixteen thousand defenders survived within the city, and on the night of February 11, they attempted a breakout, but only around eight hundred managed to breach the Russian encirclement and reach German lines. The survivors included 170 men of *Florian Geyer* and *Maria Theresia*; the rest had perished or had been taken captive.[127]

One cannot attribute this spiritually and strategically disastrous defeat to the incompetency of the *Volksdeutsche* soldiers defending Budapest, though many were recent inductees from Hungary and other parts of the southeast with little incentive to fight except basic survival. At this point, quality no longer differentiated divisions such as *Maria Theresia* and *Florian Geyer*, consisting mostly of *Volksdeutsche*, from the "classic" divisions, including the elite of the elites, Leibstandarte SS *Adolf Hitler*, which by April 1945 was down to 1,500 men and, according to some, "wandering aimlessly."[128] It is noteworthy that at Budapest five *Volksdeutsche* of *Florian Geyer* earned the Knight's Cross of the Iron Cross, the Reich's highest military honor. Their military service converged at Budapest but coincidentally originated in distant, disparate homelands—Slovakia, Latvia, South Tyrol, the Dobrudja, and Bessarabia.[129]

From Budapest to the Final Surrender

With the fall of Budapest, the bloodied and depleted Waffen-SS divisions began a fighting withdrawal westward toward Austria. In the first week of March 1945, a number of these undermanned SS divisions, including the elites *LSSAH* and *Das Reich* along with *Hitlerjugend* and *Hohenstaufen*, rallied long enough for a counterattack near Hungary's northern oilfields along Lake Balaton. Nothing came of this futile sortie except more casualties. These demoralized SS "firemen" limped toward Vienna and their final stand. By then, desertions had became commonplace, as soldiers understood the war was lost—especially the ethnic Germans of the southeast, who realized that after finally fighting close to home, retreat only carried them farther away.[130]

In March, the Red Army started its final push toward Vienna, with Waffen-SS remnants alongside Wehrmacht bits and pieces still resisting. By April 7 the Soviets had reached Vienna, and on April 13 the city fell. The badly mauled SS troops, including tens of thousands of ethnic Germans, abandoned Vienna and fled westward and northward, fighting only for survival and hoping to reach the Anglo-American lines to surrender. Remnants of *Totenkopf* surrendered to the Americans, but relief turned to shock when their captors handed them over to the Soviets to face execution or lengthy captivity in Soviet slave-labor camps—the common misfortune of Soviet prisoners. Similar fates awaited the men of *Das Reich*, *LSSAH*, *Wiking*, *Hitlerjugend*, and *Reichsführer SS*.[131] As for *Horst Wessel*, also containing large numbers of *Volksdeutsche*, some ended up in Czechoslovakia, others in Silesia—the former surrendering to Czechs and Soviets, the latter to the Soviets alone.[132] The ethnically diverse *Nordland*, whose Scandinavians and *Volksdeutsche* had one more fight left in them, defended Berlin to the end but was ultimately wiped out by the Russians.[133] Grim too was the denouement of non-Germans, including the Ukrainians of *Galizien*, who reached Anglo-American lines but in accordance with wartime diplomacy were repatriated as "Soviet citizens."[134] All were either executed as traitors or shipped to Siberia.

The men of the newly formed "paper" SS divisions, the majority being the most recent recruits, fared no better. *Böhmen-Mähren*, with its Czechoslovakian ethnic Germans as well as coerced Hungarian *Volksdeutsche* from Batschka, retreated to central Czechoslovakia only to be destroyed by the Russians on the last day of the war.[135] Another patched-together unit with many *Volksdeutsche* was *30 Januar*, assembled near Frankfurt and sent to defend Berlin; only a few escaped alive.[136] The 33rd SS Division, the sorriest of all, was made up of *Volksdeutsche* well beyond their prime. Known derisively as the "Slouch Hat Division," it hardly fought, but many of its elderly *Volksdeutsche* ended up imprisoned in Austria.[137] Another last-second creation was the 37th SS Freiwillige Kavallerie Division *Lützow*, with hardly more than a few hundred cavalry survivors of Budapest. Some surrendered to the Soviets in Austria; others made it west to American lines.[138] The last of these so-called divisions, the 38th *Nibelungen*, created in southern Germany, skirmished Americans along the upper Danube before surrendering in early May.[139] One should mention the fate of another mostly *Volksdeutsche* division, the 24th SS Gebirgs Division *Karstjäger*, operating in northeastern Italy. Never more than a brigade, these Tyrolean mountain troops had fought Italian and Slovenian partisans as well as the British before capitulating to the latter in May.[140]

The End of *Prinz Eugen*

While much of the Waffen-SS converged on Budapest in late 1944, the men of *Prinz Eugen* continued a running battle with Soviet, Bulgarian, and Partisan forces in eastern Croatia.[141] By December, this much-reduced division remained the only SS "fire brigade" still operating in the Balkans and into 1945 doggedly held its own between the Save and Drava Rivers in the vicinity of Osijek and Vukovar. Evidently, that many of these *Volksdeutsche* were fighting closer to their homes had strengthened their will to fight. Division Commander Kumm observed proudly: "They had lost fear of the enemy," and their battle cry had become, "We want our Banat back!"[142] By tying down the enemy in eastern Croatia, they relieved pressure on the German position in Hungary. This final mission, following their heroic stand at Kraljevo, entitled the men of *Prinz Eugen* to claim equality with the elite units of the Waffen-SS, which, after all, had failed to break the Soviet siege of Budapest.

After losing their former commander Arthur Phleps as a casualty in September, in January 1945 *Prinz Eugen* lost a second, Otto Kumm, who was transferred to *LSSAH* in time to command it at Budapest. August Schmidhuber resumed command, holding it until final capitulation.[143] Being the sole Waffen-SS force still operating south of the Danube, *Prinz Eugen* dispersed its men to douse fresh "fires" in the region. In February and March, units returned to Bosnia to check the advancing Partisans near Sarajevo and Mostar. But the situation in Croatia required their return, and in mid-April they abandoned forever their familiar Bosnian battlegrounds.[144]

Unable to hold eastern Croatia for long, *Prinz Eugen* packed up for Zagreb for yet another installment of their incremental hold-fight-retreat from the Balkans. By April's end, they left the Croatian capital and turned northwest toward Maribor and Ljubljana.[145] As they departed, they moved even farther from their homes. Not knowing the state of their families and leaving rather than defending their homelands, these ethnic Germans finally and bitterly acknowledged their tragic fate. Dismay struck hard, and even the most optimistic lost hope; many at long last deserted and reversed their paths, back to homes and families, heedless of the consequences—shot as deserters if caught by Germans or as traitors if captured by Yugoslavs. Others, already resigned to loss of homes and loved ones and fearing the horrendous prospects of capture by the enemy, resolved to fight on.

In the first week of May, the remnants of *Prinz Eugen* reached Celje (Cilli) in Slovenia, not far from the Austrian border, where on May 8 they received orders to lay down their weapons and capitulate.[146] Four days later, just before their surrender, a regimental band struck up the "Deutschlandlied" for the last time.[147] Officers tried to negotiate surrender to the British at Villach, but the latter remained insistent that German forces in Yugoslavia must surrender to the Partisans. Expecting the worst, the officers released their men from all further obligations, leaving them to do as they pleased. Some decided to fight their way to Austria or the Reich; others hoped to blend in with the ragtag multitudes of retreating soldiers, civilians, and refugees; still others surrendered to the Partisans and prayed for the best. According to reports, the Partisans summarily executed some 1,600 captured men of *Prinz Eugen* and thousands of other German POWs. In all, the Yugoslavs accepted the surrender of some 150,000 German combatants, including many of Löhr's two hundred thousand men still with Army Group E. Löhr too had tried to surrender to the British, with the same result. The Partisans drove their mass of captives southward in what survivors referred to as a "death and hunger march," in which an estimated one-third perished.[148]

For the men of *Prinz Eugen* reaching British and American zones of occupation, the war was not over, since their captors complied with all Yugoslav requests for the extradition of alleged German war criminals. The Yugoslavs subsequently held show trials of the extradited, found all guilty, and executed them—hanging August Schmidhuber, its last division commander. Otto Kumm escaped Tito's rope thanks to American insistence on retaining him for interrogation. Incarcerated at Dachau, Kumm escaped and surfaced only after postwar tensions between the Western Allies and the Soviets, along with their communist partner Tito, precluded any further cooperation.[149]

In his wartime memoirs, Milovan Djilas confessed without remorse to the maltreatment of German POWs as well as civilian captives but declared it was "foreordained"—retaliation for German wartime atrocities perpetrated against the Yugoslav population. He admitted to the deplorable conditions in detention camps for combatants as well as civilian *Volksdeutsche* but added that these were understandable and justifiable—as were the postwar expulsions of all surviving ethnic Germans.[150] In the minds of most Yugoslavs, all Germans, above all the men of *Prinz Eugen*, deserved no mercy—a judgment having nothing to do with their fighting qualities. Yugoslav vengeance cared little whether they had been "dregs or gems"; they all wore the same gray uniforms. This was consequence for the *Volksdeutsche* of Hitler's rise to power.

This survey suggests that as the quality of the Reich's overall fighting forces went, so did the *Volksdeutsche*. In the prewar years and in the pre-Barbarossa phases of the war, little distinguished them from the Reich Germans in the Waffen-SS. With the 1942–1943 reversal of Germany's military fortunes and the concomitant growth of SS ambitions, the SS dipped into its manpower pool much deeper than limited resources allowed, diluting its quality. As it turned increasingly to the ethnic Germans of the southeast, the SS ignored all restraints and grabbed as many *Volksdeutsche* as fast as it could, going beyond reasonable limits and resorting to ruthless measures to dragoon as many men as possible. It stands to reason that the overall quality of ethnic Germans declined. But just as the "scraping of the barrel" in the southeast eroded *Volksdeutsche* competence, the simultaneous drawing from the dwindling Reich manpower pool likewise resulted in poorer Reich German soldiers. One must keep in mind that the classic Waffen-SS divisions, just as much as the 1943 expansion divisions, lost their luster and combat prowess as the war ground on—hardly different from *Prinz Eugen*, *Florian Geyer*, and other units relying mostly on *Volksdeutsche*.

By 1944, as the eastern front collapsed and, as of June, a viable western front came into being, divisions on both fronts, Wehrmacht as well as Waffen-SS—experienced destruction and disintegration while failing to halt the enemy's relentless drive. At the same time, the *Volksdeutsche* of *Prinz Eugen* continued to fight, as evidenced in their covering the retreat of three hundred thousand German troops from Greece, and then as the last Reich forces south of the Danube. One must also recall the siege of Budapest, where the doomed ethnic Germans of *Florian Geyer* and *Maria Theresia* fought to their end, while the elite "fire brigades" tried but failed to break Soviet entrapment. Indeed, when comparing collective performance, by the end of the war it was impossible to distinguish Reich from ethnic Germans in the Waffen-SS, and, as the Yugoslavs concluded, as they wreaked vengeance, all Germans had worn the same field-gray uniforms. In the cautious estimate of this author, though much research on the subject still lies ahead, it seems doubtful that fresh results will disclose any significant differences between the combat effectiveness of the two sets of German Waffen-SS men, the Reich Germans and the *Volksdeutsche*.

11   Project 100,000 in the Vietnam War and Afterward

Thomas Sticht

In August 1966, U.S. Secretary of Defense Robert S. McNamara stood before the Veterans of Foreign Wars and announced that in addition to fighting the war in Vietnam, the military services were also going to help fight President Lyndon Johnson's War on Poverty at home.[1] They would start taking in hundreds of thousands of under-educated, disadvantaged young men who were being rejected for service because their mental aptitude scores were at the lower end of the Armed Forces Qualification Test (AFQT). Because the plan was to enlist about one hundred thousand lower aptitude recruits a year, it was called Project 100,000.

The Project 100,000 men entered the military with three strikes against them. First, they bore the burden of participating in the Vietnam War at a time when the military's image was at its lowest. The nation was being rocked by civil rights riots. A controversial "War on Poverty" was being advocated by the president. In this context, the *Army Times* editorialized, "Are the services likely to get any reasonable mileage from such people? Past performance indicates not. . . . Is this any time to require the services to take on a large scale 'poverty-war' training mission? We would think not. The services more than have their hands full with the fighting war."[2]

Second, the Project 100,000 men suffered the burden of being introduced by Robert Strange McNamara, arguably the most contro-versial secretary of defense in our nation's history. At first admired for his intelligence and analytical prowess, he later became one of the most hated men in America by the officers and enlisted person-nel he had led. Shapley notes in her biography of McNamara that the Pentagon Papers revealed his belief early on that the Vietnam

War was not winnable, yet he continued to urge the fighting on, and because of this, "doubts about McNamara in many military quarters turned to hatred."[3]

Third, the Project 100,000 recruits worked under the stigma of demeaning stereotypes about the "lower mentality group." They were undereducated, and their scores on the military's "aptitude" or "literacy" tests were in the lower range. This brought down on them all the negative stereotypes and prejudices developed in the twentieth century for those who score low on such tests. McNamara himself noted that Project 100,000 was sometimes referred to as "McNamara's Moron Corps."[4]

Speaking at Defense Appropriations hearings in 1965, just a year before McNamara's announcement of Project 100,000, Senator Saltonstall revealed this type of negative bias against those who score lower on the military's aptitude tests in a reply to a statement about the "lower mental groups" made by General Earle Wheeler, the chairman of the Joint Chiefs of Staff:

> What you are saying General, is that, in substance, the great problem that we face throughout this country today when we see these terrible crimes that are being committed everywhere are being committed by the lower mentality which you say, and I agree with you, you have kept out of the Army and, therefore, you have a lower disciplinary area in the Army because they have a higher intellect. Those poorer ones are cluttering up our jails and committing crimes and attacking women today.[5]

Jumping forward some forty years reveals this same type of negative stereotyping of the less well-educated young adults who score at lower levels of the Armed Forces Qualification Test (AFQT). A *New York Times* opinion editorial discussed Project 100,000 and concluded that it was a "failed experiment." The article was entitled "Don't Dumb Down the Army."[6]

The *Times* editorial followed a long line of negative reports of Project 100,000 in the 1970s, 1980s, and 1990s. Seven years after the conclusion of Project 100,000, Baskir and Strauss wrote, "In the opinion of many military leaders, social planners and liberal critics, Project 100,000 proved a failure."[7] Almost a decade later, writing in *The New Republic* magazine, a lieutenant colonel in the U.S. Marine Corps commented about Project 100,000: "The results were neither satisfactory nor equitable. The 'New Standards' men flunked out of basic training at twice the usual rate, were court-martialed and dismissed with premature discharges twice as often."[8]

In 1990, at congressional hearings on the results of a three-year analysis of Project 100,000, the director of accession policy for the Department of Defense summarized the performance of Project 100,000 personnel (or New Standards men, as they were called by the DoD) in the military and stated, "In general, the New Standards men performed less well in the military than their higher aptitude peers. They had lower completion rates for both basic and skill training; their premature attrition rates were higher, and they had higher rates of indiscipline."[9] At the same hearing, testimony was also given by the DoD contractor who had led the research on Project 100,000 regarding how well the Project 100,000 veterans had fared some twenty years later: "these results suggest that Project 100,000 was less than successful in its stated goal of providing low-aptitude and disadvantaged youth an avenue for upgrading their skills and potential through military service."[10]

A Different Perspective on Project 100,000

From the foregoing, it is clear that there were two main concerns about Project 100,000, one dealing with the war in Vietnam and the other with the War on Poverty at home. For the war in Vietnam, concern was for how well the Project 100,000 personnel would perform in their military jobs. In the terms of the *Army Times* editorial, the question was, "Are the services likely to get any reasonable mileage from such people?" The second concern was with how well the Project 100,000 personnel would perform as veterans after their military service. Did they escape the so-called cycles of poverty that Project 100,000 was supposed to help overcome as its contribution to the War on Poverty?

Regarding the military performance of the Project 100,000 personnel, all the negative reports cited above were based on considering the differences between Project 100,000 personnel and a comparison group of fully qualified personnel in higher-aptitude categories in terms of "rates" of attrition, recycles in training, completion of the term of service, rank attained, or indiscipline (for example, court-martials and nonjudicial punishment). However, this comparative approach to evaluating the success of Project 100,000 fails to answer directly the primary question asked by the *Army Times*.

To answer this question, the analyses required are those that compare the performance of the Project 100,000 personnel to the expectations of the makers of military manpower policy before they initiated the project. In this case, all of the young men who were being denied service in the military because of their lower aptitude scores were considered to be equal risks for enlistment. That is, 100 percent of them were projected to fail; that is why they were being excluded from military service. So the proper evaluation should be based on how well the entire cohort of Project 100,000 men actually performed compared to the projection of 100 percent failure. The first part of this chapter examines the performance of the Project 100,000 personnel from this perspective and presents comparative data with fully qualified personnel to illustrate the differences in these approaches.

The second part takes up the question of how well the Project 100,000 personnel did as veterans after leaving the military. Once again, there are two ways to look at the project. One way is to compare the lives of the Project 100,000 men before they were enlisted in the military to their lives afterward, with a focus upon employment and income. This focus is the most relevant, since Project 100,000 was part of President Johnson's War on Poverty.

The second approach is to compare the lives of the Project 100,000 veterans to a group of civilians who were comparable to the Project 100,000 personnel at the time the latter enlisted or were drafted into the military. Here the question is whether or not military service was equally, more, or less effective in breaking the cycles of poverty than not serving in the military. This is the approach taken in the 1990 report to Congress by the Department of Defense's director of accession policy and the DoD contractor mentioned above.

The Military Performance of Project 100,000 Personnel

There have been three major analyses of the military performance of the Project 100,000 personnel.[11] Because these resources provide a detailed presentation of the data for Project 100,000 personnel, only a summary of some of the major findings will be given in this chapter.

Demographics and AFQT Scores of Project 100,000 Personnel

The following data are for the total Department of Defense. The data for each of the four military services differed somewhat from these totals.[12] The average age of the Project 100,000 personnel was twenty years, 46.9 percent were high school graduates or higher, the average number of school grades completed was 10.7, and the median reading grade level was 6.4. Some 61.8 percent were white, 36.7 percent were black, and 1.5 percent were "other."

DoD records indicate that from October 1, 1966, through June 30, 1971, instead of some 475,000 who would have been accessioned in the fifty-seven months that the program was in operation, only a total of 341,127 Project 100,000 personnel were accessioned. Reasons for this difference have not been found. But of the 341,127 accessioned personnel, 91 percent (over three hundred thousand) were new mental-standards recruits, and the remainder were new physical-standards recruits. Focusing on the mental-standards recruits, almost all (99.8 percent) of the Project 100,000 accessions had AFQT scores at or below the 30th percentile, with some 3.6 percent at or below the 9th percentile.

Basic Training Performance of Project 100,000 Personnel

All new military personnel first go through basic military training to convert them from civilian to military personnel. Policies regarding acceptable performance levels for all military personnel changed during Project 100,000. One set of policies held from October 1966 to June 1969; a different set held from June 1969 to June 1970. Basic training completion rates for the first time period for Project 100,000 personnel ranged from 96.3 percent for the Army to 88.9 for the Marine Corps, with an overall DoD completion rate of 94.6 percent. For the second time period, completion rates ranged from 94.5 percent for the Army to 62.2 percent for the Marine Corps, with an overall DoD rate of 87.6 percent. For a comparison group of fully qualified personnel with AFQT scores above the 30th percentile, the DoD rates of completion of basic training for the two time periods were 97.5 and 95.6 percent, respectively.[13]

Why the completion rates for both Project 100,000 and comparison groups fell during the second period above is not known. Laurence and Ramsberger speculated that "the fact that there was a reduction of some 60,000 troops stationed in Vietnam may help to explain DoD willingness to eliminate greater numbers of those who were not performing well even at the very start of their military careers."[14] No explanation has been found for why the Marine Corps differed so drastically from the other three services in their completion rates for both Project 100,000 and comparison personnel.

Using the DoD total data from above for the second period, it can be seen that the Project 100,000 personnel had a completion rate of 87.6 percent or, stated negatively, a 12.4 percent attrition rate. For the comparison group, the attrition rate was 4.4 percent. It is thus accurate to say that the Project 100,000 personnel had an attrition rate from basic training that was almost three times (12.4/4.4 = 2.8) that of the comparison group. However, this totally misrepresents the performance of the total cohort of Project 100,000 personnel, in which over 87 percent were successful during this period.

Job Training Performance of Project 100,000 Personnel

Following their completion of basic military training, personnel generally go into job training, though in the Navy and Air Force some go directly to a job position for on-the-job training).[15] Once in a formal job training course, there are two major indicators of performance, recycles and course completion. Recycles occur when a student fails a week of training and has to be held back to repeat that week. This adds time to the training system and is to be avoided if possible. For Project 100,000, a special analysis of the records for some 238,757 project personnel indicated that for the total DoD, 94.1 percent were never recycled.[16] This compares well to 98.3 percent with no recycles in the higher-aptitude comparison group.

Concerning job skills training course completion, this ranged from a high of 92.8 percent for the Army to a low of 86.8 percent for the Navy. For the comparison group, the completion rates ranged from a high of 96.8 for the Marine Corps to a low of 91.3 percent for the Navy.[17] For the overall DoD, with a sample of 177,449 Project 100,000 personnel, the completion rate was 86.2 percent, while for the comparison group it was 86.6 percent.[18] Clearly, the Project 100,000 men were largely successful in completing their entry-level job skills training and were prepared to enter into their military jobs.

Job Performance of Project 100,000 Men

One goal of Project 100,000 was to provide training and work experience for the civilian job market. Practically all military jobs have civilian counterparts; even many combat-skills jobs are in demand for security workers, armed guards, police and so forth. The major occupational areas to which the Project 100,000 men were assigned are indicated in Table 1. About a third of the Project

Table 1. Job Assignments of Project 100,000 Personnel and Comparison Group

Occupational Area	Project 100,000 (%)	Comparison Group (%)
Infantry, gun crews, seamen	34.4	23.1
Service and supply handlers	22.9	12.8
Electrical/mechanical equipment repair	16.1	22.0
Administration specialists and clerks	12.8	17.7
Craftsmen	6.2	4.8
Communications and intel specialists	4.0	5.8
Electronic equipment repairmen	1.8	7.5
Medical and dental specialists	1.4	4.0
Other technical and allied specialists	00.4	2.3
Total	100%	100%

Source: Sticht, Armstrong, Hickey, and Caylor (1987), 50, Table 17.

100,000 personnel and a quarter of the comparison group were assigned to the infantry and related combat jobs. This reflects the military's need for combat specialists in the Army and Marine Corps during the Vietnam war and the role played by aptitude testing in job placement, which restricted the assignment of Project 100,000 personnel into the more technical jobs.

Importantly, and contrary to the claims of critics, two-thirds of the Project 100,000 personnel were assigned to a variety of jobs with knowledge and skills useful in civilian life. These jobs included service occupations, mechanical repair, clerical occupations, and certain technical occupations in communications and electrical repair. Furthermore, supervisor's ratings of the job performance of the Project 100,000 personnel showed that over 96 percent of those in the Army were rated "good or excellent," and, at the low end of the ratings, in the Marine Corps over 85 percent were rated as "good" or "excellent."[19] Aggregated across all four military services, 91 percent of Project 100,000 and 96 percent of comparison group personnel had supervisor ratings of "above average" job performance.[20]

In addition to supervisor ratings, another indicator of how well the Project 100,000 personnel performed is indicated by the pay grade that they achieved after nineteen to twenty-one months of service. Overall, 66.7 percent of Project 100,000 and 81.6 percent of the comparison group had achieved pay grades of E-4 to E-5, pay grades that placed them in positions of some leadership over other personnel. In the Army, some 85 percent of Project 100,000 personnel achieved these higher pay grades.[21]

Another indicator of how well the Project 100,000 personnel performed in the military is the extent to which they received nonjudicial or court-martial disciplinary actions during their service. This addresses the sort of concern that Senator Saltonstall expressed in the Congressional hearings cited above: "the great problem that we face throughout this country today when we see these terrible crimes that are being committed everywhere are being committed by the lower mentality." But contrary to the fear that Project 100,000 personnel would wreak criminal havoc, over 96 percent of the Project 100,000 men in the Army and some 95 percent in the Marine Corps were never court-martialed; this compared to 99.4 and 95.3 percent for comparison groups in these services. Navy and Air Force Project 100,000 and comparison groups had incidents between the extremes of the Army and Marine Corps.[22] According to the former director of Project 100,000, the annual court-martial rate for Project 100,000 men was less than 3 percent, a figure he found encouraging.[23]

One final indicator of how well the Project 100,000 personnel performed is given by their rates of completion of periods of service studied by the DoD. For the total DoD, for Project 100,000 personnel with from thirteen to twenty-four months of service (an average of eighteen months of service), 83.8 percent completed their service, compared to 91.6 percent for a comparison group of higher-aptitude personnel.[24] Of the 16.2 percent of Project 100,000 men who did not complete the studied period of service, 10.5 percent failed for unsatisfactory performance or behavior, 2.6 percent for medical reasons, 2.0 percent for hardship or similar nonperformance reasons, and 0.4 percent for death.

Did the Services Get Reasonable Mileage from the Project 100,000 People?

The data on the performance of the Project 100,000 personnel in the armed services now makes it possible to answer the question asked by the *Army Times* before the project began: "Are the services likely to get any reasonable mileage from such people?" The answer has to clearly be "Yes!" Some 94 percent completed basic training with no recycles, 86 percent completed job skills training with no recycles, 91 percent received above average ratings by their supervisors, and some 84 percent completed the period of service studied by the DoD (eighteen months of service on average).[25]

These data indicate that hundreds of thousands of young men who would have been denied volunteer service (some 54 percent were volunteer enlistments)[26] or been excluded from the draft if Project 100,000 had not been implemented were found to perform well above the expectations of the naysayers. Apparently, the services got a lot of mileage from them. And, as indicated next, the Project 100,000 men themselves appear to have benefited as veterans later on.

The Project 100,000 Veterans

The second major question in evaluating Project 100,000 involves how well the Project 100,000 personnel performed as veterans after their military service. Did they escape the so-called cycles of poverty that Project 100,000 was supposed to help overcome as its contribution to the War on Poverty?

Two studies have been found that provide data showing both how well the Project 100,000 personnel achieved in civilian life as veterans after their military service and comparing their achievements to nonveterans of comparable mental qualities who did not serve in the military.

A 1970s Follow-up Study of Project 100,000

To determine the effects of veteran status on Project 100,000 men, Beusse reported the findings of a follow-up study of a stratified random sample of 477 of the Army's 22,009 Project 100,000 who entered the military between October 1966 and March 1967.[27] He compared them to a sample of 477 low-aptitude nonveterans matched as closely as he could on age, race, geographic location as a veteran (i.e., rural, urban, etc.), educational level, and AFQT score.

Table 2 summarizes the major findings reported by Beusse. Project 100,000 veterans had a higher proportion of full-time students than did the nonveterans. Both veteran and nonveteran groups had the same rates of full- and part-time employment, with an overall rate of some 90 percent. Nine percent of the nonveterans but only 6 percent of Project 100,000 veterans were unemployed. This contrasts sharply with the approximately 38 percent unemployment status of the sample of Project 100,000 personnel at the time of their enlistment in 1966 and 1967.

Table 2. Postservice Benefits to Project 100,000 Veterans in Relation to a Comparison Group of Nonveterans

Status at Time of Study	Project 100,00 Veterans	Nonveteran Comparison Group	Advantage to Veterans
Student[a]	4%	1%	+3%
Employed	90%	90%	0
Full-time	82%	82%	0
Part-time	8%	8%	0
Unemployed	6%	9%	+3[b]
High school graduate			
Before study	40%	40%	0
At study	53%	46%	+7%
Weekly wages by education			
Non–high school graduate	$131	$116	+$15
High school graduate	$132	$122	+$10
Weekly wages by race			
White	$138	$123	+$15
Black	$121	$113	+$8

(a) 68 percent of Project 100,000 veteran students were using the G.I. Bill.
(b) Expressed as + to indicate positive fact of 3 percent less unemployment for veterans
Source: Beusse (1974).

Beusse found that Project 100,000 veterans were more likely than nonveterans to have completed their high school education or obtain a General Education Development (GED) high school equivalency certificate. Project 100,000 veterans, both whites and blacks, earned more per week than did the nonveterans.

Sixteen years after he performed his research, Beusse was invited to provide testimony on the outcomes of Project 100,000 at the same 1990 congressional hearings as those referenced above.[28] In his testimony, Beusse noted that the Project 100,000 group had an AFQT mean of 12.9, compared to a mean of 10.1 for the nonveterans. But when analyses were controlled for these slight aptitude differences, "the economic advantage accruing to the veterans remained."[29]

The Project 100,000 Veterans Fifteen to Twenty Years Later
In 1986 and 1987, surveys of samples of Project 100,000 veterans and a comparison group of low-aptitude nonveterans were conducted.[30]

Table 3. Weekly Income for Project 100,000 and National Longitudinal Survey Sample in the 1966–1971 Period

Weekly Income (dollars)	Project 100,000		NLS Sample	
	N	%	N	%
0	75,234	46	1	<1
1–100	66,780	41	425	80
101–200	20,117	12	99	19
201+	682	<1	7	1
Total	162,813	100	532	100

Source: Laurence et al. (1985), 15–16, Tables 10–11. Data are for the percentage of cohort with weekly preservice income known.

The results included information of relevance to the question of whether or not Project 100,000 had helped the participants escape poverty, which was one of the key goals of the project.

As indicated in Table 3, when Project 100,000 was initiated, the young men brought into the military had low incomes as civilians. Laurence et al. reported that 46 percent of Project 100,000 entrants had earnings of zero, suggesting an unemployment rate of 46 percent or, conversely, an employment rate of 54 percent.[31] But by the time of the 1986–1987 interviews, some 88.5 percent were employed, 85 percent full time and 3.5 percent part time.[32] This is a large increase in the employment rate for the Project 100,000 personnel over what they experienced before entering the military.

Using the data of Table 3 for the Project 100,000 personnel and the midpoints of the ranges of income given, a weighted average weekly income of $39.88 was computed for the Project 100,000 men before they started their military service. Multiplying by forty-eight weeks (the procedure used by Laurence et al[33] to convert from weekly to annual incomes) translates the $39.88 into an annual income of $1,914, which is $96 *below* the poverty threshold for a single person in 1970 ($2,010), near the midpoint of Project 100,000.[34]

By the time of the follow-up study in 1986–1987 by Laurence et al.,[35] most of the Project 100,000 veterans were married, with an average of 1.9 children. The median income for all Project 100,000 veterans working both full- and part-time was $16,524, which was 50 percent more than the average threshold poverty-level income of $10,989 for a family of four in 1985.[36] Thus, not only had the Project 100,000 veterans as individuals raised themselves out of poverty, but they were also supporting a family with wages well above the poverty level for their family.

When asked how their military service had affected their post-military careers, 49.8 percent said it had helped, 36.6 percent said it had no effect, and only 13.6 said it had hurt their careers.[37] For those who said it had helped their careers, the five top reasons given were that their service had increased their maturity (37.9 percent), they benefited from the training they received (25.5 percent), "other" reasons (16.5 percent), the discipline they received (10.3 percent), and the educational assistance they received (6.9 percent).[38]

Project 100,000 Veterans Compared to Nonveterans

The report by Laurence et al.[39] was the basis for the testimony of the director of accession policy for the Department of Defense and Janice Laurence, the senior author of the report, to the U.S. Congress in 1990.[40] In their testimony, both of these witnesses claimed that the research on Project 100,000 and comparable low aptitude non-veterans indicated that Project 100,000 alumni did not achieve as well as the nonveterans. With respect to income, Laurence reported that "veterans fared significantly less well than their non-veteran counterparts."[41]

However, subsequent analyses indicated that the testimony was based on the achievements of the nonveteran group, which, as it turns out, was not comparable to the Project 100,000 sample. A RAND report questioned the design of the study because

it did not control for selectivity bias based on unobserved characteristics. Individuals were not randomly assigned to the control and test groups. Thus, if the veterans groups differed systematically from the non-veteran groups in some unobserved characteristic—such as level of maturity—then the results may be partially or fully attributable to these unobserved differences rather than to the effects of military experience relative to civilian experience.[42]

In a footnote on page 28, Asch also noted that the aptitude scores for the nonveteran comparison group were not based on AFQT scores, as were the Project 100,000 veterans. Instead, the aptitude levels for the nonveterans were "inferred" using a variety of intelligence and aptitude tests used in different high schools around the country. Nowhere in any of the reports by Laurence et al. are distributions or averages of aptitude scores of either the Project 100,000 veterans or the nonveteran comparison group given.

In addition to the lack of information about the actual comparability of aptitude scores for the Project 100,000 veterans and the nonveterans, a second major omission of the 1989 Laurence et al. report is that it failed to correct for the obvious differences in employment rates and income between the Project 100,000 veterans and nonveterans in the mid-sixties, when the project was started. As Table 3 shows, 46 percent of Project 100,000 men had no earnings before they started their military service, which is evidence for a 46 percent unemployment rate for the Project 100,000 men. This contrasts greatly with the nonveteran comparison group, where less than 1 percent had zero income, suggesting a less than 1 percent unemployment rate.

In their report of veteran and nonveteran employment rates, Laurence et al. indicated that some 11.5 percent of Project 100,000 veterans but only 8.4 of nonveterans were not working.[43] But despite the fact that the Project 100,000 veterans had *reduced* their unemployment rates from 46 percent to 11.5 percent and the nonveterans had *increased* their unemployment rates from less than 1 to over 8 percent, Laurence never made this point and instead reported to the U.S. Congress that with regard to unemployment status the data were "in favor of the non-veterans."[44]

The failure of Laurence et al. to correct for unemployment differences between the Project 100,000 veterans and the nonveteran comparison group was compounded by a similar failure to adjust for differences in income between the two groups when Project 100,000 started in the mid-1960s. As indicated above, the annual income estimated for Project 100,000 veterans in the mid-1960s was $1,914, while some twenty years later it was reported by Laurence et al. to be $16,524. When the latter is divided by $1,914, the result is an estimated rate of increase of income of 8.6.

In contrast, using the data of Table 3 and the same weighted averaging method as for the Project 100,000 men, the estimated annual income for the nonveterans in the mid-1960s was $3,384, almost twice the estimated annual income of the Project 100,000 men before they entered the military. When the income for the nonveterans twenty years later in 1989 was reported by Laurence et al., it was $20,912.[45] When the latter is divided by $3,384, the result is an estimated rate of increase of income of 6.2, which is less than three-fourths (72 percent) as high as the rate of income growth for the Project 100,000 veterans.

The data reported above for changes in unemployment rates and the growth rates for income over the time period from the mid-1960s to the time of the 1986–1987 survey suggest that military service provided a significant "leg up" for the Project 100,000 veterans over the nonveterans. This is consistent with the conclusion of Beusse,[46] who used data carefully matched for the Project 100,000 veterans and nonveterans, but directly contradicts the conclusions of Laurence et al., who used data unmatched for employment and income between the Project 100,000 veterans and the nonveteran comparison group.

In addition to their failure to match Project 100,000 veterans and nonveterans on premilitary service employment and income data, Laurence et al.[47] compared these two groups using sample sizes well below what they stated were necessary for drawing reliable conclusions about the postservice lives of the Project 100,000 men. For instance, while it was stated that a sample size of four hundred was appropriate for drawing reliable conclusions, the actual sample sizes used to compare Project 100,000 veterans to nonveterans on employment and income ranged from below one hundred to around 260. No information is provided as to how well matched these various subsamples of veterans and nonveterans were when statistical tests of the reliability of the differences in employment and income were performed. This raises considerable questions about selectivity bias in the Laurence et al. 1989 research, as stated by Asch,[48] and consequently challenges the validity of the entire study and the subsequent congressional testimony, stories in the public press, and the book[49] that resulted from it.

Summary and Discussion

Given the foregoing analyses, it now appears that many of the criticisms of Project 100,000 as a failure were not valid. First, regarding their military service, despite that the Project 100,000 personnel did not perform exactly as well as their higher-aptitude peers, they actually did exceed by a large margin the negative expectations for their performance as a group. Instead of finding a 100 percent failure rate, which was the expected rate, given that all the Project 100,000 men were taken from a group that had been excluded from service because of their low aptitude, it was found that some 85 percent or more actually performed well in basic training, job training, and on the job, without criminal or lesser disciplinary actions, and completed their tour of duty with honor.

Returning to the *Army Times* editorial, the issues raised of whether the services would get "any reasonable mileage from such people" and the statement that "Past performance indicates not" can now be addressed. The data indicate that indeed the military services got much more than just "reasonable mileage" from the Project 100,000 personnel. Furthermore, research by Sticht et al. indicated that during World War II hundreds of thousands of lower-aptitude, poorly literate personnel performed over 90 percent as well as higher-aptitude personnel and served their nation with honor.[50]

During the Korean War, there were more low-aptitude personnel enrolled than during Project 100,000,[51] but not much was made of this. After Project 100,000, during the late 1970s and early 1980s, the military made an error in its mental testing and accidentally enlisted more low-aptitude personnel than had participated in Project 100,000. These personnel also performed 85 to 95 percent as well as higher-aptitude personnel.[52] These findings indicate that the *Army Times* statement about the past performance of lower-aptitude men was not accurate. Before, during, and after Project 100,000, the large majority of lower-aptitude, undereducated members of the armed services have performed with satisfaction, and some with distinction.

The goal for Project 100,000 as a part of the War on Poverty was that the military service of lower-aptitude, economically disadvantaged young men would help them escape the "cycles of poverty" considered prevalent at the time. The data presented above, concerning the employment and income status of Project 100,000 personnel after they left the military, confirms that the War on Poverty goal was reached for the large majority of Project 100,000 veterans. Before their service, 46 percent were unemployed, and, on average, the Project 100,000 personnel were earning below-poverty wages for an individual. Years after their service, more than 80 percent were employed, and they were earning well above the poverty level for a family of four. Their increase in their rate of earnings from the mid-1960s to the mid-1980s was well above that of the nonveterans. These data challenge the validity of those who claimed that military service did not provide a "leg up" for the veterans over lower aptitude nonveterans.[53]

Given the preponderance of data indicating that Project 100,000 was a resounding success both for the war in Vietnam and the War on Poverty, why the numerous and continuing negative reports about the project? First, the three strikes discussed at the outset of this chapter no doubt cast a pale over the entire project: it occurred during the riots and widespread civil disturbances of the 1960s and a war that tarnished the image of the military services; second, it was announced by Robert S. McNamara, a hugely unpopular secretary of defense; and third, it played on racial and mental-ability biases prevalent then and now.

The importance of the mental-ability bias is indicated by the failure of the various studies, the congressional testimony of 1990, and popular press stories to place the focus of their analyses on the actual performance of the Project 100,000 personnel, instead looking at the differences between the lower-aptitude Project 100,000 personnel and the higher-aptitude military personnel. This mental-ability bias is also blatant in recent headlines like "Don't Dumb Down the Army," which captioned Greenhill's 2006 opinion article in the *New York Times*.

Finally, was Project 100,000 good for the military? Clearly, it helped the military meet its manpower requirements for the Vietnam War. It demonstrated that the pool of manpower available to perform well in the armed services was much larger than what was thought to be useful. Also, it produced hundreds of thousands of veterans, at least half of whom had positive feelings about the armed services. It is likely that these veterans passed on some of this positive affect for the military to their spouses and children. This helps to instill respect for and interest in the military in the civilian population, which is important and useful for a nation that depends upon volunteers to populate its defense forces.

Conclusions

Sanders Marble

We have looked at how five different countries have used different groups of substandard men in their armies at different times. Given the span of a century between the first and last examples, the limited number of examples, and the various cultural factors at play, it would be rash to draw definitive conclusions. Yet it is fair to say that substandard men can play a useful and at times important role in an army. German reservists in 1914 not only fought well, but their presence in the ranks was crucial for German strategy; the Veteran Reserve Corps held the forts at Washington D.C. for a vital day. They can often perform less-demanding roles in rear areas (including as occupation troops) and in quiet sectors. The Germans did this with their bodenstandig divisions, and some of the Soviet divisions were in low-priority sectors. The British found that Bantam troops could not perform as well as others but chose not to keep the units in secondary sectors. Motivation is a key, just as it is for "better" troops: the Balkan Volksdeutsche fought hard and effectively when their homes were threatened. The Soviets also applied enough compulsion to some units that they could get useful service from penal troops; thus motivation can depend on the regime's scruples. Conversely, low expectations can sabotage performance, as it did for French reserve units and African American units. But armies face changing circumstances, and the troops that are adequate to man coastal fortifications can be inadequate for a mobile battle. Because the stakes of a lost battle can be national survival, few generals would ask for second-rate troops. And managing substandard troops can be extremely hard, as the United States found with Limited Service men: too broad a category (either General Service or Limited) meant that a job could not be matched to a man. If there is a lesson on how to use substandard manpower, it seems to be to form special units, assign them tasks within their capabilities, and trust them.

All these examples are from the Industrial Age, and as the world moves to the Information Age, these examples may not offer as much information for public policy decisions. Yet they might offer more context, as computers and long-range weapons make "desk warriors" more important. How fit does the person controlling a drone have to be? One monitoring computers? As prostheses improve to the point that they are more energy efficient than a live limb,[1] the question will arise of whom the military can use. And other developments will also affect who can serve, and where. While the "powered armor" of *Starship Troopers* is currently science fiction, the U.S. Department of Defense is working on something similar. What will physical standards be then? Who can serve? Already a blind officer is retained on active duty in the U.S. Army, and amputees are not just staying in the military but returning to combat, as infantry.[2]

All these case studies offer scope for more study, and there is opportunity to look at other countries, other time periods, and naval and air forces. Other examples also exist for study, especially in colonial forces, the earlier Invalid Corps, and Oriental or Asian armies. Military historians need to broaden beyond studies of elites and the memoir- and oral history–driven interest in the everyman to think about the scrapings. Disability historians can ponder how disabled these men were, given that they were serving their countries. Historians can study how the various societies viewed disability and military service, how military service affects societies' definitions of "disabled," and how the various armies viewed those questions. In World War II alone there are several examples that could be studied:

> The British created a Pioneer Corps for labor and assigned to it men of lower intellect.
> The Finns had to mobilize both older and younger men to maintain the strength of their forces.
> The Japanese mobilized Koreans despite ethnic disdain.

Each of these case studies could shed light on different countries and different facets of "substandard." Moving slightly beyond World War II, from 1946 into at least the mid-1950s, the U.S. Army had a program to retain (rather than discharge) some amputees; its genesis and development could shed interesting light on who was fit enough for military service.

There are also many avenues for exploration of these specific examples.

Paul Cimbala's chapter shows what the Veteran Reserve Corps did and how motivated these wounded men were. The Confederate States had a corresponding Invalid Corps that bears study. In addition, the officers of the VRC were strongly engaged in Reconstruction, but did they have a postwar political impact in the Grand Army of the Republic out of proportion to their numbers?

Dennis Showalter humanizes the German reserve system and shows how the Kaiserheer gained valuable service from men who were not the best. The Germans had further categories for men as they aged, the Landwehr and Landsturm. How those units were conceptualized and utilized can be examined. The moves by Hindenburg and Ludendorff from late 1916 to reduce levels of garrison troops, shifting the men into newly formed front-line divisions, are also ripe for investigation.

Andre Lambelet is convincing on how the French army viewed reservists and pithy on how quickly the tune changed in combat. Yet the French, like the Germans, had still older men in service in Territorial divisions. Unlike the Germans, who pulled these men into action later in the war, the French largely pulled their Territorial divisions out of action. Why this happened, amid continuing French manpower mobilization—including troops from the colonies—deserves investigation.

Peter Simkins gives a wonderfully detailed look at the Bantam phenomenon in the British army. Yet we have little idea why the British leadership did not assign the Bantams to a mission they could accomplish—there were quiet sectors of the western front—instead of essentially abolishing the Bantams. Another topic of investigation could be how the divisions that were reformed with B2 manpower in 1918 after the heavy losses of the spring were used and how they performed. The Garrison Battalions, formed for defensive purposes but ultimately used on the attack, at least in the Middle East, are also worth study.

Steven Short describes the African American experience in World War I through an important facet, the officers, and the broader experience (throughout the period of segregated service) has been well examined. However, there can still be focused studies of how and where blacks were recruited over the decades of segregation, given that they knew they were going to be treated poorly. African American National Guard units can also be studied, especially in comparison with white units from the same states.

I described the problems of managing a mix of standard and substandard manpower. However, the U.S. Army, like the British, did not decide to form weaker units for lesser missions; that decision (or lack of a decision) could be probed. The evolution of both physical standards and the physical "profile" can also be usefully studied.

Walter Dunn looked at "substandard" in the Wehrmacht, using a single division as the example. There were many other bodenstandig divisions and security divisions for rear-area duties, and their combat performance should also be assessed. The process and problems of implementing (and managing) a system that classified men in five grades of fitness is also worthy of study.

David Glantz gave an excellent overview of how the Red Army used several categories of substandard manpower. It may take years to develop the sources, but divisional histories could assess how well various units fought and whether they were handled differently because of their component manpower. There were also undoubtedly many substandard men used behind the lines and in nondivisional units (such as the fortified regions), and the tasks the Soviet leadership identified for substandard men can be probed.

Valdis Lumans looks at both recruitment and combat performance of ethnic Germans in the Waffen-SS. He suggests one topic for exploration, how the "elite" SS divisions performed in comparison to their "lesser" *Volksdeutsche* counterparts later in the war. Another topic to examine is how the Wehrmacht handled the *Volksdeutsche*, specifically the Poles that the Germans assessed as largely to partly Germanic through the Deutsche *Volksliste* (German People's List). The *Volksliste* gave those who showed more Nazi political support higher status, and while *Volksliste* IV (the lowest category) were certainly drafted for the Wehrmacht, there were restrictions on them. The military and political thinking, as well as the equation of political support with quality, are interesting topics.

Thomas Sticht looked at the U.S. Army's Project 100,000. The other services had their share of "New Standards" men, and their experience can also be studied. The small number of men who were physically below standard can also be examined.

Fitness for military service is far more flexible than has generally been imagined. Just as "normal" is a social construct with different answers in different countries and time periods, so is "substandard" both in society in general and in the military. It is intuitive that in major wars, when millions are mobilized, standards have to be lowered, but how that is handled can vary dramatically. It is also easy to imagine a wide range of postwar effects. Disability historians have indeed looked at veterans and the postwar implications of groups (especially amputees and those with facial wounds) becoming more accepted by society: of disfigurements becoming "honorable wounds." These groups especially, but others with humbler injuries as well (such as frostbite), can also tell us something about how the body was viewed. It is certainly worth examining a society's view of an amputee veteran, but it is also worth looking at an older, less-fit man still in service. We owe it to the men who served despite their perceived—or ascribed—problems not to leave them out of history.

Notes

Introduction
Sanders Marble

1. Warren Treadgold, *Byzantium and Its Army* (Stanford, Calif.: Stanford University Press, 1995), 11, citing *Codex Theodosianus* 7.22.8. Clyde Pharr's translation *The Theodosian Code and Novels and the Sirmondian Constitutions* (Union, N.J.: Lawbook Exchange, 2001), 184, gives slightly different details than Treadgold's.

2. "Army Recruiting Remains on Track Despite Challenges," http://www.2010military.com/military-news-story.cfm?textnewsid=2718. Accessed June 4, 2010.

3. Susan Birch, ed., *Encyclopedia of American Disability History* (New York: Facts On File, 2009).

4. The U.S. Army Military History Institute had fourteen bibliographies about blacks and thirteen about women and the military available on June 4, 2010. Books on elites look both at high-ranking and privileged elites and elite units; examples are Roger Beaumont, *Military Elites* (London: R. Hale, 1976); and A. Hamish Ion and Keith Neilson, eds., *Elite Military Formations in War and Peace* (New York: Praeger, 1996).

1. Federal Manpower Needs and the U.S. Army's Veteran Reserve Corps
Paul A. Cimbala

1. General Orders, no. 105, April 28, 1863, Adjutant General's Office, War Department, Library, United States Army Military History Institute, Carlisle, Penn. Hereinafter cited as GO with number and AGO, USAMHI.

2. *Washington* (D.C.) *Daily National Intelligencer*, December 15, 1863; also see Col. R. H. Rush to P. R. Freas (Germantown, Penn., *Telegraph*), July 3, 1863, Letters Sent (LS), vol. 1, Veteran Reserve Corps, Records of the Provost Marshal General's Office, Record Group 110, National Archives Building, Washington, D.C. Hereinafter cited as VRC, RG 110.

3. Capt. J. W. De Forest to Brig. Gen. J. B. Fry, November 30, 1865, in United States War Department, *The War of the Rebellion: A Compilation of the Official Records of the Union and Confederate Armies* (Washington, D.C.: Government Printing Office, 1880–1891), series 3, vol. 5, 543, 565–567. Hereinafter cited as *Official Records*. For an overview of the VRC, see Paul A. Cimbala, "Union Corps of Honor," *Columbiad* 3 (Winter 2000): 59–91. The following essay is based on initial research first presented in the above noted article as well as "Soldiering on the Home Front: The Veteran Reserve Corps and the Northern People," in *Union Soldiers and the Northern Home Front: Wartime Experiences, Postwar Adjustments*, ed. Paul A. Cimbala and Randall M. Miller (New York: Fordham University Press, 2002), 182–218; and "Lining Up to Serve: Wounded and Sick Union Officers Join the Veteran Reserve Corps during the Civil War, Reconstruction," *Prologue: Quarterly of the National Archives and Records Administration* 35 (Spring 2003): 1–12; as well as a complete reading of the VRC records housed in the National Archives Building, Washington, D.C.

4. For a discussion of the means by which the Northern states and the federal government raised troops, see Paul A. Cimbala, *American Soldiers' Lives: The Civil War* (Westport, Conn.: Greenwood Press, 2008), 39–57. Also see Duane C. Young, "Army, United States (1861–1865)," in *Encyclopedia of the American Civil War: A Political, Social, and Military History*, ed. David S. Heidler and Jeanne T. Heidler, 5 vols. (Santa Barbara, Calif.: ABC-CLIO, 2000), 1:110. James M. McPherson provides manpower estimates in *Ordeal by Fire: The Civil War and Reconstruction*, 3rd ed. (Boston: McGraw Hill, 2001), 166–173; and *Battle Cry of Freedom: The Civil War Era* (New York: Oxford University Press, 1988), 306–307n, 322.

5. James W. Geary, *We Need Men: The Union Draft in the Civil War* (DeKalb: Northern Illinois University Press, 1991), 15, 84; Fred Albert Shannon, *The Organization and Administration of the Union Army, 1861–1865*, 2 vols. (Cleveland, Ohio: Arthur H. Clark Company, 1928), 1:169–171.

6. McPherson, *Ordeal by Fire*, 166–173; Richard Nelson Current, *Lincoln's Loyalists: Union Soldiers from the Confederacy* (Boston: Northeastern University Press, 1992), 32, 46–49, *passim*. Geary, *We Need Men*, 81, 83–85, 133; Jim Leeke, ed., *A Hundred Days to Richmond: Ohio's "Hundred Days" Men in the Civil War* (Bloomington: Indiana University Press, 1999), xi–xvii, *passim*; Shannon, *The Organization and Administration of the Union Army*, 1:90–91; Ira Berlin, Joseph P. Reidy, and Leslie S. Rowland, eds., *Freedom: A Documentary History of Emancipation, 1861–1867*, series 2: *The Black Military Experience*

(Cambridge: Cambridge University Press, 1982), 12, 14; Laurence M. Hauptman, *Between Two Fires: American Indians in Civil War America* (New York: Free Press, 1995); D. Alexander Brown, *The Galvanized Yankees* (Urbana: University of Illinois Press, 1963); Michèle Tucker Butts, *Galvanized Yankees on the Upper Missouri: The Face of Loyalty* (Boulder: University Press of Colorado, 2003).

7. Stephen W. Sears, ed., *Mr. Dunn Browne's Experiences in the Army: The Civil War Letters of Samuel W. Fiske* (New York: Fordham University Press, 1998), 172–173.

8. De Forest to Fry, November 30, 1865, *Official Records*, series 3, vol. 5, 543.

9. Ibid., 543–544.

10. For example, see Michael Mann, *The Veterans* (Norwich: Michael Russell, 1997), which discusses the English use of old soldiers and invalids from the late seventeenth century down into the 1860s and briefly notes the French experience that had influenced the English.

11. Harry M. Ward, *The War for Independence and the Transformation of American Society* (London: UCL Press, 1999), 141–142.

12. De Forest to Fry, November 30, 1865, *Official Records*, series 3, vol. 5, 544. The Confederacy made use of invalids and also passed legislation to establish a formal Invalid Corps in February 1864. However, the Confederate Invalid Corps only provided a fraction of the organization achieved by its Yankee counterpart, ultimately having only some few thousand men on its rolls. H. H. Cunningham, *Doctors in Gray: The Confederate Medical Service*, 2nd ed. (Baton Rouge: Louisiana State University Press, 1960), 42–43; Kenneth Radley, *Rebel Watchdog: The Confederate States Army Provost Guard* (Baton Rouge: Louisiana State University Press, 1990), 19–20, 25–26, 29.

13. De Forest to Fry, November 30, 1865, *Official Records*, series 3, vol. 5, 544–545; Col. M. N. Wisewell to Fry, October 24, 1864, Annual Reports, 7, VRC, RG 110.

14. Rush to Fry, November 6, 1863, Annual Reports, 1; Wisewell to Fry, October 24, 1864, Annual Reports, 7, VRC, RG 110; Fry to E. M. Stanton, November 17, 1863, *Official Records*, series 3, vol. 3, 1052.

15. Wisewell to Fry, October 24, 1864, Annual Reports, 7, VRC, RG 110.

16. Circular no. 14, May 26, 1863, Provost Marshal General's Office (PMGO), *Official Records*, series 3, vol. 3, 225–227; GO 212, July 9, 1863, Adjutant General's Office (AGO), *Official Records*, series 3, vol. 3, 474; De Forest to Fry, November 30, 1865, *Official Records*, series 3, vol. 5, 546, 548–549.

17. GO 212, July 9, 1863, AGO, *Official Records*, series 3, vol. 3, 475–477.

18. Rush to Lt. Col. R. H. Coolidge, August 25, 1863; Circular [—], October 1, 1863, Letters Sent, vol. 2, VRC, RG 110.

19. H. Tilley to parents, June 4, 11, 20, 28, July 1, 5, 1863, Hiram Tilley Letters, Pearce Civil War Documents Collection, Navarro College, Corsicana, Tex.

20. Circular no. 14, May 26, 1863, PMGO, *Official Records*, series 3, vol. 3, 225–227; De Forest to Fry, November 30, 1865, *Official Records*, series 3, vol. 5, 546, 548–549.

21. De Forest to Fry, November 30, 1865, *Official Records*, series 3, vol. 5, 556, 559.

22. Rush to Lt. Martin Reichenbacker, May 20, 1863, LS, vol. 1; Wisewell to Fry, October 24, 1864, Annual Reports, 1–37, VRC, RG 110; Lt. R. F. Andrews to Lt. Col. G.A. Washburn, June 30, 1864, 20th VRC, Regimental Papers; Special Orders, no. 32, July 1, 1864, 20th VRC, Regimental Papers; Special Orders, no. 28, January 28, 1865, 9th Regiment, VRC, Regimental Papers, Records of the Adjutant General's Office, Record Group 94, National Archives Building, Washington, D.C. (hereinafter cited as AGO, RG 94); Cimbala, "Lining Up to Serve," 38–39.

23. Circular no. 14, May 26, 1863, PMGO, *Official Records*, series 3, vol. 3, 225–227; GO 290, August 19, 1863, AGO, *Official Records*, series 3, vol. 3, 691; De Forest to Fry, November 30, 1865, *Official Records*, series 3, vol. 5, 547. African American veterans, however, would not be among the new members of the corps. In August 1864, the secretary of war reminded Gen. Nathaniel P. Banks, then commander of the Department of the Gulf, and Wisewell that they had "no authority for the establishment of an invalid corps of colored troops under any name whatever." C. W. Foster to Banks, August 12, 1864, Letters Received (LR), box 2, VRC, RG 110.

24. De Forest to Fry, November 30, 1865, *Official Records*, series 3, vol. 5, 547–548.

25. Ibid.

26. Capt. James McMillan to Col. John R. Lewis, February 1, March 8, April 28, 1865; McMillan to Cahill, February 24, 1865, LS, vol. 4, VRC, RG 110. Also see Rush to Fry, November 6, 1863, Annual Reports, 1, VRC, RG 110.

27. De Forest to Fry, November 30, 1865, *Official Records*, series 3, vol. 5, 550, 566.

28. Wisewell to Fry, October 24, 1864, Annual Reports, 8, VRC, RG 110. The name change did not have that effect; as noted earlier and suggested below, direct enlistments into the corps were always fewer than the bureaucrats had optimistically expected.

29. For example, see the correspondence from Col. E. B. Alexander to Fry, during the spring, summer, and fall of 1863 in LR, box 1, VRC, RG 110.

30. GO 105, April 28, 1863, AGO, USAMHI; Rush to W. Schouler, September 30, 1863, LS, vol. 2, VRC, RG 110; De Forest to Fry, November 30, 1865, *Official Records*, series 3, vol. 5, 557.

31. Orson H. Woodworth to Fry, August 28, 1863, LR, box. 53, VRC, RG 110.

32. GO 304, September 10, 1863, *Official Records*, series 3, vol. 3, 783.

33. Wisewell to Col. A. J. Johnson, December 29, 1863; Wisewell to Col. F. D. Sewall, March 19, 1864; Wisewell to J. W. Forney, January 5, 1864, all in LS, vol. 3, VRC, RG 110.

34. De Forest to Fry, November 30, 1865, *Official Records*, series 3, vol. 5, 550–551.

35. A. S. Diven to Fry, June 26, 1863, LR, box 13, VRC, RG 110.

36. R. H. Welch to Adj. Genl. Penn [A. L. Russell], May 26, 1865, LR, box 2, VRC, RG 110.

37. J. T. Burgess to E. M. Stanton, September 18, 1863, which includes all material for Pvt. J. T. Burgess Inquiry Proceedings, October 3, 1863, LR, box 4, VRC, RG 110; Paul A. Cimbala, "Private John N. Underwood Objected to His Transfer to the Union Army's Invalid Corps," *America's Civil War* (September 2005): 64, 69.

38. G. Whitman to Ruth Whitman, March 5, 1865, George Whitman File, Civil War Misc. Collection (CWMC), United States Army Military History Institute (USAMHI), Carlisle, Penn.; A. O. Goodrich to Abraham Lincoln, January 28, 1864, LR, box 21, VRC, RG 110.

39. E. C. Fisk to [Levi] Hines, February 1, 1864, Levi Hines file, Schoff Civil War Soldiers' Letters, William L. Clements Library, University of Michigan, Ann Arbor.

40. For a detailed examination of officers' motivations, see Cimbala, "Lining Up to Serve," 38–49.

41. Benjamin Hawkes to Fry, November 30, 1863, LR, box 23, VRC, RG 110.

42. Resolution dealing with the formation of an Invalid Corps, Officers of Burnside Barracks, near Indianapolis, Indiana, [October 22,] 1863, George Wagner Collection, Hargrett Rare Book Room and Manuscript Library, University of Georgia, Athens.

43. For examples, see Wisewell to Col. J. D. Green, February 1, 1864, Letters Sent by 3rd Division, vol. 1; Col. James C. Strong to Fry, December 11, 1863, LR, box 46; Capt. W. Spencer to Fry, January 15, 1864, LR, box 46, VRC, RG 110.

44. Wisewell to Green, February 1, 1864, Letters Sent by 3rd Division, vol. 1, VRC, RG 110.

45. De Forest to Fry, November 30, 1865, *Official Records*, series 3, vol. 5, 548; Allen Douchy to [M. E. Saunders], November 28, 1864, Mary Elizabeth Saunders Correspondence, Connecticut Historical Society, Hartford.

46. Rush to Maj. Mathews, July 6, 1863, LS, vol. 1, VRC, RG 110; Wisewell to Maj. F. A. H. Gaebel, November 29, 1864, Regimental Records, 16th Regiment VRC, AGO, RG 94; De Forest to Fry, November 30, 1865, *Official Records*, series 3, vol. 5, 549.

47. GO 21, July 6, 1864, Headquarters, 1st Brigade VRC, Regimental Papers, 9th Regiment VRC; Lt. J. G. Shephard to Capt. C. D. Lyon, August 3, 1864, Headquarters, 4th Regiment VRC, Regimental Letter Book; Circular, June 6, 1865, Post Headquarters, Camp Douglas, Illinois, Regimental Papers, 15th Regiment VRC; Circular, June 4, 1865, and Circular, October 4, 1865, Headquarters Garrison, Washington, D.C., 9th Regiment VRC, AGO, RG 94.

48. Cahill to Fry, December 11, 1863, LR, box 16, VRC, RG 110.

49. Wisewell to Pvt. W. Treadwell, January 30, 1864, vol. 3, LS, VRC, RG 110.

50. Rush to Col. C. M. Prevost, August 11, 1863, LS, vol. 1; Rush to Capt. R. Touty, August 28, 1863, LS, vol. 2, VRC, RG 110.

51. Capt. James M. Davenport to Lt. George W. Corliss, October 12, 1865, Hartford, Conn. Depot Camp, Regimental Papers, 3rd Regiment VRC, box 5022, AGO, RG 94.

52. Cimbala, "The Veteran Reserve Corps and the Northern People," 205–208.

53. GO 9, August 2, 1863, Headquarters, Invalid Corps, Camp Anderson, District of Columbia, General Orders and Circulars, 1863–1864, vol. 133/242DW, United States Army Continental Commands, 1821–1920, Record Group 393, National Archives Building, Washington, D.C. Hereinafter cited as USACC, RG 393.

54. Rush to Touty, August 28, 1863; Rush to Col. B. S. Porter, October 3, 1863, LS, vol. 2; Wisewell to Col. J. B. McIntosh, January 15, 1864; Wisewell to Lt. Col. Allan Rutherford, March 9, 1864, Letters Sent by the Third Division, vol. 1, VRC, RG 110.

55. Asst. Surg. C. A. McCall to Wisewell, November 30, 1863, LR, box 33, VRC, RG 110.

56. Rush to Fry, November 6, 1863, Annual Reports, 2, VRC, RG 110; De Forest to Fry, November 30, 1865, *Official Records*, series 3, vol. 5, 556.

57. De Forest to Fry, November 30, 1865, *Official Records*, series 3, vol. 5, 566.

58. Rush to Fry, November 6, 1863, Annual Reports, 1, 2, VRC, RG 110.

59. Judith A. Bailey and Robert I. Cottom, eds., *After Chancellorsville: Letters from the Heart: The Civil War Letters of Private Walter G. Dunn and Emma Randolph* (Baltimore: Maryland Historical Society, 1998), 25, 36.

60. Rush to Fry, November 6, 1863, Annual Reports, 1; Wisewell to Fry, October 24, 1864, Annual Reports, 9, VRC, RG 110; J. J. Hayes to J. Campbell, March 1, 1864, VRC Misc. Papers, box 5199, AGO, RG 94; Maj. William Austine to the Provost Marshal General, July 11, 1865, Historical Reports of the State Acting Assistant Provost Marshal General and District Provost Marshals, 1865, roll 5, National Archives Microfilm Publication M1163 (hereinafter cited as Historical Reports, M1163 with appropriate roll number); J. K. Barnes to Stanton, October 31, 1865, *Official Records*, series 3, vol. 3, 966.

61. Maj. John Devereux to Maj. C. C. Gilbert, December 9, 1863; Capt. William Brian to Surg. J. J. Hayes, September 13, 1864, LR, box 14, VRC, RG 110.

62. Lt. Richard Goebel to W. P. Moore, May 31, 1864, LR, box 24, VRC, RG 110.

63. For some Second Battalion men who failed to live up to standards, see Capt. J. C. Peterson to Wisewell, March 19, 1864, LR, box 40; Surg. Chas. O'Leary to Sewall, October 14, 1864, LR, box 38; J. M. Cuyler to Surgeon General USA, October 28, 1864, LR, box 16, VRC, RG 110.

64. Rush to Fry, November 6, 1863, Annual Reports, 2; Wisewell to Fry, October 24, 1864, Annual Reports, 5–7, VRC, RG 110; De Forest to Fry, November 30, 1865, *Official Records*, ser. 3, vol. 5, 560–565.

65. Lt. Col. Garrick Mallery to Fry, October 20, 1865, LR, box 36, VRC, RG 110.

66. These various duties are documented in the Regimental Papers, 3rd Regiment VRC, box 5022, AGO, RG 94.

67. De Forest to Fry, November 30, 1865, *Official Records*, ser. 3, vol. 5, 561.

68. Lt. Col. Garrick Mallery to Fry, October 20, 1865, LR, box 36, VRC, RG 110.

69. Entries for Jan.-Feb. 1865, Diary, Gideon W. Burtch Papers, CWMC, USAMHI.

70. *After Chancellorsville*, pp. 19, 28, 182, 185, 215; Benjamin F. Turley to brother, July 3, 1864, Jonathan Turley Papers, Indiana State Library, Indianapolis.

71. Acting Assistant Surg. L. D. Lays to Surg. W. J. Sloan. Feb. 23, 1865, box 5199, VRC Misc. Papers, AGO, RG 94; Maj. William Austine to Provost Marshal General, July 11, 1865, roll 5, Historical Reports, M1163.

72. Cimbala, "Soldiering on the Home Front," pp. 203–215.

73. Maj. W. Austine to the Provost Marshal General, July 11, 1865, Historical Reports, roll 5, M1163; De Forest to Fry, November 30, 1865, *Official Records*, ser. 3, vol. 5, 562, 563.

74. E. C. Fisk to [Levi] Hines, Feb. 1, 1864, Levi Hines file, Schoff Civil War Soldiers' Letters, William L. Clements Library, University of Michigan, Ann Arbor.

75. Capt. Lewis Hollman to Col. [A. Y.] Johnson, November 21, 1863, VRC Misc. Papers, box 5204, AGO, RG 94.

76. Lt. S.D. Underwood to Corliss, October 14, 1865, Regimental Papers, 3rd Regiment VRC, box 5022, AGO, RG 94.

77. Cimbala, "Soldiering on the Home Front,"187–89.

78. C. D. Robbins, History of Operations, June 1, 1865, roll 4, Historical Reports, M1163.; Cimbala, "Soldiering on the Home Front,"197.

79. Capt. Garett Nagle to De Forrest, October 17, 1865, LR, box 37, VRC, RG 110; De Forest to Fry, November 30, 1865, *Official Records*, ser. 3, vol. 5, 561.

80. Gaebel, "Report of the History and Operations of the 16th Regt. V. R. Corps," enclosed in Gaebel to De Forest, October 19, 1865, LR, box 23, VRC, RG 110.

81. Col. C. Johnson to Fry, Sept. 30, 1864, LR, box 28; Col. Charles Johnson to De Forest, October 12, 1865; Surg. W. C. Roller and other surgeons to Capt. R. L. Orr, June 12, 1864, LR, box 29, VRC, RG 110; De Forest to Fry, November 30, 1865, *Official Records*, ser. 3, vol. 5, 553–556.

82. Wisewell to Fry, October 24, 1864, Annual Reports, 9, 10, 11, VRC, RG 110.

83. Entries for November 1864, Peter S. Ludwig Diary, CWMC, USAMHI.

84. Cimbala, "Soldiering on the Home Front," 215–218; John William De Forest, *A Union Officer in the Reconstruction*, ed. James H. Croushore and David Morris Potter (New Haven, Conn.: Yale University Press, 1948), xiv–xv.

85. De Forest to Fry, November 30, 1865, *Official Records*, ser. 3, vol. 5, 559, 567.

86. Cimbala, "Soldiering on the Home Front," 209.

87. Nagle to De Forrest, October 17, 1865, LR, box 37, VRC, RG 110.

88. Col. M. O. Mansfield to De Forrest, October 17, 1865, enclosed in Mansfield to De Forrest, October 18, 1865, LR, box 36, VRC, RG 110.

89. McMillan to Commanding Officer, 3rd Regiment VRC, May 25, 1865, Post Orders of Depot Camp, Hartford, Conn., vol. 97/260, USACC, RG 393.

90. Underwood to Corliss, October 14, 1865, 3rd Regiment VRC, Regimental Papers, box 5022, AGO, RG 94.

91. G. Whitman to Ruth Whitman, April 10 [1865], George Whitman File, CWMC, USAMHI; John T. Sumny to [A. L. Russel], Adjutant General of Pennsylvania, [filed under Pennsylvania, State of] May 13, 1865, LR, box 42, VRC, RG 110.

92. GO 56, August 1, 1866; GO 92, November 23, 1866, AGO, USAMHI.

93. McIntosh to Bvt. Maj. Gen. J. F. Barstow, December 7, 1866, LS, vol. 1, Records of the 42nd Regiment Infantry, Records of the United States Regular Army Mobile Units, Record Group 391, National Archives Building, Washington, D.C. Hereinafter cited as USA Mobile Units, RG 391.

94. Capt. Tully McCrea to General, April 28, 1867, Company Reports and Officers' Reports, 1867, 42nd Regiment Infantry, USA Mobile Units, RG 391.

95. McIntosh to Bvt. Maj. Gen. Harvey Brown, December 29, 1869; McIntosh to Maj. R.E. Morgan, January 7, 1867; McIntosh to Capt. Charles F. Greene, February 13, 1867, McIntosh to Bvt. Lt. Col. T. W. [Grutry?], May 1, 1867, LS, vol. 1, 42nd Regiment Infantry; Lt. Col. G. A. Woodward to Bvt. Maj. Gen. A. B. Dyer, August 9, 1867; Woodward to Adjt Genl U.S. Army, February 15, 1868, LS, vol. 1, 45th Regiment Infantry, USA Mobile Units, RG 391.

96. Maj. F. E. Trotter to Lt. W.A. Coulter, November 8, 1866; Capt. J. H. Donovan to Adj. Genl U.S.A., May 19, 1868, Letters Sent, vol. 1, 44th Regiment Infantry, USA Mobile Units, RG 391.

97. GO 116, June 17, 1865; GO 155, October 26, 1865; GO 165, November 24, 1865; GO 56, August 1, 1866; GO 92, November 23, 1866; GO 24, July 24, 1868; GO 16, March 11, 1869, AGO, USAMHI.

98. GO 165, November 24, 1865, AGO, USAMHI.

99. Lt. W. F. DeKnight to Erastus W. Everson, March 16, 1866, Erastus W. Everson Papers, South Carolina Historical Society, Charleston.

100. Cimbala, "Lining Up to Serve," 46–48.

101. For a brief look at the Freedmen's Bureau and its work, see Paul A. Cimbala, *The Freedmen's Bureau: Reconstructing the American South after the Civil War* (Malabar, Fla.: Krieger Publishing, 2005).

102. Lt. D. J. Connolly to Brig. Gen. E. D. Townsend, August 2, 1865, LR, box 13, VRC, RG 110.

103. Endorsement of Maj. Gen. O. O. Howard on Capt. Edward S. E. Newbury to Howard, August 21, 1865, LR, box 37, VRC, RG 110.

104. Howard to Fry, March 21, 1866, April 23, 1866, LR, box 27, VRC, RG 110.

105. Cimbala, *The Freedmen's Bureau*, 20–22.

106. De Forest, *A Union Officer in the Reconstruction*, 39.

107. Ibid., xxix.

108. Ibid., 30. For another representation of the commonly shared experiences of VRC officers serving with the Freedmen's Bureau, see Suzanne Stone Johnson and Robert Allison Johnson, eds., *Bitter Freedom: William Stone's Record of Service in the Freedmen's Bureau* (Columbia: University of South Carolina Press, 2008).

109. Capt. William H. Merrell to Bvt. Brig. Gen. John Ely, April 6, 1866, enclosed in Ely to Capt. H. S. Browne, April 9, 1866, LR, BRFAL, roll 74, M752.

110. Ibid.

111. James E. Sefton, *The United States Army and Reconstruction, 1865–1877* (Baton Rouge: Louisiana State University Press, 1967), 261–262.

112. Cimbala, "Lining Up to Serve," 47–48; Paul A. Cimbala, *Under the Guardianship of the Nation: The Freedmen's Bureau and the Reconstruction of Georgia, 1865–1870* (Athens: University of Georgia Press, 1997), 76–77; Pension File of Jabez Blanding, Civil War Pension Files, Record Group 15, National Archives Building, Washington, D.C.

113. Ely to Fry, June 9, 1865, Historical Reports, roll 3, M1163; Ely to Browne, April 9, 1866, LR, roll 74, BRFAL, M752.

2. A Grand Illusion? German Reserves, 1815–1914
Dennis Showalter

1. Heinz Stuebig, "Heer und Nation: Zur Entwicklung der paedagogisch-politischen Ideen Hermann von Boyen," *Militaergeschichtliche Mitteilungen* 58 (1999): 1–22, discusses the Prussian intellectual roots of this process. For general comparative background, cf. Thomas Hippler, *Citizens, Soldiers, and National Armies: Military Service in France and Germany, 1789–1839* (New York: Routledge, 2008).

2. For details of the Landwehr's origins and early years, see Dennis Showalter, "The Prussian Landwehr and Its Critics, 1813–1819," *Central European History* 4 (1971): 3–33; and Dorothea Schmidt, *Die preussische Landwehr: Ein Beitrag zur Geschichte der allgemeinen Wehrpflicht in Preussen zwischen 1815 und 1830* (Berlin: Militaerverlag der DDR, 1981). The analysis in Dierk Walter, *Preussische Heeresreformen 1807–1870.*

Militaerische Innovation und der Mythos der "Roonschen Refom"
(Paderborn: Schoeningh, 2003), 326–386, is excellent.

3. Curt Jany, *Geschichte der preussischen Armee vom 15. Jahrhundert
bis 1914*, vol. 4 (Osnabrueck: Biblio, 1967), 178ff., summarizes the major
troop movements. On the Landwehr, cf. Manfred Messerschmidt, "Die
Preussische Armee," in *Deutsche Miliaergeschchte*, vol. IV/2 (Frankfurt:
Bernard & Graefe, 1979), *passim*. Robert Sackett, "Die preussische
Landwehr am linken Niederrhein um die Mitte des 19. Jahrhunderts,"
Annalen des Historischen Vereins fuer den Niederrhein, 194 (1991):
167–188, focuses on the western provinces. For background and detail,
cf. R. de l'Homme de Courbiere, *Die preussische Landwehr in ihrer
Entwicklung von 1815 bis zur Reorganisation von 1859* (Berlin: Mittler,
1867); and Conrad Canis, "Der preussische Militarismus in der Revolution
von 1848" (dissertation, Rostock, 1965).

4. The issue of reduced service is a major theme of *Militaerische
Schriften Kaiser Wilhelms des Grossen Majestaet*, ed. kgl.
Pr.Kriegsministerium, 2 vols. in 1 (Berlin: Mittler, 1897), which includes a
large amount of relevant correspondence dating to 1833 in 1:142, *passim*.
The issue is summarized in Walter, *Preussische Heeresreformen
1807–1870*, 345–358, from a perspective sympathetic to the shorter
service.

5. Contemporary commentaries by external observers, like "Die
Heeresreform in Preussen," *Allgemeine Militaer-Zeitung* 35 (1860); and
"Die Praeszenszeit," *Allgemeine Militaer-Zeitung* 37 (1862) tended to take
two-year service for granted.

6. "Motive und Vorschlaege zu einer Reorganisation fuer die
Preussische Armee (Konzept des Oberstleutnant von Clausewitz),
Juli 1857," in *Militaerische Schriften Kaiser Wilhelms*, 2:326ff. Cf. the
discussion in Walter, *Preussische Heeresreformen 1807–1870*, 288ff.; and
H. Witte, *Die Reorganisation des preussischen Heeres durch Wilhelm I*
(Halle: Niemeier, 1910), 37ff.—the latter still useful for details.

7. Dieter Langewiesche, "Reich, Nation und Staat," *Historische
Zeitschrift* 254 (1992): 341–381; and L. Haupts, "Die liberale Regierung in
Preussen in der Zeit der 'Neuen Aera,'" *Historische Zeitschrift* 227 (1978):
45–85.

8. "Bemerkungen und Entwuerfe zur vaterlaendischen
Heeresverfassung," in *Militaergeschichtliche Schriften Kaiser Wilhelms*,
2:344ff.; and in Albrecht von Roon, *Denkwuerdigkeiten aus dem Leben
des Generalfeldmarschalls Kriegsministers Grafen von Roon*, 2nd ed.,
3 vols. (Breslau: Trewendt, 1892), 3:521ff. Dierk Walter, "Roon, the
Prussian Landwehr, and the Reorganization of 1860," *War in History*

16 (2009): 269–297, deftly shreds the myth of Roon's central role and the limited direct impact of this memo.

9. Rolf Helfert, *Der preussische Liberalismus und die Heeresreform von 1860* (Bonn: Holos, 1989); and "Die Taktik preussischer Liberaler von 1858 bis 1862," *Militaergeschichtliche Mitteilungen* 53 (1994): 33–48, are the most detailed on the politics of military reform. For the economics, see Klaus Erich Pollmann, "Heeresverfassung und Militaerkosten im preussisch-deutschen Verfassungsstaat 1860–1868," in *Parliamentaerische und oeffentliche Kontrolle von Ruestung in Deutschland, 1700–1970*, ed. J. Duellfer (Düsseldorf: Droste, 1992), 45–61.

10. Walter, *Preussische Heeresreformen 1807–1870*, 477.

11. *Allerhoechsten Verordnungen ueber die groesseren Truppenuebungen* (Berlin, 1861); and the brief commentary in Jany, *Geschichte der preussischen Armee*, 231–232.

12. For background on this issue, see Klaus Latzel, *Vom Sterben im Krieg: Wandlungenin deDroster Einstllungzum Soldatentod vom Siebenjaehrigen Krieg bis zum II. Weltkrieg* (Warendorf: Fahlbusch, 1988).

13. Walter, "Roon," 283.

14. Willerd Fann, "On the Infantryman's Age in Eighteenth-Century Prussia," *Military Affairs* 41 (1977): 165–170.

15. Walter, "Roon," 285.

16. Statistics on the Landwehr are from Jany, *Geschichte der preussischen Armee*, 4:264–265; exact figures vary slightly. Hermann Rahne, *Mobilmachung: Militaerische Mobilmachungsplanung und Technik in Preussen und im Deutschen Reich vom Mitte des 19. Jahrhunderts bis zum Zweiten Weltkrieg* (East Berlin: Militaerverlag der DDR, 1983), 50–51, criticizes Prussian planners for significantly underestimating personnel requirements of even a relatively short war in an industrial context.

17. The point is well demonstrated in Margaret Anderson, *Practicing Democracy: Elections and Political Culture in Imperial Germany* (Princeton, N.J.: Princeton University Press, 2000).

18. Ute Frevert, "Das Militaer als 'Schule der Maennlichkeit.' Erwartungen, Angebote, Erfahrungen im 19. Jahrhundert," in *Militaer und Gesellschaft im 19. und 20. Jahrhundert* (Stuttgart: Klett-Cotta, 1997), 134–163.

19. *Facsimile Querschnitt durch die Berliner Illustrierte*, ed. F. Luft (Munich, 1965), 46ff.

20. Cf. the surveys by Holger Afflerbach, "'Bis zum Letzten Mann und letztewn Groschen?' Die Wehrpflicht im Deutschen Reich und

ihre Auswirkung auf die militaerische Fuehrungsgedenken im Ersten
Weltkrieg" in *Die Wehrpflicht*, ed. R. G. Foerster (Munich: R. Oldenbourg,
1994), 71–90; and Jack Dukes, "Militarism and Arms Policy Revisited:
The Origins of the German Army Law of 1913," in *Another Germany: A
Reconsideration of the Imperial Era*, ed. J. Dukes and J. Remak (Boulder,
Colo.: Westview, 1988), 19–40.

21. Volker Berghahn, *Der Tirpitz-Plan: Genesis und Verfall einer
innenpolitischen Krisenstrategie unter Wilhelm I* (Düsseldorf: Droste,
1971).

22. Dennis Showalter, "German Grand Strategy: A Contradiction in
Terms?" *Militaergeschicthliche Mitteilungen* 48 (1990): 65–102, and, from
a different perspective, Stig Foerster, "Facing 'People's War': Moltke the
Elder and Germany's Military Options after 1871," *Journal of Strategic
Studies* 10 (1987): 209–230.

23. Cf. Jehuda Wallach, *The Dogma of the Battle of Annihilation: The
Theories of Clausewitz and Schlieffen and Their Impact on the German
Conduct of Two World Wars* (Westport, Conn.: Greenwood, 1986); and
Antulio Echevarria, *After Clausewitz: German Military Thinkers before
the Great War* (Lawrence: University of Kansas Press, 2000).

24. The best example is Isabel V. Hull, *Absolute Destruction: Military
Culture and the Practices of War in Imperial Germany* (Ithaca, N.Y.:
Cornell University Press, 2005).

25. See Stig Foerster, "Militaer und staatsbuergerlich Partizipation.
Die allgemeine Wehrpflicht im Deutschen Kaiserreich, 1871–1914," in *Die
Wehrpflicht*, 55–70.

26. Jany, *Geschichte der preussischen Armee*, 326–329.

27. Except where otherwise noted, the following is based on Dennis
Showalter, "Army and Society in Imperial Germany: The Pains of
Modernization," *Journal of Contemporary History* 18 (1983): 583–608;
and "The Army as an Instrument of Social Integration in Imperial
Germany," in *Another Germany*, 1–18. For contemporary color, see
the excerpts in *Untertan in Uniform. Militaer und Militarismus im
Kaiserreich 1871–1914*, ed. B. Ulrich, J. Vogel, and B. Ziemann (Frankfurt
am Main: Fischer, 2001), 57–64; and, judiciously, Haupt Heydemark,
Soldatendeutsche (Berlin, 1934).

28. Cf. Benjamin Ziemann, *War Experiences in Rural Germany,
1914–1923*, trans. A. Skinner (New York: Berg, 2007); Dieter Dreetz,
"Methoden der Ersatzgewinnung fuer das deutsche Heer 1914–1918,"
Militaergeschichte 16 (1977): 701–706; and especially for the statistics,
Hermann Gauer, *Von Bauerntum Buergertum, und Arbeitertum in der
Armee* (Heidelberg: Schulze, 1936).

29. Ute Frevert, *A Nation in Barracks: Modern Germany, Military Conscription, and Civil Society*, trans. A. Boreham and D. Brueckenhaus (New York: Berg, 2004), offers an alternative and far less sympathetic interpretation of this process and its long-term consequences.

30. Cf. L. Mertens, "Das Privileg des Einjaehrig-Freiwilligen Militaerdienst im Kaiserreich und seine gesellschaftliche Bedeutung," *Militaergeschichtliche Mitteilungen* 39 (1986): 59–66; and Hartmut John, *Das Reserveoffizierkorps im deutschen Kaiserreich 1890–1914* (Frankfurt: Campus, 1981).

31. John, *Das Reserveoffizierkorps*, 471.

32. See Alexander Watson, "Junior Officership in the German Army during the Great War, 1914–1918," *War in History* 14 (2007): 429–453.

33. As did the future Protestant clergyman Adolf Clarenbach, *Heitere Erinnerungen aus dem Leben eines westfaelischen Landesgeistlichen* (Borgeln: Kirchengemeinde, 1981), 31–32.

34. Hartmut Wiedner, "Soldatenmisshandlungen im Wilhelminischen Kaiserreich (1890–1914)," *Archiv fuer Sozialgeschichte* 22 (1982): 159–199.

35. This is by no means a specifically German phenomenon. Drill instructors in all mass armies not infrequently deliberately single out such a recruit as a warning to the rest that their lot can always get worse.

36. Cf. U. Broeckling, "Psychopathische Minderwertigkeit? Moralischer Schwachsinn? Krankhafter Wandertrieb? Zur Pathologisierung von Deserteuren im Deutschen Kaiserreich Vor 1914," in *Armeen und ihre Deserteure. Vernachlaessigte Kapitel einrt Militaergeschichte der Neuzeit*, ed. U. Broeckling and M. Sikora (Goettingen: Vandenhoek & Ruprecht, 1998), 161–186.

37. Harold C. Deutsch, "Training, Organization, and Leadership in the German Reserve System: The Eve of World War I," in "German and Allied Army Reserves in 1914," HERO report prepared for the Office of the Assistant Secretary of Defense, February 1980, 16–18.

38. "Wie man als Reservist behandelt wird," *Dresdner Volkszeitung* (August 8, 1911), in Politisches Archiv des Auswaertigen Amtes, Deutschland 121/16.

39. Paul Plaut, "Psychographie des Kriegers," in *Beihefte zur Zeitsschrift fuer angewandte Psychologie* 21 (1920): 11ff. Cf. Bernd Ulrich, "Kriegsfreiwillige. Motivationen, Erfahrungen, Wirkungen," in *August 1914: Ein Volk zieht in den Krieg*, ed. Berliner Geschichtswerkstaat (Berlin, 1989), 232–241.

40. Jeffrey Verhey, *The Spirit of 1914: Militarism, Myth, and Mobilization in Germany* (Cambridge: Cambridge University Press, 2000).

41. Cf. the distinguished works by Michael Schmid, *Der Eiserne Kanzler und die Generaele Deutsche Ruestungspolitik in der Aera Bismarck (1871–1890)* (Paderborn: Schoeningh, 2002); and Stig Foerster, *Der doppelte Militarismus. Die deutsche Heeresruestungspolitik zwischen Status-Quo-Sicherung und Aggression 1890–1913* (Stuttgart: Steiner, 1985).

42. The most up-to-date reference and compendium on this issue is *Der Schlieffenplan: Analysen und Dokumente*, ed. by Hans Ehlert, M. Epkenhans, and G. Gross (Paderborn: Schoeningh, 2006).

43. For background, see Foerster, *Doppelte Militarismus*, 165ff.

44. See the skeleton *Aufmarschplaene* from 1893/94 to 1913/14, reproduced in *Der Schlieffenplan*, 345–477.

45. In 1914, half the fourteen reserve corps were from a single district. In addition to the reserve divisions that took the field, three others were formed as the "main reserve" of major fortresses, to reinforce the regular garrisons, and provide some tactical flexibility.

46. Jany, *Geschichte der preussischen Armee*, 281, 301–304, *passim*.

47. For these anomalous and amorphous formations, see Eric Dorn Brose, *The Kaiser's Army: The Politics of Military Technology during the Machine Age, 1870–1918* (Oxford: Oxford University Press, 2001), 81.

48. Theodor W. Fuchs, "The Readiness and Performance of German Army Reserves in 1914, with Particular Reference to the Combat of the XXV German Reserve Corps at Lodz, Poland," in "German and Allied Reserves," 20–31.

49. *Der Weltkrieg, 1914 bis 1918, Kriegsruestung und Kriegswirtschaft*, ed., Reichsarchiv Abt. III, vol. 1 (Berlin: Mittler, 1930), 107–108. For context, see Annika Mombauer's excellent *Helmuth von Moltke and the Origins of the First World War* (Cambridge: Cambridge University Press, 2001), 86–105.

50. Schlieffen was so concerned at the reserve corps' weakness in artillery that in 1912 he recommended amalgamating reserve and active units in the same corps—another probably unintended acknowledgement of the old Landwehr/Line connection. Schlieffen to Freytag-Loringhoven, August 14, 1912, in *Generalfeldmarschall Schlieffen. Briefe*, ed. E. Kessel (Goettingen, 1958), 317–318.

51. Fuchs, "The Readiness and Performance of German Army Reserves," 32–36.

52. Deutsch, "Training, Organization, and Leadership," 11–13; and *Die Schlacht in Lothringen und in den Vogesen, die Feuretaufe der Bayerischen Armee* (Munich, 1929), 1–33.

53. Most recent and comprehensive is Alex Watson, "The Identity and Fate of the German Volunteers, 1914–1918," *War In History* 14 (2005): 44–74. Cf. also Karl von Unruh, *Langemarck: Legende und Wirklichkeit* (Koblenz: Bernard & Graefe, 1986); and H. Kopetzky, *In den Tod, Hurra. Deutsche Jugendregimenter im Ersten Weltkrieg* (Cologne: Pahl-Rugenstein, 1981).

54. Erwin Rommel, *Attacks*, trans. J. R. Driscoll (Vienna,Va.: Athena, 1979), 3ff.; Walter Bloem, *The Advance from Mons*, trans. G. C. Wynne (London: Davies, 1930), 66ff.

55. Holger Herwig, *The Marne, 1914* (New York: Random House, 2010), is the latest and best general work to affirm the overall combat performance of German reservists during the war's early stages.

56. H. Linnenkohl, *Vom Einzelschuss zur Feuerwalze. Der Wettlauf zwischen Technik und Taktik im Ersten Weltkrieg* (Koblenz: Bernard & Graefe, 1990).

57. Cf. Wallach, *The Dogma of the Battle of Annihilation*; Terence Zuber, *Inventing the Schlieffen Plan: German War Planning, 1871–1914* (New York: Oxford University Press, 2002); and Robert T. Foley, *German Strategy and the Path to Verdun: Erich von Falkenhayn and the Development of Attrition, 1870–1916*, (Cambridge: Cambridge University Press, 2005).

58. S. D. Jackman, "Shoulder to Shoulder: Close Control and 'Old Prussian Drill' in German Offensive Infantry Tactics, 1879–1914," *Journal of Military History* 68 (2004): 73–104; and "Led into Hell: Conservative Influence on German Offensive Infantry Tactics, 1871–1918" (dissertation, University of Nebraska, 2002), effectively present and support this position.

59. The most effective statements of that position are Terence Zuber, *The Battle of the Frontiers: Ardennes, 1914* (Stroud: Tempus); and *The Mons Myth: A Reassessment of the Battle* (Stroud: History Press, 2010). See also Herwig, *The Marne, 1914*. Simon J. House, "The Battle of the Ardennes 22 August 1914: A Comparative Study" (dissertation, King's College London, 2011) substantiates the initial effectiveness of German reservists from a French perspective.

60. *Histories of 251 Divisions of the German Army Which Participated in the War (1914–1918): Compiled from Records of Intelligence Section of the General Staff, American Expeditionary Forces* (Washington, D.C.: Government Printing Office, 1920).

61. A fact—or a perspective—affirmed by no less an authority than Erich Ludendorff in *Meine Kriegserinnnerungen 1914–1918* (Berlin: Mittler, 1919), 532.

62. Wilhelm Deist, "Verdeckter Militaerstreik im Jahre 1918?" in *Krieg des kleinen Mannes. Eine Militaergeschichte von unten*, ed. W. Wette (Munich: Pieper, 1992), 146–167.

63. This is a significant theme in Dieter Storz, *Kriegsbild und Ruestung vor 1914. Europaeische Landstreitkraefte vor dem Ersten Weltkrieg* (Herford: Mittler, 1992). Cf. Ralf Raths, *Vom Massensturm zur Stosstruppen: die Deutsche Landkrigtaaktik im Spiegel von Dienstvorschriften und Publizistik 1906 bis 1918* (Freiburg: Rombach, 2009).

3. Manifestly Inferior? French Reserves, 1871–1914
André José Lambelet

1. Marshal Joseph Joffre, *The Personal Memoirs of Joffre, Field Marshal of the French Army*, trans. Bentley T. Mott (New York: Harper & Brothers, 1932), 61. Joffre died in January 1931; his memoirs were not published (in French or English) until the year after his death.

2. Robert A. Doughty, *Pyrrhic Victory: French Strategy and Operations in the Great War* (Cambridge, Mass.: Harvard University Press, 2005), 42.

3. Joffre, *Memoirs*, 62.

4. See Robert A. Doughty, "French Strategy in 1914: Joffre's Own," *Journal of Military History* 67, no. 2 (2003).

5. Charles de Gaulle, *La France et son armée* (Paris: Plon, 1938), 271. The mathematician Pierre Boutroux, who carefully examined wartime statistics, claims that the army expected 10 percent. Pierre Boutroux, "Nos Effectifs (août 1914 - mars 1918)," *Revue de Paris* (August 15, 1919): 819.

6. Quoted in David Avrom Bell, *The First Total War: Napoleon's Europe and the Birth of Warfare as We Know It* (Boston: Houghton Mifflin, 2007), 148.

7. Alan I. Forrest, *The Soldiers of the French Revolution* (Durham, N.C.: Duke University Press, 1990), 83. See also Isser Woloch, "Napoleonic Conscription: State Power and Civil Society," *Past and Present* 111 (May 1986): 103–104; Bell, *First Total War*, 210. That French soldiers were not always convinced by the exhortations to sacrifice is made plain in Forrest, *Conscripts and Deserters: The Army and French Society During the Revolution and Empire* (New York: Oxford University Press, 1989).

8. Forrest, *Soldiers of the Revolution*, 84.

9. Michael Howard, *War in European History* (Oxford: Oxford University Press, 2001), 95.

10. In 1814, the restored Bourbon monarchy abolished conscription in favor of a system built on voluntary recruitment.

11. Jean-Charles Jauffret, *Parlement, gouvernement, commandement: l'armée de métier sous la 3e République 1871–1914*, 2 vols. (Vincennes: Ministère de la Défense. Etat-Major de l'Armée de Terre. Service Historique, 1987), 1:56–57.

12. David Ralston, *The Army of the Republic: The Place of the Military in the Political Evolution of France, 1871–1914* (Cambridge, Mass.: The MIT Press, 1967), 11.

13. Raoul Girardet, *La Société militaire de 1815 à nos jours* (Paris: Perrin, 1998), 131; Ralston, *Army*, 10–11.

14. Ralston, *Army*, 20.

15. Jauffret, *Parlement*, 60.

16. See Allan Mitchell, *Victors and Vanquished: The German Influence on Army and Church in France after 1870* (Chapel Hill: University of North Carolina Press, 1984), 3–15.

17. Mitchell, *Victors*, 82. Stoffel published his reports in 1871. His admiration for the Prussian system of military organization is apparent. See Eugène Stoffel, *Rapports militaires écrits de Berlin, 1866–1870*, 2nd ed. (Paris: Garnier frères, 1871). One of the most celebrated indictments of the French army came from General Louis Trochu, who called for the expansion of military service and a reduction in the duration of service. He declared that this could only happen once public mores had adapted but acknowledged that such an adaption was unlikely. Louis Trochu, *L'armée française en 1867* (Paris: Amyot, 1867), 279–280.

18. For a full discussion of the Niel reforms, see Jean Casevitz, *Une Loi manquée: la loi Niel, 1866–1869; l'armée française à la veille de la guerre de 1870* (Rennes: 1960).

19. Alain Plessis, *De la fête impériale au mur des fédérés 1852–1871* (Paris: Éditions du Seuil, 1973), 216–217. The National Guard, created in 1789, was never a front-line force; instead, its primary purpose was the maintenance of order. See Georges Carrot, *La Garde nationale (1789–1871). Une force politique ambiguë* (Paris: L'Harmattan, 2001).

20. Michael Howard, *The Franco-Prussian War: The German Invasion of France, 1870–1871* (London: Routledge, 1999); and Geoffrey Wawro, *The Franco-Prussian War: The German Conquest of France in 1870–1871* (Cambridge: Cambridge University Press, 2003) are excellent treatments of the military aspects of the Franco-Prussian War.

21. Alain Plessis, *The Rise and Fall of the Second Empire, 1852–1871*, trans. Jonathan Mandelbaum (Cambridge: Cambridge University Press, 1987), 168–169.

22. Plessis, *Second Empire*, 170; Jean-Marie Mayeur, *Les Débuts de la IIIe République 1871–1898* (Paris: Seuil, 1973), 14.

23. On the Paris Commune, see Robert Tombs, *The Paris Commune, 1871* (London: Longman, 1999); Stewart Edwards, ed., *The Communards of Paris, 1871* (Ithaca, N.Y.: Cornell University Press, 1973).

24. The commission's full name was *La commission chargée de présenter un ensemble de dispositions législatives, sur le recrutement et l'organisation des armées de terre et de mer.* Its rapporteur was the Marquis de Chasseloup-Laubat. For an extremely detailed discussion of these debates, see Jauffret, *Parlement.*

25. "Loi sur le recrutement de l'armée," July 27, 1872, J. B. Duvergier, ed., *Collection complète des lois, décrets, ordonnances, règlements et avis du conseil d'état* (Paris: Charles Noblet, 1872), 72:332–363; "Loi relative à l'organization générale de l'armée," July 24, 1873, Duvergier, *Collection complète*, 73:263–276; "Loi relative à la constitution des cadres et des effectifs de l'armée active et de l'armée territoriale," March 13, 1875, Duvergier, *Collection complète des lois*, 75:166–206.

26. Howard, *Franco-Prussian War*, 3; Howard, *War in European History*, 97–104.

27. Mitchell, *Victors*, provides an important account of the impact of German ideas on French debates about the army and the Church.

28. François Marquis de Chasseloup-Laubat, Rapporteur, "Rapport au nom de la commission chargée de présenter un ensemble de dispositions législatives, sur le recrutement et l'organisation des armées de terre et de mer," Annexe N° 975, March 12, 1872, *Journal officiel de la République française*: 2380–2400, 2380. Hereafter *JO*.

29. Cited in Raoul Girardet, *La Société militaire dans la France contemporaine, 1815–1939* (Paris: Librairie Plon, 1953), 166–167. But see the section below on Jaures' proposals thirty years later.

30. Charles de Freycinet, *La Guerre en province pendant le siège de Paris, 1870–1871: précis historique* (Paris: M. Lévy frères, 1871), 331.

31. Farcy, a former naval officer, sat on the extreme left and was a member of the *Union républicaine*. Adolphe Robert, Edgar Bourloton, and Gaston Cougny, *Dictionnaire des parlementaires français*, 5 vols. (Paris: Bourloton, 1891), 599.

32. Jauffret, *Parlement*, 274–275.

33. *JO* (1872): 3760.

34. Ibid., 3761.

35. Ralston, *Army*, 46–47.

36. Léon Gambetta, Speech to Republican Committees of the Gironde, June 26, 1871, in Léon Gambetta, *Discours et plaidoyers politiques*

de M. Gambetta, ed. Joseph Reinach, 11 vols. (Paris: G. Charpentier, 1880–1885), 2:23–24.

37. Ralston, *Army*, 39.

38. Jules Louis Lewal, *Etudes de guerre* (Paris: J. Dumaine, 1873), 30.

39. *JO* (1872): 2383.

40. Ibid., 2384, 2386.

41. Mitchell, *Victors*, 36.

42. Ibid., 33–36.

43. Article 1 of the law of July 27, 1872, declared, "All French men owe military service"; article 36 spelled out how the years would be divided. Duvergier, *Collection complète des lois*, 72:334, 349. The division of military obligations into four different components would survive, more or less intact, until the abolition of compulsory military service in 1997.

44. For budgetary reasons, the members of the first portion were usually released early; virtually all of the men who were subject to the five-year period served less than four years in the active army. See detailed figures in Jauffret, *Parlement*, 355–356.

45. Léon Gambetta, speech to the National Assembly, June 12, 1872, *JO* (1872): 3965.

46. Joseph Monteilhet, "L'avènement de la nation armée," *Revue des Études napoléoniennes* 14 (1918): 137–138.

47. "Loi relative à l'organisation générale de l'armée," July 24, 1873, in Duvergier, *Collection complète des lois*, 73:262–276; "Loi relative à la constitution des cadres et des effectifs de l'armée active et de l'armée territoriale," in Duvergier, *Collection complète des lois*, 75:166–206.

48. For the complete detail, see articles 3–6 of the law of 1875: Duvergier, *Collection complète des lois*, 75:174–176, as well as the tables on unit strengths, 75:193–206.

49. Jean Doise and Maurice Vaïse, *Diplomatie et outil militaire, 1871–1991* (Paris: Seuil, 1992), 37.

50. Mitchell, *Victors*, 29–31.

51. Article 29, law of 1873.

52. The difference in recruiting was not as clear cut as the law suggested. Odile Roynette notes that the recruitment system was in effect "mixed." Units of the active army would be brought from their peacetime strength to full combat strength by an infusion of reservists and men on disponibilité domiciled in the region. Odile Roynette, *"Bons pour le service": l'expérience de la caserne en France à la fin du XIXe siècle* (Paris: Belin, 2000), 201.

53. Article 34, law of 1873.

54. For a useful history of French officers, see Claude Croubois, *Histoire de l'officier français des origines à nos jours* (Saint-Jean-d'Angély: Editions Bordessoules, 1987). An excellent discussion of the relationship between professional officers and the nation is to be found in William Serman, *Les Officiers français dans la nation, 1848–1914* (Paris: Aubier Montaigne, 1982).

55. "Loi Gouvion-Saint-Cyr du 18 mars 1818," cited in Serman, *Officiers,* 10. On the promotion of *sous-officiers,* see Terry W. Strieter, "An Army in Evolution: French Officers Commissioned from the Ranks, 1848–1895," *Military Affairs* 42, no. 4 (1978).

56. Strieter, "Army in Evolution," 78.

57. Article 39 of the law of 1875. See discussion in Jean-Charles Jauffret, "L'Officier français (1871–1919)," in Croubois, *Histoire de l'officier français,* 300–302.

58. Jauffret, "Officier français," 302.

59. See Douglas Porch, *The March to the Marne: The French Army, 1871–1914* (Cambridge: Cambridge University Press, 1981), 81–83, for a skeptical look at republican attempts to reform officers' schools; Girardet offers a somewhat more generous assessment: *Société militaire* (1998), 140.

60. Article 43, law of 1872.

61. Roynette, *Service,* 325–331, provides a useful discussion of the impact of the annual maneuvers on reservists and active soldiers alike.

62. Capitaine Henri Choppin, *L'Armée française 1870–1890* (Paris: Albert Savine, 1890), 192, cited in Roynette, *Service,* 329.

63. Roynette, *Service,* 331.

64. Gambetta, *Discours,* 5:241.

65. Ralston, *Army,* 96–115, provides a succinct account of these very tedious deliberations.

66. In 1892, the law would be modified again. The reserve component was increased to ten years, again without changing the number of periods of actual presence under the colors. The obligation to serve in the territorial reserve obligations was correspondingly reduced to six years. Doise and Vaïse, *Diplomatie,* 122.

67. Ibid., 122. This includes a modification in 1892.

68. Etienne Lamy served as a republican representative from the Jura to the National Assembly from 1871 to 1875 and as a member of the Chamber of Deputies from 1876 to 1881. He broke with his republican colleagues over the education laws of Jules Ferry in 1881, because he believed they were an assault on religion, and was warmly received by the right. Robert, Bourloton, and Cougny, *Parlementaires français,* 3:572.

69. "Armée et démocratie II," 850.

70. "Armée et démocratie I," 418.

71. Ibid., 419.

72. Ibid., 860.

73. See Benjamin F. Martin, *Count Albert de Mun, Paladin of the Third Republic* (Chapel Hill: University of North Carolina Press, 1978).

74. *Journal officiel de la République française. Débats parlementaires. Chambre des députés*, (Paris: Impr. du Journal officiel, 1887), 1141–1142.

75. On the Dreyfus Affair, see the very readable Jean-Denis Bredin, *The Affair: The Case of Alfred Dreyfus*, trans. Jeffrey Mehlman (New York: George Braziller, 1986).

76. Ralston, *Army*, 114–115.

77. Doise and Vaïse, *Diplomatie*, 34.

78. Eugène Carrias, *La Pensée militaire française* (Paris: Presses Universitaires de France, 1960), 272.

79. Michael Howard, "Men against Fire: The Doctrine of the Offensive in 1914," in *Makers of Modern Strategy from Machiavelli to the Modern Age*, ed. Peter Paret (Princeton, N.J.: Princeton University Press, 1986), 513.

80. Ardant du Picq's *Etudes*, having only been circulated privately, had no significant impact on the debates in the early 1870s. In 1876 and 1877, however, the *Bulletin de la Réunion des officiers* published extracts of the *Etudes* that focused on the battles of antiquity. In 1880, Hachette issued an edition containing both the studies of ancient warfare and the unfinished discussion of modern warfare. Though incomplete, this edition had an enormous influence on French military thinking, which was already retreating from its postwar commitment to the defensive. Stefan T. Possony and Etienne Mantoux, "Du Picq and Foch: The French School," in *Makers of Modern Strategy: Military Thought from Machiavelli to Hitler*, ed. Edward Mead Earle (New York: Atheneum, 1970), 218. A more complete edition was published by Chapelot in 1903, in time to boost the offensive just as critics of that doctrine were beginning to make their voices heard. Jean Norton Cru, *Témoins: essai d'analyse et de critique des souvenirs de combattants édités en français de 1915 à 1928* (Nancy: Presses Universitaires de Nancy, 1993), 75. See Robert A. Nye, *The Origins of Crowd Psychology: Gustave LeBon and the Crisis of Mass Democracy in the Third Republic* (London: Sage, 1975), 2:127–129.

81. Colonel Charles Ardant du Picq, *Etudes sur le combat, combat antique et combat moderne* (Paris: Librairie Hachette et Cie., 1880), 110.

82. Carrias, *Pensée militaire*, 276–302.

83. Ibid., 276.

84. Ibid., 290. Generals Kessler and de Négrier both believed that firepower had become the predominant factor on the battlefield.

85. Howard notes that General Langlois founded the *Revue militaire générale* "very largely to combat 'acute transvaalitis,' the term he coined to describe 'this abnormal dread of losses on the battlefield.'" Howard, "Men against fire," 517.

86. Ministère de la guerre, *Décret du 28 octobre 1913 portant règlement sur la conduite des grandes unités (service des armées en campagne)* (Paris: Librairie militaire Berger-Levrault, 1914), 48.

87. Carrias, *Pensée militaire*, 272.

88. Ibid., 276; Doise and Vaïse, *Diplomatie*, 122–123.

89. Doise and Vaïse, *Diplomatie*, 123.

90. Carrias, *Pensée militaire*, 284.

91. Joffre, *Memoirs*, 6.

92. Doise and Vaïse, *Diplomatie*, 223.

93. Jauffret, "Officier français," 302.

94. Ibid., 303–304.

95. Doise and Vaïse, *Diplomatie*, 224.

96. Porch, *Marne*, 197–200, 206; Jauffret, *Parlement*, 519, citing 1N10, procès-verbaux manuscrits, SHAT.

97. Ralston, *Army*, 344.

98. General Louis André, *Cinq ans de ministère* (Paris: Louis Michaud, 1907), 178.

99. François Lescazes, "Réservistes et territoriaux," *Nouvelle revue* (April 1, 1908): 393.

100. de Gaulle, *France et son armée*, 245.

101. Lescazes, "Réservistes," 396.

102. The *affaire des fiches* (affair of the files) exploded in October 1904, when a nationalist deputy revealed that members of Minister of War General Louis André's cabinet had been using Masonic files to vet officers for promotion. A number of the participants in the affair wrote self-serving accounts: Jean Bidegain, *Le Grand Orient de France* (Paris: Librairie Antisémite, 1905); Jules-Henry Mollin, *La Vérité sur l'affaire des fiches* (Paris: Librairie Universelle, 1905); André, *Cinq ans de ministère*. A more recent account is to be found in François Vindé, *L'Affaire des fiches, 1900–1904. Chronique d'un scandale* (Paris: Editions Universitaire, 1989), which seems to be based largely on Bidegain's self-interested account. See also Ralston, *Army*, 269–280; Porch, *Marne*, 92–104; Serman, *Officiers*, 80–83.

103. Jauffret, "Officier français," 271.

104. General Metzinger, *La Transformation de l'armée 1897–1907* (Paris: Société d'édition Belleville, 1909), 4.

105. Ibid., 36. On Metzinger, see Jack L. Snyder, *The Ideology of the Offensive* (Ithaca, N.Y.: Cornell University Press, 1984), 74–75.

106. Serman, *Officiers*, 105.

107. Jean-Noël Jeanneney, foreword to Jean Jaurès, *L'Armée nouvelle* (Paris: Imprimerie nationale, 1992), 10.

108. Jean Jaurès, *L'Armée nouvelle*, ed. Georges Duby (Paris: Imprimerie nationale, 1992), 57, 58, 256, 292.

109. Ibid., 128–129.

110. Ibid., 252–253. France experimented with premilitary training in the 1880s, but these efforts quickly petered out. See Philippe Marchand, "Les Petits soldats de demain: les bataillons scolaires dans le département du Nord. 1882–1892," *Revue du Nord* 68, no. 266 (1985).

111. Ralston, *Army*, 350.

112. See Eugen Weber, *The Nationalist Revival in France, 1905–1914* (Berkeley: University of California Press, 1959).

113. Ibid., 111.

114. See Gerd Krumeich, *Armaments and Politics in France on the Eve of the First World War: The Introduction of Three-Year Conscription, 1913–1914*, trans. Stephen Conn (Dover, N.H.: Berg, 1984).

115. Doise and Vaïse, *Diplomatie*, 208.

116. Doughty, *Pyrrhic Victory*, 17.

117. The plan was finalized in February 1914 and given ministerial approval in May 1914. Doughty, "French Strategy," 438–442.

118. Doise and Vaïse, *Diplomatie*, 209–211.

119. Michel Huber, *La Population de la France pendant la guerre, avec un appendice sur les revenus avant et après la guerre* (Paris: Les Presses universitaires de France, 1931), 90.

120. de Gaulle, *France et son armée*, 271.

121. General Joseph Joffre, Grand Quartier Général, 3e Bureau, "Ordre Général No. 8," 18 August 1914, in *Les Armées françaises dans la grande guerre* (Paris: Imprimerie nationale, 1931), I:2 Annexes vol. 1, p. 83, No. 90. Hereafter *AFGG*. Millerand fully agreed with Joffre and threatened those who did not display proper discipline and military bearing with courts-martial. Alexandre Millerand, letter to generals commanding army corps regions, No. 2921 d, September 5, 1914, in *AFGG* I:2 Annexes vol. 2, pp. 760–64, No. 2461.

122. Colonel Pierre Guinard, Jean-Claude Devos, and Jean Nicot, *Inventaire sommaire des Archives de la Guerre, Série N 1872–1919* (Troyes: Imprimerie La Renaissance, 1975), 213, citing SHAT 6N 58.

123. Barbara W. Tuchman, *The Guns of August* (New York: Ballantine, 1994), 230, 354. These "over-age reservists fought valiantly outside Cambrai to delay the arrival of the German II Corps." John Keegan, *The First World War* (New York: Random House, 1999), 102.

124. *AFGG* II:4–5.

125. General Joseph Joffre. 17 November 1914. 4100. *AFGG* II Annexes 1:163.

126. *AFGG* II:143.

127. *AFGG* II:385.

4. "Each One a Pocket Hercules": The Bantam Experiment and the Case of the Thirty-fifth Division
Peter Simkins

I am greatly indebted to John Bourne, Sanders Marble, Stephen McGreal, Tony Richards, John Richardson, William Spencer, and Michael Stedman for their help and advice in the preparation of this chapter.

1. "Each one a Pocket Hercules" is from a popular verse, "The British Bantams," published c. early 1915. "Bantam" is defined in the *Oxford English Dictionary* as a small kind of domestic fowl, of which the cock bird is pugnacious, or a "small but spirited person."

2. *Parliamentary Debates, House of Commons, 1911–1914*, LXV, col. 2082; *The Times*, August 7, 1914. For a detailed account and analysis of army expansion and voluntary recruiting in 1914–1915, see Peter Simkins, *Kitchener's Army: The Raising of the New Armies* (Manchester: Manchester University Press, 1988); also Peter Simkins, "The Four Armies, 1914–1918," in *The Oxford Illustrated History of the British Army*, ed. David Chandler and Ian F. W. Beckett (Oxford: Oxford University Press, 1994), 241–262.

3. Daily recruiting returns, August 30 to September 5, 1914, The National Archives (TNA), WO 162/3; Simkins, *Kitchener's Army*, 66.

4. *The Times*, September 11, 1914; telegram from Adjutant-General's Department to OCs Districts, September 11, 1914, TNA WO 159/18; Recruiting Memorandum, no. 72, September 17, 1914, WO 159/18.

5. Army Council Instruction (ACI 251), October 22, 1914; Simkins, *Kitchener's Army*, 104.

6. Stephen McGreal, *Cheshire Bantams: 15th, 16th, and 17th Battalions of the Cheshire Regiment* (Barnsley: Pen & Sword, 2006), 17–42; Alfred Bigland, *The Call of Empire* (London: Cecil Palmer, 1922), 23–35; Sidney Allinson, *The Bantams: The Untold Story of World War I* (London: Howard Baker, 1981), 37–49; Simkins, *Kitchener's Army*, 120–121; Arthur

Crookenden, *The History of the Cheshire Regiment in the Great War* (Chester: Evans, n.d.), 346–347; Lieutenant Colonel H. M. Davson, *The History of the 35th Division in the Great War* (London: Sifton Praed, 1926), 1–2; *Birkenhead News*, November 18, 1914; *Daily Sketch*, December 1, 1914; Major A. F. Becke, *Order of Battle of Divisions, Part 3B* (London: HMSO, 1945), 51–59.

7. J. J. Hutchinson, quoted in Allinson, *The Bantams*, 205.

8. Information supplied to the author by Michael Stedman, January 30, 2009; see also Michael Stedman, *Manchester Pals: 16th, 17th, 18th, 19th, 20th, 21st, 22nd, and 23rd Battalions of the Manchester Regiment* (London: Leo Cooper, 1994), 34–35; McGreal, *Cheshire Bantams*, 44; Allinson, *The Bantams*, 69; *Manchester Guardian*, November 26, 1914.

9. Major John Ewing, *The Royal Scots, 1914–1919* (Edinburgh: Oliver and Boyd, 1925), 1:10; McGreal, *Cheshire Bantams*, 46–47; Allinson, *The Bantams*, 65–66, 78; *Army Debates, House of Commons, Session 1914–15* (London: HMSO, 1916), see February 10 and March 1, 1915, cols. 1166, 1173, 1174, 1197, 1703.

10. McGreal, *Cheshire Bantams*, 43–49; Allinson, *The Bantams*, 68, 75–77, 80, 82–83; Michael Stedman, *Salford Pals: 15th, 16th, 19th, and 20th Battalions, Lancashire Fusiliers. A History of the Salford Brigade* (London: Leo Cooper, 1993), 54–56; Maurice Bacon and David Langley, *The Blast of War: A History of Nottingham's Bantams, 15th (S) Battalion, Sherwood Foresters* (Nottingham: Sherwood Press, 1986), 3–12; John Sheen, *Durham Pals: 18th, 19th, and 22nd Battalions of the Durham Light Infantry: A History of Three Battalions Raised by Local Committee in County Durham* (Barnsley: Pen and Sword, 2007), 54–57; Davson, *The History of the 35th Division*, 2–3; see also Becke, *Order of Battle of Divisions*, 54–55.

11. Becke, *Order of Battle of Divisions*, 51–59; Davson, *The History of the 35th Division*, 2–4. Frank Richards of the Second Royal Welsh Fusiliers, who later served under Pinney, called him "a bun-punching crank . . . more fitted to be in command of a Church Mission hut at the Base than a division of troops." However, Sir Douglas Haig had a much higher opinion and was quick to note the transformation in the Thirty-third Division once Pinney took over, saying he "could be sure" when Pinney's Thirty-third Division was in the line. Pinney retained command of the Thirty-third Division, being the second-longest-serving divisional commander in the BEF by the Armistice. See Frank Richards, *Old Soldiers Never Die* (London: Faber, 1933), 217; John Bourne, *Who's Who in World War I* (London: Routledge, 2001), 234; Haig Diary, October 28, 1916, TNA WO 256/13; Gary Sheffield and John Bourne, eds., *Douglas*

Haig: War Diary and Letters, 1914–1918 (London: Weidenfeld and Nicolson, 2005), 249.

12. Lieutenant Colonel F. E. Whitton, *History of the 40th Division* (Aldershot: Gale and Polden, 1926), 7–10; Becke, *Order of Battle of Divisions*, 101–108; McGreal, *Cheshire Bantams*, 57–59; Simkins, *Kitchener's Army*, 121; Allinson, *The Bantams*, 130–155 (139 for Cunningham quote).

13. Allinson, *The Bantams*, 175–201.

14. Ibid., 106, 239.

15. Bacon and Langley, *The Blast of War*, 22–24.

16. See, for instance, Philip Gibbs, "Gallant Bantams," *Daily Chronicle*, June 19, 1916; Nigel Hamilton, *Monty: The Making of a General, 1887–1942* (London: Hamish Hamilton, 1981), 96; Allinson, *The Bantams*, 114–115.

17. Lieutenant Colonel Harrison Johnston, *Extracts from an Officer's Diary: Being the Story of the 15th and 16th Service Battalions, The Cheshire Regiment (Originally Bantams)* (Manchester: Geo. Falkner and Sons, 1919), 23, 26. Harrison Johnston, who crossed to France with the Fifteenth Cheshires in 1916, was placed in command of the battalion and was awarded the DSO the following year; see McGreal, *Cheshire Bantams*, 182.

18. A copy of the June 9, 1916, Corps Routine Order, conveying the congratulatory messages, is in the diary of Major General Sir Reginald Pinney, Pinney MSS, Imperial War Museum (IWM) 66/257/1.

19. Johnston, *Extracts from an Officer's Diary*, 66–67; Gibbs, "Gallant Bantams."

20. Pinney Diary, July 2, 1916.

21. Becke, *Order of Battle of Divisions*, 52.

22. A recent analysis of the problems between the British Fourth Army and the French Sixth Army in the Guillemont sector is in Peter Simkins, "For Better or For Worse: Sir Henry Rawlinson and His Allies in 1916 and 1918," in *Leadership in Conflict, 1914–1918*, ed. Matthew Hughes and Matthew Seligmann (Barnsley: Leo Cooper/Pen and Sword, 2000), 16–22.

23. GHQ to Fourth Army (OAD 123), August 24, 1916, Fourth Army MSS, IWM, vol. 5; Robin Prior and Trevor Wilson, *Command on the Western Front: The Military Career of Sir Henry Rawlinson, 1914–18* (Oxford: Blackwood, 1992), 222–223; Robin Prior and Trevor Wilson, *The Somme* (New Haven, Conn.: Yale University Press, 2005), 167–168; Peter Simkins, "Haig and the Army Commanders," in *Haig: A Reappraisal Seventy Years On*, ed. Brian Bond and Nigel Cave (Barnsley: Leo Cooper/Pen and Sword, 1999), 86.

24. 16th Cheshires, War Diary (WD), WO 95/2487; 105th Infantry Brigade, WD, WO 95/2485; 35th Division WD, WO 95/2468; Davson, *The History of the 35th Division*, 31–33; McGreal, *Cheshire Bantams*, 110–116. Davson states that three officers were killed or died of wounds and a further six, including the CO, were wounded in this action, while thirty-two other ranks were killed, 194 wounded, and seven posted as missing, a total of 242. McGreal's overall total is 244. The action was sufficiently significant for mention in Haig's dispatch of December 23, 1916: see Lieutenant Colonel J. H. Boraston, ed., *Sir Douglas Haig's Despatches, December 1915–April 1919* (London: Dent, 1979), 34.

25. 15th Sherwoods WD, WO 95/2488; 104th Brigade WD, WO 95/2482; 105th Brigade WD, WO 95/2485; 35th Division WD, WO 95/2468; Davson, *The History of the 35th Division*, 34–36; Captain Wilfrid Miles, *Military Operations, France and Belgium, 1916*, vol. 2 (London: Macmillan, 1938), 111–112 (hereafter *OH, 1916*); Bacon and Langley, *The Blast of War*, 25–29; Allinson, *The Bantams*, 210; McGreal, *Cheshire Bantams*, 116–117. The orders issued to the Sherwood Foresters are reproduced in Bacon and Langley, *The Blast of War*, 27–29. The Official Historian (Miles, see above) gives a higher combined casualty total for the two battalions (over 450) than either Davson or Bacon and Langley.

26. Judge Advocate General's Records: Proceedings of Field General Court Martial and associated papers, TNA WO 71/489; Register of Field General Courts Martial, TNA WO 213/10 and 213/11 (hereafter JAG FGCM Proceedings and Register); Gerard Oram, *Death Sentences Passed by Military Courts of the British Army, 1914–1924* (London: Francis Boutle, 1998), 40; Julian Putkowski and Julian Sykes, *Shot at Dawn: Executions in World War One by Authority of the British Army Act* (Barnsley: Wharncliffe, 1989), 111–112; Cathryn Corns and John Hughes-Wilson, *Blindfold and Alone: British Military Executions in the Great War* (London: Cassell, 2001), 151–153; Bacon and Langley, *The Blast of War*, 26. On the same day that Wilton was tried, another soldier of the Fifteenth Sherwood Foresters, Private J. Moffit, was also sentenced to death for quitting his post, though the sentence was reduced to five years' penal servitude.

27. 18th Lancashire Fusiliers WD, WO 95/2484; 104th Brigade WD, WO 95/2482; Davson, *The History of the 35th Division*, 37; *OH, 1916*, 2:114.

28. 17th Royal Scots WD, WO 95/2490; 17th West Yorkshire WD, WO 95/2490; 106th Brigade WD, WO 95/2489; Davson, *The History of the 35th Division*, 39; Ewing, *Royal Scots*, 1:305.

29. Davson, *The History of the 35th Division*, 45; McGreal, *Cheshire Bantams*, 119–122; Bacon and Langley, *The Blast of War*, 37; Sheen, *Durham Pals*, 109.

30. 105th Brigade WD, WO 95/2485; 16th Cheshires WD, WO 95/2487; 14th Gloucesters WD, WO 95/2488; McGreal, *Cheshire Bantams*, 121–122; Davson, *The History of the 35th Division*, 47–49; Corns and Hughes-Wilson, *Blindfold and Alone*, 153–154; Pinney diary, entries for August 20 and 22. It should be noted that Davson, the divisional historian and himself an artillery officer, was not wholly convinced that British "short-shooting" had occurred, claiming that subsequent investigation showed much damage from German artillery and that hostile high-angle fire from a flank could have been mistaken for "friendly fire" from the rear.

31. 35th Division WD, WO 95/2468; 104th Brigade WD, WO 95/2482; 17th Lancashire Fusiliers WD, WO 95/2484; *OH, 1916*, 2:199–201; Davson, *The History of the 35th Division*, 50–51; Pinney diary, August 25, 1916.

32. JAG FGCM Proceedings and Register, WO 71/518, WO 71/519, WO 213/12; Oram, *Death Sentences*, 86, 101; Corns and Hughes-Wilson, *Blindfold and Alone*, 154–157. McQuade had a poor disciplinary record. Described by his commanding officer as "absolutely useless as a soldier," he had been left behind when his battalion crossed to France. When sent to rejoin his unit in June 1916, he had not only gone missing from his draft but was tried on July 5 for disobeying an order, receiving a one year's suspended sentence to hard labor.

33. Captain B. L. Montgomery to his mother, August 27, 1916, Montgomery MSS, IWM BLM 1/55; Pinney diary, entries for August 25, 27, 29, and 31, 1916; McGreal, *Cheshire Bantams*, 123. Davson, *The History of the 35th Division*, 53, states that the weeding out was generally recognized as necessary but began later.

34. For a detailed breakdown of losses in the infantry battalions, see Davson, *The History of the 35th Division*, appendix 2.

35. This finding is based on a detailed survey of a sample of 281 attacks carried out by New Army divisions on the Somme, all mentioned in the relevant volumes of the British Official History.

36. 35th Division WD, WO 95/2468; 104th Brigade WD, WO 95/2482; 105th Brigade WD, WO 95/2485; 106th Brigade WD, WO 95/2489; 17th Lancashire Fusiliers WD, WO 95/2484; 19th DLI WD, WO 95/2490; 15th Sherwoods WD, WO 95/2488. Detailed analyses and discussions of the events of the night of November 25–26, 1916 can also be found in Sheen, *Durham Pals*, 128–134, 273–294; Corns and Hughes-Wilson,

Blindfold and Alone, 157–175; Davson, *The History of the 35th Division*, 74–80; and Bacon and Langley, *The Blast of War*, 41.

37. JAG FGCM Proceedings and Register, WO 71/534, WO 71/535, WO 213/13; 35th Division WD, WO 95/2468; 106th Brigade WD, WO 95/2489; Record of Service for Private J. S. Dunn (Burnt Documents), TNA WO 363/D1148; Corns and Hughes-Wilson, *Blindfold and Alone*, 162–175; Oram, *Death Sentences*, 45–46; Sheen, *Durham Pals*, 273–294; Putkowski and Sykes, *Shot at Dawn*, 175–178.

38. JAG FGCM Proceedings, WO 71/534.

39. Sheen, *Durham Pals*, 290, 335–353; JAG FGCM Proceedings, WO 71/534, WO 71/535; Corns and Hughes-Wilson, *Blindfold and Alone*, 169, 172; Davson, *The History of the 35th Division*, 80.

40. General Sir Aylmer Haldane, *A Soldier's Saga* (Edinburgh: Blackwood, 1948), 335; see also Davson, *The History of the 35th Division*, 80; Sheen, *Durham Pals*, 132; and Allinson, *The Bantams*, 244.

41. 35th Division WD, WO 95/2468; Assistant Director of Medical Services (ADMS), 35th Division, WD, WO 95/2472; Davson, *The History of the 35th Division*, 80–81.

42. Ernest Sheard, *My Great Adventure: The Great War, 1914–1918*, unpublished MS account, n.d., IWM PP/MCR/133 and P 285, 267–268; Harrison Johnston, *Extracts from an Officer's Diary*, 121.

43. 35th Division WD, WO 95/2468; ADMS 35th Division, WD, WO 95/2472; Becke, *Order of Battle of Divisions*, 58; Sheen, *Durham Pals*, 132; McGreal, *Cheshire Bantams*, 135; Davson, *The History of the 35th Division*, 81–82; Haldane, *A Soldier's Saga*, 335–336. From evidence in Haldane's account, the unnamed brigade commander is most likely Brigadier General H, O'Donnell of 106th Brigade.

44. See, for example, Davson, *The History of the 35th Division*, 82; Becke, *Order of Battle of Divisions*, 58; and *OH, 1916*, 2:92–93. However, in a sample of four battalions—the Fifteenth Cheshires, Fifteenth Sherwoods, Seventeenth Lancashire Fusiliers, and Nineteenth DLI—very few (1.3 percent or less) of the post-1916 casualties listed in *Soldiers Died in the Great War* can be positively identified as having come from cavalry or Yeomanry units.

45. 35th Division WD, WO 95/2468; ADMS 35th Division, WD, WO 95/2472; Davson, *The History of the 35th Division*, 84–85, 90.

46. Charles Messenger, *Call to Arms: The British Army, 1914–1918* (London: Weidenfeld and Nicolson, 2005), 231–233; Sheen, *Durham Pals*, 132–133, 335–353; McGreal, *Cheshire Bantams*, 138–141; Davson, *The History of the 35th Division*, 82.

47. 35th Division WD, WO 95/2468; 104th Brigade WD, WO 95/2482; Davson, *The History of the 35th Division*, 92–94, 101–105; Captain Cyril Falls, *Military Operations, France and Belgium, 1917* (London: Macmillan, 1940), 1:529n1.

48. 105th Brigade WD, WO 95/2486; 15th Sherwoods WD, WO 95/2488; Davson, *The History of the 35th Division*, 114–115; Bacon and Langley, *The Blast of War*, 43–45.

49. Davson, *The History of the 35th Division*, 118–128; K. W. Mitchinson, *Epéhy* (Barnsley: Leo Cooper/Pen and Sword, 1998), 69–73, 101–108; Becke, *Order of Battle of Divisions*, 51; General Sir Martin Farndale, *History of the Royal Regiment of Artillery: Western Front, 1914–18* (London: Royal Artillery Institution, 1986), 186.

50. Davson, *The History of the 35th Division*, 134–137; Mitchinson, *Epéhy*, 104–105; McGreal, *Cheshire Bantams*, 157–158; Bacon and Langley, *The Blast of War*, 46.

51. Davson, *The History of the 35th Division*, 137–149; 105th Brigade WD, WO 95/2486; 106th Brigade WD, WO 95/2489; 15th Cheshires WD, WO 95/2487; 15th Sherwoods WD, WO 95/2488; 18th HLI WD, WO 95/2490; Mitchinson, *Epéhy*, 104–108; McGreal, *Cheshire Bantams*, 157–168; Sheen, *Durham Pals*, 184–186; Bacon and Langley, *The Blast of War*, 46–48.

52. These figures have been compiled from those published in appendix 2 ("Casualty Lists") of Davson, *The History of the 35th Division*.

53. Its action at Houthulst Forest was not considered sufficiently important to merit more than a passing and indirect reference in the British Official History volume dealing with that offensive; see Brigadier General Sir James Edmonds, *Military Operations, France and Belgium, 1917* (London, Macmillan), 2:348.

54. The numerical weakness of 106th Brigade is indicated by the fact that the combat strength of the Seventeenth West Yorkshires had been reduced to 450 rifles; see Davson, *The History of the 35th Division*, 160n2. For the background to the Houthulst Forest attack, see Edmonds, *Military Operations*, 343–344, 348; Davson, *The History of the 35th Division*, 157–160; Nigel Steel and Peter Hart, *Passchendaele: The Sacrificial Ground* (London: Cassell, 2000), 281.

55. 35th Division WD, WO 95/2469; 104th Brigade WD, WO 95/2482; 105th Brigade WD, WO 95/2486; 17th Lancashire Fusiliers WD, WO 95/2484; 16th Cheshires WD, WO 95/2487; 14th Gloucesters WD, WO 95/2488; Davson, *The History of the 35th Division*, 161–171; McGreal, *Cheshire Bantams*, 173–180; Bacon and Langley, *The Blast of War*, 48–49.

56. Davson, *The History of the 35th Division*, 169–171; McGreal, *Cheshire Bantams*, 179–180.

57. These sample statistics have been compiled from a detailed analysis of casualties named in *Soldiers Died in the Great War* (CD-Rom version published by the Naval and Military Press), the list of original other ranks of the Nineteenth DLI in Sheen's *Durham Pals*, 335–353, and the Roll of Honour of the Fifteenth Sherwoods published by Bacon and Langley in *The Blast of War*, 86–99.

58. Both Becke, *Order of Battle of Divisions*, 56n38; and Brigadier E. A. James, *British Regiments, 1914–18* (London: Samson, 1978), 103, state that the drafts of dismounted Glasgow Yeomanry personnel included 146 other ranks, though Davson, *The History of the 35th Division*, 152, gives a figure of 250.

59. Becke, *Order of Battle of Divisions*, 54–56; Davson, *The History of the 35th Division*, 183–185; McGreal, *Cheshire Bantams*, 184–185.

60. 35th Division WD, WO 95/2469; 105th Brigade WD, WO 95/2486; 106th Brigade WD, WO 95/2489; 15th Cheshires WD, WO 95/2487; 15th Sherwoods WD, WO 95/2488; Davson, *The History of the 35th Division*, 193–196, 205–206; Brigadier General Sir James Edmonds, *Military Operations, France and Belgium, 1918*, 5 vols. (London: Macmillan, 1935), 1:413–418 (hereafter *OH, 1918*); Bacon and Langley, *The Blast of War*, 53; McGreal, *Cheshire Bantams*, 196–197.

61. 35th Division WD, WO 95/2469; 104th Brigade WD, WO 95/2483; 106th Brigade WD, WO 95/2489; 12th HLI WD, WO 95/2490; 19th DLI WD, WO 95/2484; *OH, 1918*, 1:473–475; Davson, *The History of the 35th Division*, 199–204; Sheen, *Durham Pals*, 220; Bacon and Langley, *The Blast of War*, 53; McGreal, *Cheshire Bantams*, 197–199. Lieutenant Colonel W. H. Anderson, commanding the Twelfth HLI, organized and led two counterattacks by his battalion on March 25, 1918, first at Favière Wood and later at Maricourt. He was killed in the second of these actions but was posthumously awarded a Victoria Cross.

62. Third Army WD, WO 95/369; VII Corps WD, WO 95/867; 35th Division WD, WO 95/2469; 104th Brigade WD, WO 95/2483; 105th Brigade WD, WO 95/2486; 106th Brigade WD, WO 95/2489; *OH, 1918*, 1:488–489, 508–517, 532, 538–544, 2:12; Davson, *The History of the 35th Division*, 205–213; McGreal, *Cheshire Bantams*, 199–201.

63. 35th Division WD, WO 95/2469; 104th Brigade WD, WO 95/2483; 105th Brigade WD, WO 95/2486; 106th Brigade WD, WO 95/2489; 19th DLI WD, WO 95/2484; 17th Lancashire Fusiliers WD, WO 95/2484; 18th Lancashire Fusiliers WD, WO 95/2484; 18th HLI WD, WO 95/2490; 15th Cheshires WD, WO 95/2487; Bacon and Langley, *The Blast of War*,

53–54; McGreal, *Cheshire Bantams*, 201–203; Sheen, *Durham Pals*, 220–222; Davson, *The History of the 35th Division*, 210–217; *OH, 1918*, 2:34, 54–55, 94, 113, 457, 491; K. W. Mitchinson, *Pioneer Battalions in the Great War: Organized and Intelligent Labour* (Barnsley: Leo Cooper/ Pen and Sword, 1997), 220. The Fifteenth Cheshires' losses of fifty-five officers and men killed and 385 other ranks wounded or missing indicate the scale of casualties suffered by battalions in the March fighting.

64. For an overview of British divisional performance in the final offensive and the methodology for calculating divisional success rates, see Peter Simkins, "Co-Stars or Supporting Cast? British Divisions in the 'Hundred Days,' 1918" in *British Fighting Methods in the Great War*, ed. Paddy Griffith (London: Cass, 1996), 50–69.

65. 35th Division WD, WO 95/2470; 106th Brigade WD, WO 95/2489; Davson, *The History of the 35th Division*, 257–268; *OH, 1918*, 5:59, 61, 68, 77–79, 85–86, 89.

66. 35th Division WD, WO 95/2470; 104th Brigade WD, WO 95/2483; 106th Brigade WD, WO 95/2489; 19th DLI WD, WO 95/2484; Davson, *The History of the 35th Division*, 268–284; *OH, 1918*, 5:274, 279, 286, 289–290, 428–430, 432; Sheen, *Durham Pals*, 258.

67. 35th Division WD, WO 95/2470; 104th Brigade WD, WO 95/2483; Davson, *The History of the 35th Division*, 284–288, 290–293; *OH, 1918*, 5:444, 447–448, 548–549, 556.

5. Scraping the Barrel: African American Troops and World War I
Steven Short

1. Jack D. Foner, *Blacks and the Military in American History: A New Perspective* (New York: Praeger, 1974), 3–5.

2. Philip Foner, *Blacks in the American Revolution* (London: Greenwood Press, 1975), 53–55.

3. Gerald Astor, *The Right to Fight: A History of African Americans in the Military* (Novato, Calif.: Presidio Press, 1998), 22.

4. Part of the measures to create black units in the South stemmed from the Confiscation Act of July 1862, which authorized the use of "contrabands" to help put down the rebellion. In the North, a revised Militia Act provided for the enlistment of qualified or competent African Americans in military or naval service. On the early use of black troops in the Civil War, see James G. Hollandsworth, *The Louisiana Native Guards: The Black Military Experience during the Civil War* (Baton Rouge: Louisiana State University Press, 1995).

5. The exploits and attitudes toward black troops in the Civil War is well documented. See Joseph T. Glatthaar's *Forged in Battle: The Civil War Alliance of Black Soldiers and White Officers* (New York: The Free Press, 1990) and James McPherson's *The Negro's Civil War: How American Blacks Felt and Acted During the War for the Union* (New York: Vintage, 1965) as excellent sources.

6. Astor, *The Right to Fight*, 32.

7. James M. McPherson, *Ordeal by Fire: The Civil War and Reconstruction* (New York: Alfred A. Knopf, 1982), 351. After the war, leaders generally accepted that white officers could command black troops, but the question of black officers in command positions remained a sticking point, even of black officers commanding black troops.

8. Bernard Nalty, *Strength for the Fight: A History of Black Americans in the Military* (New York: The Free Press, 1986), 58–59.

9. The three West Point graduates were Henry O. Flipper, John H. Alexander, and Charles Young.

10. Graham A. Cosmas, *An Army for Empire: The United States Army in the Spanish-American War* (College Station: Texas A&M University Press, 1994), 129–130. The existing black units were the Ninth and Tenth Cavalry Regiments and the Twenty-fourth and Twenty-fifth Infantry Regiments created in 1866.

11. Nalty, *Strength for the Fight*, 67.

12. Marvin Fletcher, *The Black Soldier and Officer in the United States Army, 1891–1917* (Columbia: University of Missouri Press, 1974), 239–241.

13. Charles Johnson Jr., *African American Soldiers in the National Guard: Recruitment and Deployment during Peacetime and War* (Westport, Conn.: Greenwood Press, 1992), 76–77.

14. Emmett J. Scott, *Scott's Official History of the American Negro in the World War* (New York: Arno Press, 1969), 33. The number of ten thousand National Guardsmen is a rather high figure and is likely closer to five thousand, based on the size of regiments.

15. John D. Weaver, *The Brownsville Raid* (New York: W.W. Norton, 1970), 97–99.

16. The nomenclature between state militia and state National Guard units was inconsistent at this time. Some states had already changed their militia designations to that of National Guard.

17. United States Government, *Congressional Record, 64th Congress, 1st Session*. "An Act for making further and more official provisions for the national defense and other purposes." The National Defense Act of 1916 also called for an increase in the size of state militias, established

the Reserve Officers' Training Corps (ROTC) at various colleges, and an increase in the size of the cadet corps at the United States Military Academy at West Point.

18. Marvin A. Kreidberg and Merton G. Henry, *History of Military Mobilization in the United States Army, 1775–1945* (Washington, D.C.: GPO, 1955), 221.

19. United States, *Congressional Record, 63rd Congress, 2nd Session.*

20. Baltimore *Afro American Ledger*, September 19, 1914. The reference to British and French troops was to their employment of colonial troops.

21. *The Crisis* 11, no. 6 (April 1916): 310.

22. Kenneth E. Hamburger, *Learning Lessons in the American Expeditionary Forces* (Washington, D.C.: U.S. Army Center of Military History, 1997), 9.

23. Arthur E. Barbeau and Florette Henri, *The Unknown Soldiers: African-American Troops in World War I* (Philadelphia, Penn.: Temple University Press, 1974), 56–57.

24. Baltimore *Afro American Ledger*, March 10, 1917. Original letter not dated but probably written in early March 1917.

25. Letter from George Austin to Joel Spingarn, January 4, 1917. Joel E. Spingarn Papers, box 95–1, folder 31; Manuscript Division, Moorland-Spingarn Research Center, Howard University. Future references to the Spingarn Papers will be designated by his initials JES Papers, and the Moorland-Spingarn Research Center at Howard University will be designated MSRC.

26. Thomas M. Gregory Papers, box 37–1, folder 23; Manuscript Division, MSRC. Future references to the Gregory Papers will be cited as TMG Papers.

27. Spingarn note to himself. JES Papers, MSRC, box 95–13, folder 533. Underline is in original.

28. Letter from George Brice to Spingarn, March 14, 1917. JES Papers, MSRC, box 95–2, folder 61.

29. Baltimore *Afro American Ledger*, March 31, 1917. Capital letters in original newspaper publication but not in Young's original letter, JES Papers, MSRC, box 95–4, folder 138.

30. Hal Chase, "Struggle for Equality: Fort Des Moines Training Camp for Colored Officers, 1917," *Phylon* 39 (December 1978): 302.

31. United States, *Congressional Record, 64th Congress, 1st Session.*

32. United States, *Order of Battle of the United States Land Forces in the World War*, vol. 3, pt. 1 (Washington, D.C.: GPO, 1931–1949), 79–81.

33. Letter to Stephen Newman from Ralph Hayes, May 12, 1917. JES Papers, MSRC, box 95-5, folder 200. There is no record of Baker's decision-making process.

34. TMG Papers, MSRC, box 37-1, folder 7.

35. The training camp established at Fort Des Moines was not related to the Plattsburg camps or the preparedness movement. The Fort Des Moines camp was created by Secretary Baker and the War Department as an official U.S. Army training camp.

36. National Archives and Records Administration (hereafter referred to as NARA), Record Group 165, box 139, report #13290. Memorandum to Chief of Staff (hereafter CoS) from Joseph Kuhn (May 6, 1917) and memorandum to CoS from Henry G. Sharpe (May 8, 1917).

37. Ibid. Memorandum from General Sharpe to General Scott (May 8, 1917).

38. NARA, RG 165, box 139, report #13290. Memorandum from General Kuhn to General Scott (May 6, 1917).

39. NARA, RG 165, microfilm set M1024 roll 261 frame 436. Memorandum to Adjutant General (hereafter AG) from CoS (May 17, 1917). Hereafter listed in the following format: M1024/261/436.

40. NARA, RG 165, box 143, item #8142-17.

41. Some of the applicants refer to their previous military experience as "militia" duty, the earlier term for National Guard service.

42. JES Papers, MSRC, box 95-13, folder 530. The first two groups of applicants contained 352 men. The first list contained applicants with college degrees (162 men); the second list contained applicants either enrolled in college or scheduled to begin college in the fall of 1917 (190 men).

43. Gerald W. Patton, *War and Race: The Black Officer in the American Military, 1915–1941* (Westport, Conn.: Greenwood Press, 1981), 56–57.

44. NARA, RG 165, box 139, item #13290. Letter from Secretary Baker to Congressman Murray Hurlbert (May 26, 1917).

45. Jerome Dowd, *The Negro in American Life* (New York: Century, 1926), 233–234.

46. NARA, RG 407, box 1169, file "Ft. Des Moines" #354.16. Memorandum from AG to W. T. Johnston.

47. Iowa *Bystander*, June 29, 1917.

48. Des Moines *News*, July 5, 1917.

49. NARA, RG 407, box 1169, folder "Ft. Des Moines." Report from Commanding Officer 17th Provisional Training Regiment (hereafter CO, 17th PTR) to AG, July 10, 1917, 2–3.

50. NARA, RG 407, box 1168, file "Ft. Des Moines," item #354.16. Memorandum to Commanding General, Central Department from the AG, May 29, 1917.

51. Ibid. Report from CO, 17th PTR to AG, July 10, 1917, 1–2.

52. Ibid., 2.

53. Ibid. Venereal disease rates during the World War I period were surprisingly high; five cases was a remarkably small number among 1,250. It is also likely that Ballou included these cases in his report because most African Americans were viewed as immoral and second-class citizens. Army disease rates varied from .59 percent in Oregon recruits to 8.90 percent in Florida, while Fort Des Moines's rate was under .01 percent.

54. Ibid., 3–4.

55. Ibid., 5.

56. NARA, RG 165, box 139, item #13290. Memorandum to CoS from General Joseph Kuhn, May 6, 1917.

57. Ibid., Memorandum for CoS from General Lochridge, War College Division, August 31, 1917.

58. Chicago *Defender*, October 20, 1917.

59. NARA, RG 107, box 2, file C. Memorandum for Emmett J. Scott from AG, November 1, 1917. An attachment to the memorandum includes official War Department numbers regarding the number of commissions, ranks, and post assignments. There is also a discrepancy in the actual number of graduates. War Department records indicate both 624 and 639. At the October graduation, however, the number stood at 624, with several additional commissions subsequently issued.

60. Ibid., Memorandum for the Secretary of War from AG, September 4, 1917.

61. NARA, RG 165, box 139, item #13290. Memorandum for CoS from Acting Chief of War College Division, August 31, 1917. NARA, RG 165, box 139, item #13290. Memorandum from Chief of Staff to Adjutant General of the Army, September 1, 1917. The black draftees would not be mobilized until early October 1917.

62. Ibid., Memorandum for Scott from AG, November 1, 1917.

63. Ibid., Memorandum to Chief of Staff from General Kuhn, May 6, 1917.

64. Baker's decision as Secretary of War came from both political and social pressure that black communities might protest against the government for failing to use black officers and men in combat positions. If this happened, then the War Department could be a target of retribution.

65. United States, *Order of Battle* (Washington, D.C.: GPO, 1931–1949), 2:437.

66. Kreidberg and Henry, *History of Military Mobilization*, 222.

67. United States War Department, *War Department Annual Reports, 1917*, 911.

68. United States War Department, *Report of the Acting Chief of the Militia Bureau, 1918* (Washington, D.C.: GPO, 1918), 112–120. African Americans enjoyed much greater access to military service in National Guard units, because the decision to organize those units rested upon the states and not the federal government.

69. Scott, *The American Negro in the World War*, 197–198.

70. Barbeau and Henri, *The Unknown Soldiers*, 70–71.

71. Johnson, *African American Soldiers in the National Guard*, 99.

72. United States, *Order of Battle*, 12:437. A discrepancy exists surrounding the regimental designations. Although archival records indicate the orders were issued in December 1917, contemporary accounts indicate that the regimental commanders were not informed until arriving in France in early 1918.

73. Johnson, *African American Soldiers in the National Guard*, 99–102; NARA, RG 120, box 1, file 293–13.6. Memorandum from Secretary of War organizing the Ninety-third Division.

74. William S. Bradden, *Under Fire with the 370th Infantry, AEF* (Chicago: Published by the author, n.d.), 437.

75. Edward M. Coffman, *The War to End All Wars* (New York: Oxford University Press, 1968), 24–25, 27.

76. United States, *First Report of the Provost Marshal General to the Secretary of War* (Washington, D.C.: GPO, 1917), 30–31.

77. Scott, *The American Negro in the World War*, 66–67.

78. Ibid., 31. The total number of eligible men increases to 24,234,021 when the 325,445 registrants from U.S. territories are added. The number 9.58 percent is slightly lower than the percentage arrived at by other historians. This variation is attributable to discrepancies in the total number of men registered for the draft; the number I used is higher, while the number of blacks registered remained the same. It is likely that some Puerto Ricans were considered black, but War Department documentation supporting this is missing.

79. United States, *Order of Battle*, 3:392–393. This volume contains the postwar report of the Provost Marshal General's Department.

80. Ibid., 3:371–372.

81. United States, *Second Report of the Provost Marshal General to the Secretary of War* (Washington, D.C.: GPO, 1919), 188–192. These numbers

reflect the amount of men entered into Class I status and not necessarily the number of men who actually served during the war.

82. Ibid., 458–459. Most Southern states shared a similar experience in that blacks served at a higher rate than whites.

83. TMG Papers, box 37–1, folder 22, MSRC.

84. NARA, RG 107, box 2, file "MISC." Memorandum from Secretary Baker to Special Assistant Scott, November 22, 1917.

85. NARA, RG 107, box 2, file "SPP." Press release signed by Baker. No date is on the release, but it is likely on February 12, 1918.

86. United States, *Order of Battle*, 3:403.

87. NARA, RG 407, box 1169, file "Ft. Des Moines, IA." Memorandum for AG from CoS, August 2, 1917.

88. NARA, RG 407, box 1169, file "Ft. Des Moines, IA." Memorandum for CoS from the Chief of War College Division, August 2, 1917.

89. NARA, RG 407, box 1109, file "Ft. Des Moines, IA." Memorandum from Chief of Ordnance to AG, August 31, 1917. The unwillingness to integrate units or even to have segregated regiments within the same division not only reflects the racism within the War Department and American society at large but also provided them a quick means of eliminating African Americans from more specialized branches. In doing so, the army eliminated the opportunity for black soldiers and officers to prove themselves capable and it reinforced negative stereotypes for these "bottom of the barrel" soldiers.

90. NARA, RG 407, box 1169, file "Ft. Des Moines, IA" #652. Memorandum for Secretary of War from CoS, September 19, 1917.

91. NARA, RG 165, box 144, report #13597. Memorandum from Captain Hammond, General Staff, to CoS, September 27, 1917.

92. NARA, RG 165, box 144, file #13597. Memorandum for CoS from Captain Hammond of the General Staff, September 27, 1917.

93. NARA, RG 165, box 149, report #14150. Memorandum from Colonel Leitch to CoS, October 9, 1917. These decisions were reached before the official announcement of the formation of the Ninety-second. Concerns stemmed from the Houston riot and the earlier riot in East St. Louis, Missouri.

94. NARA, RG 165, box 144, report #13597. Memorandum from Colonel Lochridge to CoS, October 21, 1917. The limitation in rank of black officers would also gradually weed out higher-ranking black officers in the Ninety-third Division. Limiting the advancement in rank of African American officers was a direct result of racism and the belief that black troops and officers constituted the bottom of the barrel.

95. NARA, RG 165, box 146, file #13825, "Instructions Pertaining to the Training of a Division in Trench Warfare, and the Establishment of Divisional Schools," August 31, 1917.

96. For more thorough examinations of the black combat experience during World War I, see Henri and Barbeau, *The Unknown Soldiers*, Foner, *Blacks and the Military in American History*, and Bernard Nalty, *Strength for the Fight: A History of Black Americans in the Military*, to name a few.

97. David Trask, *The AEF and Coalition Warmaking, 1917–1918* (Lawrence: University of Kansas Press, 1993), 4–6. Trask provides an excellent explanation of the amalgamation issue and goes into great detail about Pershing's and Wilson's personal feelings toward it.

98. NARA, RG 120, boxes 1–2, file "Cable History of Colored Soldiers," item 7–12.5, cable #592.

99. Bradden, *Under Fire with the 370th Infantry*, 73–74.

100. United States, *Order of Battle*, 2:439–440.

101. Chester Heywood, *Negro Combat Troops in the World War: The Story of the 371st Infantry* (Worcester: n.p., 1928), 193–194. Memorandum referenced from General Garneir Duplessix to 157th and 161st French Divisions, which included the American Ninety-third Division regiments, October 7, 1918.

102. United States Army War College, *Colored Soldiers in the U.S. Army* (Washington, D.C.: GPO, 1942), 82–88.

103. NARA, RG 120, box 61, file 43. Memorandum from General Hay to commanding officer U.S.S. *Mt. Vernon*, June 18, 1918.

104. NARA, RG 120, box 61, file 43. Memorandum from Major Mason, 366th Infantry, to Commanding General onboard USS *Mt. Vernon*, June 15, 1918.

105. John J. Pershing, *My Experiences in the World War* (New York: Stokes, 1931), 2:45–47.

106. NARA, RG 120, box 4, file 292–50.4. Training Memorandum Number 2 issued by Ballou, July 21, 1918.

107. NARA, RG 120, box 1, file 292–11.4. "Operations of 92d Division."

108. United States, *United States Army in the World War*, 9:67.

109. NARA, RG 120, box 1, file 292–11.4. "Operation of 92d Division."

110. Coffman, *War to End All Wars*, 314.

111. Barbeau and Henri, *Unknown Soldiers*, 153–155.

112. Shipley Thomas, *The History of the AEF* (New York: Doran, 1920), 256–258.

113. Robert Bullard, *Personalities and Reminiscences of the War* (New York: Doubleday, Page, 1925), 294–296.

114. Barbeau and Henri, *Unknown Soldiers*, 162–163.

115. NARA, RG 120, box 1, file 292–50.4. Memorandum of training issued by Colonel Greer, December 6, 1918. Greer was second in command of the Ninety-second and implemented many of the orders and regulations against the men of the Ninety-second.

116. Robert R. Moton, "Negro Troops in France," *Southern Workman* 48 (May 1919): 220–221. This article is based on Moton's visit to black troops in France in late 1918 to assess their morale.

117. NARA, RG 120, box 2, file 293–23.9. Memorandum from Commanding Officer, 371st Infantry to Town Majors of Marat la Grande, Marats la Petit, and Rembercourt aux Pots, of the Department of the Meuse, August 31, 1918.

118. Moton, "Negro Troops in France," 220–221.

119. W. E. B. Du Bois, "The History of the Black Man," *The Crisis* 17 (June 1919): 63–65.

120. United States, *Order of Battle*, 2:435, 442.

121. Kreidberg and Henry, *History of Military Mobilization*, 377–379.

122. United States Army War College, file 127. Questionnaire concerning the use of African-American manpower in the army. Memorandum from Colonel Vernon Caldwell to War College, March 14, 1920; memorandum from Colonel James Parsons to War College, August 30, 1924.

123. That story is told in Ulysses Lee, *The Employment of Negro Troops* (Washington, D.C.: GPO, 1966), in the United States Army in World War II series.

6. Below the Bar: The U.S. Army and Limited Service Manpower

Sanders Marble

1. Marvin Kreidberg and Merton Henry, *History of Military Mobilization in the United States Army, 1775–1945* (Washington, D.C.: Department of the Army, 1955), 228.

2. John W. Chambers II, *To Raise an Army: The Draft Comes to Modern America* (New York: Free Press, 1987), 154.

3. Memo, Tasker Bliss to TAG, May 12, 1917. NARA RG165, roll 210, ref. 8591–5.

4. *Regulations Governing Physical Examinations* (Washington, D.C.: GPO, July 1917). This is a case of the rules saying you can break the rules.

5. *Regulations Governing Physical Examinations, Compiled Rulings through 27 August 1917* (Washington, D.C.: GPO, 1917).

6. Sheila Nataraj Kirby and Harry J. Thie, "Enlisted Personnel Management: A Historical Perspective," RAND Corporation report (1996), 74.

7. See Kreidberg and Henry, *History of Military Mobilization*, 298–309, for details on AEF plans and their effects on the draft and mobilization.

8. Ibid., 262–263.

9. Ibid., 273; Albert Love, *Defects Found in Drafted Men: Statistical Information Compiled from the Draft Records Showing the Physical Condition of the Men Registered and Examined in Pursuance of the Requirements of the Selective-Service Act* (Washington, D.C.: GPO, 1920), 74, table.

10. John H. Quayle, "Reclamation Camps for the Physically Unfit," *Forum* 58 (November 1917): 579–584.

11. No evidence has been found that Pomerene ever actually submitted a bill. I am indebted to Mrs. Ellen Milhiser for research in Congress and the Library of Congress on this point.

12. E.g., Edwin Bowers, "Fitting the Unfit," *Everybody's Magazine* 37-B (December 1917): 128–132; "Reclaiming Our Man-Power for War," *Literary Digest* 6 (April 1918): 32–33.

13. Provost Marshal General, *Second Report to the SecWar on the Operations of the Selective Service System to December 20, 1918* (Washington, D.C.: GPO, 1919), 153–154.

14. A. G. Crane, *Medical Department of the U.S. Army in the World War*, vol. 13, *Physical Reconstruction and Vocational Education*, 205–216, covers Development Battalions. (Hereafter *MDWW* with volume number.) See also *MDWW*, vol. 4 (*Activities Concerning Mobilization Camps and Ports of Embarkation*), 24–26; Leonard L. Lerwill, "The Personnel Replacement System in the United States Army, vol. 1: Colonial Period – World War I," unpublished MS (Office of the Chief of Military History, 1952), 292–295; and the War Department General Staff files in serial 10014, National Archives RG165, roll 308.

15. They were also established in the AEF. Maj. Gen. W. C. Gorgas, *Confidential Report to Secretary of War, Inspection of Medical Services with American Expeditionary Forces* (Washington, D.C.: GPO, 1919), 21–22.

16. *MDWW*, 13:216. 0.4% deserted and 0.7% died.

17. *MDWW*, vol. 10 (*Neuropsychiatry*) (Washington, D.C.: GPO, 1929) is the official history.

18. Ibid., 10:513.

19. Ibid., 10:164. Some of these were rejected by their draft boards, and it is not clear whether neuropsychiatrists played a role there or not.

20. Richard T. von Mayrhauser, *The Triumph of Utility: The Forgotten Clash of American Psychologies in World War I* (Ph.D. diss., University of Chicago, 1986), 83. Yerkes kept his goals; in July he still hoped to test 15–20%—those identified as high- or low-scoring by mass testing—individually.

21. Much has been written on the World War I intelligence tests, partly since the data were used to support racial theories and immigration quotas. See, for instance, Daniel J. Kelves, "Testing the Army's Intelligence: Psychologists and the Military in World War I," *Journal of American History* 55, no. 3 (December 1968), 565–581; James Reed, "Robert M. Yerkes and the Mental Testing Movement," in *Psychological Testing and American Society, 1890–1930*, ed. Michael M. Sokal (New Brunswick, N.J.: Rutgers University Press, 1987); John Carson, "Army Alpha, Army Brass, and the Search for Army Intelligence," *Isis* 84 (1993): 278–309; Stephen Jay Gould, *The Mismeasure of Man* (New York: Norton, 1981), esp. chap. 5.

22. Robert M. Yerkes, *Psychological Examining in the United States Army* (Washington, D.C.: GPO, 1921), 101.

23. King was a physician and Medical Department staff officer, head of the Division of Special Hospitals and Physical Reconstruction. It has not been possible to trace any contact between King and the CCP or to shed any light on where King got the idea.

24. King would clearly be a "manager" in Brian Linn's intriguing categorization. *The Echo of Battle: The Army's Way of War* (Cambridge, Mass.: Harvard University Press, 2007).

25. NARA RG165 M912, roll 14, frame 074.

26. RG165 M91,2 roll 267, Memo for the CoS subj: Classification of men unfit for full military duty, April 10, 1918; and Memo for TAG (same subject), April 12, 1918.

27. RG165 roll 295, ref. 9796–104, –134, –137, –325; March 1, 7, and 9, and May 29, 1918, respectively.

28. RG165 roll 305, ref. 9948–153, April 11, 1918; RG165 roll 334, ref. 10351–5, August 15, 1918.

29. RG165 roll 349, ref. 10856–23, October 18, 1918. The men were not historians but photo archivists.

30. RG165 roll 298, ref. 9860–37, September 9, 1918.

31. RG165 roll 363, ref. 11064–1, July 9, 1918.

32. RG165 roll 214, ref. 8689–132, April 4–19, 1918; RG165 roll 298, ref. 9860–42, September 21, 1918.

33. RG165 roll 298, ref. 9860–29, July 13, 1918; CCP, *History of the Personnel System*, 1:189–193. The first revised TOEs were published in November 1918, and others were in the pipeline, being published through March 1919.

34. RG165 roll 298, ref. 9860–63, November 15 and 16, 1918.

35. The CCP's vol. 2, *The Personnel Manual*, was the how-to system that was intended to sit on the shelf for future dusting off.

36. CCP, 1:141–142. The November 1, 1918, CCP card had a flip side that recorded details on physical condition, allowing for more efficient personnel management, but it was clearly too late to matter.

37. Provost Marshal General, *Second Report*, 154, 156.

38. Mobilization Regulation (MR) 1–5 ("Standard of Physical Examination during those Mobilizations for which Selective Service is Planned," December 5, 1932) would define LS, but the definition would still be a grey area, men who do "not come within the standards of unconditional acceptance, or of unconditional rejection."

39. Kreidberg and Henry, *History of Military Mobilization*, 390.

40. This might have earned LS a mention in the IMPs but apparently did not. Only the 1936 IMP has been found, in the University of Richmond Library.

41. MR 1–3 "Classification of Enlisted Men," December 10, 1935; MR 1–9 "Reception of Selective Service Men," January 15, 1934.

42. MR 1–1 "Procurement and Reception of Volunteers During Mobilization," March 27, 1934; MR 1–9, "Reception of Selective Service Men," January 15, 1934.

43. Army War College Curricular Archives AWC 381-A-1, "The Procurement of Personnel by Voluntary Enlistment in the Early Stages of the Mobilization for a Major Emergency; The Procurement of Special Service Enlisted Men," MG C. H. Bridges, October 6, 1931. USAMHI.

44. MR 1–1 "Procurement and Reception of Volunteers during Mobilization," WD, March 27, 1934.

45. MR 1–4 "Personnel Procurement Through Selective Service," May 16, 1934. MR 1–9 of 1932 even saw medical/surgical remediation of men up to LS standards, presumably as a way of further reducing the labor turmoil incident to a draft.

46. Address to Army War College, May 14, 1929, Merritte Ireland Papers, National Library of Medicine. While Ireland was speaking off the cuff, 50 percent was later accepted in World War II. Charles Wiltse, *Medical Department, U.S. Army, Physical Standards in World War II* (Washington, D.C., 1967), 77.

47. Kreidberg and Henry, *History of Military Mobilization*, 464, 473.

48. AWC Conference report, "Manpower," November 12, 1937, AWC Curricular Archive 1–1938-1, USAMHI. This was seen as not only more efficient for the army but for the nation, as it would create fewer veterans who would cost the taxpayers money for benefits.

49. MR 1–1 "Personnel," September 1, 1939. There was a renumbering of some of the MRs; the old 1–1 became 1–5.

50. MR 1–5 "Procurement and Reception of Volunteers during Mobilization," October 1, 1940.

51. MR 1–4, May 16, 1934; repeated in MR 1–1 "Personnel," September 1, 1939.

52. Public Law 783, September 16, 1940.

53. This was through May 31, 1941. Arthur P. Black, "Measures of Preventive Medicine Recommended by the Federal Medical Services to Insure the Maximum Improvement of the Selectee of 1961 over Him of 1941," *Military Surgeon* 91, no. 6 (December 1942): 619–637.

54. MR 1–1 "Personnel," September 1, 1939; MR 1–5 "Procurement and Reception of Volunteers During Mobilization," October 1, 1940.

55. An editorial, "With Emphasis on the Word Selective," *Military Surgeon* 87, no. 6 (December 1940): 265–266. *Military Surgeon* was a semiofficial publication of the Army and Navy medical services.

56. *Selective Service* 1, no. 5 (May 1941).

57. *Selective Service* 1, no. 11 (November 1941). This would be stopped in early 1942 as not being worthwhile, especially given the wartime reduction of physical standards. L. G. Rowntree, "Wartime Problems of Selective Service," *Military Surgeon* 92, no. 2 (February 1943): 149–162. Rowntree's paper was presented in November 1942 and published three months later.

58. Editorial, "Selective Service Examinations," *Military Surgeon* 88, no. 6 (June 1941): 674. This is six months after the same journal had called for the strictest standards. L. G. Rowntree, "Some Problems of Selective Service," *Military Surgeon* 90, no. 3 (March 1942): 238–245. Rowntree's paper was presented in October 1941 and published five months later.

59. In November 1943, the 7,700,000-man army had five thousand slots in development battalions. Kreidberg and Henry, *History of Military Mobilization*, 629.

60. Rowntree, "Some Problems of Selective Service."

61. Lerwill, "The Personnel Replacement System," 142. See also Staff, Personal Research Section, Classification and Enlisted Replacement Branch, the Adjutant General's Office, "Personnel Research in the Army," *Psychological Bulletin* 40 (1943). This was a seven-part article covering various facets.

62. See AR 615–26, Enlisted Men: Index and Specifications for Civilian and Military Occupational Specialists, September 15, 1942; and Technical Manual 12–425, Personnel Classification, June 17, 1944.

63. AR 615–25, Enlisted Men Initial Classification, July 31, 1942, 3–4.

64. See Robert R. Palmer, "The Procurement of Enlisted Personnel: The Problem of Quality," in *The Procurement and Training of Ground Combat Troops*, ed. Robert R. Palmer, Bell I. Wiley, and William R. Keast (Washington, D.C.: GPO, 1948), 4–86, esp. 4–13, which also explains how the Navy and Army Air Forces obtained intelligent men disproportionately to the ground combat troops.

65. See Robert J. Lewinski, "Military Considerations of Mental Deficiency," *Military Surgeon* 95, no. 5 (November 1944): 385–390.

66. Palmer's chapter may have set the trend for this.

67. Kreidberg and Henry, *History of Military Mobilization*, 642.

68. AR 615–28, May 28, 1942.

69. There were two specifically-LS drafts, one of one thousand men in June 1942 as an experiment and then 25,000 men in August. Research Section, National Headquarters Selective Service System, "World War II Experience of Selective Service with the Registrant Found Acceptable to the Armed Forces for Limited Service Only" (Washington, D.C., 1951), 3. For the Selective Service System, the category I-B was shortly abolished, with the men classified I-A or IV-F. Then in mid-1943 I-A(L) for limited was recreated. *Selective Service* 2, no. 7 (July 1942); *Selective Service* 2, no. 8 (August 1942); *Selective Service* 3, no. 7 (July 1943). When LS was abolished, I-A(L) would be abolished in October 1944. *Selective Service* 4, no. 10 (October 1944).

70. *Annual Report of the Surgeon General, Fiscal Year 1943*, 42, on file, Office of Medical History. The rationale for all this is unclear.

71. Palmer, "The Procurement of Enlisted Personnel," 40.

72. WD Circular 327, Utilization of Limited Service Enlisted Personnel, September 27, 1942.

73. Eli Ginzberg et al., *The Lost Divisions* (New York: Columbia University Press, 1959), 69–70, puts this in the best light, as commanders probably did at the time. For examples of problems for units, see Leo P. Brophy and George J. B. Fisher, *The Chemical Warfare Service: Organizing for War* (Washington, D.C.: GPO, 1959), 149–150; and Blanche D. Coll, Jean E. Keith, and Herbert H. Rosenthal, *The Corps of Engineers: Troops and Equipment* (Washington, D.C.: GPO, 1958), 299–300. For a discussion of other kinds of personnel turmoil in the army, see John Brown, *Draftee Division: The 88th Infantry Division in World War II* (Lexington: University of Kentucky Press, 1985), esp. chaps. 2 and 9 and appendix 1.

74. Lerwill, "The Personnel Replacement System," 145. See also Philip A. Langehough, *When Hearts Were Brave Again and Arms Were Strong: A Limited Service Soldier's Great Adventure, 1943–1945* (Great Falls, Va.: Information International, 2005), where Langehough was somewhat indignant about being labeled LS and insisted he did not want any consideration.

75. Comments of LTG Henry Aurand, *Presentation of Organization and Functions of the Office of The Surgeon General to the Director of Logistics, General Staff, USA, 16 Dec 1948*, 28–31. Aurand noted that many LS men came in with relevant training but also claimed that they were eager to serve. He also reminisced that MPs who suppressed a race riot had been reclassified as LS after combat wounds.

76. John McMinn, draft chapter, "The Early War Period in the Zone of the Interior, 1941–1943," 260. RG 112, entry 31a, box 424.

77. Ibid., 261–262. In April 1943, the surgeon general experimented with training LS men before sending them to a hospital, but the experiment was a mixed success. Wiltse, *Physical Standards*, 235–236. It is unclear how many high-AGCT LS men were available in late 1942, but the Army Air Forces was able to obtain over one thousand in exchange for GS men in the autumn of 1944. Robert J. Parks, *Medical Training in World War II* (Washington, D.C.: GPO, 1974), 218.

78. WD Circular 395, December 5, 1942.

79. Palmer, "The Procurement of Enlisted Personnel," 41–42. It would take until September for AR 615–25 change 5 to stop sending LS men (by then an obsolete term) to combat units, combat support units, and for training as combat replacements.

80. John McMinn and Max Levin, *Medical Department, U.S. Army, Personnel in World War II* (Washington, D.C.: GPO, 1963), 235–236; "Effects of Physical Standards and Regulations on Selective Service Procurement," Research and Statistics Division, National Headquarters Selective Service System, January 10, 1944, 4.

81. For more on the Troop Basis, see Robert R. Palmer, "The Mobilization of the Ground Army," Army Ground Forces Historical Section Study no. 4, 1946.

82. WD Circular 161, July 14, 1943. While this is after the cut Troop Basis, the War Department may not have been nimble enough for Circular 161 to be a response.

83. See Palmer, "The Procurement of Enlisted Personnel," 43, on the difficulties. Circular 293 had to repeat the removal of the term LS, and MR 1–9 of April 19, 1944, still used it, showing how many separate bureaucratic moving parts the army had.

84. Wiltse, *Physical Standards*, 21, 104–106; Palmer, "The Procurement of Enlisted Personnel," 45, Ginzberg et al, *The Lost Divisions*, 75–78. Statistics overlap, but from November 1940 to October 1943 the army discharged 95,000 LS men as "not adaptable to military service" (an administrative discharge) plus 42,000 for physical reasons, "Effects of Physical Standards and Regulations."

85. Ginzberg et al, *The Lost Divisions*, 77–78.

86. Circular 293 was issued on November 11 but was preceded by an emergency radiogram on November 3. Albert J. Glass and Robert J. Bernucci, *Neuropsychiatry in World War II, Zone of Interior* (Washington, D.C.: GPO, 1966), 207–209. Lerwill, "The Personnel Replacement System," 146, says it took two months to disseminate a change and two months to get reports back to check results; thus it would take six months to implement a correction. Considered against this standard, at 121 days the change from Circular 161 to 293 was nimble.

87. Wiltse, *Physical Standards*, 105.

88. WD Circular 312, November 30, 1943.

89. Report of the Commission of Physicians Appointed to Examine the Requirements for Admission to the Army, Navy, and Marine Corps, February 29, 1944.

90. The AGF role in this is retold in Palmer, "The Procurement of Enlisted Personnel," 64–69. Almost any system that changed the assignment system would provide the AGF men with better AGCT scores.

91. See Wiltse, *Physical Standards*, 68–76, for more detail.

92. Kreidberg and Henry, *History of Military Mobilization*, 643. The adjutant general's office had tried to provide some fine tuning of using LS men, matching particular defects (presuming the remaining capabilities) against particular positions. No details have been found, but given the chaos around the LS policy it cannot have worked particularly well. Staff, Classification and Replacement Branch, the Adjutant General's Office, "Selection, Classification, and Assignment of Military Personnel in the Army of the United States During World War II," September 1947. Center of Military History files, 4–1.4 BA.

93. Technical Manual 12–425, Personnel Classification, June 17, 1944, 2.

94. WD memorandum W 40–44, May 18, 1944, described C as Limited Service, so the term was still in use—by officials—even after repeated changes to Limited Assignment. Presumably LS was the familiar term and, after all, was essentially the same as Limited Assignment.

95. Palmer, "The Procurement of Enlisted Personnel," 69.

96. WD Circular 164, April 26, 1944.

97. WD Circular 212, May 29, 1944.

98. History of Classification and Replacement Division, Ground, Adjutant General's Section, Headquarters Army Ground Forces, March 1, 1943–December 31, 1945, Center of Military History files, 6–1 AE. Footnote 61 of Palmer, "The Procurement of Enlisted Personnel" (the underlying documents for which have not been found), suggests this was the result of a conference in late July because of a buildup of low-quality manpower that could not be utilized regardless of policy.

99. WD Circular 370, September 12, 1944.

100. History of Classification and Replacement Division, January 24, 1945.

101. The Information-Education Division of the European Theater of Operations produced an illustrated booklet in June 1945, "*Why* Limited Assignment?" explaining, presumably to the combat wounded, why they could not go home. It quoted Circular 164, 1944, then explained how their new rear-area jobs would also be important.

102. Personnel Division, G-1, War Department, "The Physical Profile—An Element in Classification," *Military Review* 25, no. 3 (June 1945): 62–65.

103. Headquarters, Replacement Training Command, U.S. Army Pacific, "Personnel Audit and Recovery Program U.S. Army Forces Pacific Ocean Areas and Middle Pacific 15 October 1944 to 10 September 1945," USAMHI. The G-1 team was more optimistic about using LS men and, when given the authority to overrule unit commanders, identified 3,130 positions in addition to the 7,927 already filled with LS men. This totaled around 33 percent of the positions examined, reasonably in line with prewar projections.

104. Forrest J. Agee, "Limited Assignment Men Serve in Forward Areas," *Military Review* 26, no. 5 (August 1946): 65–66.

105. Col. George R. Evans, "Not So Disabled," *Army Information Digest* 1, no. 8 (December 1946): 43–45.

106. "Disabled Personnel," *Health of the Army* (July 1953): 8–13, was a ten-year review.

107. See three lectures at the Industrial College of the Armed Forces, Maj. Gen. Lewis Hershey (director of Selective Service), April 10, 1946; Lt. Col. F. P. Greer, February 3, 1947; and Dr. E. A. Fitzpatrick, February 21, 1947; as well as Leonard Carmichael and Leonard Mead, eds., *The Selection of Military Manpower: A Symposium* (Washington, D.C.: National Academy of Sciences, 1951), 130, 250.

7. Soviet Use of "Substandard" Manpower in the Red Army, 1941–1945
David Glantz

1. S. V. Lipitsky, "Voennaia reforma 1924–1925 godov [The military reforms of 1924–1925]," *Kommunist* [The communist] 4 (March 1990): 105.

2. First-line cadre divisions had 6,300 permanent cadre and 12,300 mobilization personnel, and second-line cadre divisions had 604 permanent personnel and 11,750 mobilization personnel. The three manning levels (first, second, and third line) in territorial divisions consisted of 2,400, 604–622, and 190 cadre and 10,681, 11,734–11,750, and over 12,000 men, respectively. In some cases, one territorial division could form the nucleus for up to three new divisions. See I. Berkhin, "O territorial'no-militsionnom stroitel'stve v Sovetskoi Armii [Concerning the territorial-militia construction in the Red Army]," *Voenno-istoricheskii zhurnal* [Military-historical journal] 12 (December 1960): 15–16. Hereafter cited as *VIZh* with appropriate article.

3. I. G. Pavlovsky, *Sukhoputnye voisk SSSR* [The ground forces of the USSR] (Moscow: Voenizdat, 1985), 65–68.

4. N. A. Mal'tsev, "Kadrovaia ili militsionnaia [Cadre or militia]," *VIZh* 11 (November 1989): 38.

5. Iurii Gor'kov, *Gosudarstvennyi komitet oborony postanovliat, 1941–1945: Tsifry, dokumenty* [The State Defense Committee decrees, 1941–1945: Figures and documents] (Moscow: Olma Press, 2002), 117; and *Liudskie poteri SSSR v period Vtoroi Mirovoi voiny: Sbornik statei* [Personnel losses of the USSR in World War II: A collection of articles] (St. Petersburg: Russian Academy of Sciences, 1995), 72.

6. For specific formations, see, V. V. Gradosel'sky, "Natsional'nye voinskie formirovaniia v Krasnoi Armii (1918–1938 gg.) [National military formation in the Red Army (1918–1938)]," *VIZh* 10 (October 2001): 4.

7. Ibid., 4.

8. See, for example, Stavka directive no. 170578, August 20, 1942, to the commander of the Trans-Caucasus Front about measures to reinforce the defenses along the Prokhlodnyi axis, archival citation *TsAMO*, f. 48a, op. 3408, d. 72, l. 224; and Soviet General Staff order no. 994168, August 20, 1942, to the commander of the Trans-Caucasus Front about removing Armenians, Azerbaijanis, and Dagestanis from the Sixty-first Rifle Division, *TsAMO*, f. 48a, op. 3408, d. 72, l. 164, quoted verbatim and translated in David M. Glantz, *The Struggle for the Caucasus: Combat Chronology and Documents*, Vol. 1, *21 July–18 November 1942* (Carlisle, Penn.: The author, 2008), 88–89. This bias against non–Great Russian soldiers even extended to Ukrainians. For example, Russian historians

have heaped praise on General Rodimtsev's Thirteenth GRD for its stoic defense of the city of Stalingrad in the fall of 1942 while almost ignoring the performance of Colonel Batiuk's 284th RD, which made even greater contributions to the Soviet victory. They lavished this praise largely because Rodimtsev's division consisted of Great Russians while Batiuk's contained primarily Ukrainians, one of whom was Valerii Zaitsev, the Soviet sniper commemorated in the book and movie *Enemy at the Gates*.

9. See V. A. Zolotarev, ed., "Stavka VGK: Dokumenty i materialy 1942 [The Stavka VGK: Documents and materials 1942]," in *Russkii arkhiv: Velikaia Otechestvennaia, 16 (5–2)* [The Russian archives: The Great Patriotic War, 16 (5–2)] (Moscow: TERRA, 1996), 88–89.

10. "Boevaia kharakteristika na 121 sd [The combat characteristics of the 121st Rifle Division]," from "Boevye rasporiazheniia shtaba Voronezhskogo fronta [The combat orders of the Voronezh Front]," *TsAMO*, f. 417, op. 10564, d. 252, l. 12.

11. "Boevaia kharakteristika na 248 otdel'nuiu kursantskuiu strelkovuiu brigadu [The combat characteristics of the 248th Student Rifle Brigade]," from "Boevye rasporiazheniia shtaba Voronezhskogo fronta [The combat orders of the Voronezh Front]," *TsAMO*, f. 417, op. 10564, d. 252, l. 13.

12. "Komandiram 1, 2, 3 armeiskikh zagradotriadov. 16. 3. 43g. No. 0224 [Order no. 0224, March 16, 1943, to the commanders of the First, Second, and Third Army Blocking Detachments]," in "Direktivy SVGK, GSh, KA voiskam Brianskogo fronta, 13A, 2. 1–20. 7. 43 [Directives of the Stavka of the Supreme High Command to the Briansk Front and Thirteenth Army, January 2–July 20, 1943]," *TsAMO*, f. 361, op. 6079, d. 173, l. 105.

13. See V. A. Zolotarev, ed., "Prikazy narodnogo komissara oborony SSSR 1943–1945 [The orders of the People's Commissar of Defense of the USSR, 1943–1945]," in *Russkii arkhiv: Velikaia Otechestvennaia, 13 (2–3)* [The Russian archives: The Great Patriotic War, 13 (2–3)] (Moscow: TERRA, 1997), 216. Hereafter cited as Zolotarev, "NKO 1943," with appropriate pages.

14. Ibid., 219.

15. David M. Glantz, *Red Army Officers Speak* (Carlisle, Penn.: The author, 1998), 116–117. The interview is with Iu. A. Naumenko, the commander of the Ninety-seventh Guards Rifle Division's 289th Guards Rifle Regiment, which served in the Fifth Guards Army's Thirty-second Guards Rifle Corps.

16. Simeon Aria, "From Tanks to Katiushas," in *Memories of War: The Experiences of Red Army Veterans of the Great Patriotic War* (Carlisle, Penn.: The author, 2001), 5:21.

17. These two historians are Kazimiera J. Cottam, who has written several books, including *Women in War and Resistance: Selected Biographies of Soviet Women Soldiers* (Nepean, Canada: New Military Publishing, 1998); and Reina Pennington, who wrote the recent study *Wings, Women, and War: Soviet Airwomen in World War II Combat* (Lawrence: University Press of Kansas, 2001).

18. M. M. Kozlov, ed., *Velikaia Otechestvennaia voina 1941–1945: Entsiklopediia* [The Great Patriotic War 1941–1945: An encyclopedia] (Moscow: Sovetskaia entsiklopediia, 1985), 269–270.

19. Cottam, *Women in War and Resistance*, xx.

20. See Zolotarev, "NKO 1941," 13 (2–2), 113. This NKO order was numbered 0099.

21. Ibid., 184–185. This NKO order was numbered 0058.

22. Ibid., 196. The NKO order was numbered 0065.

23. Ibid., 212–213. This NKO order was numbered 0284.

24. Ibid.

25. Ibid., 214–215, 396n40. These NKO orders were numbered 0296 and 0297.

26. Ibid., 217–218. This NKO order was numbered 0325.

27. Zolotarev, "NKO 1943," 13 (2–3), 13–14.

28. Ibid., 115.

29. *Liudskie poteri*, 74.

30. Krivosheev, *Rossiia i SSSR v voinakh XX veka*, 96–100; and *Liudskie poteri*, 74.

31. Krivosheev, *Rossiia i SSSR v voinakh XX veka*, 263.

32. Ibid., 312–313.

33. Ibid., 109–110.

34. Zolotarev, "NKO 1943," 13 (2–3), 198. This order was numbered 0413.

35. For further details concerning the 123rd Penal Company, see S. Khomenko, "A Disciplinary Battalion Joins Battle" *Soviet Soldier* 11 (November 1990): 36–38.

36. Krivosheev, *Rossiia i SSSR v voinakh XX veka*, 441.

37. Ibid.

38. Igor Mangazeev, "A 'Penal' Corps on the Kalinin Front," *Journal of Slavic Military Studies* 15, no. 3 (September 2002): 120–121.

39. Ibid., 120.

40. Ibid., 123.

41. Ibid.

42. Ibid., 124–125.

43. Ibid., 126.

8. German Bodenstandig Divisions
Walter Dunn

1. For an explanation of how the replacement system worked, see "German and Soviet Replacement Systems in World War II, Final Report," Historical Evaluation and Research Organization, July 1975. [Editor's note.]

2. Wehrkreise were military districts that mainly administered the manpower system. [Editor's note.]

3. On occupation forces in Norway during 1942–1943, including the bodenstandig divisions, see *The German Northern Theater of Operations, 1940–1945* (Washington, D.C.: Center of Military History, 1989), chaps. 11–12. [Editor's note.]

4. There is relatively little written about the Walcheren campaign. It is mentioned in the British official history (L. F. Ellis, *Victory in the West*, vol. 2: *The Defeat of Germany* [London: HMSO, 1968], 66–123). Gerald Rawling, *Cinderella Operation: The Battle for Walcheren, 1944* (London: Cassell, 1980), is apparently the only book focused on it. The broader question of opening Antwerp for shipping has received much more attention but goes far beyond the 70th Infantry Division. [Editor's note.]

9. Recruiting *Volksdeutsche* for the Waffen-SS: From Skimming the Cream to Scraping the Dregs
Valdis O. Lumans

1. This scene is constructed from the testimony of M.R., an ethnic German of Franzfeld in the Yugoslavian Banat, testifying May 6, 1957, doc. nr. 5, 65–67, in vol. 2 of *Dokumentation der Vertreibung, Das Schicksal der Deutschen aus Ungarn*, as well as other pieces of testimony and documentation in this series. Consult this published series as well as its compiler, the German Bundesministerium für Vertriebene, Flüchtling und Kriegsgeschädigte, *Dokumentation der Vertreibung der Deutschen aus Ost-Mitteleuropa*, ed. Theodor Scheider (1953–1961). The series is also available in English translation as *Documents on the Expulsion of the Germans from East Central Europe*, ed. Theodor Scheider (1960–1961). See also Bundesarchiv Koblenz (BAK), R142/15, 176, and English translation by Georga Beichl, 65. This and other documentation can be found in a series of U.S. extradition cases against former ethnic German Waffen-SS men, for which this author served as expert witness, including *USA vs. Johann Breyer*.

2. For introductions to the Waffen-SS, see George H. Stein, *The Waffen-SS: Hitler's Elite Guard at War, 1939–1945* (Ithaca, N.Y.: Cornell University Press, 1966), esp. 1–8; Bernd Wegner, *Hitlers*

Politische Soldaten: Die Waffen-SS, 1933–1945 (Paderborn: Schöningh, 1982); Robert L. Koehl, *The Black Corps: The Structure and Power Struggles of the Nazi SS* (Madison: University of Wisconsin Press, 1983); Charles W. Sydnor, *Soldiers of Destruction: The SS Death's Head Division, 1933–1945* (Princeton, N.J.: Princeton University Press, 1977); and James J. Weingartner, *Hitler's Guard: The Story of the Leibstandarte SS Adolf Hitler, 1933–1945* (Carbondale: University of Southern Illinois Press, 1974).

3. Stein, *The Waffen-SS*, 189. For an introduction to Waffen-SS involvement with the ethnic Germans, refer to Stein's account and Koehl, *The Black Corps*, 135–141. In addition, see Robert Herzog, *Die Volksdeutsche in der Waffen-SS* (Tübingen: Institut für Besetzungsfragen, 1955), in *Studien des Instituts für Besatzungsfragen in Tübingen zu den Deutschen Bessetzungen im 2. Weltkrieg*, nr. 5; Leo Daugherty, "The Volksdeutsche and Hitler's War," *Journal of Slavic Military Studies* 8, no. 2 (June 1995): 296–318; and Valdis O. Lumans, *Himmler's Auxiliaries: The Volksdeutsche Mittelstelle and the German National Minorities of Europe, 1933–1945* (Chapel Hill: University of North Carolina Press, 1993), 211–216, and other relevant sections; Lumans, "The Military Obligation of the Volksdeutsche of Eastern Europe toward the Third Reich," *Central European History* 15, no. 3 (1982): 266–297; Ronald Smelser and Enrico Syring, eds., *Die SS: Elite unter dem Totenkopf; 30 Lebensläufe* (Paderborn: Schöningh, 2000).

4. *USA vs. Johann Breyer*, govt. documents 1324–0082, 2.

5. Stein, *The Waffen-SS*, 192n65; Chris Bishop, *SS: Hitler's Foreign Divisions: Foreign Volunteers in the Waffen-SS, 1940–1945* (London: Amber Books, 2005), 19; John Keegan, *Waffen-SS: The Asphalt Soldiers* (New York: Ballantine Books, 1970), 143.

6. Felix Steiner, *Die Freiwilligen der Waffen-SS: Idee und Opfergang* (Preuss. Oldendorf: K.W. Schütz KG, 1973), 263.

7. Gordon Williamson, *Loyalty Is My Honor: Personal Accounts from the Waffen-SS* (Osceola, Wis.: Motorbooks International, 1995), 72–73.

8. Stein, *The Waffen-SS*, 192; Keegan, *Waffen-SS*, 109; Tim Ripley, *The Waffen-SS at War: Hitler's Praetorians, 1925–1945* (St. Paul, Minn.: Zenith Press, 2004), 10.

9. Lumans, *Auxiliaries*, 22–23; Wilhelm Winkler, *Statistisches Handbuch der europäischen Nationalitäten* (Vienna: Wilhelm Braumüller, 1931), and *Deutschtum in aller Welt: Bevölkerungsstatistische Tabellen* (Vienna: Verlag Franz Deuticke, 1938).

10. Lumans, *Auxiliaries*, 22–23; see relevant statistics in Winkler, *Statistisches Handbuch*.

11. Lumans, "Military Obligation." Much of the material and documentation in this chapter has been shared with this article on the Volksdeutsche military obligation, cited fully in note 3, above. In the interest of space, for fuller citations refer to the original article.

12. For a thorough study of VoMi, see Lumans, *Auxiliaries*.

13. Karl H. Theile, *Beyond "Monsters" and "Clowns": The Combat SS: De-Mythologizing Five Decades of German Elite Formations* (New York: University Press of America, 1997), 237; Paul Hausser, *Soldaten wie Andere auch: Der Weg der Waffen-SS* (Osnabrück: Munin Verlag, 1966), 93; Lumans, *Auxiliaries*, 211–216.

14. Ernst-Gunther Krätschmer, *Die Ritterkreuzträger der Waffen-SS* (Preuss. Oldendorf: Verlag K.W. Schütz KG, 1982), 376–377, 474–478, 602–603, 905, 914–915.

15. Theile, *Beyond "Monsters" and "Clowns,"* 129; Krätschmer, *Die Ritterkreuzträger der Waffen-SS*, 513, 578–579, 842, 863, 941–942.

16. Krätschmer, *Die Ritterkreuzträger der Waffen-SS*, 566–567.

17. Lumans, *Auxiliaries*, 80–93, 216–221; Lumans, "The Ethnic German Minority of Slovakia and the Third Reich, 1938–1945," *Central European History* 15, no. 3 (1982): 266–297; see also L'ubomir Liptak, "The Role of the German Minority in Slovakia in the Years of the Second World War," *Studia Historica Slovaca* 1 (1963): 150–178.

18. Krätschmer, *Die Ritterkreuzträger der Waffen-SS*, 238–240.

19. Krätschmer, *Die Ritterkreuzträger der Waffen-SS*, 779, 841, 857, 916–917.

20. See relevant passages in Lumans, *Auxiliaries*; Lumans, "Slovakia"; also Mark W. A. Axworthy, *Axis Slovakia: Hitler's Slavic Wedge, 1938–1945* (Bayside, N.Y.: Axis Europa Books, 2002), 222–223. Refer also to Lumans, "Military Obligation," 311.

21. Stein, *The Waffen-SS*, 46; Axworthy, *Slovakia*, 215, 222–224.

22. Axworthy, *Slovakia*, 75.

23. Stein, *The Waffen-SS*, 46; Axworthy, *Slovakia*, 75, 99, 179–186, 199–206, 223, 248–255, 316.

24. Stein, *The Waffen-SS*, xxxii–xxxiv, 28. For the authoritative study on the TK, see Sydnor, *Soldiers of Destruction*.

25. Stein, *The Waffen-SS*, xxxiv, 46, 50; Marc J. Rikmenspoel, *Waffen-SS: The Encyclopedia* (Garden City, N.Y.: Military Book Club, 2000), 75–76.

26. Krätschmer, *Die Ritterkreuzträger der Waffen-SS*, 844; Williamson, *Loyalty*, 29.

27. Lumans, *Auxiliaries*, 131–140, 152–170; also Dietrich Loeber, ed., *Diktierte Option: Die Umsiedlung der Deutsch-Balten aus Estland und*

Lettland, 1939–1941 (Neumünster: Karl Wacholz Verlag, 1972); Lumans, "Military Obligation," 308.

28. Lumans, *Auxiliaries*, 131–141. See also Robert L. Koehl, *RKFDV: German Resettlement and Population Policy, 1939–1945* (Cambridge, Mass.: Harvard University Press, 1957).

29. Lumans, *Auxiliaries*, 184–198; Lumans, "Military Obligation," 308–309.

30. Lumans, *Auxiliaries*, 213–214; Gerhard Rempel, "Gottlob Berger: Ein Schwabengeneral der Tat," in Smelser and Syring, *Die SS*, 48–49; Lumans, "Military Obligation," 308–309.

31. Krätschmer, *Die Ritterkreuzträger der Waffen-SS*, 582, 607, 789, 831, 693. See also Valdis O. Lumans, "A Reassessment of Volksdeutsche and Jews in the Volhynia-Galicia-Narew Resettlement," in *The Impact of Nazism: New Perspectives on the Third Reich and Its Legacy*, ed. Alan E. Steinweis and Daniel E. Rogers (Lincoln: University of Nebraska Press, 2003), 81–100.

32. Bishop, *SS*, 37, 58.

33. Rikmenspoel, *Waffen-SS: The Encyclopedia*, 77, 83, 99–101; Williamson, *Loyalty*, 28; Steiner, *Die Freiwilligen*, 83; Hausser, *Soldaten wie Andere auch*, 74–75.

34. Theile, *Beyond "Monsters" and "Clowns,"* 292; Rikmenspoel, *Waffen-SS: The Encyclopedia*, 84–85, 100–101; Bishop, *SS*, 47.

35. Rikmenspoel, *Waffen-SS: The Encyclopedia*, 85, 101; Kurt-Georg Klietmann, *Die Waffen-SS: Eine Dokumentation* (Osnabrück: Verlag 'der Freiwillige, 1965), 133–37; Keegan, *Waffen-SS*, 93.

36. Stein, *The Waffen-SS*, 107.

37. Bishop, *SS*, 13–16, 27, 49; Rikmenspoel, *Waffen-SS: The Encyclopedia*, 24–25, 101, 109; Klietmann, 133–37.

38. Bishop, *SS*, 27; Rikmenspoel, *Waffen-SS: The Encyclopedia*, 85.

39. Krätschmer, *Die Ritterkreuzträger der Waffen-SS*, 238–240; Rikmenspoel, *Waffen-SS: The Encyclopedia*, 99–100.

40. Krätschmer, *Die Ritterkreuzträger der Waffen-SS*, 649; Stein, *The Waffen-SS*, 46; Theile, *Beyond "Monsters" and "Clowns,"* 237.

41. Rempel, "Gottlob Berger," 48–49.

42. Stein, *The Waffen-SS*, 94, 169; Richard Landwehr, *Romanian Volunteers of the Waffen-SS, 1944–1945* (Brookings, Or.: Siegrunen, 1991), 34; Bishop, *SS*, 90.

43. Klietmann, *Die Waffen-SS*, 76–77, 87. See also Chris McNabb, *World War II Data Book: The SS, 1923–1945; The Essential Facts and Figures for Himmler's Stormtroopers* (London: Amber Books, 2009), 61–68.

44. Lumans, "Military Obligation," 315n35. For those interested in copious archival sources on the subject, in the interest of economizing the text length of this chapter, references will be given to secondary citations.

45. Stein, *The Waffen-SS*, 169; Rikmenspoel, *Waffen-SS: The Encyclopedia*, 77; Theile, *Beyond "Monsters" and "Clowns,"* 237; Steiner, *Die Freiwilligen*, 42–43; Klietmann, *Die Waffen-SS*, 76–77, 87.

46. Herzog, *Die Volksdeutsche in der Waffen-SS*, 12; Keegan, *Waffen-SS*, 93; Rikmenspoel, *Waffen-SS: The Encyclopedia*, 77–78; Stein, *The Waffen-SS*, 169, 192; Theile, *Beyond "Monsters" and "Clowns,"* 237; Steiner, *Die Freiwilligen*, 42–43; Klietmann, *Die Waffen-SS*, 76–77.

47. Lumans, "Military Obligation," 313n24.

48. Ibid., 314.

49. Cited in SS Richter beim RFSS Per. Stab, 19 Feb. 1945, "Wehrpflicht der Deutschen aus den Volksgruppen," T-175/74/259-1954-55 (refers to microfilms; Records of the RFSS, reel 74, series 259, frames 1954–1955). This 1945 memo refers to events in 1942.

50. Lumans, "Military Obligation," 312n18–19; Lumans, *Auxiliaries*, 215.

51. Dr. Juraj Spiler, Reich official in Serbia, testifying in October 1947; Nuremberg testimony, NO-5693, National Archives. Also Himmler's communication to Werner Lorenz of VoMi, as cited in Max Jamst, "Die Ausschopfung der Wehrkraft der deutschen Volksgruppen in Sudosteuropa durch die SS" (a study on Volksdeutsche in the Waffen-SS), found in Folder DC Volkstum-Ausland, 1951, at the Berlin Document Center. Lumans, "Military Obligation," 312n21.

52. Lumans, "Military Obligation," 313n24.

53. Ibid., 313n26.

54. Ibid., 314.

55. Enver Redzic, *Bosnia and Herzegovina in the Second World War*, trans. Aida Vidan (New York, 2005), 6, 29. See also Lumans, "Military Obligation," 314n29.

56. Testimony of Josias Kumpf, in *USA vs. Josias Kumpf*, case no. 03 C 0944; Lumans, "Military Obligation," 314n30–31.

57. Redzic, *Bosnia and Herzegovina*, 29.

58. Lumans, "Military Obligation," 314n33–34.

59. Kammerhofer NO-2904.

60. Lumans, "Military Obligation," 311–313; Lumans, *Auxiliaries*, 214–216n18–20.

61. Ibid., 315n35–36.

62. Ibid., 315n39.

63. Ibid., 316.

64. Ibid., 316–317.

65. Peter Kaip of the Banat, doc. #6, "Aushebung von Volksdeutschen der Jahrgange 1919–1920 im Herbst 1941 zum Polizeidienst im Banat," testifying December 14, 1958, *Das Schicksal der Deutschen aus Ungarn*, 68–70.

66. J.H. from Batchka (part of Hungarian Banat/Voivodina), doc. #8, "Die Waffen-SS Aktionen von 1942–1944 . . . Erfassung der Wehrdiensttauglichen unter Gewissenszwang und Terror für den Dienst in der Waffen-SS," *Das Schicksal der Deutschen aus Ungarn*, 74–78, testifying April 13, 1958.

67. Lumans, "Military Obligation," n48.

68. Rudolf Melzer, "Wehrdienst der Karpatendeutschen in der Waffen-SS . . ." in *Karpaten Jahrbuch 1995*, 61.

69. Report to Vienna re: Recruiting Ethnic Germans for the Waffen-SS, August 28, 1942. Transl. of govt. exhibit 3.89 (1324–55).

70. Also in the same Beichl translation.

71. Klietmann, *Die Waffen-SS*, 247–248; Bishop, *SS*, 149; Rikmenspoel, *Waffen-SS: The Encyclopedia*, 44; Paul Hausser, *Waffen-SS im Einsatz* (Gottingen: Plesse Verlag K.W. Schutz, 1953), 158; Roland Kaltenegger, *Mountain Troops of the Waffen-SS, 1941–1945* (Atglen, Penn.: Schiffer Military/Aviation History, 1995), 34; Theile, *Beyond "Monsters" and "Clowns,"* 351.

72. SS Obergruppenführer Konstantin Kammerhofer, SS authority in Croatia, 1943–1945, testifying in January 1948; Nuremberg affidavit, NO-5815.

73. Konstantin Kammerhofer, Sworn Testimony, April 19, 1947, NO-2904, National Archives. Kammerhofer worked on recruiting for the SS under Berger. Kammerhofer affidavit, NO-5815.

74. Lumans, "Military Obligation," 320n59–60.

75. "D.H." of Sibiu (Hermannstadt), "Heranziehung der Rumänien-Deutschen zum Dienst in der Waffen-SS," *Das Schicksal Deutschen der Rumänien Transylvania 1957*, doc. nr. 9, 46–53. *Das Schicksal der Deutschen in Rumänien*, 55E–56E National Archives Document, dated August 20, 1951, addressed to James J. Norris, European Director NCWC, Frankfurt/Main-Hoechst, from St. Raphaels-Verein, Generalsekretariat, Verbindungstelle zur NCWC, re: "Material to the Problem of the Involuntary Drawing-in of German Ethnics into the Waffen-SS." The same memo of August 20, 1951: "3. State-Agreement about the Involuntary Drawing in of German Ethnics from Romania to the Waffen-SS."

76. Ibid.

77. Testimony of Josef Wittje, *USA vs. Josef Wittje*, case no. 03 C 6367.

78. Jamst, "Die Ausschopfung der Wehrkraft," 7; F.N., of Romanian Banat, testified on August 20, 1956, doc. #11, *Das Schicksal der Deutschen der Rumänien*, 58–60.

79. Lumans, "Military Obligation," 319n53–54.

80. J.H. from Batchka, doc. #8, "Die Waffen-SS Aktionen von 1942–1944 . . . Erfassung der Wehrdiensttauglichen unter Gewissenszwang und Terror für den Dienst in der Waffen-SS," *Das Schicksal der Deutschen aus Ungarn*, 74–78, testifying April 13, 1958.

81. Charles Trang, *La Division Florian Geyer*, trans. John Lee (Bayeux: Heidal, 2000), 91.

82. Jamst, "Die Ausschopfung der Wehrkraft," 1–7.

83. Axworthy, *Slovakia*, 214–215.

84. In "Security Service of the Reichsführer SS, Prague, Events in Slovakia, 12 February 1943," govt. exhibit 3.94 (1324–60).

85. Report on a Trip to Slovakia, by H. J. Wernicke, March 27, 1943, govt. exhibit 3.96 (1324–62), 2.

86. Refer to Rudolf Melzer, "Wehrdienst der Karpatendeutschen in der Waffen-SS von 1939 bis 1945," *Karpaten Jahrbuch 1995*, 59–81. BAK (Federal Archives Koblenz) R142/15, 176 (footnote 19 and 20 in Melzer). English translation by Georga Beichl, 65.

87. Lumans, *Auxiliaries*, 216n23.

88. Bishop, *SS*, 134; Theile, *Beyond "Monsters" and "Clowns,"* 338.

89. Herzog, *Die Volksdeutsche in der Waffen-SS*, 14; Lumans, *Auxiliaries*, 243–249.

90. An example is the Hegewald settlement in the Ukraine in a study by Wendy Lower, *Nazi Empire Building and the Holocaust in Ukraine* (Chapel Hill: University of North Carolina Press, 2005), 171–179.

91. Lumans, "Military Obligation," 319n57.

92. Benedikt Pfuhl, farmer from Batchka, testimony of May 1958, doc. #10, "Zwangsmassnahmen und Mishandlungen bei der Aushebung von Volksdeutschen aus Bukin zum Dienst in der Waffen-SS," *Das Schicksal der Deutschen aus Ungarn*, 80–81.

93. Lumans, "Military Obligation," 320n59–61.

94. Klietmann, *Die Waffen-SS*, 275–276; Bishop, *SS*, 159; Theile, *Beyond "Monsters" and "Clowns,"* 355; Axworthy, *Slovakia*, 316.

95. Rikmenspoel, *Waffen-SS: The Encyclopedia*, 30, 42–43; Hausser, *Einsatz*, 126; Steiner, *Die Freiwilligen*, 85; Klietmann, *Die Waffen-SS*, 233–237; Theile, *Beyond "Monsters" and "Clowns,"* 350; Bishop, *SS*, 145; Trang, *La Division Florian Geyer*, 143–44, 165, 172–173.

96. Theile, *Beyond "Monsters" and "Clowns,"* 340–341; Rikmenspoel, *Waffen-SS: The Encyclopedia*, 37–38; Philip W. Blood, *Hitler's Bandit*

Hunters: The SS and the Nazi Occupation of Europe (Washington, D.C.: Potomac Books, 2006), 141; Klietmann, *Die Waffen-SS*, 203–205; Trang, *La Division Florian Geyer*, 143, 147, 150–154.

97. Theile, *Beyond "Monsters" and "Clowns,"* 225.

98. Rikmenspoel, *Waffen-SS: The Encyclopedia*, 52; Bishop, *SS*, 145.

99. Rikmenspoel, *Waffen-SS: The Encyclopedia*, 56–57.

100. Stein, *The Waffen-SS*, 173; Herzog, *Die Volksdeutsche in der Waffen-SS*, 16–17.

101. Hausser, *Einsatz*, 15; Hausser, *Soldaten*, 75; Stein, *The Waffen-SS*, 168–169.

102. Stein, *The Waffen-SS*, 46, 75, 168–169.

10. The Ethnic Germans of the Waffen-SS in Combat: Dregs or Gems?
Valdis O. Lumans

1. For an introduction to the background and nature of the Waffen-SS, see notes 2 and 3 of the previous chapter. Notes to this chapter continue the short form from the previous chapter.

2. Adolf Hitler, *Secret Conversations with Hitler*, ed. Edouard Calic, trans. Richard Barry (repr., 1969; New York: John Day Co., 1971), 178; Stein, *The Waffen-SS*, 199, 212–213; Theile, *Beyond "Monsters" and "Clowns,"* 197.

3. Stein, *The Waffen-SS*, 192–193, 296–297; Wegner, *Hitlers Politische Soldaten*, 281.

4. Stein, *The Waffen-SS*, 242–243; Williamson, *Loyalty*, 13; Theile, *Beyond "Monsters" and "Clowns,"* 198, 204; Mark Axworthy et al., *Third Axis Fourth Ally: Romanian Armed Forces in the European War, 1941–1945* (London: Arms and Armour, 1995), 116.

5. Ripley, *The Waffen-SS at War*, 25; Theile, *Beyond "Monsters" and "Clowns,"* 224–228; Williamson, *Loyalty*, 29; Stein, *The Waffen-SS*, 45.

6. Stein, *The Waffen-SS*, 9–10; also Syring, "Hausser," in Smelser and Syring, *Die SS*, 190–207; Keegan, *Asphalt Soldiers*; Rikmenspoel, *Waffen-SS: The Encyclopedia*, 195–199, 251–252.

7. Stein, *The Waffen-SS*, 28, 56–57; Williamson, *Loyalty*, 12.

8. Rikmenspoel, *Waffen-SS: The Encyclopedia*, 18–20, 197; Stein, *The Waffen-SS*, 32–34; Hausser, *Soldaten*, 90–91.

9. Rikmenspoel, *Waffen-SS: The Encyclopedia*, 16–17; Stein, *The Waffen-SS*, 32–34.

10. Stein, *The Waffen-SS*, 56, 60; Williamson, *Loyalty*, 12; Rikmenspoel, *Waffen-SS: The Encyclopedia*, 16–24.

11. Ahmet Donlagic, Zarko Atanackovic, and Dushan Plenca, *Yugoslavia in the Second World War*, trans. Lovett F. Edwards (Belgrade: Interpress, 1967), 21. This book provides an official, approved communist interpretation of events. See also U.S. Army, *German Anti-Guerilla Operations in the Balkans, 1941–1944* (Washington, D.C.: U.S. Government Printing Office, 1954; 1989), 21–22. One Yugoslav *Volksdeutsche* to fare poorly under the Germans was Herta Has, a communist and former wife of the partisan leader Josip Broz, better known by his nomme de guerre as Tito. The Germans imprisoned Has, who had a German father, releasing her in a 1943 prisoner exchange. Milovan Djilas, *Wartime*, trans. Michael B. Petrovich (New York: Harcourt & Brace Jovanovich, 1977; 1980), 242.

12. Christopher R. Browning, "The Wehrmacht in Serbia Revisited," in *Crimes of War: Guilt and Denial in the Twentieth Century*, ed. Omer Bartov, Atina Grossmann, and Mary Nolan (New York: The New Press, 2002), 31–40; U.S. Army, *Anti-Guerilla*, 64–65, 76–77.

13. Williamson, *Loyalty*, 52–53; Klietmann, *Die Waffen-SS*, 501; Rikmenspoel, *Waffen-SS: The Encyclopedia*, 21–22.

14. Ripley, *The Waffen-SS at War*, 73; Rikmenspoel, *Waffen-SS: The Encyclopedia*, 26; Williamson, *Loyalty*, 52–53.

15. Bishop, *SS*, 166.

16. Williamson, *Loyalty*, 53.

17. Hausser, *Einsatz*, 68; Bishop, *SS*, 122; U.S. Army, *Anti-Guerilla*, 15–16, 22–26, 43, 53–54.

18. Bishop, *SS*, 19, 90, 115; Kaltenegger, *Mountain Troops*, 19; Rikmenspoel, *Waffen-SS: The Encyclopedia*, 78; Klietmann, *Die Waffen-SS*, 151–153; Otto Kumm, *Prinz Eugen: The History of the 7. SS-Mountain Division Prinz Eugen* (Winnipeg: J. J. Federowicz, 1995), 16–17. See also original German version, Otto Kumm, '*Vorwarts Prinz Eugen!' Geschichte der 7. SS Freiwillien-Division 'Prinz Eugen'* (Osnabrück: Munin Verlag, 1978), 38–45; Ripley, *The Waffen-SS at War*, 87, 203; Stein, *The Waffen-SS*, 170; Hausser, *Einsatz*, 103–104; Steiner, *Die Freiwilligen*, 45.

19. Herzog, *Die Volksdeutsche in der Waffen-SS*, 86; Donlagic et al., *Yugoslavia in the Second World War*, 48–49, 87–89.

20. Krätschmer, *Die Ritterkreuzträger der Waffen-SS*, 509–512; Steiner, *Die Freiwilligen*, 45, 178, 219–220; Kumm, *Prinz Eugen*, 8–10, 16–17; Hausser, *Soldaten*, 58; Theile, *Beyond "Monsters" and "Clowns,"* 322; Stein, *The Waffen-SS*, 170; Hausser, *Einsatz*, 103–109; Marc C. Yerger, *German Cross in Gold: Holders of the SS and Police*, vol. 2, *"Das Reich"*

(San Jose, Calif.: R. James Bender, 2005), 365; Blood, *Hitler's Bandit Hunters*, 109, 322; Rikmenspoel, *Waffen-SS: The Encyclopedia*, 85–86; Kaltenegger, *Mountain Troops*, 38.

21. Krätschmer, *Die Ritterkreuzträger der Waffen-SS*, 899–901; Steiner, 219–220; Theile, *Beyond "Monsters" and "Clowns,"* 200; Kumm, *Prinz Eugen*, 10, 16; Blood, *Hitler's Bandit Hunters*, 109; Kaltenegger, *Mountain Troops*, 38; Rikmenspoel, *Waffen-SS: The Encyclopedia*, 78; Stein, *The Waffen-SS*, 170.

22. Kumm, *Prinz Eugen*, 17.

23. Ibid., 17.

24. Ibid., 16–17.

25. Rempel, "Gottlob Berger," 45–46.

26. Steiner, *Die Freiwilligen*, 219; Kumm, *Prinz Eugen*, vii; Krätschmer, *Die Ritterkreuzträger der Waffen-SS*, 509–510.

27. Kumm, *Prinz Eugen*, viii, 16.

28. Steiner, *Die Freiwilligen*, 219; Hausser, *Einsatz*, 194.

29. Krätschmer, *Die Ritterkreuzträger der Waffen-SS*, 510–511.

30. Kumm, *Prinz Eugen*, 20–21; Bishop, *SS*, 19–20; Stein, *The Waffen-SS*, 170; Theile, *Beyond "Monsters" and "Clowns,"* 39.

31. Klietmann, *Die Waffen-SS*, 152–53; Krätschmer, *Die Ritterkreuzträger der Waffen-SS*, 509–510.

32. Stein, *The Waffen-SS*, 273–274; Karl Sauer, *Die Verbrechen der Waffen-SS: Eine Dokumentation der VVN Bund der Antifaschisten* (Frankfurt a. M.: Roderberg Verlag, 1977), 35.

33. Koehl, *Black Corps*, 207.

34. Herzog, *Die Volksdeutsche in der Waffen-SS*, 96–97. Browning, "The Wehrmacht in Serbia Revisited," 36.

35. Robert E. Herzstein, *Waldheim: The Missing Years* (New York: Arbor House/William Morrow, 1988), 67; Browning, "The Wehrmacht in Serbia Revisited," 31–33.

36. Sauer, *Die Verbrechen der Waffen-SS*, 46.

37. Kumm, *Prinz Eugen*, 269–270; Theile, *Beyond "Monsters" and "Clowns,"* 237, 322, 394–95; Kaltenegger, *Mountain Troops*, 8; Steiner, *Die Freiwilligen*, 45, 219; Hausser, *Einsatz*, 106; see also Browning, "The Wehrmacht in Serbia Revisited," 31–33.

38. Theile, *Beyond "Monsters" and "Clowns,"* 395.

39. Djilas, *Wartime*, 215, 290.

40. Bishop, *SS*, 20, 90, 122; Kumm, *Prinz Eugen*, 270; Erich Schmidt-Richtberg, *Der Endkampf auf dem Balkan: Die Operationen der Heeresgruppe E von Griechenland bis zu den Alpen* (Heidelberg: Scharnhorst Buchkameradschaft, 1955), 52–53.

41. Kaltenegger, *Mountain Troops*, 21; Theile, *Beyond "Monsters" and "Clowns,"* 322; Kumm, *Prinz Eugen*, 22; Rikmenspoel, *Waffen-SS: The Encyclopedia*, 28; Bishop, *SS*, 123; Hausser, *Einsatz*, 106; Krätschmer, *Die Ritterkreuzträger der Waffen-SS*, 509–510.

42. Kumm, *Prinz Eugen*, 122; Steiner, *Die Freiwilligen*, 226–227.

43. Trang, *La Division Florian Geyer*, 6–9, 11–16, 27.

44. In April 1945, Hitler ordered Fegelein shot as a suspected traitor, even though Fegelein's wife was Eva Braun's sister, thereby making Fegelein posthumously Hitler's brother-in-law. For a biographical sketch, refer to Volker Riess, "Hermann Fegelein: Parvenu ohne Skrupel," in Smelser and Syring, *Die SS*, 160–172; Blood, *Hitler's Bandit Hunters*, 320; Bishop, *SS*, 125; Trang, *La Division Florian Geyer*, 6–9.

45. Rikmenspoel, *Waffen-SS: The Encyclopedia*, 28–30; Bishop, *SS*, 20, 97, 125–126; Klietmann, 157–159; Theile, *Beyond "Monsters" and "Clowns,"* 323–324; Georg Tessin, *Verbände und Truppen der deutschen Wehrmacht und Waffen SS im Zweiten Weltkrieg, 1939–1945, Dritter Band: Die Landstreitkrafte 6–14* (Frankfurt am Main: Verlag E. S. Mittler und Sohn, 1967), 119–120.

46. Blood, *Hitler's Bandit Hunters*, 121, 140, 297; Theile, *Beyond "Monsters" and "Clowns,"* 324; Ripley, *The Waffen-SS at War*, 200; Rikmenspoel, *Waffen-SS: The Encyclopedia*, 29–30; Bishop, *SS*, 125–126.

47. Sauer, *Die Verbrechen der Waffen-SS*, 33–34, 43.

48. Bishop, *SS*, 97, 125; Trang, *La Division Florian Geyer*, 85.

49. Bishop, *SS*, 125–126; Kleitmann, *Die Waffen-SS*, 157–159; Rikmenspoel, *Waffen-SS: The Encyclopedia*, 28–29, 77; Stein, *The Waffen-SS*, 202–203; Trang, *La Division Florian Geyer*, 82–88, 789.

50. For a biographical sketch of Willi Bittrich, see Horst Muhleisen, "Wilhelm Bittrich: Ritterlicher Gegner und Rebel," 79–80, in Smelser and Syring, *Die SS*, 77–87; Trang, *La Division Florian Geyer*, 93.

51. Bishop, *SS*, 126; Theile, *Beyond "Monsters" and "Clowns,"* 325; Stein, *The Waffen-SS*, 275; Kleitmann, *Die Waffen-SS*, 157–161; Rikmenspoel, 29–30; Trang, *La Division Florian Geyer*, 99, 101.

52. Blood, *Hitler's Bandit Hunters*, 153–156, 219.

53. Ibid., 163–164, 172.

54. Ibid., 162–164.

55. Klietmann, *Die Waffen-SS*, 505; Stein, *The Waffen-SS*, 203.

56. Klietmann, *Die Waffen-SS*, 505–509; Theile, *Beyond "Monsters" and "Clowns,"* 191, 224; Bishop, *SS*, 20.

57. Stein, *The Waffen-SS*, 171; Keegan, *Asphalt Soldiers*, 104; Bishop, *SS*, 23.

58. Kumm, *Prinz Eugen*, 10, 74; Rikmenspoel, *Waffen-SS: The Encyclopedia*, 11–12; Hausser, *Einsatz*, 104; Kaltenegger, *Mountain Troops*, 9; Blood, *Hitler's Bandit Hunters*, 141–142, 322; Ripley, *The Waffen-SS at War*, 204.

59. Stein, *The Waffen-SS*, xxxi, 204; Keegan, *Asphalt Soldiers*, 91, 143; Rikmenspoel, *Waffen-SS: The Encyclopedia*, 80–81.

60. Wegner, *Hitlers Politische Soldaten*, 291–292; Stein, *The Waffen-SS*, 171, 204, 287; Hausser, *Soldaten*, 91–92; Rikmenspoel, *Waffen-SS: The Encyclopedia*, 80; Keegan, *Asphalt Soldiers*, 91, 143; Bishop, *SS*, 21.

61. Rikmenspoel, *Waffen-SS: The Encyclopedia*, 80–81; Wegner, *Hitlers Politische Soldaten*, 291–292; Blood, *Hitler's Bandit Hunters*, 157; Axworthy, *Third Axis*, 116.

62. Herzstein, *Waldheim*, 94.

63. Kumm, *Prinz Eugen*, 30–31; Blood, *Hitler's Bandit Hunters*, 102; Redzic, *Bosnia and Herzegovina in the Second World War*, 35–37; U.S. Army, *Anti-Guerilla*, 25–26, 41–43.

64. Donlagic et al., *Yugoslavia in the Second World War*, 107–09; Kumm, *Prinz Eugen*, 30–31; Blood, *Hitler's Bandit Hunters*, 102; Redzic, *Bosnia and Herzegovina in the Second World War*, 35–37.

65. Donlagic et al., *Yugoslavia in the Second World War*, 107–109, 113; U.S. Army, *Anti-Guerilla*, 36–37.

66. Djilas, *Wartime*, 215–216; Blood, *Hitler's Bandit Hunters*, 259; Krätschmer, *Die Ritterkreuzträger der Waffen-SS*, 510; Herzstein, *Waldheim*, 85; Kumm, *Vorwärts!*, 56–72.

67. Herzstein, *Waldheim*, 86–87; Redzic, *Bosnia and Herzegovina in the Second World War*, 39–40; Donlagic et al., *Yugoslavia in the Second World War*, 116–117, 124; U.S. Army, *Anti-Guerilla*, 37–38.

68. Herzstein, *Waldheim*, 88.

69. Ibid., 88–89.

70. Sauer, *Die Verbrechen der Waffen-SS*, 35, 47–48, DOK D-940 (GB 550). The document citations refer to Nuremberg, IMT proceedings.

71. Herzstein, *Waldheim*, 91; Donlagic et al., *Yugoslavia in the Second World War*, 126–127.

72. Herzstein, *Waldheim*, 91, 95.

73. Kumm, *Prinz Eugen*, 43, 57; Djilas, *Wartime*, 247, 282–283; Ripley, *The Waffen-SS at War*, 204–205; Hausser, *Einsatz*, 208; Kaltenegger, *Mountain Troops*, 21.

74. Kumm, *Prinz Eugen*, 43, 47; U.S. Army, *Anti-Guerilla*, 49–50.

75. Sauer, *Die Verbrechen der Waffen-SS*, 46–47, DOK D-578 (GB 553); Sauer, *Die Verbrechen der Waffen-SS*, 58–49 DOK D-944 (GB 566).

76. U.S. Army, *Anti-Guerilla*, 41–42.

77. Kumm, *Prinz Eugen*, 58–59; Krätschmer, *Die Ritterkreuzträger der Waffen-SS*, 510–511; Kaltenegger, *Mountain Troops*, 21; Blood, *Hitler's Bandit Hunters*, 109, 244; Hausser, *Einsatz*, 107; Bishop, *SS*, 123.

78. Hausser, *Einsatz*, 107.

79. Herzstein, *Waldheim*, 85, 93–97, 102–105; U.S. Army, *Anti-Guerilla*, 44.

80. Kumm, *Prinz Eugen*, 89–90; Kumm, *Vorwärts!*, 139–148; U.S. Army, *Anti-Guerilla*, 49–50.

81. Kumm, *Prinz Eugen*, 89–90, 90, 96; Kaltenegger, *Mountain Troops*, 21.

82. Kumm, *Prinz Eugen*, 89, 96–97.

83. Ibid., 87–88.

84. Djilas, *Wartime*, stresses this theme throughout his memoirs.

85. Rikmenspoel, *Waffen-SS: The Encyclopedia*, 21–26; Steiner, *Die Freiwilligen*, 260–261; Trang, *La Division Florian Geyer*, 136–37, 141–147.

86. Klietmann, *Die Waffen-SS*, 123.

87. Rikmenspoel, *Waffen-SS: The Encyclopedia*, 43–44, 92–94, 98; Theile, *Beyond "Monsters" and "Clowns,"* 331; Bishop, *SS*, 29.

88. Bishop, *SS*, 138, 166; Rikmenspoel, *Waffen-SS: The Encyclopedia*, 39; Klietmann, *Die Waffen-SS*, 215–217; Theile, *Beyond "Monsters" and "Clowns,"* 344; Blood, *Hitler's Bandit Hunters*, 141; Ripley, *The Waffen-SS at War*, 87.

89. Keegan, *Asphalt Soldiers*, 119; Rikmenspoel, *Waffen-SS: The Encyclopedia*, 33–38; Theile, *Beyond "Monsters" and "Clowns,"* 327–330, 341; Williamson, *Loyalty*, 80–83; Klietmann, *Die Waffen-SS*, 181–183.

90. Stein, *The Waffen-SS*, 221; Ripley, *The Waffen-SS at War*, 89; Blood, *Hitler's Bandit Hunters*, 110.

91. Kumm, *Prinz Eugen*, 106–107, 250; Rikmenspoel, *Waffen-SS: The Encyclopedia*, 219; Yerger, *German Cross in Gold*, 365.

92. Kumm, *Prinz Eugen*, 100–101; Bishop, *SS*, 123, 250.

93. Kumm, *Prinz Eugen*, 117–144; Blood, *Hitler's Bandit Hunters*, 260–262; Kumm, *Vorwärts!*, 178–224, for a full discussion of this operation; also U.S. Army, *Anti-Guerilla*, 65–66.

94. Kumm, *Prinz Eugen*, 124–26, 144–45; U.S. Army, *Anti-Guerilla*, 65–66.

95. Kumm, *Prinz Eugen*, 121–129; Blood, *Hitler's Bandit Hunters*, 261–262.

96. Kumm, *Prinz Eugen*, 125, 144, 148.

97. Ibid., 125; Blood, *Hitler's Bandit Hunters*, 260–261; Kumm, *Vorwärts!*, for a report on "free hunting."

98. Kumm, *Prinz Eugen*, 128.

99. Krätschmer, *Die Ritterkreuzträger der Waffen-SS*, 899–901; Kumm, *Vorwärts!*, 335–336.

100. Kaltenegger, *Mountain Troops*, 24–25; Kumm, *Prinz Eugen*, 233; Theile, *Beyond "Monsters" and "Clowns,"* 337; Blood, *Hitler's Bandit Hunters*, 259; Krätschmer, *Die Ritterkreuzträger der Waffen-SS*, 899–901; Redzic, *Bosnia and Herzegovina in the Second World War*, 41–42, 53.

101. Kleitmann, *Die Waffen-SS*, 510; Theile, *Beyond "Monsters" and "Clowns,"* 350; Rikmenspoel, *Waffen-SS: The Encyclopedia*, 43.

102. Bishop, *SS*, 142–144; Kumm, *Prinz Eugen*, 236; Rikmenspoel, *Waffen-SS: The Encyclopedia*, 42; Klietmann, *Die Waffen-SS*, 229–231; Kaltenegger, *Mountain Troops*, 28; Williamson, *Loyalty*, 106.

103. Axworthy, *Axis*, 190–191; U.S. Army, *Anti-Guerilla*, 66–67.

104. Axworthy, *Axis* 198–199; Kumm, *Prinz Eugen*, 171; Herzstein, *Waldheim*, 127–128.

105. Kumm, *Prinz Eugen*, 11; Steiner, *Die Freiwilligen*, 292; Hausser, *Einsatz*, 160; Krätschmer, *Die Ritterkreuzträger der Waffen-SS*, 512; Theile, *Beyond "Monsters" and "Clowns,"* 323; Blood, *Hitler's Bandit Hunters*, 322.

106. For more on the Slovak uprising, see note 17 of the previous chapter.

107. Rempel, "Gottlob Berger," 54.

108. Axworthy, *Slovakia*, 293–300, 316; Hausser, *Einsatz*, 161; Bishop, *SS*, 138, 166; Theile, *Beyond "Monsters" and "Clowns,"* 344–345; Trang, *La Division Florian Geyer*, 137, 143–144, 165.

109. Bishop, *SS*, 134; Axworthy, *Slovakia*, 310.

110. Axworthy, *Slovakia*, 289, 293, 307, 312–313.

111. Donlagic et al., *Yugoslavia in the Second World War*, 164–165, 179–180.

112. Kumm, *Prinz Eugen*, 171–173; Kaltenegger, *Mountain Troops*, 21; Klietmann, *Die Waffen-SS*, 152–153; Herzstein, *Waldheim*, 127; Erich Schmidt-Richberg, *Der Endkampf Auf Dem Balkan: Die Operationen der Heeresgruppe E von Greichenland bis zu Alpen* (Heidelberg: Kurt Vauinckel Verlag, 1955), 27–28.

113. Herzstein, *Waldheim*, 127, 147; Klietmann, *Die Waffen-SS*, 152–53; Kumm, *Prinz Eugen*, 171–76, 198–215; Kumm, *Vorwärts!*, 256–294; Schmidt-Richberg, *Endkampf*, 51–52.

114. Donlagic et al., *Yugoslavia in the Second World War*, 179.

115. Kumm, *Prinz Eugen*, 198–199; Kumm, *Vorwärts!*, 295–336.

116. Kumm, *Vorwärts!*, 316–317.

117. Herzstein, *Waldheim*, 128, 147–150; Hausser, *Einsatz*, 111–117; Klietmann, *Die Waffen-SS*, 153; Yerger, *German Cross in Gold*, 365; Rikmenspoel, *Waffen-SS: The Encyclopedia*, 219; Theile, *Beyond "Monsters" and "Clowns,"* 323; Kaltenegger, *Mountain Troops*, 21; Kumm, *Prinz Eugen*, 176, 159–60, 209, 219–224; Ripley, *The Waffen-SS at War*, 206.

118. Tessin, *Verbände und Truppen*, 6, 119–120; Trang, *La Division Florian Geyer*, 143–147, 154–155; Axworthy, *Third Axis*, 200; Karl Cerff, *Die Waffen SS im Wehrmachtbericht* (Osnabrück: Munin Verlag, 1971), 77.

119. Kumm, *Prinz Eugen*, 111, 171–79; Axworthy, *Third Axis*, 194–200; Bishop, *SS*, 145; Hausser, *Einsatz*, 160; Cerff, *Die Waffen SS im Wehrmachtbericht*, 77.

120. U.S. Army, *Anti-Guerilla*, 69.

121. Herzstein, *Waldheim*, 147.

122. Trang, *La Division Florian Geyer*, 143–147, 150–151, 165–169, 172–175.

123. Two understrength divisions of pro-Nazi Hungarians were also formed, the 25th and 26th Waffen-Grenadier Divisions.

124. Ripley, *The Waffen-SS at War*, 301–307; Krätschmer, *Die Ritterkreuzträger der Waffen-SS*, 835–836; Stein, *The Waffen-SS*, 233; Steiner, *Die Freiwilligen*, 293; Theile, *Beyond "Monsters" and "Clowns,"* 317.

125. Klietmann, *Die Waffen-SS*, 107, 133–137; Rikmenspoel, *Waffen-SS: The Encyclopedia*, 25–26; Steiner, *Die Freiwilligen*, 292–293; Stein, *The Waffen-SS*, 233; Hausser, *Soldaten*, 117–118.

126. Rikmenspoel, *Waffen-SS: The Encyclopedia*, 22–26, 33, 37–39, 94–95; Steiner, *Die Freiwilligen*, 292–293; Bishop, *SS*, 130, 138, 166; Tessin, *Verbände und Truppen*, 6, 257; Klietmann, *Die Waffen-SS*, 96–98, 107, 133–137, 181–183, 203–205, 215–217; Stein, *The Waffen-SS*, 233; Ripley, *The Waffen-SS at War*, 309–310; Theile, *Beyond "Monsters" and "Clowns,"* 340–345; Hausser, *Einsatz*, 161; Axworthy, *Slovakia*, 310.

127. Bishop, *SS*, 127; Steiner, *Die Freiwilligen*, 304–305; Hausser, *Einsatz*, 160; Klietmann, *Die Waffen-SS*, 233–234; Rikmenspoel, *Waffen-SS: The Encyclopedia*, 30, 43; Williamson, *Loyalty*, 106; Trang, *La Division Florian Geyer*, 141–147.

128. Williamson, *Loyalty*, 106, 126–27.

129. Krätschmer, *Die Ritterkreuzträger der Waffen-SS*, 789, 839–840, 843–844. Those receiving the Cross were Friedrich Buck, Bessarabia; Hermann Maringgele, South Tyrol; Albert Klett, Dobrudja; Gustav Wendrinsky, Slovakia; Harry Phönix, Latvia.

130. Ripley, *The Waffen-SS at War*, 314–317; Williamson, *Loyalty*, 106; Rikmenspoel, *Waffen-SS: The Encyclopedia*, 22; Klietmann, *Die Waffen-SS*, 96–98, 107.

131. Klietmann, *Die Waffen-SS*, 96–98, 107, 133–137, 181–183; Rikmenspoel, *Waffen-SS: The Encyclopedia*, 22, 25–26; Ripley, *The Waffen-SS at War*, 317; Theile, *Beyond "Monsters" and "Clowns,"* 318; Tessin, *Verbände und Truppen*, 257; Williamson, *Loyalty*, 106.

132. Bishop, *SS*, 138; Rikmenspoel, *Waffen-SS: The Encyclopedia*, 39; Klietmann, *Die Waffen-SS*, 215–217; Theile, *Beyond "Monsters" and "Clowns,"* 344–345.

133. Bishop, *SS*, 130.

134. Theile, *Beyond "Monsters" and "Clowns,"* 338.

135. Klietmann, *Die Waffen-SS*, 275–276; Bishop, *SS*, 159; Rikmenspoel, *Waffen-SS: The Encyclopedia*, 51; Hausser, *Einsatz*, 161; Ripley, *The Waffen-SS at War*, 88; Antonio J. Munoz, *The Last Levy: Waffen-SS Officer Roster, March 1st, 1945* (Bayside, N.Y.: Axis Europa Books, 2001), 68.

136. Rikmenspoel, *Waffen-SS: The Encyclopedia*, 52; Bishop, *SS*, 145.

137. Rikmenspoel, *Waffen-SS: The Encyclopedia*, 52; Williamson, *Loyalty*, 108; Trang, *La Division Florian Geyer*, 175–179.

138. Klietmann, *Die Waffen-SS*, 303; Theile, *Beyond "Monsters" and "Clowns,"* 359; Rikmenspoel, *Waffen-SS: The Encyclopedia*, 56; Bishop, *SS*, 163.

139. Rikmenspoel, *Waffen-SS: The Encyclopedia*, 56–57.

140. Hausser, *Einsatz*, 158; Kaltenegger, *Mountain Troops*, 34; Theile, *Beyond "Monsters" and "Clowns,"* 351; Bishop, *SS*, 149; Rikmenspoel, *Waffen-SS: The Encyclopedia*, 44; Klietmann, *Die Waffen-SS*, 247–248.

141. Hausser, *Einsatz*, 193; Kumm, *Prinz Eugen*, 245–246; Kumm, *Vorwärts!*, 351–356, 365; Steiner, *Die Freiwilligen*, 306–307; Schmidt-Richberg, *Endkampf*, 92–95.

142. Kumm, *Prinz Eugen*, 250–255.

143. Ibid.; Bishop, *SS*, 124; Hausser, *Einsatz*, 193; Rikmenspoel, *Waffen-SS: The Encyclopedia*, 28.

144. Steiner, *Die Freiwilligen*, 306–307; Kaltenegger, *Mountain Troops*, 22; Kumm, *Prinz Eugen*, 265; Kumm, *Vorwärts!*, 371–375; Schmidt-Richberg, *Endkampf*, 105–108, 124.

145. Kaltenegger, *Mountain Troops*, 22; Kumm, *Prinz Eugen*, 256, 263.

146. Hausser, *Einsatz*, 194; Kumm, *Prinz Eugen*, 265–266; Kumm, *Vorwärts!*, 376–379; Kaltenegger, *Mountain Troops*, 22; Tessin, *Verbände und Truppen*, 82; Schmidt-Richberg, *Endkampf*, 130–131; Donlagic et al., *Yugoslavia in the Second World War*, 211–212.

147. Kumm, *Prinz Eugen*, 265; Kumm, *Vorwärts!*, 382–383.

148. Herzstein, *Waldheim*, 153–155; Kumm, *Prinz Eugen*, 266–69; Blood, *Hitler's Bandit Hunters*, 273.

149. Kumm, *Prinz Eugen*, 272–273; Steiner, *Die Freiwilligen*, 308–309.

150. Djilas, *Wartime*, 423–424.

11. Project 100,000 in the Vietnam War and Afterward
Thomas Sticht

1. Janice Laurence and Peter Ramsberger, *Low-Aptitude Men in the Military: Who Profits, Who Pays?* (New York: Praeger, 1991).

2. Lawrence Baskir and William Strauss, *Chance and Circumstance: The Draft, the War, and the Vietnam Generation* (New York: Vintage, 1978), 126.

3. Deborah Shapley, *Promise and Power: The Life and Times of Robert McNamara* (Boston: Little, Brown, 1993), xii.

4. Thomas Sticht, William Armstrong, Daniel Hickey, and John Caylor, *Cast-off Youth: Policy and Training Methods From the Military Experience* (New York: Praeger, 1987), 190.

5. U.S. Congressional Record, *Department of Defense Appropriations, 1965. Hearings before the Subcommittee of the Committee on Appropriations, United States Senate, Eighty-Eighth Congress, Second Session on H.R. 10939, Part 2* (Washington, D.C.: U.S. Government Printing Office, 1964), 761–762.

6. Kelly Greenhill, "Don't Dumb Down the Army," *New York Times* (February 17, 2006).

7. Baskir and Strauss, *Chance*, 131.

8. David Evans, "The Army and the Underclass: A Losing Battle," *New Republic* (June 1986): 10–13.

9. U.S. Congressional Record, *Readjustment of Project 100,000 Veterans. Hearing before the Subcommittee on Oversight and Investigations of the Committee on Veteran's Affairs, House of Representatives, One Hundred First Congress, First Session, Serial No. 101-38, Testimony of Wayne S. Sellman* (Washington, D.C.: U.S. Government Printing Office, 1990), 3.

10. Ibid., testimony of Janice H. Laurence, 6.

11. Sticht et al., *Cast-off*, 90; Thomas Sticht, *How Military Service Helped Low-aptitude, Economically Disadvantaged Young Men of the Mid-1960s Escape Poverty*, Research Note no. 1 (El Cajon, Calif.: Applied Behavioral & Cognitive Sciences, Inc., January 1992); Janice Laurence, Peter Ramsberger, and Monica Gribben, *Effects of Military Experience*

on the Postservice Lives of Low-aptitude Recruits: Project 100,000 and the ASVAB Misnorming. Final Report 89–29. HumRRO FR-PRD-89-29 (Alexandria, Va.: Human Resources Research Organization, December 1989).

12. Sticht et al., Cast-off, Tables 11–13.

13. Ibid., Table 15.

14. Laurence and Ramsberger, Low-aptitude, 44.

15. Ibid., 45.

16. Thomas Sticht, "Military Testing and Public Policy: Selected Studies of Lower Aptitude Personnel," in Test Policy in Defense: Lessons from the Military for Education, Training, and Employment, ed. Bernard Griffin and Linda Wing (London: Kluwer Academic Publishers, 1992), 1–77.

17. Sticht et al., Cast-off, 48, Table 16.

18. Sticht, Military Testing, 27, Table 4.

19. Sticht et al., Cast-off, 54, Table 20.

20. Sticht, Military Testing, 34, fig. 4.

21. Sticht et al., Cast-off, 53, Table 19.

22. Laurence and Ramsberger, Low-aptitude, 49.

23. Irving Greenberg, "Project 100,000: The Training of Former Rejectees," Phi Delta Kappan 50 (1969): 570–574.

24. Sticht et al., Cast-off, 51, Table 18.

25. Sticht, Military Testing, 34, fig. 4.

26. Laurence and Ramsberger, Low-aptitude, 37.

27. William Beusse, The Impact of Military Service on Low-aptitude Men. AFHRL-TR-74-15 (Brooks AFB, Tex.: Air Force Human Resources Laboratory, 1974).

28. U.S. Congressional Record, Readjustment of Project 100,000 Veterans . . . Testimony of William Beusse (Washington, D.C.: U.S. Congressional Record, 1990), 6.

29. Ibid., 8.

30. Laurence et al., Effects of Military Experience.

31. Janice Laurence, Jane Heisey, Barbara Means, and Brian Waters, Demographic Comparison of Low-aptitude Military and Nonmilitary youth. Final Report 85–1, HumRRO FR-PRD-85-1 (Alexandria, Va.: Human Resources Research Organization, February 1985), 15, Table 10.

32. Laurence et al., Effects of Military Experience, 72, Table 19.

33. Laurence et al., Demographic, 15, Table 10.

34. U.S. Bureau of the Census, Historical Poverty Tables (Washington, D.C.: U.S. Department of Commerce). Accessed January 4, 2007. http://www.census.gov/hhes/poverty/histpov/histpov1.html. Using the Table 3 data for the Project 100,000 personnel and the midpoints of the ranges of

income given, the author computed a weighted average weekly income of $39.88 for the Project 100,000 personnel before they started their military service: $[(75,234 \times 0) + (66,780 \times 50) + (20,117 \times 150) + (682 \times 201)]/162,813 = 6,493,632/162,813 = \$39.88$.

35. Laurence et al., *Effects of Military Experience*.

36. U.S. Bureau of the Census, *Historical Poverty Tables*.

37. Laurence et al., *Effects of Military Experience*, 114, Table 48.

38. Ibid., 116, Table 50.

39. Ibid.

40. U.S. Congressional Record, *Readjustment*.

41. Ibid., 5.

42. B. Asch *Military Support for Youth Development: An Exploratory Analysis* (Santa Monica, Calif.: RAND Corporation, 1994), 29.

43. Laurence et al., *Effects of Military Experience*, 72, Table 19.

44. U.S. Congressional Record, *Readjustment*, 5.

45. Laurence et al., *Effects of Military Experience*, 90, Table 30.

46. Beusse, *The Impact of Military Service*.

47. Laurence et al., *Effects of Military Experience*, 25.

48. Asch, *Military Support*.

49. Laurence and Ramsberger, *Low-aptitude*.

50. Sticht et al., *Cast-off*, 79.

51. Ibid., 14.

52. Ibid., 79.

53. Laurence et al., *Effects of Military Experience*, 92.

Conclusions

Sanders Marble

1. See http://www.timesonline.co.uk/tol/sport/olympics/article3946860.ece.

2. See http://www.cbsnews.com/stories/2010/09/05/sunday/main6837189.shtml and http://www.military.com/news/article/double-amputee-returns-to-combat.html.

Contributors

Paul A. Cimbala is Professor of History at Fordham University, in the Bronx, New York. He is the author of *Under the Guardianship of the Nation: The Freedmen's Bureau and the Reconstruction of Georgia, 1865–1870*, which received the Malcolm and Muriel Barrow Bell Award of the Georgia Historical Society; and *The Freedmen's Bureau: Reconstructing the American South after the Civil War*. He has also co-edited several essay collections dealing with the Civil War era, including *The Great Task Remaining Before Us: Reconstruction as America's Continuing Civil War*. He most recently published *Soldiers North and South: The Everyday Experiences of the Men Who Fought America's Civil War*.

Walter S. Dunn Jr. received his Ph.D. from the University of Wisconsin in 1971. In a forty-year career in museums and historical societies, including the Buffalo & Erie County Historical Society and the Iowa Science Center, he wrote a number of studies of the frontier of British North America around the time of the American Revolution. He also published many works on World War II, focusing especially on the Wehrmacht and Red Army. On that subject, his titles include *Hitler's Nemesis: The Red Army, 1930–1945*, *The Soviet Economy and the Red Army, 1930–1945*, *Stalin's Keys to Victory: The Rebirth of the Red Army*, *Soviet Blitzkrieg: The Battle for White Russia, 1944*, *Kursk: Hitler's Gamble, 1943*, *Second Front Now, 1943: An Opportunity Delayed*, and *Heroes or Traitors: The German Replacement Army, the July Plot, and Adolf Hitler*. His health deteriorated before revisions of his chapter in this work could be completed.

Col. David M. Glantz is a graduate of the Virginia Military Institute, the University of North Carolina at Chapel Hill, and the U.S. Army's Command and General Staff College, Defense Language Institute,

Institute for Russian and Eastern European Studies, and War College. He served for over 30 years in the U.S. Army before retiring in 1993. At Fort Leavenworth in 1986, he helped found and later directed the U.S. Army's Soviet (later Foreign) Military Studies Office (FMSO), where he remained until his retirement in 1993. While at FMSO, he established the *Journal of Slavic Military Studies,* a scholarly journal for which he still serves as chief editor. A member of the Russian Federation's Academy of Natural Sciences, he has written or co-authored more than twenty commercially published books, over sixty self-published studies and atlases, and over one hundred articles dealing with the history of the Red (Soviet) Army, Soviet military strategy, operational art, and tactics, Soviet airborne operations, intelligence, and deception, and other topics related to World War II. In recognition of his work, he has received several awards, including the Society of Military History's prestigious Samuel Eliot Morrison Prize for his contributions to the study of military history.

André José Lambelet teaches history and the humanities at Quest University Canada, in Squamish, British Columbia. He is particularly interested in questions of cultural, ethnic, national, and political identity: how identities are created, how people come to identify themselves as part of a group, and how people choose between or reconcile competing identities. The chapter in this volume is based on his broader research on citizenship, republicanism, and conscription in modern France.

Valdis O. Lumans earned his undergraduate degree in history at the University of Florida and Ph.D. in history at the University of North Carolina, Chapel Hill. He at present serves as Chair of the Department of History and Political Science at the University of South Carolina–Aiken, where he holds the Leora Toole Murray Chair in History. He is also a USC Carolina Trustee Professor. He has published two major books, *Himmler's Auxiliaries: The Volksdeutsche Mittelstelle and the German Minorities of Europe, 1933–1945,* and *Latvia in World War II.* He is currently working on a third, *The Baltic Guard: Baltic Paramilitary Auxiliaries in the U.S. Army in Post-WWII Germany.* He has also served as an expert witness in six federal SS denaturalization and extradition cases.

Sanders Marble received his AB from the College of William & Mary and his MA and PhD from King's College of the University of London. He worked for eHistory.com, the National Museum of American History of the Smithsonian Institution, and has had two stints at the U.S. Army's Office of Medical History, sandwiched around a period as historian at Walter Reed Army Medical Center. He has written a variety of works on artillery (especially British artillery) in World War I and on military medicine.

Steven W. Short earned his doctoral degree from Texas Tech University, where he studied African American history and U.S. military history. His research interests include the black experience in World War I, racism and violence in the aftermath of the war, and the military as a medium of social change. He is currently working on a manuscript about the creation of the black officer corps in World War I. Dr. Short also serves on the editorial review board of the *East Texas Historical Journal* and teaches U.S. and African American history at Collin College in McKinney, Texas.

Dennis Showalter is Professor of History at Colorado College and past president of the Society for Military History. Joint editor of *War in History*, he specializes in comparative military history. His recent monographs include *The Wars of German Unification*, *Patton and Rommel: Men of War in the Twentieth Century*, and *Hitler's Panzers*.

Peter Simkins was born in northwest London in 1939. In 1963 he joined the staff of the Imperial War Museum, London, becoming Keeper of the Department of Exhibits from 1965 to 1976 and later the Museum's Senior Historian and Head of its Research and Information Office. On his retirement in 1999 he was awarded the MBE for his services to the museum. For the next eleven years he was Honorary Professor in Modern History at the University of Birmingham. In that capacity, and more recently as Visiting Lecturer, he has helped to teach that University's MA course in First World War studies since 2005. He is also currently a vice president of the Western Front Association, a fellow of the Royal Historical Society, and a member of the Army Records Society and British Commission for Military History. His numerous publications include *Kitchener's Army*, which was awarded the Templer Medal by the Society for Army Historical Research.

Thomas G. Sticht is an international consultant in adult education. He received his Ph.D. in experimental psychology from the

University of Arizona. His research and development activities have centered on applications of cognitive science, communications technology, and computer technology to the literacy, education, and training needs of underserved youth and adults, with a focus upon military personnel. He directed a research team that first integrated and reported analyses of both the performance of Project 100,000 personnel during the Vietnam war and the performance of hundreds of thousands of personnel of lower aptitude that entered the military services when a mistake was made in the use of Armed Services Vocational Aptitude Battery. He was the only researcher to interview Robert S. McNamara about the outcomes of Project 100,000 and to report on McNamara's reaction to the research findings. The results of this work and the interview are covered in his 1987 book *Cast-off Youth: Policy and Training Methods from the Military Experience.*

Index